"*Husserl and Spatiality* is a whirlwind expedition through central Husserlian concepts in relation to the central problem of what constitutes a space. As I read about DuFour's childhood memories, and his descriptions from his rich ethnographic study of the spaces and practices of the Brazilian religion Candomblé, his writing seemed to linger and cling to the walls of my room, building tangible horizons and creating ripples of effect in my understanding also of my own surrounding environment. This book will inspire interpretations of the world that favour empathy over power, bodily engagement over subjective self-centeredness, and historical meaningfulness over relational flatness. It is a much-needed call to reinterpret spatial relationships in ways that allow the past to gently touch the future."
— **Henriette Steiner**, *Associate Professor, Section for Landscape Architecture and Planning, University of Copenhagen*

"Part radical re-reading of Husserl, part phenomenology of Afro-Brazilian ritual, DuFour's is an astoundingly original take on space as the constitutive ground of all lived experience. The ethnography of ritual here becomes the litmus test of the deepest stakes of human experience—both condition of possibility and the generative source of human relationships, replete with embodied history and affective significance. This is what DuFour calls environmentality—a tour de force of life-driven conceptual creativity."
— **Martin Holbraad**, *Professor of Social Anthropology and Head of the Department of Anthropology, University College London*

Cover image: black and white photograph of the Candomblé *caboclo* ritual of Tupiniquim. © Tao DuFour

Husserl and Spatiality

Husserl and Spatiality is an exploration of the phenomenology of space and embodiment, based on the work of Edmund Husserl. Little known in architecture, Husserl's phenomenology of embodied spatiality established the foundations for the works of later phenomenologists, including Maurice Merleau-Ponty's well-known phenomenology of perception. Through a detailed study of his posthumously published and unpublished manuscripts on space, DuFour examines the depth and scope of Husserl's phenomenology of space. The book investigates his analyses of corporeity and the "lived body," extending to questions of intersubjective, intergenerational, and geo-historical spatial experience, what DuFour terms the "environmentality" of space.

Combining in-depth architectural philosophical investigations of spatiality with a rich and intimate ethnography, *Husserl and Spatiality* speaks to themes in social and cultural anthropology, from a theoretical perspective that addresses spatial practice and experience. Drawing on fieldwork in Brazil, DuFour develops his analyses of Husserl's phenomenology through spatial accounts of ritual in the Afro-Brazilian religion of Candomblé. The result is a methodological innovation and unique mode of spatial description that DuFour terms a "phenomenological ethnography of space." The book's profoundly interdisciplinary approach makes an incisive contribution relevant to academics and students of architecture and architectural theory, anthropology and material culture, and philosophy and environmental aesthetics.

Tao DuFour is an Assistant Professor at the Department of Architecture at Cornell University. He holds a BArch from The Cooper Union, and obtained his MPhil and PhD in the History and Philosophy of Architecture from the University of Cambridge. He directs the Landscape and Urban Environmentalities Lab at Cornell.

Routledge Research in Architecture

The *Routledge Research in Architecture* series provides the reader with the latest scholarship in the field of architecture. The series publishes research from across the globe and covers areas as diverse as architectural history and theory, technology, digital architecture, structures, materials, details, design, monographs of architects, interior design, and much more. By making these studies available to the worldwide academic community, the series aims to promote quality architectural research.

Architectural Anthropology
Exploring Lived Space
Edited by Marie Stender, Claus Bech-Danielsen and Aina Landsverk Hagen

Writing the Materialities of the Past
Cities and the Architectural Topography of Historical Imagination
Sam Griffiths

Louis I. Kahn in Rome and Venice
Tangible Forms
Elisabetta Barizza

Cybernetic Architectures
Informational Thinking and Digital Design
Camilo Andrés Cifuentes Quin

Jørn Utzon and Transcultural Essentialism
Adrian Carter and Marja Sarvimäki

Husserl and Spatiality
A Phenomenological Ethnography of Space
Tao DuFour

For more information about this series, please visit: https://www.routledge.com/Routledge-Research-in-Architecture/book-series/RRARCH

Husserl and Spatiality
A Phenomenological
Ethnography of Space

Tao DuFour

LONDON AND NEW YORK

First published 2022
by Routledge
2 Park Square, Milton Park, Abingdon, Oxon, OX14 4RN

and by Routledge
605 Third Avenue, New York, NY 10158

Routledge is an imprint of the Taylor & Francis Group, an informa business

© 2022 Tao DuFour

The right of Tao DuFour to be identified as author of this work has been asserted by him in accordance with sections 77 and 78 of the Copyright, Designs and Patents Act 1988.

All rights reserved. No part of this book may be reprinted or reproduced or utilised in any form or by any electronic, mechanical, or other means, now known or hereafter invented, including photocopying and recording, or in any information storage or retrieval system, without permission in writing from the publishers.

Trademark notice: Product or corporate names may be trademarks or registered trademarks, and are used only for identification and explanation without intent to infringe.

Library of Congress Cataloging-in-Publication Data
Names: DuFour, Tao, author.
Title: Husserl and spatiality : a phenomenological ethnography of space / Tao DuFour.
Description: New York : Routledge, 2022. |
Series: Routledge research in architecture | Includes bibliographical references and index. |
Identifiers: LCCN 2021019133 (print) | LCCN 2021019134 (ebook) | ISBN 9780815361558 (hardback) | ISBN 9781032103099 (paperback) | ISBN 9781351116145 (ebook)
Subjects: LCSH: Husserl, Edmund, 1859–1938. | Space and time. | Candomblé (Religion)
Classification: LCC B3279.H94 D86 2022 (print) |
LCC B3279.H94 (ebook) | DDC 114—dc23
LC record available at https://lccn.loc.gov/2021019133
LC ebook record available at https://lccn.loc.gov/2021019134

ISBN: 9780815361558 (hbk)
ISBN: 9781032103099 (pbk)
ISBN: 9781351116145 (ebk)

DOI: 10.4324/9781351116145

Typeset in Sabon
by codeMantra

*Ninguém pode mais passar pela encruzilhada
sem pagar alguma coisa a Exu.*
[No one may any longer pass through the crossroads
without paying something to Exu.]

Orixá myth fragment from Reginaldo Prandi, *Mitologia dos Orixás*

Welchen Sinn hat das Ansich der Natur gegenüber dem wirklichen und möglichen Eingreifen der Subjekte, von denen sie doch nicht abtrennbar gedacht werden kann? Was liegt für ein Ansich beschlossen und als Idee konstruierbar in der Idee der Einstimmigkeit möglicher Erfahrung—erfahrender Subjekte?
[What sense does the in-itself of nature have in relation to the actual and possible intervention of subjects, apart from which nature cannot at all be conceived? What kind of an in-itself is this that is included (and, as idea, is construable) in the idea of the concordance of possible experience—experiencing subjects?]

Edmund Husserl, *Analysen zur passiven Synthesis* (1923)

pentru Iulia

Contents

List of figures		xi
Acknowledgements		xiii
	Introduction: spatial description	1
1	Phenomenon and method	23
	Fieldwork as methodological clue 29	
	Sensing history 39	
2	Corporeity and spatiality	49
	Constitution and experience 51	
	Visual space 53	
	The spatial phantom and time 68	
	Tactual space, motility, and the lived body 72	
	Corporeity and time 78	
3	Space and the other	106
	The genesis of space 109	
	Empathic spatiality 123	
	Generative space 138	
4	A phenomenological ethnography of space	168
	The reunião *184*	
	Epilogue: *Umweltlichkeit*	218
	Glossary	225
	Bibliography	227
	Index	241

Figures

2.1 View towards the table in the room where the Candomblé ritual—the *caboclo reunião*—takes place. Photo by the author 55
2.2 Detail of the *caboclo* "figurine." Photo by the author 57
2.3 View towards the table. Photo by the author 58
2.4 Detail at the table. Photo by the author 61
2.5 Diagram of the spatial structure of thing "phantom" perception. Sketch by the author, digitised by Gracie Meek 63
2.6 Detail at the table, towards the vase and foliage. Photo by the author 64
2.7 View towards the table with the lights turned off. Photo by the author 65
2.8 View towards the ceiling. Photo by the author 71
2.9 The table partially set. Photo by the author 77
2.10 View towards the ceiling. Photo by the author 85
2.11 Diagram of the retention-protection structure of the temporality of perception after Husserl. Sketch by the author, digitised by Gracie Meek 88
3.1 *Filho-de-santo* being incensed. Photo by the author 126
3.2 *Filha-de-santo* incensing. Photo by the author 127
3.3 Detail at the ground at the front gate. Photo by the author 130
3.4 *Filha-de-santo* being incensed. Photo by the author 136
3.5 *Filha-de-santo* being incensed. Photo by the author 136
3.6 *Filhas-de-santo* singing at the table. Photo by the author 142
4.1 Plan of the room where the *reunião* takes place. Sketch by the author 177
4.2 *Filhas-de-santo* attending to dress. Photo by the author 182
4.3 *Filha-de-santo* marking her body with scented powder. Photo by the author 182
4.4 View towards the table. Photo by the author 185
4.5 *Filha-de-santo* lies prostrate before the *mãe-de-santo*. Photo by the author 189
4.6 *Filhas-de-santo* in prayer at the table. Photo by the author 192

Acknowledgements

My regard was first turned towards certain spatial practices in the Caribbean, as sites of intellectual sounding, by James Wylie. James's seminars, which I took as an undergraduate at The Cooper Union, revealed the poetics of ritual through Haitian literature. The descriptions of life that I was exposed to in these seminars reverberated in memory and animated my imagination; I am thankful to James for this and for his generous correspondence in the years following. The literary and personal encounter motivated interests that would extend to Brazil, inspired by an urbanism studio on Brasília that I took with Diana Agrest who, in this context, introduced me to anthropology. My interest in Brazil deepened, and this book stems from later pursuits as a doctoral student at the Department of Architecture at the University of Cambridge. Although it is based on my dissertation, the problems and ideas taken up here branch off in directions not anticipated at that time, making this work substantially different in content, structure, and argument. Nevertheless, it is at Cambridge where the ideas distinctly emerged and were explored.

I am thankful to the institutions that financially supported my doctoral studies, namely Cambridge University, the Cambridge Commonwealth Trust, Trinity College, and the Overseas Research Students Award Scheme. In addition, I thank at Cambridge the Department of Architecture, the Centre of Latin American Studies, and Kettle's Yard for further financial support that made possible my fieldwork in Brazil. This book is to a significant extent the result of research I undertook subsequent to my doctoral studies, specifically in 2018 as a Visiting Researcher at the Center for Subjectivity Research (CFS) at the University of Copenhagen, and then in 2019 as a Visiting Scholar at the Husserl Archives at the Institute of Philosophy, KU Leuven. I thank Dan Zahavi for hosting me at the CFS, and for his invaluable insights and intellectual generosity in discussions about my research. The CFS is an exceptional environment for phenomenological research; I thank colleagues whom I met there, specifically Hynek Janousek for our lengthy discussions on the history of the phenomenology of space. At the Husserl Archives, I was welcomed by Julia Jansen and Thomas Vongehr, to whom I express my appreciation. I thank Emanuele Caminada for his generous correspondence and for granting permission to quote from Husserl's unpublished manuscripts, and to use the excerpt from Husserl's *Analysen zur passiven Synthesis* as one of the book's opening epigraphs. For the English translation of this epigraph, I thank Sara Martínez at Springer Nature for permission to use the translation by Anthony J. Steinbock of the excerpt from Husserl's *Analyses Concerning Passive and Active Synthesis*, originally published by Kluwer Academic Publishers. My research at the CFS and Husserl Archives was funded by the College of Architecture, Art, and Planning at Cornell University, and I thank Dean J. Meejin Yoon, Andrea Simitch, Kent Kleinman, and Mark Cruvellier for their support.

To staff at the following libraries and archives I express my thanks: Cornell University Library, the Husserl Archives, the Philosophy Collection in the Department of Communication at the University of Copenhagen, Cambridge University Library, the Middleton Architectural Library at Cambridge University, Trinity College Library, and the British Library; in Salvador, the library of the Centro de Estudos Afro-Orientais (CEAO) of the Universidade Federal da Bahia, the map room of the Biblioteca Central, the map library of Fundação Gregório de Mattos, and the map library of the Secretaria de Planejamento da Prefeitura Municipal do Salvador. To Martha Walker and Carla Bahn in the Mui Ho Fine Arts Library at Cornell, I express my appreciation for assistance in the later stages of writing, during the pandemic. I am grateful to the editors at Routledge, Grace Harrison, Krystal Racaniello, and Christine Bondira, for their support and patience in seeing this book project through to production, and to Irina du Quenoy for copyediting. I thank the two anonymous reviewers for their close reading of the manuscript, and for their important observations and suggestions on the theme of space. I am especially thankful to my student research assistants: Edward Aguilera Perez, Gracie Meek, who digitally reproducing my hand-drawn diagrams, and Daniel Friedman for meticulously going over my English translations of German texts. I include a note on translation in the Introduction.

Marcio Goldman's guidance, both in intellectual and pragmatic matters related to my fieldwork in Brazil, was invaluable. Conversations with Wolfgang Reiber, Juana Elbein dos Santos, Carlos and Ayeola Moore, Fabio Lima, and Miriam Rabelo offered important insights into the social constitution of Salvador and its forms of religiosity. I thank Reginaldo Prandi for permission to use the excerpt from his *Mitologia dos Orixás* as one of the opening epigraphs of this book. Mãe Juta and her household welcomed me with immediacy and warmth to the Centro do Caboclo Tupiniquim, and I thank the members of the family, and the *terreiro* as a family. I am thankful to Gilmara for slowly and with care walking me through her own understanding of the *caboclo* ritual. I thank Joice and Viviane for their help. To Mãe Juta, I express profound gratitude, from the place of a *filho*, that is, one of deep respect and love. In this vein, I wish also to express my heartfelt

Acknowledgements xv

thanks to Equede Sinha, who with warmth and solicitude introduced me to the more intimate life of the *candomblé* Ilé Axé Iyá Nassô Oká or *terreiro* Casa Branca. Although in the writing I was not able to expand the scope of my research to study this historically significant *terreiro*, the experience profoundly enriched my understanding of Candomblé as a lived reality. I thank all those who welcomed me at Casa Branca, specifically Pãe Mauro Nunes, Ogan Antônio Marques, Edney, and Paula.

In the long course of their formation and eventual articulation, the ideas explored in this book reflect the influence of teachers, colleagues, and friends. At Cambridge, I was privileged to have been taught by the late Dalibor Vesely, and in this way to have participated in an inheritance that touched directly the thought of Jan Patočka and thus Husserl. To Peter Carl, my doctoral supervisor, I owe a special debt of gratitude. Peter's wisdom, wit, and patience, even where it seemed that I had taken a less secure route, illuminated my way. I thank Wendy Pullan and Dermot Moran, who examined my doctoral thesis, for their generous engagement with the work. I thank Maximilian and Claudia Sternberg for their warmth, generosity, and friendship. Of my cohort in the graduate programme in the History and Philosophy of Architecture, I am thankful to Alex Dougherty, Heba Mostafa, Anita Bakshi, Konstantin Kastrissianakis, and Barry Phipps for their inspiration and friendship. Martin Holbraad and Rebecca Empson introduced me to an extraordinary sphere of anthropological thinking at Cambridge, which contributed significantly to my understanding of their discipline. Cornell University has been a wonderful institutional home, and I am grateful to my colleagues in the Department of Architecture, specifically the Department Chair Caroline O'Donnell, Lily Chi, Esra Akcan, and Val Warke. I thank Bruno Bosteels, Tom McEnaney, and John Zissovici for enrapturing conversations in Amazonia, Havana, and at the DeWitt Cafe. In a similar vein, I thank Jenny Sabin, Gerard Aching, and Neil Hertz. Natalie Melas and Jeremy Foster read draft chapters of the manuscript, and I express my deep appreciation for their comments and insights. Conversations I had with Jorge Otero-Pailos on architecture and phenomenology were inspiring, and I thank him for his intellectual generosity. I was able to present and work through aspects of this study in various forums, and I thank in particular Henriette Steiner and Ellen Braae for hosting me at the Section for Landscape Architecture and Planning at the University of Copenhagen; Leslie Hewitt and Omar Berrada at The Cooper Union; Marina Lathouri at the Architectural Association School of Architecture; and Gareth Doherty at the Graduate School of Design at Harvard University. A special note of thanks is due to Anthony Vidler, Eric Parry, Mark Raymond, Sue Gussow, Jean Khalfa, and Mary Jacobus, who in different and essential ways have been mentors, interlocutors, colleagues, and friends.

In the Caribbean, familial and affine relations extend like the proverbial "pumpkin vine," intertwining like the roots of a mangrove. The solicitude of many relatives and friends shaped lived experiences that motivated and informed my thinking about themes explored in this book. To those who constituted this lacework of care I express deep gratitude. Of those whom I acknowledged explicitly in my dissertation I am especially grateful to Sujin Huggins, Baba Sule, the De Fours, Winniefred Francois, and Andre Francois for their emotional support as this book developed, and to Steve Regis and Ken Reyes for their friendship. I thank Nnandi Lecointe for her help in the field, my aunt Maria Dürsteler for sharing her memories of Nenny, Ion and Elena Stătică, my siblings, and my parents, Soyini Sule and Chi Kamose, for their love and support. I acknowledge the memory of my grandparents Harold and Earline (DuFour) Herbert, to whom my dissertation was dedicated, Fidalin Furlonge, and Cynthia Gill (Nenny). Iulia Stătică-DuFour has been my spiritual and intellectual complement, and my life's light; with patience, care, and love she has been with me along the way. I dedicate this book to her.

Introduction
Spatial description

In his reflections on the rhythms of the Jamaican countryside, Stuart Hall describes the life of his grandmother's house as "one memory which stills holds me."[1] In an analogous way, there is an image from my formative years in Trinidad that retains its vividness each time it emerges from the haze of memory. It was evening. In Trinidad twilight lingers until after 6 pm, so that as we drove towards the short bridge, looking through the car window as a small boy I glimpsed the features of the slope rising to our left and the ravine dropping to our right. The vegetation in Carenage—a fishing village on the northwest coast of the island, a thickly forested peninsula leased by the British to the United States during the Second World War—was lush and interspersed with small houses peering through the landscape on both sides of the ravine. Twilight tarried with us as we made our way along the dirt trail that led up the slope to Nenny's house, a modest structure—I think it was wooden, perhaps on a poured concrete foundation. Nenny was the person who raised my father from his infancy, and in this way I knew her as a grandmother.[2] That night there was a feast, and as I write the memories flood back. Inside the living room the space had a blue-grey aura, the colour of twilight. Relatives and neighbours were gathered around her in a loose circle. I stood by the front door, near the threshold between the interior and the small porch from where, if one looked out, one could see the forested hillside, sometimes in a cloud of mist through which, at moments like this, could be heard the "sounds of drumming from the shacks buried in the ravines."[3] My grandmother was dressed in white, a long flowing dress, her head wrapped in white cloth. As the drums echoed in the opacity of the night, her body articulated their rhythms; her eyes seemed to be looking into her thoughts, the "black lacquer of her skin" seemed to glow as if illuminated from within, and as she moved "the blood rose near the surface and mingled in the blackness, and glints the color of wine appeared in her cheeks."[4]

The style of event that I witnessed, and the fact of having witnessed it at a young age, is not unique to my personal biography. It is an example of a typical experience of religious praxis and social life that one finds in communities throughout the Caribbean and Latin America. I could

DOI: 10.4324/9781351116145-1

2 Introduction: spatial description

therefore draw on narrative descriptions of writers from the region—Stuart Hall, Simone Schwarz-Bart, and C. L. R. James—that seem to coincide with my own experience.[5] The landscapes harbour within them histories of everyday life whose traces are to be found less in official archives, than in practices handed over in the intergenerational negotiation of the lived experience of tradition. What these writers capture in their descriptions are both a mode or "style" of experiencing and the manner in which the environment—the room, the house, the landscape, environing sounds, the bodies of others in movement—appears as pregiven in typical and familiar ways. Between the experiencing life and the experienceable surrounding world lie spatial horizons. This book aims to describe the structure and sense of this spatiality. It is not, therefore, a study of the design, construction, or social production of space; nor is it a history or genealogy of the concept of space. Rather, it is a study of the manner in which space is given in embodied, lived experience.[6] This does not mean that either the agency implied in design or the background of social production is denied. These phenomena instead emerge, in varying levels of significance, appositeness, and distinctness, out of the affective level of embodiment. The memorial image with which I started thus serves to indicate and open up the problem of the spatial description of lived experience. It points to a certain possibility of being immersed in the truth of a situation as an ethical claim; of being enchanted by the life of a situation; and thus of being open to its modes of givenness and self-disclosure.

The idea of spatial description proposed here is not geometrical. I am not referring to a geometrically describable "space," in the modern mathematico-epistemic sense, which Edward Casey characterises as absolute, extensive, relative, panoptic, and formal.[7] The spatial understanding at stake here is akin to Henri Lefebvre's plenal, intricately woven and rich analyses of the "architectonics" of space, specifically his thematisation of "the fleshy (spatio-temporal) body" whose lived experience is "firmly anchored in the here and now" of the living present.[8] In this sense descriptions of spatiality are inherently descriptions of lived bodily experience. The body's corporeity is thus to be understood in its expressivity and affectivity, as constitutive of its spatiality. The interpretation of space from the perspective of embodiment introduces a range of problems: Sara Heinämaa's phenomenology of embodied sexual difference, for example, implies the sense of space in its inherent sexuality; Dan Zahavi points to the problem of the intersubjective experience of space; and Anthony Steinbock indicates the nature of space as constituted intergenerationally and historically.[9] While I explore these issues in detail in the following chapters—specifically Chapters 2 and 3—I want to emphasise with these introductory remarks that spatial description is a *qualitative* problem. At the same time, I am interested not only in a description of the *sense* of spatial experience but also in the *structures* of spatiality.

Concerning the problem of space—of lived spatiality—sense and structure are inextricably interlaced. There are different ways to approach the matter, and I propose initially the path of the experience of "immersement." It suggests that one finds oneself, from the start, as already enraptured, enmeshed in the fibrils of space given beforehand as structured and sensible. The problem, therefore, is to describe this intertwining from within its claims. The idea of immersement is introduced by anthropologist Marilyn Strathern in her meditations on the nature of fieldwork and its relation to writing. Strathern speaks of a "moment of immersement" that implicates both the lived experiences of fieldwork and the subsequent activity of writing, of ethnographic description.[10] For Strathern, the activity of writing itself is enfolded in the moment of immersement, and description can thus be understood as a modality of lived experience. The ethnographer must negotiate a paradoxical tension between "being dazzled" by the ethnographic moment *totally*, yet not completely yielding to this very claim of total commitment to the moment.[11] The distance that both unites and separates the experience of the field and that of writing is the site through which this tension is worked over. Strathern—quoting Annelise Riles—describes this moment as "a figure seen twice."[12] Implicated here is thus a peculiar spatio-temporal distancing, which at the same time connects and makes possible both modes of experience: the anticipatory, futural orientation of fieldwork towards writing, and the orientation of ethnography towards the concreteness of the lived sense of the past experience in the field. This "figure" indicates the space between perception and writing, which points to a notion of temporality that implies transformation in the possibilities of understanding an experiential situation due to modes of distancing from its lived duration. There is a hermeneutic implied in this distancing, in which the discursive intent of writing is necessarily intertwined with the facticity of spatial experience, and in this way writing can be understood as a problem of *spatial description*.[13]

Ethnography, of course, is not limited to spatial description, nor does it as a method, in principle, depend on fieldwork, although this has historically tended to be the case.[14] Caroline Humphrey, for example, suggests that ethnography can be undertaken through, or at least supplemented by, imaginative literature.[15] But even in this case, literature has its basis in the typicality of lived experience, which is Humphrey's point. While I do not claim to have either the scope of interests or the training of an anthropologist, I am inspired by the principle of its ethnographic method and the intrinsic value it places on the epistemological significance of a description of lived experience. This refers not only to the subjects and events being described but also to the lived experience of the ethnographer herself. The problem of spatial description, therefore, implicates the writer, and this involvement in the situation through the writing is a moment inherent to the knowledge produced about space.

It is important to recognise here the role of imagination. Strathern notes, for example, that "field immersement is repeated in the subsequent study away from the field" and that a part of the task of writing is that of "re-creating some of those effects [of fieldwork] in the context of writing about them."[16] This involves imagination: "The writing only works [...] as an imaginative re-creation of some of the effects of fieldwork itself."[17] Humphrey's suggestion of the supplementary value of imaginative literature implies a distance not limited to that between fieldwork and writing, but one that involves wider social and temporal horizons, in that "because some thoughts cannot be readily expressed in the form most ethnographic interaction takes [...] it is there [through imaginative literature] that we have access to another, more far-flung, dimension of what people may intimate about their worlds."[18] Humphrey's methodological innovation, however, is still oriented towards the problem of lived experience, through a more expansive understanding of the "field." The field is a surrounding world, a spatial environment that is pregiven and affectively saturated, into which the researcher is immersed sense perceptually "in the flesh" or imaginatively through the literary work. The two, of course, are not coincident, as I can close the book, but in the reading the world of the story, like the world described ethnographically in the traditional sense, still has affective allure grounded in the facticity of the living environment towards which it descriptively points. On the pregivenness and affectivity of the field, Strathern notes: "I am not referring to the products of discourse [...] I want rather to find a way of acknowledging the fact that my attention has been transfixed at certain (ethnographic) moments I have never been able—wanted—to shake off."[19] The value that I draw from the principle of description in ethnographic fieldwork and writing is not merely methodological; it is also ethical. For one to be "dazzled," to be "transfixed" by the life of the field, immersement has to be characterised by an openness to the way in which the field as a surrounding world of life discloses itself in levels of environmental experienceability, that is, levels of familiarity and opacity.

This implies levels of intersubjective, generative—temporalities of birth, ageing, and death—and geo-historical depth. An approach to spatial description inspired by methodological and ethical principles of ethnography, in which the reflexive nature of descriptive practice is inherent as a mode of knowledge, is necessarily concerned, therefore, with questions of depth levels of sense.[20] There are levels of sensibility and understanding that depend in part on one's ability to experience different strata of meaning—for example, questions of familiarity, facility, and so forth—and in part on the mode of givenness and self-disclosure of that which is experienced. The problem of describing the structure of spatiality begins at the level of sense perception and embodiment, which means that the task, at this level, is to describe the structure of sense perceptual experience. The problem is a very peculiar one, in that it requires examples of actual sense perceptual experiences in their specificity and contingency, even though the descriptions have a generalised character. This study presents one such example, through which it offers a concrete description of the sense and structure of spatiality in its givenness in lived experience. It is precisely in the selection of the *example*, however, where a conflict or tension may seem to arise between a certain descriptive generality and situated experience. I will first introduce the example.

The events that guide this study were not those of the familiar memorial landscapes of Trinidad, with which I began this introduction. Although I had not experienced anything quite like them in their specificity before, I could still follow their contours, initially as if seen through mist. The events were *reuniões*, meaning "gatherings," that took place weekly—to my knowledge, they may have been more frequent, but I was only invited on Thursdays—in a relatively open room in the upper floor of a house in a neighbourhood in the greater metropolitan area of the city of Salvador, in the state of Bahia in the Brazilian Northeast. The *reuniões*—to use the Portuguese term—were part of the ritual structure of an Afro-Brazilian religion called Candomblé. They were intimate and had a familial and welcoming feel, as if at a dinner party with close friends and relatives. In fact, they took place around a long table, which was typically spread with ritual implements, a figurine, leaves, and certain items of food; unlike at a dinner party, however, nothing was consumed at the table. The events involved dialogue, prayer, chanting and singing, dancing, incensation, smoking of cigars, and ecstatic moments of trance or the "arrival" (*chegar* in Portuguese) of entities called *caboclos* expressed in the bodily gestures and speech of women. The head of both the domicile and the religious household—called a *terreiro*, a Portuguese word for a public square or yard, but here also for Afro-Brazilian religious grounds—was a woman called a *mãe-de-santo* or "mother-of-saint," who would "manifest" a *caboclo*—"an entity [...] identified as being of indigenous origin"[21]—called Tupiniquim. Everyone, including myself, was typically dressed in white. This ritual—a Candomblé *caboclo reunião* of Tupiniquim—serves as the example for my study of the sense and structure of the lived experience of spatiality. In describing it I aim to be true to the event, to my experience of having been "dazzled" by it, and thus to describe *its* modes of givenness and self-disclosure. I will refer to it throughout the following chapters with a detailed, concrete description, which I have termed a phenomenological ethnography of space. It is instructive, in this light, to compare Strathern's consideration of fieldwork and writing—that is, ethnographic description—with Anthony Steinbock's characterisation of descriptive problems associated with "practicing phenomenology," which requires one:

> to be attentive to what give themselves in the way that they give themselves, even if these "matters" do not conform to our usual habits of thought and preconceptions about what can appear. No matter how paradoxical this may sound, it requires *being open to* being struck by

the matters, even if one cannot anticipate being struck by what might appear. It requires being open to the possibility that there might be modes of givenness, kinds of evidence, and modalities of experience that do not follow the strict pattern of the way in which objects of perception and objects of thought give themselves to an individual perceiver or to an autonomous thinker. [...] If we restrict in advance what is going to count as experienceable, we may just be cutting short fundamental aspects of who we are as persons and as living creatures.[22]

With the above considerations and the example of the *caboclo reunião* in mind, I return to the matter of the tension between the specificity and contingency of sense and a certain generality that characterises the structure of spatial experience.

Spatial experience is embodied experience that is necessarily sense perceptual. The problems of sense perception and embodiment were taken up by Maurice Merleau-Ponty in his celebrated work, *Phenomenology of Perception*, first published in French in 1945.[23] According to Fr. Hermann Leo Van Breda, the Belgian Franciscan priest who established the Husserl Archives in Louvain, Merleau-Ponty was the first researcher outside of Louvain to consult the archives, in 1939, a year after Husserl's death.[24] In Merleau-Ponty's words: "Since 1938 [1939] [...] I have been allowed to consult some of Husserl's unpublished texts at the Husserl Archives in Louvain [...]. I have stayed in contact with the Archives ever since."[25] Although it is well known that Merleau-Ponty's phenomenology of perception is indebted to his readings of Husserl, the extent of this debt is little known or recognised outside of specialist circles in philosophy. Dan Zahavi, for example, traced the contours of Husserl's phenomenology of embodiment and perception, noting that "there is far more *continuity* between Husserl and the later phenomenologists than is normally assumed."[26] Regarding a more general neglect of Husserl's contribution to phenomenology—a philosophical paradigm that he founded—Klaus Held notes that

> little more than Husserl's name is known by the average person interested in philosophy—even in Germany. There is one main reason for this: Husserlian phenomenology may easily constitute the most important presupposition for the important early works of Heidegger and Sartre [...], but because Husserl was Jewish, his later writings could no longer appear in the Third Reich. Thus continued analysis of Husserl's thought was interrupted, whereas in the 1950s and 1960s, Heidegger and Sartre were again discussed intensely.[27]

In this study, I approach the problem of spatial description as it is found in select writings of Husserl. A primary reason for this is that Husserl's phenomenological descriptions of space not only pervade his phenomenology of perception and embodiment but are implicated in his concrete phenomenological investigations of problems of habituality, "empathy" and intersubjectivity, intergenerational relations and generativity, historicity, problems of interspecies relations ("animality"), and the experiential givenness of what he terms "ground" or "earth."[28] As I demonstrate in the following chapters, an analysis of the concreteness of spatial experience limited to a phenomenology of perception and embodiment would be inadequate.

In architecture, my home discipline, the content proper of Husserl's philosophy has received relatively little attention. His phenomenology when acknowledged, tends to be either passed over in favour of the work of later thinkers or met with a critical reception that refers only to programmatic works published in his lifetime, specifically his *Ideas* and *Crisis*.[29] An exception to this tendency is Filip Mattens, who has explored the phenomenology of space and embodiment in Husserl. His work, however, is more expansive, investigating concepts of space in the thought of other phenomenologists and precursors to phenomenology, including Carl Stumpf and Erwin Strauss.[30] Husserl's phenomenology of *space* in particular is little known in architecture, although there are well-established and important paradigms of architectural theory that engage with phenomenology more broadly, referred to in shorthand as "architectural phenomenology." This phenomenological orientation in architectural theory derives its philosophical underpinning from phenomenologists following Husserl, specifically the works of Martin Heidegger and Merleau-Ponty. Jacques Derrida's deconstruction, understood by philosophers as lying within the phenomenological tradition, within architecture tends to be associated with post-structuralism.[31] The literature on architectural phenomenology is extensive and increasing with varying critical dispositions. Scholars, including Jorge Otero-Pailos in his *Architecture's Historical Turn* and M. Reza Shiraz in *Towards an Articulated Phenomenological Interpretation of Architecture*, have mapped the genealogy of architectural phenomenology, from the early works of figures such as Jean Labatut and Christian Norberg-Schulz to the substantial contributions of Kenneth Frampton and Juhani Pallasmaa.[32] The work of architectural historian and theorist Alberto Pérez-Gómez has been significant for the development and articulation of architectural phenomenology, as has been the writings of architects Steven Holl and Peter Zumthor, among others.[33]

Czech architectural theorist and pedagogue Dalibor Vesely significantly influenced phenomenological approaches to architecture, specifically through his teaching at the University of Essex, the Architectural Association in London, and then at Cambridge University, where he taught until his death in 2015. The volume edited by José de Paiva and dedicated to Vesely, *The Living Tradition of Architecture*, speaks to his legacy through contributions from colleagues and former students, whose works have also significantly informed phenomenological approaches to architectural history, theory, pedagogy, and practice.[34] The Czech philosopher Jan Patočka was an important influence on Vesely, and the latter's engagement

8   *Introduction: spatial description*

with Husserl's philosophy is indicated in terms of his appropriation of the concept of "the natural world" from Patočka and the mediation of Merleau-Ponty's phenomenology.[35] The primary philosophical underpinning of Vesely's thinking, however, which orients the argument of his major work, *Architecture in the Age of Divided Representation*, is the phenomenological hermeneutics of Heidegger and Hans-Georg Gadamer; the same can be said of the thought of Peter Carl.[36] Building critically on Vesely's and Carl's work, the volume co-edited by Henriette Steiner and Maximilian Sternberg, *Phenomenologies of the City*, expands the breadth of phenomenological inquiry in architecture through its attention to the complex institutional, atmospheric, and *agonic* structures of the city.[37] The latter theme is exemplified in the work of Wendy Pullan and her collaborators on urban conflict.[38] The 2018 volume of the journal *Log*, guest-edited by Bryan Norwood and titled *Disorienting Phenomenology*, is a critical contribution that challenges traditional approaches to phenomenology in architecture.[39] Contributors to this volume interrogate and critique inherited tendencies in architectural phenomenology, foregrounding topics and themes that carry their own theoretical weight, within which phenomenology as a philosophical paradigm proper is implicated. These include questions of race through critical race and postcolonial theories; questions of gender and sexuality in queer and feminist thought; and theories of disability, all approached in relation to the task of historicising and theorising architecture.[40] Recent scholarship on the contribution of phenomenology in the Husserlian tradition to postcolonial thought, and to decolonising and antiracist ethical imperatives, has foregrounded its significance for social and political *critique*. In their examination of Frantz Fanon's contribution to psychiatry, Dan Zahavi and Sophie Loidolt have shown that "he is part of a long history of critical approaches in psychopathology and psychiatry, which has firm roots in the phenomenological tradition, and which keeps up its critical work today."[41] In a similar vein, Jean Khalfa's thorough investigation of Fanon's writings on psychiatry and his psychiatric work has pointed to the significance of key thinkers and concepts in the phenomenological tradition for Fanon's thought, such as the notion of the "corporeal schema"—a concept that Merleau-Ponty appropriated from early neurophysiology, but gave a new phenomenological sense informed by his study of Husserl's then unpublished research manuscripts.[42] I take up these Husserlian themes concerning space and embodiment in this study, in the context of Afro-Brazilian religious praxis. It is the situational specificity of the topic of the spatiality of the Candomblé ritual itself that I aim to foreground *through* phenomenological description, which includes its interlaced horizons of intersubjectivity and historicity.

In parallel and in dialogue with architectural theorists' engagement with phenomenology are works of philosophers interested in architecture from the perspective of phenomenology, and specifically the phenomenology of *place*. To Edward Casey's *The Fate of Place*, already mentioned, and his *Getting Back into Place*, should be added the writings of Karsten Harries, specifically his *The Ethical Function of Architecture*, as well as the work of Andrew

Benjamin, Fred Rush, and Jeff Malpas.[43] The works of both theorists of architectural phenomenology and philosophers of place and architecture reflect the profound influence of the writings of later phenomenologists, especially Heidegger and Merleau-Ponty. Although programmatic aspects of Husserl's philosophy are regarded in these overlapping paradigms, with varying levels of depth and sympathy, the specific problems of a phenomenology of spatial experience and the constitution of space as developed in Husserl's concrete descriptions and analyses are not addressed. An exception to this is the relatively recent book by James Dodd, *Phenomenology, Architecture and the Built World*.[44] Dodd's perspective emphasizes phenomenology's "classical expression in the work of Edmund Husserl and the early Martin Heidegger," and in this way aspects of his analyses address questions of the constitution of space in Husserl's phenomenology.[45] For sustained Husserlian interpretations, however, one must turn to the contemporary philosophical literature on Husserl specifically and, of course, Husserl's writings themselves.

The importance of Filip Mattens's work has already been mentioned. The published volume to date dedicated exclusively to the problem of spatiality in Husserl is Ulrich Claesges's untranslated work, *Edmund Husserls Theorie der Raumkonstitution* (Edmund Husserl's Theory of the Constitution of Space).[46] I follow Claesges's analyses closely in Chapter 2 of this study. Fred Kersten's doctoral dissertation was a study of "Husserl's Investigations toward a Phenomenology of Space" (1964), and Noel Mouloud explored Husserl's work on space in "Le principe spatial d'individuation" ("The spatial principle of individuation") (1956).[47] Numerous volumes in the Husserliana series of Husserl's complete works, which I discuss below, have been published since these studies, including Husserl's lectures on *Thing and Space* (1973), his *Analyses Concerning Passive Synthesis* (1966), and a series of late manuscripts on spatiality published in Peter McCormick and Frederick Elliston's edited volume, *Husserl: Shorter Works* (1982).[48] My study takes this material into account, together with later publications of Husserl's writing on the themes of "intersubjectivity" and "generativity," which have important implications for his concept of space. That said, Husserl studies has in recent decades witnessed a blossoming. I have already mentioned the work of Anthony Steinbock, Dan Zahavi, and Sara Heinämaa. To this I would add Donn Welton's research on Husserl's "systematic" phenomenology, David Carr's on problems of history, and the investigations of Dermot Moran and Robert Sokolowski, whose works, among others, I draw upon for this study.[49] My elaboration of Husserl's description of space constitution in terms of bodily motility also has affinities with Jaana Parviainen's study of kinaesthetic structures in the writings of Husserl and Edith Stein.[50]

One of the aims of this book, therefore, is to introduce aspects of this rich and dynamic philosophical conversation on Husserl to an architectural audience and in this way, through a focus on *space*, to offer architectural theoretical readings of Husserl. Implied here is a double movement: a *phenomenological* description of spatial experience concerned with clarifying "transcendental" structures, and a *spatial ethnography* aimed at understanding the contingent sense of an exemplary situation. The nature of the problem is such that the tension has to be worked out in the very *activity of description*. It is a "zig-zag" process, to use a Husserlian expression, in which the concrete conditions being described function as "leading clues" to more general insights. In the following chapters I work through this tension by way of a sustained and detailed description of spatial experience and modes of givenness of spatiality, following the guiding thread of the ethnographic example of the *caboclo reunião*.

For the reader unfamiliar with Husserl, a short biography may be useful, but this cannot take the form here of an introduction to Husserl's thought; volumes have been and continue to be written on Husserl's vast corpus, and even Husserl himself framed his own writings published during his lifetime as "introductions" to his phenomenology. Edmund Husserl was born on April 8, 1859, in Prossnitz, Moravia—then part of the Austro-Hungarian Empire, now Prostejov in the Czech Republic—into a "middle-class family of assimilated non-religious Jews."[51] As Klaus Held notes, there is "nothing 'spectacular' to tell about the inconspicuous scholarly life" of Husserl.[52] Between 1867 and 1881, he studied mathematics, physics, and astronomy in Leipzig, and later mathematics and philosophy in Berlin. He received his doctorate in mathematics in 1882 from the University of Vienna, where he studied from 1884 to 1886 under Franz Brentano, whose influence on him was profound.[53] His two-volume *Logical Investigations* (1900–1901), "written at a turning point in Husserl's philosophical development," as Dermot Moran notes, was followed over a decade later by his seminal programmatic text on phenomenology, the first volume of his *Ideas Pertaining to a Pure Phenomenology and to Phenomenological Philosophy* (1913), and the only of three intended volumes published during his lifetime.[54]

As I explore in Chapter 2, Husserl had by this time developed in painstaking detail his phenomenology of embodiment and descriptions of the experiential givenness of space. His last major work, *The Crisis of European Sciences and Transcendental Phenomenology*, was published in part in Belgrade in 1937, one year before his death.[55] Between his *Ideas* and *Crisis*, Husserl published only three substantial works: parts of his *Lectures on Internal Time Consciousness*, based on texts compiled by Edith Stein and edited for publication in 1928 by Martin Heidegger, both of whom were his former assistants; *Formal and Transcendental Logic* (1929); and *Cartesian Meditations*, published in French translation by Emanuel Levinas and Gabrielle Peiffer in 1931.[56] With the rise of National Socialism in Germany in 1933, Husserl was suspended from Freiburg University, with his teaching license withdrawn and eventually his German citizenship revoked in 1935.[57] He died in Freiburg in Breisgau on April 27, 1938. In the fall of that year, Fr. H. L. Van Breda miraculously secured the transportation from Freiburg to Louvain, of over 40,000 pages of Husserl's unpublished shorthand manuscripts as well as some 10,000 pages of transcriptions by his assistants, thus founding the Husserl Archives in Louvain.[58] Since the publication of the first volume of Husserliana—the collected works of Husserl—in 1950, forty-three volumes have been published to date.[59] In this study of Husserl's phenomenology of space, I draw primarily on posthumously published writings in the Husserliana series and corresponding English translations, including references to select unpublished manuscripts. In light of the extraordinary work of the Husserl Archives in making this material available, Dan Zahavi's comments, written in 1994, are today even more pertinent:

> It has for a long time been permissible to present a traditional (that is quasi-Cartesian) Husserl-interpretation, as long as one simply added that there might be more refined reflections in Husserl's unpublished research manuscripts. By now so many volumes of the Husserliana have appeared, however, that this excuse is simply no longer viable [...] more than enough has already appeared to refute once and for all any interpretation oblivious to the decisive differences between a traditional (be it Cartesian or Kantian) philosophy of subjectivity and Husserl's phenomenology.[60]

At this point we can turn expressly to the problem of *phenomenological* description. In this work, I propose to *carry out* a phenomenological description of space, employing a concrete example.[61] I do not thematise the descriptive method itself but rather show how it works by example. Some preliminary considerations concerning the theory of phenomenological description are, however, appropriate. The matter gets to the heart of Husserl's phenomenology, and can only be indicated in this introduction. Robert Sokolowski approaches the issue in terms of questions of presence and absence, of the appearance of things in modes of givenness, inherent to which belong modes of concealment and withdrawal.[62] It is not that there is something lying behind appearances or that there is "a screen of ideas that comes between us and the object as it really exists;" rather, the thing itself is given in the manner proper to its way of appearing.[63] Starting with the sensuously perceivable thing, the descriptive problem does not aim at its special features, but rather through these at "the ways in which it can be experienced [...] the modes of experience and modes of presentation."[64] What this problem indicates is an inherently reflexive condition, in which the perceiving subject is also given to itself in its way of self-disclosure in terms of its relation to the thing. Husserl proposes that this *relationship* itself can be described as a structural condition of the possibility of the experience of things. In this sense, as being concerned with descriptions of the structure of experience, phenomenological description is a description of "transcendental structures."[65] It is not possible to fully flesh out this matter within the space of this introduction. Here I can only point to the issues and their resolution by others, as my aim in this book is not to present the phenomenological method but to put it into practice.

David Carr approaches the question of the meaning of the motif of the transcendental for phenomenology's descriptive method by discussing the relationship between "subjectivity" and "intentionality," in the way that Husserl uses these terms.[66] Carr notes that Husserl emphasises the "descriptive, non-explanatory character of phenomenological investigations" in clarifying the manner in which things are given in experience.[67] The sense of "experience" Husserl foregrounds is that of "living through" something:

> Husserl wants to distinguish the awareness that belongs to this "living through" from any kind of awareness of objects. [...] In perception, for example [...] I perceive some object—for example, a tree in the garden—but I "experience" or "live through" (*ich erlebe*) the perception itself. I do not "live through" the tree, and unless I explicitly reflect, I do not perceive my perception.[68]

This experience as a "living through" process is *directed* towards the object: "In perception something is perceived, in imagination something is imagined [...] in desire something desired, and so forth."[69] Husserl terms this directedness towards the object as an experiential living through one's relation with it "intentionality." Carr's rich and detailed analyses are focused on Husserl's description of the structure of intentionality. The structure points to the phenomenon of meaning or *sense*—the object *as* experienced—and implicated is not merely the givenness of things, but the experience of "my surrounding world" and the "world."[70] It is in relation to the givenness of the world that the concept of transcendence acquires significance for phenomenology:

> The original *realism* of phenomenology is never abandoned [...] no attempt is made to reduce or absorb the object of intentionality into consciousness. For this reason, using the term "reduction" in place of "epoche" is very misleading. On the contrary, the *transcendence* of object and world, which is precisely their *non*-reducibility (to consciousness), is taken seriously and subjected to careful analysis. [...] the point is not to deduce or infer the world's existence—much less to explain it or indeed explain consciousness—but to clarify and describe the sense of that existence.[71]

The aim of this study is to carry out a description of the experiential sense of spatiality. In doing this, I expressly refrain, where possible, from employing technical language typically found in Husserl's programmatic works—that is, texts concerned with presenting phenomenology's aims and methods rather than actual descriptions—such as "intentionality," "transcendental subjectivity," "epochē," and "reduction." I approach the question of intentionality from the perspective of embodiment, and thus frame the question of spatial experience in terms of embodied subjectivity, what Husserl calls the "lived body." The reader familiar with Husserl's programmatic works, but less so with his posthumously published research manuscripts, may find it surprising to see that these technical terms so readily associated with Husserl recede into the background when he is engaged in concrete phenomenological description. The scholars whom I have noted above, and others not mentioned, have argued convincingly for a reassessment of Husserl's philosophical legacy, presenting his philosophy in a new light.[72] This study thus adds to this new engagement with Husserl, as an example of the possibilities of phenomenology as a descriptive practice.

The style of spatial description developed in this work can therefore be understood as a phenomenological ethnography of space, with the dual aim of developing both a concrete phenomenological description of the structure of spatiality and a spatial ethnography. In his approach to ethnographic fieldwork, anthropologist Alessandro Duranti draws explicitly on Husserl's philosophy, for example, in his *The Anthropology of Intentions*. Duranti's focus, however, is not on space but on the significance of Husserl's concept of intentionality for an approach to linguistic anthropology in terms of a method that he terms "ethnopragmatics."[73] The work of Tim Ingold is well known for its phenomenological perspective, but Ingold's approach tends to be more deeply engaged with Heidegger's philosophy than with Husserl's.[74] In their compelling co-edited volume, *Phenomenology in Anthropology*, Kalpana Ram and Christopher Houston trace the contours of the "poetics and politics of phenomenological ethnography," exemplified in descriptions of the contributors to their volume.[75] Although I would hope that my descriptions echo some of the qualities of these ethnographies by anthropologists—specifically Chapter 4—my study differs from these works in two significant ways: firstly, I do not regard the wider phenomenological tradition, such as the legacy of Heidegger and Merleau-Ponty, but develop my study with a distinct focus on Husserl; and secondly, my primary concern is with the problem of spatial experience, rather than the wide range of themes that social and cultural anthropology investigate. The 2003 special issue of the journal *Ethnography*, guest edited by Jack Katz and Thomas J. Csordas, considers the influence of phenomenological methods in ethnographic research, specifically as regards tensions in the use of phenomenological ethnography in anthropology and sociology.[76] Other important works in this vein include Michael Jackson's edited volume, *Things as They Are: New Directions in Phenomenological Anthropology* (1996) and the article by Robert Desjarlais and C. Jason Throop, "Phenomenological Approaches in Anthropology" (2011).[77] Katz and Csordas are not concerned with differentiating between phenomenological paradigms and Desjarlais and Throop's article takes a critical stance, while Jackson's volume treats the broad phenomenological spectrum. As with the volume by Ram and Houston, the question of Husserl's *specific* contribution to ethnography is not a primary concern of these works, far less questions of his phenomenology of space. The work of scholars in PEACE—"Phenomenology for East-Asian CirclE"—should also be noted, such as the volume edited by Kwok-Ying Lau, Chan-Fai Cheung, and Tze-Wan Kwan, *Identity and Alterity: Phenomenology and Cultural Traditions*.[78] This volume includes insightful interpretations of Husserl's thought by Lau and Xianghong Fang, but these do not address the problem of space specifically.[79]

I was led to the problem of spatial description via insights gained through my experience of the phenomenon of the ritual praxis itself. The matter concerns the question of how to thematise the spatiality of the situation, to describe what is properly an embodied and intersubjective experience. In Chapter 1, I introduce and discuss the path that I took to arrive at the task of drawing out and articulating a Husserlian phenomenology of space from an interest in the spatiality of the ritual. Fieldwork was essential to this process, and I present the background to field research in Salvador. The chapter introduces the anthropological context of research on Afro-Brazilian religion, and specifically Candomblé. I identify certain theoretical issues around the systematic study of Candomblé praxis foregrounded in the work of anthropologist Marcio Goldman that relate to the seminal studies of sociologist Roger Bastide, which I propose pertain to a hermeneutics of ritual. This ultimately points to problems of understanding and conceptions of time related to the ethics of ethnographic study in the field. Implied are certain possibilities for spatial experience characterised by "empathy" (*Einfühlung*) and "coevalness," concepts I draw from the philosophical and theoretical critiques of anthropology of Valentin Mudimbe and Johannes Fabian. I take up the spatio-perceptual theme that these concepts indicate. They point to the fundamental significance of lived experience as a mode of "sensing history" at the level of sense perceptual encounter, and it is in this light that I introduce the problem of a phenomenology of space as developed in Husserl's thought. To be clear, the methodological considerations of this chapter do not pertain to programmatic questions of method internal to Husserl's philosophy, as noted above, but to the path that led me from an interest in the spatiality of the ritual to a way of describing it.

In the second and third chapters, I explore Husserl's phenomenology of spatial experience in detail. Here, a few notes on translation are appropriate. The difficulty of approaching and attempting to translate Husserl's writings in German cannot be overstated. Many volumes in the Husserliana series have been translated into English, as well as some text fragments published elsewhere. I have worked primarily with these English translations of Husserl's writings. Where no such translations are available, I have consulted the original publications in German, as well as certain unpublished manuscripts. In working with German texts, I have consistently drawn on Dorion Cairns's authoritative *Guide for Translating Husserl*, as well as the dictionaries of Husserl's philosophy by John J. Drummond, and Dermot Moran and Joseph Cohen.[80] It is important to note that certain of Husserl's technical terms have been rendered in different ways in English, and for this reason I have consistently referenced the corresponding German works for key terms in working with English translations. Where I have chosen to render terms differently than given in English translations, I have noted either in the main body of the text or in the notes. Identifying intuitively a specific phrase or passage in Husserl's writings in German that stands out as of particular relevance for my interest in space is one thing, but attempting to expressly and faithfully render its meaning in English translation is another. To this end, I have benefited from extended and in-depth conversations and correspondence—sometimes limited to a single compound word—with my colleagues Maximilian Sternberg and Natalie Melas, and my doctoral research assistant Daniel Friedman. Ultimately, however, I have determined the form that these translations have taken, the meanings that they aim to convey, and the rendering of Husserl's German expressions in English. Apart from these untranslated writings of Husserl, I have worked closely, as noted earlier, with Ulrich Claesges's *Edmund Husserls Theorie der Raumkonstitution*, which is untranslated in English. These notes on translation apply equally to Claesges's study.

In developing my analyses in Chapter 2, I draw on Claesges's study of Husserl's theory of the constitution of space. I introduce certain aspects of the ritual for phenomenologically descriptive purposes as examples. Insofar as the spatial situation of the *caboclo reunião* functions as exemplary in a sustained way throughout this and the following chapter, the phenomenological description gathers increasing ethnographic significance. The distinction, therefore, between the two modes of description—phenomenological and ethnographic—becomes increasingly blurred. I begin Chapter 2 by considering two basic concepts in Husserl's technical vocabulary, that of "constitution" and "experience," drawing on the work of Sokolowski.[81] With a clarification of these concepts in hand, I explore in detail the problem of space constitution, beginning with the experience of "things" understood in an abstract way as merely sensuous phenomena, or what Husserl terms "phantoms." At this level of description, it is as if all objects experienced sense perceptually have been stripped of their layers of historical and cultural significance, appearing in merely sensible givenness. It is a methodological abstraction through which Husserl is able to describe certain structural features of spatial experience, primarily in visual and tactual givenness. I explore this, using the ritual example in a sustained way. These features of space constitution include the modes of givenness of the sensible, perceived and apperceived in structures of perspectivity, positionality, and horizonality; the peculiar mode of self-givenness of the perceiving subject as embodied, that is, the kinaesthetic structure and corporeity of the body as what Husserl terms the "lived body" (*Leib*); the integral relation between the "spontaneity" and "receptivity" of the lived body as a motivational structure tied to the *affectivity* of space; and the temporality of spatial experience as characterised by the accruing and sedimentation of sense in the form of lived bodily acquisitions and habitualities. Husserl's systematic descriptions of space constitution from the point of view of an experiencing, embodied subject for whom sense accrues immanent to it as *habitus* imply intersubjective experience. These structurally descriptive analyses of what I have termed "phantom spatiality"—space given in its mere sensibility—and lived bodily corporeity set the bases for the more concrete investigations of space as intersubjectively constituted in the following chapter.

Chapter 3 investigates in greater depth problems of the constitution of visual and tactual space, exploring the temporal density of spatial experience in the genesis, accrual, acquisition, sedimentation, and transformation of sense. Before taking this step, however, I consider the theme of *horizon* in its relation to the perceptual experience of that which is merely sensuously given, that is, phantom spatiality. Following the analyses of Zahavi, I characterise phantom spatiality in terms of the concept "horizon perception," a notion that indicates a certain structural indeterminacy in terms of which space in its mere sensibility is given. This indeterminacy that characterises the perception of horizons is an index of another, corresponding structural feature of spatial experience, namely, the principle of the *experienceability* of space in a generalised sense, which Zahavi terms "open intersubjectivity." Even in terms of the methodological abstraction of phantom experience, this structural feature of spatiality points to an open, indeterminate plurality of actual or possible perceiving subjects, which can be human or non-human.

This level of description clarifies structure, but it cannot explain the "genesis" of space, that is, the process of the constitution of sense. The problems here are intricate, having to do with the concreteness of spatial experience, where "things" are no longer thematised in their appearance as mere sensuous phantoms, but rather as the givenness of familiar surroundings or an "environing world" (*Umwelt*). We encounter here a methodological shift in Husserl's philosophy from "static" to "genetic" phenomenology, the latter term to be understood in a *phenomenological* sense concerned with *temporality*, and not an empirical-biological one related to information. In approaching this methodological shift, I draw on the analyses of Welton. The matter necessarily points to the problem of the experience, not merely of environing things but of other subjects and of the "Other," in an ethnographic sense. I take up this problem as one of elaborating the spatial implications of Husserl's theory of the experience of another embodied subjectivity through what he terms "empathy" (*Einfühlung*). Husserl uses this term with a specific phenomenological meaning, and I analyse its significance for a description of the intersubjective constitution of space as a more concrete mode of spatial experience that I term "empathic spatiality." With reference to the exemplary function of the *caboclo reunião*, I introduce the spatial affectivity of the gestural movements and singing voices of women. In the linguality of the sound is also embodied its occasionality, which is a spatial condition within which I myself am immersed. At this moment in my analysis, I introduce the problem of generation. The spatiality of the ritual is not merely between subjects, not merely *inter*subjective, but is an inheritance characterised by a certain traditionality, intergenerationality, and historicity. Drawing on Steinbock's "generative phenomenology" I investigate and elaborate on the problem of spatiality in its properly concrete, generative experiential givenness. What I term "generative space" is a mode of intersubjective, intergenerational, historical, and environmental (implying interspecific) experience that is inextricably intertwined with the spatiality and corporeity of the lived body. In elaborating these relations, I introduce the *phenomenological* concept of "environmentality" (*Umweltlichkeit*), which speaks of the generativity and geo-historicity of space, what Husserl sometimes terms "earth-space," "earth-ground," or simply "earth."

The fourth chapter is a spatial ethnography of the *caboclo reunião* of Tupiniquim. It begins with a consideration of the role that my photographic images of the ritual play throughout the book in supplementing phenomenological descriptions of space. In view of the environmentality of generative space—that is, space in its full concreteness within which phantom, genetic, and empathic spatialities are enmeshed—a phenomenological description of the spatiality of the ritual takes on an ethnographic style and texture. This chapter functions at the same time as an *example* of a concrete, phenomenological description of the constitution of space, that is, a description of the experiential givenness of space.

Notes

1 Stuart Hall, *Familiar Stranger: A Life between Two Islands*, ed. Bill Schwarz (Durham, NC: Duke University Press, 2017), 35.
2 Nenny was an Orisha devotee who raised my father from early childhood, he having been estranged from his biological parents. In this way, I came to also know Nenny's children as aunts and uncles.
3 Hall, *Familiar Stranger*, 50.
4 Simone Schwarz-Bart, *The Bridge of Beyond*, trans. Barbara Bray (New York: New York Review Books, 2013), 25.
5 My reference to C. L. R. James is more opaque, namely, to the opening chapter of his *Beyond a Boundary*, which he frames around "the bedroom window" through which he observes as "a small boy of six," "not a person but a stroke," entranced by the movement of Arthur Jones who "when the ball hit down outside the off-stump [...] lifted himself to his height, up went his bat and he brought it down across the ball as a woodsman puts his axe to a tree." C. L. R. James, *Beyond a Boundary* (London: Serpent's Tail, 1994), 3–5.
6 The seminal study of the social production of space, which also traces out a genealogy of the modern concept of space, is Henri Lefebvre, *The Production of Space*, trans. Donald Nicholson-Smith (Oxford: Blackwell, 1991). The literature on Lefebvre is extensive; a volume examining in breadth and depth the contours and intricacies of his thought is Kanishka Goonewardena et al., eds., *Space, Difference, Everyday Life: Reading Henri Lefebvre* (New York: Routledge, 2008).
7 Edward S. Casey, "Part Three: The Supremacy of Space," in *The Fate of Place* (Berkeley: University of California Press, 1998), 131–93.
8 Lefebvre, *The Production of Space*, 201.
9 Sara Heinämaa, *Toward a Phenomenology of Sexual Difference: Husserl, Merleau-Ponty, Beauvoir* (London: Rowman & Littlefield, 2003); Dan Zahavi, *Husserl and Transcendental Intersubjectivity*, trans. Elizabeth A. Behnke (Athens: Ohio University Press, 2001); Anthony J. Steinbock, *Home and Beyond: Generative Phenomenology after Husserl* (Evanston, IL: Northwestern University Press, 1995).
10 Marilyn Strathern, *Property, Substance and Effect: Anthropological Essays on Persons and Things* (London: Athlone, 1999), 1.
11 Strathern, *Property, Substance and Effect*, 6–11.
12 Strathern, 262, note 1.
13 I am inspired here by David Scott's notion of a "problem space," but interpreted more literally as an embodied condition, rather than a primarily discursive one. See David Scott, *Conscripts of Modernity: The Tragedy of Colonial Enlightenment* (Durham, NC: Duke University Press, 2004), 2–6.
14 The work of Bronisław Malinowski is paradigmatic in this context, specifically for the tradition of British social anthropology, the tradition which Strathern

18   Introduction: spatial description

inherits. For an overview, see Sharon MacDonald, "British Social Anthropology," in *Handbook of Ethnography*, ed. Paul Atkinson et al. (London: Sage Publications, 2002), 60–79.
15 Caroline Humphrey, "Ideology in Infrastructure: Architecture and Soviet Imagination," *Journal of the Royal Anthropological Institute* 11, no. 1 (2005): 39–58.
16 Strathern, 5.
17 Strathern, 1.
18 Humphrey, "Ideology in Infrastructure," 41.
19 Strathern, 6.
20 A seminal work interrogating the ethics, politics, and epistemological value of ethnographic writing is James Clifford and George E. Marcus, eds., *Writing Culture: The Poetics and Politics of Ethnography* (Berkeley: University of California Press, 1986). A more recent work focused specifically on material culture is Amiria Henare, Martin Holbraad, and Sari Wastel, eds., *Thinking through Things: Theorising Artefacts Ethnographically* (London: Routledge, 2007). On the work of Marilyn Strathern specifically, see Martin Holbraad and Morten Axel Pedersen, "Relational Ethnography: Strathern's Comparisons and Scales," in *The Ontological Turn: An Anthropological Exposition* (Cambridge, UK: Cambridge University Press, 2017), 110–56. See also Eduardo Viveiros de Castro and Marcio Goldman, "Slow Motions: Comments on a Few Texts by Marilyn Strathern," *Cambridge Anthropology* 28, no. 3 (January 2008): 23–42.
21 Jocélio Teles dos Santos, *O Dono da Terra: O Caboclo nos Candomblés da Bahia* (Salvador: SarahLetras, 1995), 9.
22 Anthony Steinbock, *Limit-Phenomena and Phenomenology in Husserl* (London: Rowman & Littlefield, 2017), ix–x.
23 Maurice Merleau-Ponty, *Phenomenology of Perception*, trans. Colin Smith (London: Routledge, 1989); Maurice Merleau-Ponty, *Phénoménologie de la perception* (Paris: Gallimard, 1945).
24 H. L. Van Breda, "Merleau-Ponty and the Husserl Archives at Louvain," in Maurice Merleau-Ponty, *Texts and Dialogues: On Philosophy, Politics, and Culture*, ed. Hugh J. Silverman and James Barry Jr. (Amherst, NY: Humanity Books, 2005), 151.
25 Van Breda, "Merleau-Ponty and the Husserl Archives at Louvain," 161.
26 Dan Zahavi, "Husserl's Phenomenology of the Body," *Études Phênoménologiques*, 19 (1994): 63.
27 Klaus Held, "Husserl's Phenomenological Method," in *The New Husserl: A Critical Reader*, ed. Donn Welton (Bloomington: Indiana University Press, 2003), 3.
28 These themes do not cover the extent of Husserl's investigations. Anthony Steinbock, for example, has explored problems of what he terms "limit-phenomena" in Husserl, which, apart from generativity, include those of "vertical givenness," "vocational experience," "moral emotions," and "loving"; meanwhile, Janet Donohoe has investigated Husserl's ethics. See, for example, Steinbock, *Limit Phenomena and Phenomenology in Husserl* and Janet Donohoe, *Husserl on Ethics and Intersubjectivity: From Static to Genetic Phenomenology* (Toronto: University of Toronto Press, 2016). Research on Husserl has been flourishing among phenomenologists interested in his legacy and I refer to relevant works in the chapters to follow.
29 W. R. Boyce Gibson's English translation, published in 1930, is the standard reference; see Edmund Husserl, *Ideas: General Introduction to Pure Phenomenology*, trans. W. R. Boyce Gibson (London: Routledge, 2012), and Edmund Husserl, *The Crisis of European Sciences and Transcendental Phenomenology: An Introduction to Phenomenological Philosophy*, trans. David Carr (Evanston, IL: Northwestern University Press, 1970). A recent example of this critical

reading focused on the opening lines of Husserl's *Ideas* is Mark Jarzombek, "Husserl and The Problem of Worldliness," in *Disorienting Phenomenology, Log 42*, ed. Cynthia Davidson and Bryan E. Norwood (New York: Anyone Corporation, 2018), 67–79.
30 See, for example, Filip Mattens, "From the Origin of Spatiality to a Variety of Spaces," in *The Oxford Handbook of the History of Phenomenology*, ed. Dan Zahavi (Oxford: Oxford University Press, 2018), 558–78.
31 On deconstruction in architecture see Mark Wigley, *The Architecture of Deconstruction: Derrida's Haunt* (Cambridge, MA: MIT Press, 1993). For an intellectually generous and expansive approach that also engages with psychoanalysis see Anthony Vidler, *The Architectural Uncanny: Essays in the Modern Unhomely* (Cambridge, MA: MIT Press, 1992). On Derrida and phenomenology, see Dermot Moran, "Jacques Derrida: From Phenomenology to Deconstruction," in Moran, *Introduction to Phenomenology* (London: Routledge, 2000), 435–74. Considered more broadly, not only post-structuralism, but structuralism itself can be seen as having its basis in phenomenology. See Elmar Holenstein, *Roman Jakobson's Approach to Language: Phenomenological Structuralism*, trans. Catherine Schelbert and Tarcisius Schelbert (Bloomington: Indiana University Press, 1976), and Beata Stawarska, *Saussure's Philosophy of Language as Phenomenology: Undoing the Doctrine of the Course in General Linguistics* (Oxford: Oxford University Press, 2015).
32 Jorge Otero-Pailos, *Architecture's Historical Turn: Phenomenology and the Rise of the Postmodern* (Minneapolis: University of Minnesota Press, 2010); M. Reza Shirazi, *Towards an Articulated Phenomenological Interpretation of Architecture: Phenomenal Phenomenology* (London: Routledge, 2014).
33 Pérez-Gómez is a prolific author who established a distinct phenomenological approach to architectural history and theory in his influential book, *Architecture and the Crisis of Modern Science* (Cambridge, MA: MIT Press, 1985). See Steven Holl, Juhani Pallasmaa, and Alberto Pérez-Gómez, *Questions of Perception: Phenomenology of Architecture* (San Francisco, CA: William Stout, 2006), and Peter Zumthor, *Atmospheres: Architectural Environments, Surrounding Objects* (Basel: Birkhäuser, 2006).
34 José de Paiva, ed. *The Living Tradition of Architecture* (London: Routledge, 2017). Contributors to this volume include Frampton and Pérez-Gómez mentioned above, Christian Frost, Dagmar Weston, David Leatherbarrow, Gabriele Bryant, Joseph Rykwert, Karsten Harries, Mari Hvattum, Patrick Lynch, Robin Middleton, Stephen Witherford, Werner Oechslin, as well as Eric Parry and Daniel Libeskind. Also significant has been the work of Adam Sharr and Jonathan Hale. Joseph Bedford has examined Vesely's contribution to architectural phenomenology, specifically in the sphere of architectural education, in his doctoral dissertation. Bedford's dissertation was in progress and later embargoed, in anticipation of its publication, during my work on this book. I was therefore unable to consult it, but I benefitted from multiple conversations with him, for which I express my thanks. See Joseph Bedford, "Creativity's Shadow: Dalibor Vesely, Phenomenology and Architectural Education (1968–1998)" (PhD diss., Princeton University, 2018).
35 I consider Vesely's appropriation of the concept of "the natural world" in Patočka, and explore the concept in Patočka's thought in Tao DuFour, "Toward a Somatology of Landscape: Anthropological Multinaturalism and The 'Natural' World," in *Routledge Research Companion to Landscape Architecture*, ed. Ellen Braae and Henriette Steiner (London: Routledge, 2019), 156–70.
36 Dalibor Vesely, *Architecture in the Age of Divided Representation: The Question of Creativity in the Shadow of Production* (Cambridge, MA: MIT Pres, 2004). Vesely and Carl taught together from the 1980s in the graduate programme in the History and Philosophy of Architecture at the Department of

20 Introduction: spatial description

Architecture at Cambridge University. See the preface by Eric Parry in de Paiva, *The Living Tradition of Architecture*, ix–xi.
37 Henriette Steiner and Maximilian Sternberg, eds., *Phenomenologies of the City: Studies in the History and Philosophy of Architecture* (Farnham: Ashgate, 2015).
38 See, for example, Wendy Pullan and Britt Baillie, eds. *Locating Urban Conflicts: Ethnicity, Nationalism, and the Everyday* (Basingstoke: Palgrave Macmillan, 2013).
39 Davidson and Norwood, *Disorienting Phenomenology*. For Jarzombek's contribution on Husserl see my note above.
40 See, for example, Sara Ahmed, *Queer Phenomenology: Orientations, Objects, Others* (Durham: Duke University Press, 2006); and the recent volume, published subsequent to the *Log* issue by Davidson and Norwood, by Gail Weiss, Ann V. Murphy, and Gayle Salamon, eds., *50 Concepts for a Critical Phenomenology* (Evanston, Illinois: Northwestern University Press, 2020).
41 D. Zahavi and S. Loidolt, "Critical Phenomenology and Psychiatry," *Continental Philosophy Review* (in press, 2022). I thank Dan Zahavi for kindly granting me permission to quote from the manuscript of this article. It may be relevant here to note a wider contemporary antagonism directed not only at "architectural phenomenology"—a term that is perhaps too general, as it includes what are actually diverse approaches—but of phenomenology more broadly. For a response to these more recent antagonisms see Dan Zahavi, "The End of What? Phenomenology vs. Speculative Realism," *International Journal of Philosophical Studies* 24, no.3 (2016): 289–309.
42 See Jean Khalfa, "Fanon and Psychiatry," *Nottingham French Studies* 54, no. 1 (2015): 52–71. I thank Jean Khalfa for directing me to his article and for sharing with me in conversations his profound insights into Fanon's engagement with phenomenology. Achille Mbembe also indicates the influence of phenomenology on Fanon's thought and practice, noting, for example, that "Fanon maintains, 'the constant concern to refer each gesture, each word, each facial expression of the patient' to the illness afflicting him." See Achille Mbembe, *Necropolitics*, trans. Steven Corcoran (Durham, NC: Duke University Press, 2019), 144. On Merleau-Ponty and Husserl see Van Breda, "Merleau-Ponty and the Husserl Archives at Louvain," cited above. See also Donald A. Landes, "Merleau-Ponty from 1945 to 1952: The Ontological Weight of Perception and the Transcendental Force of Description," in Zahavi, *The Oxford Handbook of the History of Phenomenology*, 360–79.
43 Edward Casey, *Getting Back into Place* (Bloomington: Indiana University Press, 1993) and Casey, *The Fate of Place*; Karsten Harries, *The Ethical Function of Architecture* (Cambridge, MA: MIT Press, 1997); Andrew Benjamin, *Architectural Philosophy: Form, Function and Alterity* (London: Athlone Press, 2001); Fred Rush, *On Architecture* (London: Routledge, 2008); Jeff Malpas, *Place and Experience: A Philosophical Topography* (Cambridge, UK: Cambridge University Press, 1999).
44 James Dodd, *Phenomenology, Architecture and the Built World: Exercises in Philosophical Anthropology* (Leiden: Brill, 2017). I thank David Carr for drawing my attention to this important work.
45 See, for example, "Adumbration, Sensation and Movement," in Dodd, *Phenomenology, Architecture and the Built World*, 130–41.
46 Ulrich Claesges, *Edmund Husserls Theorie der Raumkonstitution* (Den Haag: Martinus Nijhoff, 1964).
47 Frederick Irving Kersten, "Husserl's Investigations toward a Phenomenology of Space" (PhD diss., New School for Social Research, 1964); Noel Mouloud, "Le principe spatial d'individuation: Fondement phénoménologique et signification géométrique," *Revue de Métaphysique et de Morale*, 1 (January–March 1956): 259–82.

48 Edmund Husserl, *Ding und Raum: Vorlesungen 1907*, Husserliana, vol. 16, ed. Iso Kern (The Hague: Martinus Nijhoff, 1973) (English translation, *Thing and Space: Lectures of 1907*, trans. Richard Rojcewicz [Dordrecht: Kluwer, 2010]); idem., *Analysen zur passiven Synthesis. Aus Vorlesungs- und Forschungsmanuskripten 1918–1926*, Husserliana, vol. 11, ed. Margot Fleischer (The Hague: Martinus Nijhoff, 1966) (English translation, *Analyses Concerning Passive and Active Synthesis: Lectures on Transcendental Logic*, trans. Anthony Steinbock [Dordrecht: Kluwer, 2001]); Peter McCormick and Frederick Elliston, eds., *Husserl: Shorter Works* (Notre Dame, IN: University of Notre Dame Press, 1981), 211–70. The German texts translated for this volume were published in different venues. I refer to these in Chapter 3 of this book.

49 See, for example, Donn Welton, *The Other Husserl: The Horizons of Transcendental Phenomenology* (Bloomington: Indiana University Press, 2000); David Carr, *Phenomenology and the Problem of History: A Study of Husserl's Transcendental Philosophy* (Evanston, IL: Northwestern University Press, 1974); Dermot Moran, *Husserl's Crisis of the European Sciences and Transcendental Phenomenology: An Introduction* (Cambridge, MA: Cambridge University Press, 2012); Robert Sokolowski, *The Formation of Husserl's Concept of Constitution* (The Hague: Martinus Nijhoff, 1970).

50 Jaana Parviainen, "Choreographing Resistances: Spatial-Kinaesthetic Intelligence and Bodily Knowledge as Political Tools in Activist Work," *Mobilities* 5, no. 3 (September 2010): 311–29.

51 Dermot Moran and Joseph Cohen, *The Husserl Dictionary* (London: Continuum, 2012), 12.

52 Held, "Husserl's Phenomenological Method," 4.

53 Held, 4. See also Dermot Moran, *Edmund Husserl: Founder of Phenomenology* (Cambridge, MA: Polity Press, 2005), 15–19.

54 Edmund Husserl, *Logical Investigations*, vol. 1, trans. J. N. Findlay, ed. Dermot Moran (London and New York: Routledge, 2001), xvii; idem., *Logical Investigations*, vol. 2, ed. Dermot Moran, trans. J. N. Findlay (London: Routledge, 2001); idem., *Ideas Pertaining to a Pure Phenomenology and to Phenomenological Philosophy. First Book: General Introduction to a Pure Phenomenology*, trans. F. Kersten (The Hague: Martinus Nijhoff, 1983).

55 Husserl, *The Crisis of European Sciences*. On the chronology of Husserl's life and work, see Moran and Cohen, *The Husserl Dictionary*, 12–18.

56 Edmund Husserl, *On the Phenomenology of the Consciousness of Internal Time (1893–1917)*, trans. John Barnett Brough (Dordrecht: Kluwer, 1991); idem., *Formal and Transcendental Logic*, trans. Dorion Cairns (The Hague: Martinus Nijhoff, 1969); idem., *Cartesian Meditations*, trans. Dorion Cairns (Dordrecht: Kluwer, 1999).

57 Moran, *Edmund Husserl*, 39–40.

58 Van Breda, "Merleau-Ponty and the Husserl Archives at Louvain," 150. On the founding of the archives see H. L. Van Breda, "Le Sauvetage de l'héritage husserlien et la fondation des Archives-Husserl," in *Husserl et la pensée moderne/Husserl und das Denken der Neuzeit*, ed. H. L. Van Breda and Jacques Taminiaux (The Hague: Martinus Nijhoff, 1959), 1–42.

59 "Husserliana: Edmund Husserl Gesammelte Werke," Husserl Archives Leuven, accessed January 6, 2021, https://hiw.kuleuven.be/hua/editionspublications/husserliana-gesammeltewerke.

60 Dan Zahavi, "Husserl's Phenomenology of the Body," 82.

61 The question of the significance of the "example" for phenomenological description implies the deeper problem of the methodological significance of a phenomenology of *phantasy* for description. This concerns Husserl's method of "free-phantasy variation." The matter is beyond the scope of this study, but for an outline of the problems see Richard M. Zaner, "Examples and Possibles:

A Criticism of Husserl's Theory of Free-Phantasy Variation," *Research in Phenomenology* 3 (1973): 29–43.
62 Robert Sokolowski, "The Theory of Phenomenological Description," in *Descriptions*, ed. Don Ihde and Hugh J. Silverman (Albany: SUNY Press, 1985), 14–24.
63 Sokolowski, "The Theory of Phenomenological Description," 17.
64 Sokolowski, "Theory of Phenomenological Description," 16.
65 To illustrate the sense of "structure" in Husserl, Sokolowski uses the rhetorical example of the exchange between John Searle and Jacques Derrida, in which Derrida asserts of the written sign that "the possibility of a written survival in the absence of the one who did the writing [...] pertains, qua possibility, to the structure of the mark as such, i.e., to the structure precisely of its iterability." Sokolowski, "Theory of Phenomenological Description," 19.
66 See David Carr, "Husserl: Subjectivity and Intentionality," in *The Paradox of Subjectivity: The Self in the Transcendental Tradition* (Oxford: Oxford University Press, 1999), 67–97.
67 Carr, "Husserl: Subjectivity and Intentionality," 69.
68 Carr, "Husserl: Subjectivity and Intentionality," 70. Carr is here distinguishing between the two German expressions typically translated as "experience"—*Erlebnis* and *Erfahrung*—and is focusing on *Erlebnis*. I discuss this difference at the start of Chapter 2 of the present work.
69 Carr, "Husserl: Subjectivity and Intentionality," 70.
70 Carr, "Husserl: Subjectivity and Intentionality," 77.
71 Carr, "Husserl: Subjectivity and Intentionality," 82.
72 See, for example, contributions in Welton, *The New Husserl*, and Zahavi, *Oxford Handbook of the History of Phenomenology*.
73 Alessandro Duranti, *The Anthropology of Intentions: Language in a World of Others* (Cambridge, UK: Cambridge University Press, 2015), 6–7.
74 Ingold is a prolific author; see, for example, Tim Ingold, *The Perception of the Environment: Essays on Livelihood, Dwelling and Skill* (London: Routledge, 2000), and idem., *Making: Anthropology, Archaeology, Art and Architecture* (London: Routledge, 2013).
75 Kalpana Ram and Christopher Houston, eds., *Phenomenology in Anthropology: A Sense of Perspective* (Bloomington: Indiana University Press, 2015).
76 See Jack Katz and Thomas J. Csordas, "Phenomenological Ethnography in Sociology and Anthropology," *Ethnography* 4, no. 3 (September, 2003): 275–288.
77 Michael Jackson, ed., *Things as They Are: New Directions in Phenomenological Anthropology* (Bloomington: Indiana University Press, 1996); Robert Desjarlais and C. Jason Throop, "Phenomenological Approaches in Anthropology," *Annual Review of Anthropology* 40 (October, 2011): 87–102.
78 Kwok-Ying Lau, Chan-Fai Cheung and Tze-Wan Kwan, eds. *Identity and Alterity: Phenomenology and Cultural Traditions* (Würzburg: Königshausen & Neumann, 2010). See also Kwok-ying Lau and Chung-Chi Yu, eds. *Border-Crossings: Phenomenology, Interculturality and Interdisciplinarity* (Würzburg: Königshausen & Neumann, 2014).
79 See Kwok-Ying Lau, "Husserl, Buddhism, and the Problematic of the Crisis of European Sciences," in Lau, Cheung, and Kwan, *Identity and Alterity*, 221–33, and Xianghong Fang, "The Phenomenological Stratification of Husserl's 'Idee' and Lao Tzu's 'Tao'," in idem., 235–46.
80 Dorion Cairns, *Guide for Translating Husserl* (The Hague: Martinus Nijhoff, 1973); Moran and Cohen, *The Husserl Dictionary;* John J. Drummond, *Historical Dictionary of Husserl's Philosophy* (Lanham, MD: Scarecrow, 2008).
81 I approach this in a manner analogous to Fred Kersten's introduction to the problem of a phenomenology of space in his doctoral dissertation. See the chapter "Some Aspects of Husserl's Theory of Consciousness," in Kersten, "Husserl's Investigations," 8–20.

1 Phenomenon and method

This chapter introduces the topic of Afro-Brazilian religion, specifically Candomblé, and the particular ritual that serves as the example and concrete basis of spatial description for this study. The ritual is referred to in Portuguese as a *reunião*—translated simply as a "gathering"—and involves the manifestation of an entity called a *caboclo*, referred to by name as Tupiniquim. Experienced as masculine, the manifestation of Tupiniquim is given as "his" incarnation in/as the body of the head of a Candomblé house, a woman called a *mãe-de-santo* or "mother-of-saint." The *reunião* ritual takes place in a room of a simple house in the periphery of the city of Salvador. The chapter begins with a view towards this urban context in Brazil where I undertook fieldwork, and in relation to this it traces the contours of Candomblé, its historical formation and aspects of its praxis. The ritual practices that I encountered in the field presented spatial situations of a particular quality and character, and pointed towards ways of conceptualising spatiality tied to their modes of givenness and presentation. Implied are problems of method in approaching spatial description, where the descriptive task is aimed at the situations and experiences themselves in the way that they are concretely lived. In the following, I elaborate on the manner in which the experiences of the field provoked methodological considerations on spatial description, as discussed in the Introduction, and go on to explore these questions of method. They concern the path that led me from an interest in the spatiality of Candomblé ritual to a way of describing spatial experience, and thus to the problem of a phenomenological description of space.

*

My fieldwork to study the spatiality of Candomblé ritual was undertaken in Salvador, the capital of the state of Bahia in the Brazilian Northeast. Salvador is a major port city that forms part of a vast natural harbour called Baía de Todos os Santos (Bay of All Saints). The scale of the bay is difficult to grasp from land by the naked eye and gives the feel of a small sea into which Salvador projects, like a peninsula.[1] The Portuguese first landed in this area

DOI: 10.4324/9781351116145-2

at the turn of the sixteenth century, though the mythical *Ilha Brasil* (Brazil Island) of the European imagination appeared already in the medieval world in a fourteenth-century map.[2] Salvador lies to the eastern side of the bay. In his history of Bahia, Antonio Risério traces the initial colonisation of the bay not to the Portuguese, but to the indigenous Tupinamba.[3] The Tupinamba are one of the peoples of the Tupi-Guarani linguistic family. Anthropologist Eduardo Viveiros de Castro notes that the population of the latter in the sixteenth century was around four million: "Of the various peoples who speak closely related languages, we find the groups ranging from small bands of nomadic hunters [...] up to the enormous Tupinamba villages of the sixteenth century with their sophisticated economy."[4] A small village in the area of the bay was set up by the Portuguese in the first half of the sixteenth century, portrayed by a contemporary historical narrative as "the most complete *eurotupinambá* village of Bahia."[5] The city of Salvador proper, however, was founded in 1549, and three years later the first episcopate under the archbishop of Lisbon was established. Salvador, the first capital of the Portuguese colony of Brazil, was to retain this status until 1763.[6] The task of pacification and catechisation of the indigenous population lay primarily in the hands of the religious orders, specifically the Society of Jesus, for whom Bahia was a "Jesuit utopia," an opportunity to "reinvent the human."[7] This utopia took the form of "the wholesale slaughter and enslavement of Indians" which, coupled with virulent epidemics, meant that by the turn of the century the indigenous population of Bahia in demographic terms had dwindled to insignificance.[8]

From its origins until the nineteenth century, Salvador was essentially a port and administrative centre, which functioned as part of a colonial society built on institutionalised enslavement and based on a plantation economy divided between a rural planter and an urban merchant class.[9] The eighteenth-century city had a basic geographic and functional division: the port facing the bay formed the *cidade baixa* or low city, and atop the steep hills—the *cidade alta* or high city—were the colonial administrative and ecclesiastical centres.[10] Pierre Verger divides the traffic of enslaved Africans to Bahia into four "cycles," corresponding to the geographical regions in Africa from which persons were taken.[11] The first two cycles—the sixteenth to seventeenth centuries—saw the arrival of people from the Bantu linguistic group, in particular from Angola and the Congo. In terms of religious practices, they brought with them traditions of ancestor worship and the cult of the *inquice*.[12] The third and fourth cycles occurred in the eighteenth and nineteenth centuries, with slavery finally abolished in 1888.[13] This period saw the arrival of the Gégé and the Nagô-Yorùbá (from regions in present-day Togo, Republic of Benin, and southwestern Nigeria) who brought with them the cults of the *voduns* and the *orixás*.[14] Recent scholarship has highlighted the complexity and plasticity of the formation of identities as a consequence of the slave trade—including the denominational significance of slave ports on the African coast, geographic regions of residence, and ethno-linguistic identities—emphasising the tension between what Luis Nicolau Parés has termed *"ethnonym"* and *"meta-ethnic denomination."*[15] The former refers to modes of self-identification "internal" to social groups, while the latter term to "'external' denominations used, whether by Africans or European slavocrats, to designate a *plurality* of initially heterogeneous groups."[16] In the Bahian context Parés emphasises the process of meta-ethnic denomination, which was distinctly tied to language: "the ability of Africans to communicate with and understand one another [...] led to the absorption of these denominations as forms of self-identification and to the consequent creation of new communities or feelings of collective belonging."[17] The significance of this dialogical formation of community should not be viewed in the abstract, rather, religious practices and thus the space of ritual functioned as "a privileged context for expression."[18]

By the late nineteenth century, the population of Salvador was just over one hundred thousand.[19] Nineteenth-century Salvador, no longer the capital, but still a major city in the now independent Brazilian nation, was defined by a multilayered socio-economic structure.[20] The colonial tripartite city—the port of the low city, and the administrative and religious centres of the high city—was now spread out into various urban and rural districts. The latter comprised small farms, fishing communities, and coastal forests.[21] The ten or eleven urban districts allowed for a certain mobility across classes and races, making it possible for the veiled continuity of various African religious traditions, as Rachel Harding notes: "Many ritual activities of Candomblé were purposefully conducted clandestinely both to avoid detection and repression and because of their sui generis secretive nature. However, the public space of the street was also a site of ritual action."[22] This was even more the case in the rural districts where, according to João José Reis, "hills, woods, lagoons and rivers [...] provided ecological support for the development of an independent, quasi-clandestine African collective. The city was surrounded by mobile *quilombos* [maroon communities] and religious meeting places."[23]

Modern Salvador has, since the mid-twentieth century, expanded significantly beyond its nineteenth-century limits.[24] The process leading to the immense transformation of the city can be traced to the "new economic dynamism" of the Brazilian Northeast in the 1960s, such that today Salvador is an expansive city of roughly three million inhabitants.[25] The historic centre has retained its basic topographic integrity—the low city and the high city—though it is dwarfed by a modern skyline littered with commercial and residential towers. These latter form a cluster along the coast but overlook in the other direction towards the interior a field of low-level residential districts, which articulate the urban periphery. James Holston notes that urban peripheries

> developed in Brazil as the place of and for the laboring poor. After the 1930s, these hinterlands became practically the only areas in which

both established workers and new migrants could secure a residential foothold in Brazil's industrializing urban economies. As urban migration mushroomed in subsequent decades, so did this autoconstruction of distant hinterlands [...] At the same time, a new national state sought to modernise the organization of this urbanizing economy and society.[26]

Within this larger socio-economic framework concretely articulated by the urban fabric, resides an extraordinary, complex spiritual network. Anthropologist Marcio Goldman describes Candomblé succinctly as follows:

> Put very simply, Candomblé can be described as a religion of African origin, brought to Brazil with the traffic of slaves. Here in their new setting, Yoruba and Bantu cosmologies intermixed, blending with indigenous beliefs, popular Catholicism and European spiritualism. The essential feature of Candomblé is a cult centred on a pantheon of divinities called Orishas [orixás], who are "embodied" in certain ritually initiated followers.[27]

The systematic study of Candomblé dates to the turn of the twentieth century, but it is perhaps the works of French sociologist Roger Bastide, with his colleague and compatriot Pierre Verger in the 1950s and 1960s, that have had the most significant impact, to an extent influencing the religious discourse of Candomblé leaders themselves.[28] This resulted in the peculiar reflexive phenomenon in which Candomblé leaders, called a *mãe-* or *pai-de-santo* (mother- or father-of-saint), began to produce polemical and academic studies of their own religious practices.[29] This, however, is not the norm, and Candomblé remains a phenomenon fundamentally determined by a set of practices, handed down not through formal teaching but by means of a lengthy, highly elaborate and secretive process of practical "learning." Goldman draws on the ethnography of Gisèle Binon Cossard to describe this process, which it is useful to quote at length, as it captures the lived experience of Candomblé praxis. According to Cossard, the initiate must

> learn everything relating to ritual and the deities: how to take care of their sacred belongings, how to behave during the different ceremonies. Little by little, she tries to delve into the secrets of Candomblé, its "foundations" (*fundamento*). She is bound to face many difficulties in the process, since nobody, strictly speaking, will teach her a single chant, dance or appropriate gesture. As she cannot ask anything she is left to observe, with her head and eyes lowered, making sure never to appear too attentive or over-interested. [...] "Time dislikes whatever is done without it," say the elders. Hence much patience and perseverance is required, which enables friendships to be cultivated and, in trade for

endless hours of work, precious knowledge can be gleaned by paying attention during conversations. At the same time, the numerous chants and dance steps can be learnt by taking part in all the festivals. As time goes by, the novice becomes more confident. Knowledge of the ritual seeps into her slowly. Gestures and words, dances and melodies eventually become indissociable automatisms.[30]

The formation and development of Candomblé in nineteenth-century Bahia points to factors that are both specific to the social conditions of slavery in Brazil, as well as structural dimensions inherent to it historically as a form of religious praxis.[31] Although it is not the ethnographic focus of this study, I was fortunate during my fieldwork to have been welcomed to witness and participate in some of the more intimate aspects of one of the earliest recorded Candomblé religious houses or *terreiros* named Ilé Axé Iyá Nassô Oká, popularly known as Casa Branca. Established at some date between 1788 and 1830 and originally located in a district or *bairro* of Salvador near the historic centre, called Barroquinha, Ilé Axé Iyá Nassô Oká "is often considered to be a ritual template from which Candomblé evolved."[32] The *candomblé*—here referring to this specific religious community—initially took the form of a domestic cult linked to the black sisterhood of the Good Lord Jesus of the Martyrdoms as its patron saint.[33] The cult was organised in a large *tapia* house behind the Chapel of Our Lady of the Barroquinha. The *candomblé* was dedicated to two Yorùbá divinities, or *orixás*: the "lord of the house" was the *orixá* Xangô (the "god of storms") and the "owner of the earth" was Oxóssi (the "patron of hunters").[34] These attributes of these two *orixás*—"god of storms" and "patron of hunters"—indicate norms that also give a more general sense of how *orixás* are typically understood in Candomblé, and are not necessarily ontological characterisations regarding the "being" of the *orixás*, which is a problem fraught with difficulties.[35] I discuss the *orixás* in greater detail in Chapter 4, in terms of their apparent experiential givenness in the context of ritual praxis.[36]

At some point in the evolution of the *candomblé* of the Barroquinha there occurred a schism, involving the intrusion of a *vodun*—a divinity of Dahomean stock—called Oxumare, the "rainbow-snake."[37] Parés has foregrounded the historical presence of *voduns* within Candomblé, drawing on a *candomblé* roughly contemporaneous in its origins with Casa Branca, named Zoogodô Bogum Malê Rundô.[38] He proposes an alternative or complementary source as the genesis of the ritual and liturgical structure for Candomblé praxis that "would take the vodun cults in Africa as its *organizational model*" (and not merely the Yorùbá based *orixá* cults of Casa Branca), pointing to the complexity and cosmopolitanism of social structures in the Gbe-speaking areas of Africa—certain regions in the modern states of Togo and Nigeria, and the Republic of Benin—contemporaneous with colonial and nineteenth century Brazil.[39] In this vein Parés makes the salient point that "the plasticity and multiplicity of identity, which is typically attributed to late modernity, was a phenomenon occurring at least as early as the eighteenth century."[40] In her recent study of the largely Yorùbá-speaking origins of the candomblé Ilé Axé Iyá Nassô Oká (Casa Branca), Lisa Earl Castillo reveals the heterogeneity of the Yorùbá constitution itself of this paradigmatic *candomblé*.[41] My intention here is not to focus on the historicising of Candomblé per se, but rather to point to the insights of this scholarship, which reveals the complexity, hybridity, and interpenetration of praxes that characterised the phenomenon, as having existed from its historically accessible and interpretable beginnings. To this must be added, following Goldman, fundamental aspects of Candomblé praxis that complicate its "intra-African" heterogeneity, to use Parés's expression. In this study, I am particularly concerned with a category of "spirits" called *caboclos*. In speaking of these entities, Parés notes that

> the proliferation in Candomblé of "Brazilian" entities called *caboclos*—whether they be Indian spirits or other entities called *encantados*, associated with popular types such as the cowherd, fisherman, sailor, and so on, but in any case, entities, "created" in Brazil—seem to have occurred primarily at the end of the nineteenth century, although their presence in some cults of African origin might be much older.[42]

From its nineteenth century and perhaps earlier origins, Candomblé was therefore characterised by a certain plasticity of intra-African formation, and ritual articulation of its increasingly diverse Brazilian constitution. Although it is possible to establish a limited genealogy of certain Candomblé *terreiros*,[43] each *candomblé* is in principle an autonomous entity and the founding of a new *terreiro* does not necessarily require the sanction of anyone in particular.[44] Many *candomblés* are headed by women or *mães-de-santo* (mothers-of-saint), a topic that was explored in Ruth Landes's influential study, *The City of Women* (1947); subsequent scholarship, however, has contradicted Landes, confirming a long and continuous tradition of *candomblés* headed by men.[45] Nonetheless, the general composition (initiated participants) of *candomblés* had historically been and continues to be majority female. According to Parés, reasons for this, as well as the shift in the gender composition of Candomblé leadership, lie in the complex nature of social relations in nineteenth-century Brazil and the transformations of these relations as a consequence of abolition and processes of creolisation.[46] The scale of *terreiros*—their actual physical make-up—varies, from those that are large compounds comprising multiple structures—temples, shrines, fonts, areas of vegetation, a main ritual hall called a *barracão*, and living quarters[47]—to others that are basically the size of a modest dwelling. Today there are over fourteen hundred Candomblé *terreiros* in Salvador.[48]

Fieldwork as methodological clue

I travelled to Salvador initially on a short visit for preliminary fieldwork in 2008. During that time, I met an initiate of Candomblé, called a *filha-de-santo* or "daughter-of-saint," through a chance visit to one of the religious houses. When I returned to Brazil for intensive fieldwork, I visited the *terreiro* again and was told that the *filha-de-santo* whom I had met had moved to Rio de Janeiro. I was not given her details, nor was I welcomed as before. In effect, I had to begin again, from a field of over a thousand Candomblé houses, each more or less enclosed in religious secrecy. In the end, the phenomenon that I would ultimately have extraordinary and intimate access to was something that the literature had not prepared me for at that time: the ritual "manifestation" of a *caboclo*, or "Indian spirit."[49]

The systematic study of Candomblé: some theoretical issues

> Isabel asked me if I saw my image clearly in the mirror, and responding to her affirmatively, she explained to me that persons who are not able to see their image in the mirror are ready to die.[50]

In 1900, physician Raimundo Nina Rodrigues published his study of Afro-Brazilian religion, with the aim of proving a thesis that "African mentality [was] different from white Brazilian mentality."[51] The excerpt above is taken from his ethnography of one of the oldest and, today, most prestigious Candomblé *terreiros* in Salvador, called Gantois. The excerpt refers to the "representation" of the *orixá* Dadá—god of newborn children—which consists of a small funnel-shaped object made of cowries, with a fragment of a mirror embedded into it. The metaphor of the mirror and the theme of "mentality" point to the recurrent problem of cultural relativism. The racist and naïve psychologism of Nina Rodrigues would ultimately be repudiated by his successors, but even in this new disposition of empathy, the researcher would still not see herself "clearly" in Candomblé's mirror:

> While positivism cannot be said to forget that these things [i.e. "social data"] may be psychic representations, i.e. collective representations, it disregards their significatory values and ultimately tends to dehumanise the social. The sociology of understanding, by contrast, puts significations in the foreground, since the very purpose of understanding is to grasp them. But [... the] danger, pointed out by Lévy-Bruhl, of interpreting data pertaining to other civilizations in terms of our own values remains undiminished.[52]

The work of Bastide can be seen as initiating a new period in the study of Candomblé after the original research of Nina Rodrigues. Bastide's analyses would mark a definitive shift in the theoretical understanding of the religion away from naïve psychologisms, towards a sociology of understanding or "depth sociology," and ultimately towards an attempt to articulate an "epistemological" framework internal to Candomblé.[53] This latter concern shows Bastide's sensitivity to the problem of cultural difference. The philosopher and ethnological theorist Lucien Lévy-Bruhl, mentioned by Bastide in the quote above, framed the issue in terms of the problematic notion of "mentality"—a concept and theoretical model that even the historians of the French *Annales* school would appropriate for the study of the history of Europe.[54] For Bastide this sensitivity to difference was not a matter of psychologism, but rather of socio-cultural understandings, and thus by implication of historical situation. The fundamental concept was actually not that of "mentality," but rather of "collective representations," which Bastide awkwardly defines as "group mental images."[55]

A path through and beyond Bastide is suggested by Brazilian anthropologist Marcio Goldman in a text titled "How to Learn in an Afro-Brazilian Spirit Possession Religion: Ontology and Multiplicity in Candomblé." Here Goldman discusses the manner in which Bastide attempts to situate his theoretical ambitions in relation to three decisive paradigms of twentieth-century anthropology:

> Beginning by associating the name Lévy-Bruhl with an emphasis on participation, that of Durkheim and Mauss to the privilege given to classifications and that of Lévi-Strauss to transformations, Bastide then hesitates in the implementation of his synthesis.[56]

According to Goldman's interpretation, Bastide requalifies the three concepts in terms of the "category of action," as motivated by a "will to connect."[57] In other words, the classes are "pragmatic": they reflect a concern with the practical task of becoming closer to the *orixá*, for example through the process of initiation. This pragmatism makes the sharp conceptual separation above more fluid, drawing attention to the "fact that classifications are constantly 'manipulated.'"[58] In concluding, Goldman pushes the theme of action further, and he does this precisely by thematising *action* itself: "Hence, the key point is not the fact that manipulations are in accordance with classes or participations, but the fact of manipulations itself."[59] The significance of Goldman's astute analysis is that it puts back into relief the relationship between ethnography and the theoretical possibilities that this (ethnography) suggests; it glimpses the resistance Candomblé offers—due to its very ontological character, as opposed to an explicit ideological or political project—to conceptualisation based on predetermined epistemological models, be it psychologism or sociologism. In other words, it opens a path of empathy and attempts to subordinate discourse to the phenomenon itself.

La chose du texte

Goldman does not present his approach as hermeneutical; however, I propose to place his theoretical insights alongside the philosophy of Valentin Mudimbe. Mudimbe, a Congolese philosopher and postcolonial theorist, sets up his philosophical project comprehensively in his book, *The Invention of Africa: Gnosis, Philosophy, and the Order of Knowledge*.[60] This text is concerned with critically foregrounding the historical-methodological background to discourses on Africa—theological, anthropological, and politico-ideological—situating the legacy of the black West Indian E.W. Blyden (1832–1912) as a paradigm in which these discourses were already anticipated. Not only does the title itself suggest it, but Mudimbe speaks explicitly of his Foucauldian approach.[61] His critique, however, is also informed by hermeneutics, in terms of its concern with "unveiling *la chose du texte*," as Mudimbe himself states:

> This notion, which belongs to hermeneutics, and which according to Ricoeur's proposition calls for an *obedience* to the text in order to unfold its meaning, could be a key to the understanding of African *gnosis*.[62]

Mudimbe sets up a tension between the concepts of *gnosis* and *episteme*, which express two possible and distinct types of knowledge, foregrounding the former term.[63] The idea of *gnosis* as a form of knowledge can be traced to antiquity, specifically the writings of Plotinus in the third century A.D.[64] For Plotinus, *gnosis* has the sense of "a knowledge which does not need to articulate itself into demonstrations and propositions, since it amounts to an immediate contact and union with its object," while *episteme* implies "another knowledge which, being predicative as well as discursive, never can measure up to the wealth and immediacy of [*gnosis*]."[65] In the way that Mudimbe uses the term, *gnosis* functions as a "methodological tool": by making the very concept of "knowledge" into a problem, he enquires into the "conditions of possibility" that would determine both its normative sense and its production in relation to discourse about Africa.[66] His text thus functions as an "archaeology" in the Foucauldian sense. Where, in my view, Mudimbe goes beyond this Foucauldian paradigm is in his explicit raising of the question, directed towards himself: "who speaks and from where?"[67] In taking his lead from the notion of *Weltanschauung* (world-view)—a term associated with the hermeneutics of Wilhelm Dilthey—Mudimbe implicates the phenomenon of historical consciousness and therefore establishes in principle that the relationship between a living tradition and discourse about that tradition has a peculiar effect:

> These disciplines [social science and history of Africanist discourse] do not provide a real comprehension of the *Weltanschauungen* studied.

Yet one can also say that it is in these very discourses that African worlds have been established as realities for knowledge.[68]

In the final chapter of *The Invention of Africa*, titled "The Patience of Philosophy," Mudimbe addresses the question of "African philosophy," which he traces, as did Bastide, to the concept of "mentality" developed by Lévy-Bruhl.[69] He proceeds to review the systematic critique by African philosophers of what he terms the "Ethnophilosophical School."[70] In the final section of this chapter titled "Horizons of Knowledge," Mudimbe shifts from a critical position to a more programmatic one. He is still concerned with the theme of "African *gnosis*," but precisely what *gnosis* is Mudimbe throws open as a *question*: "What this *gnosis* attests to is thus [...] a dramatic but ordinary question about its own being: what is it and how can it remain a pertinent question mark?"[71] What Mudimbe terms "African *gnosis*" can be described broadly and formally as the productive *relation* between the *topos* of anthropology and the discourse of anthropology:

> Perhaps this *gnosis* makes more sense if seen as a result of two processes: first, a permanent reevaluation of the limits of anthropology as knowledge in order to transform it into a more credible *anthropou-logos*, that is a discourse on a human being; and, second, an examination of its own historicity.[72]

The ethical basis of this relation Mudimbe characterises as *Einfühlung*, which he translates as "sympathy";[73] in the phenomenological literature in English, however, the term is typically translated as "empathy."[74] I discuss the intricacies of *Einfühlung* as a concept pertaining to the experience of another person in Chapter 3, and for the moment follow the norm of rendering this term in English as empathy. That Mudimbe is using *Einfühlung* with some reference to the phenomenological tradition is clear, when one considers the significance of Paul Ricoeur's thought for his argument. The basis of empathy is what Mudimbe refers to as *"la chose du texte"*—the *matter* of the text—and it calls for both *"obedience* to the text" and "responsibility."[75] It is instructive here to turn to the sources of Mudimbe's theoretical-methodological insights themselves: the hermeneutical approach and, indicatively, the concrete practices.

From text to action: the interpretation of ritual as play

In "Hermeneutics and the Critique of Ideology," Paul Ricoeur suggests a movement away from interpreting "the matter of the text" as the topic of discourse via writing, to "a category that pertains to praxis."[76] Ricoeur draws the notion of "the matter of the text" from the hermeneutics of Hans-Georg Gadamer, which he further qualifies as "the sort of *world* opened up by it."[77] Although in this essay Ricoeur is concerned with qualifying discourse as a praxis in order to present the hermeneutical notion of "distanciation" as compatible with the project of a critique of ideology, we can abstract from it a more general theme.[78]

Ricoeur qualifies the sense of "world" in terms of the concept of "reference," that is, "the mode of being unfolded in front of the text."[79] What this implies is the sense in which the written text "takes hold" of or claims our understanding through its reference to a world as a structural possibility, a *mode* of being which has the character of a *mythos*, a "fable." As Ricoeur notes, here "we are developing a theme sketched by Gadamer himself, particularly in his magnificent pages on *play*."[80] Ricoeur is indeed being faithful to Gadamer, for it is precisely in terms of the theme of *mythos* as "the path of *mimēsis*, or creative imitation" that Gadamer establishes the relation between art and play.[81]

For Gadamer, the work of art "has something of the 'as if' character [...] recognized as an essential feature of the nature of play."[82] It is in terms of the concept of play that hermeneutics draws us away from discourse, from the written text as speech to phenomena that show themselves in terms of action. Of the latter, Gadamer points to the fundamental status of ritual, but he does not take us much deeper than a glimpse via a reference to Johan Huizinga's notion of "holy play."[83] Gadamer's primary concern is with the work of art, in terms of which ritual is passed over in favour of the written text.[84] In spite of this, he still provides us with a clue as to the significance of space:

> Human play requires a playing field. Setting off the playing field—just like setting off sacred precincts, as Huizinga rightly points out—sets off the sphere of play as a closed world, one without transition and mediation to the world of aims.[85]

Gadamer continues:

> The playing field on which the game is played is, as it were, set by the nature of the game itself and is defined far more by the structure that determines the movement of the game from within than by what it comes up against—i.e., the boundaries of the open space—limiting movement from without.[86]

Following Gadamer, play is thus grounded in a *structure*, and it is in terms of this structure that we come to have an understanding of the playing field as a spatial horizon. But here the question of play as action and thus the space of play is merely deferred, passed on to the notion of "structure." The *telos* of play is the very presentation of structure, such that play "is" structure: it is *self-presentation*.[87] As such, play overcomes its medium such that the medium too becomes play, and it does so absolutely. Gadamer therefore defines play as *"transformation into structure"* and total mediation.[88]

I have treated Gadamer's discussion of play formally, because he does not qualify his concepts using examples from ritual but rather constantly refers us to the work of art. This presents a methodological problem for the task of interpreting the spatiality of the *caboclo* ritual, for the notion of "art" may not be not wholly appropriate; it implies levels of differentiation and modes of representational mediation that one cannot simply assume.[89]

The clue to the methodological problem provided in advance by fieldwork

We arrived at play through Gadamer's reference to the "as if" character of the work of art, that is, the function of the work of art in mediating the experience of a reality that it itself makes structurally possible by means of *representation*. It cannot be said that what I witnessed in the field has the character an "as if," in the way that this motif is proposed by Gadamer with reference to the work of art. In the ritual context of Candomblé that I observed, the *mãe-de-santo* and others "manifest" through trance *caboclos* and in one instance an *orixá*, as I describe in Chapter 4. The *caboclo* or "Indian spirit" is not mediately present through an "as if" structure in this sense; "his" manifestation "in" the body of the *mãe-de-santo* is not metaphorical or theatrical; rather, through the lived corporeity of the *mãe-de-santo*, "he" is experienced as *immediately* present, in the flesh. In other words, the world "opened up" by the ritual is not encountered as mediated through representation, but as *presentation* in the immediacy of *lived experience*.

Mudimbe's concept of *gnosis* points to a discursive knowledge that is an inextricable interlacing of a modern episteme and traditional knowledges as a function of the historicity of coloniality. Beyond this, however, are implied the lived experiences that this *gnosis* is about. This "gnostic" discourse aims at lived experiences but cannot contain them; yet, it is necessary in order to speak about them, which is to speak about oneself as, to quote Stuart Hall, a "familiar stranger." Thus, Mudimbe states:

> *Gnosis* is by definition a kind of secret knowledge [...] a knowledge which is sometimes African by virtue of its authors and promoters, but which extends to a Western epistemological territory. [...] Does the question of how to relate in a more faithful way to *la chose du texte* necessarily imply another epistemological shift? Is it possible to consider this shift outside of the very epistemological field which makes [... this] question both possible and thinkable?[90]

It is the complexity of the historical experience of the human beings for whom the historicity of the colonial encounter *inheres* in their/our being, even as they/we continue to be the topics of an *anthropou-logos*, which makes the basic ethical disposition of empathy, in Mudimbe's sense, an imperative. It calls for a level of engagement closer than discourse and upon which discourse is grounded, which is the fundamental necessity of being actually present to *la chose du texte*, in the flesh. The fact that I have experienced the specific Candomblé ritual in person is itself a primary opening onto its truth. All further methodological considerations are founded on this presence to perception of the phenomenon.

—

I arrived in Salvador for my second, longer and more intensive period of fieldwork in March of 2010, having experienced the disappointment of not being able to study the *terreiro* I initially encountered on my first visit. I spent the first few weeks trying to gain access to a dispersed and secretive community. It was eventually through the help of a Brazilian friend that I was introduced to Mãe Juta, the *mãe-de-santo* (mother-of-saint) of a small Candomblé house in one of the peripheral districts of Salvador.[91] On the third Thursday of April I was invited to what she called a *reunião*, an everyday Portuguese word that in this context has the social sense of a "gathering." That evening I witnessed a ritual involving the phenomenon of trance, or the "arrival" of an "Indian spirit" named Tupiniquim, for whom the *mãe-de-santo* served as the "*médium*" (medium). I describe the event in detail in Chapter 4, but a few introductory comments here are needed.

Firstly, I must emphasise the uniqueness of the event. It is not merely that I witnessed it for the first time myself, but this study represents, to my knowledge, the first time that an event of this type in general has been extensively described and documented. In a correspondence with Brazilian anthropologist Marcio Goldman, he considered the *reunião*, via images I had sent him, as "peculiar," "another creation (in the artistic sense of the term) of the people of Bahia."[92] The only description of a similar type of event that I have come across in the literature is by Jocélio Teles dos Santos in his work published in 1995, *O Dono da Terra: O Caboclo nos Candomblés da Bahia*.[93] This text is exceptional in that it is a monograph dedicated solely to the cult of the *caboclos*. Scholarship on Candomblé, as I noted, tends to primarily focus on ritual and social practices involving African divinities, specifically the Yorùbá *orixás* and the Dahomean *voduns*, although peripheral mention is made of the *caboclos*. In the text by Santos, he gives a description in four pages of "Uma sessão de caboclo" (A caboclo session).[94] This *caboclo* "*sessão*" or "session" as described by Santos seems similar to the *reunião*, and it may simply be the case that the naming of the event is fluid; thus, a *sessão* is a *reunião*. Santos's description, however, is compact and is merely a fragment of a work that covers a much larger topic of the cult of the *caboclos* as a whole.

Another important ethnography is given by Jim Wafer in his book, *The Taste of Blood: Spirit Possession in Brazilian Candomblé* (1991), published four years before Santos's work. Wafer offers a vivid ethnography of a *caboclo* festival, which one also finds in Santos in the chapter, "A festa no Candomblé" (The festival in the Candomblé).[95] Although there are some common features—for example, the chants—the structure and quality of a *caboclo* festival is very different from that of a *sessão* or *reunião*, and it is for this reason that Santos treats the events as distinct types. The *caboclo* festival is a grand public affair, analogous to the well-documented public festivals for the African gods; the *reunião*, however, is intimate and for the most part private.[96] Wafer does not describe anything resembling a *sessão* or *reunião* in his ethnography, which is primarily concerned with the larger picture of *orixás*. We are left, therefore, with one written description that resembles the *reunião* in outline: Santos's "Uma sessão do caboclo." This ethnography thematises neither itself nor the phenomenon, with an explicit theoretical interest, apart from a comment at the end which characterises the *sessão* as "magic comedy," after Marcel Mauss.[97] This reference to Mauss implicates a more general discourse of anthropology, which I considered above through the mediation of Mudimbe. What truly grounds and qualifies *la chose du texte* is indeed the "matter" itself, which means, in this case, the *reunião* as a concrete *event*.

Einfühlung *and coevalness*

The notion of *Einfühlung* as used by Mudimbe—introduced earlier in this chapter and which I have rendered as "empathy"—is not only an ethical principle but also a methodological one. It is the means by which the subject matter is genuinely experienced in its self-showing. It is the subject matter that must dictate the character of *Einfühlung*. The subject matter with which Mudimbe is concerned is African *gnosis*, understood as a certain kind of "epistemological"—in a broad sense—phenomenon that is *textual*: "a knowledge which is sometimes African by virtue of its authors and promoters, but which extends to a Western epistemological territory."[98] African *gnosis* to a significant extent presupposes the historical background of European colonialism. The emergence of a more explicit historical consciousness is tied to the development of literacy.[99] Because of its essential literary-historical character, what Mudimbe has called "African *gnosis*" is a mode of historical consciousness and self-understanding that is open to hermeneutical critique. We can thus speak more generally of "*gnosis*" as a phenomenon that is the reflection of a "Western" epistemological tradition that extends far beyond the historical and geographical horizon of the "West." Perhaps Mudimbe's choice of the term *gnosis* is itself problematic, insofar as this term is closely tied to a European historical and theological self-understanding, but it is the principle of *contact* with the "West" as having generated a specific mode of historical consciousness and "knowledge" as the basis of discourse about Africa that is at issue.[100] In this regard, the discipline of anthropology has for Mudimbe a privileged position. As oriented by empathy (*Einfühlung*) for its subjects, the discipline moves in two directions: "a permanent reevaluation of the limits of anthropology as knowledge" and "an examination of its own historicity."[101] Mudimbe's study foregrounds the latter in particular, that is, an examination of the historicity of African *gnosis*, in terms of the historicity of anthropology. Mudimbe's hermeneutical critique, which asks the question of the limits of anthropology as knowledge, presupposes its dependence on fieldwork and ethnography. It is within this concrete, experiential sphere that certain fundamental problems emerge.

As I noted previously, Mudimbe employs the notion of *gnosis* as a "methodological tool," inspired by the ethnographic work of Johannes Fabian on a charismatic movement in Katanga, a province in the former Belgian Congo and Democratic Republic of the Congo.[102] Fabian addresses the methodological and phenomenological priority of ethnography for anthropology in an important and polemical work, *Time and the Other*.[103] Fabian's thesis in essence is that ethnography presupposes *coevalness*, which anthropology has historically and systematically denied. According to Matti Bunzl, "Fabian deploys the designation 'coevalness' in order to merge into one Anglicized term the German notion of '*Gleichzeitigkeit*,' a phenomenological category that denotes both contemporaneity and synchronicity/simultaneity."[104] Thus, between anthropologists and their subjects, coevalness as the condition of possibility for ethnography implies *mutual presence* to each other, in the *common present*. Fabian's book highlights the remarkable political complexity involved in such a basic condition, the implications of which he characterises in terms of the "idea of totality."[105] Like Mudimbe's, Fabian's project is for the most part epistemological/critical. The main body of the book is more or less dedicated to an identification and a radical criticism of the ways in which anthropology as a discipline has systematically denied the reality of coevalness in its engagements with, and presentation of, the "Other"; this denial Fabian terms "allochronism."[106] Fabian sees this always in a political light: the contribution of anthropology to the perpetuation of the (neo-)colonial project of domination. The overall negativity of Fabian's critique is a function of his explicitly polemical stance, but, like Mudimbe, his aim is ultimately to disclose the positive possibilities of a self-critical anthropological praxis.

Fabian develops his positive critique in the final chapter of his text. This positive side of Fabian's polemic is what is of particular importance for my study, and there are essential thematic overlaps between his and Mudimbe's critiques, though Fabian's is wider in scope. The issue is this: having made thematic the phenomenon of coevalness, how does the researcher methodologically address this condition? In consideration of this, Fabian turns critically to Hegel and Marx. Having executed such a rigorous hermeneutical critique of his discipline, Fabian certainly does not approach these thinkers naively. Rather, they function like motifs, foregrounding the themes of intersubjective historicity and material embodiment. Fabian speaks therefore of the *praxis* of a "materialist anthropology":

> Consciousness, realized by the (producing) meaningful sound, is self-consciousness. The Self, however, is constituted fully as a speaking and hearing Self. Awareness [...] is fundamentally based on hearing meaningful sounds produced by self *and* others [...] social communication is the starting point for a materialist anthropology [...] Man *is* communication and society.[107]

It seems clear, following Bunzl's interpretation, that there is a phenomenological insight in Fabian's position, here concerning the sense perceptual basis of intersubjective communication. He mentions Husserl (and Heidegger) in an endnote discussing the contribution of Alfred Schutz to the phenomenology of intersubjectivity. Here, Fabian notes that "it is in this context of intersubjectivity and of the problem of shared Time that some of the insights of phenomenological philosophy continue to influence anthropology."[108] In ethnographic work, *Einfühlung* rests on coevalness, that is, the common temporality that characterises the presence of the researcher and her subjects of study to each other, in person. This phenomenological condition implies the immediacy of sense perceptual apprehension of each other and the surroundings. I argue, therefore, that in order to methodologically address the condition of coevalness that fundamentally determines the ethnographic experience, the meaning of the sense perceptual basis of this experience must be clarified.

The priority of perception

Anyone who attends a *caboclo reunião* in person perceives the event in its immediacy, be they members of the *terreiro*, the *mãe-de-santo*, Tupiniquim "himself," or strangers. This immediacy of sense perceptual encounter implies being together in person and thus connotes *mutual* presence to each other. The ethnographer must first experience before she can write. Any methodological assumption or theoretical position taken by the ethnographer has, as the necessary basis of its truth, this condition of corporeal presence to each other as "being here together." Furthermore, the ritual unfolds temporally. Any thesis regarding the temporality of the ritual—"circular time," "regenerative time," "mythical time," "cosmic time," and so on—has as its basis "being here together in the flesh as the *reunião* happens presently." The temporality of this "being here together" is necessarily the *mutual* perceptual present. The *common* basis that sets in advance the condition of possibility of being here together, and thus the possibility for a written description of the *reunião* in any of its aspects, is therefore the experience that has the character: "here together in the common present." As Dan Zahavi notes of the experience of being with others in person:

> There is not only a coincidence of what is "there" for me and what is "here" for the other (i.e., the constitution of a common *space*), but also

a coincidence of my now and the other's now (i.e. *simultaneity* and a common *present*). What we perceive in common coexists through coincidence—and with this, there is also a coincidence between my constituted time and the other's.[109]

My concern in this study is the experience of space in the concreteness of the ritual in its performance. The togetherness that qualifies the *reunião* is necessarily based on a *common space*. The mutuality of time and space that characterises the presence of the *reunião* such that anyone who is there in person can be certain that she is there together with others, and that they are there together with the room and its "things," is a mutuality founded on *aisthēsis*: on *sense perception*. Therefore, any attempt to interpret the *reunião* in its concreteness must have—whether explicitly made thematic or not—as its methodological basis an assumption about the nature of sense perception. This is particularly the case for an interest in questions of space. It is for this reason that I have given methodological priority to a study of Husserl's phenomenology of sense perception and theory of space constitution that it indicates. Guided by Mudimbe's, as well as Fabian's philosophical interrogation of anthropology, I outlined the contours of the historicity of the *anthropou-logos* itself. But there is a layer of history—intermingled with the latter to be sure, yet determined by an historical mode of being of its own—that belongs to *la chose du texte*. As I established, for us the "matter" is the *reunião* in its lived experiential concreteness as an event. The methodological possibility of thematic access to this history must also be founded on "being here together in the flesh in the common present," that is, on the phenomenological priority of sense perception. The question, therefore, of the historicity of sense perception must be traced out.

Sensing history

It is initially as a question that I will sketch the issues. This is because they require the work of interpreting the phenomenology of perception elaborated by Husserl. The movement from sense perception to the intersubjective nature of spatial experience, its historicity and generativity, I develop in Chapters 2 and 3. In the following I must, to an extent, anticipate the content of those chapters.

The theme of history in Husserl is best known through his last major work published in his lifetime, *The Crisis of European Sciences and Transcendental Phenomenology*.[110] In light of the "matter" of the *caboclo reunião*, however, I propose to draw on a little-known text by Husserl, which is explicitly concerned with the anthropological-ethnological sense of the question of history. This is a letter that Husserl wrote to Lucien Lévy-Bruhl in 1935.[111] I have already introduced Lévy-Bruhl, in relation to our consideration of the work of Roger Bastide, as having posited the thesis of "mentality," and specifically "primitive mentality." If for Bastide the virtue of such a thesis was to put into relief the difference of various "collective representations" so as to point out the "danger [...] of interpreting data pertaining to other civilizations in terms of our own values,"[112] Mudimbe instead would point to another danger:

> It is the *episteme* of the nineteenth and early twentieth centuries that invented the concept of a static and prehistoric tradition. [...] Theorists such as Spencer and Lévy-Bruhl interpreted and classified these monstrosities as existing at the beginning of both history and consciousness.[113]

It seems to me that Husserl had anticipated this danger, having lucidly identified the problem of "anthropologism":

> Transcendental phenomenology [...] is the science that reveals the *universal taken-for-grantedness* "would and we human beings in the world" to be an *obscurity* (*Unverständlichkeit*).[114]

Not only does transcendental phenomenology disclose the fact of this "obscurity," it proceeds to enquire after this "enigma," making it "intelligible" (*verständlich*) in terms of a unique methodical approach that Husserl would describe, in somewhat enigmatic language himself, as "the sole possible way of radical self-examination."[115] He goes on to say of transcendental phenomenology, in seemingly impenetrable prose:[116]

> It is a scientificity that is novel by virtue of this radicality; it proceeds as a systematic analysis, which systematically shows the ABCs and the elementary grammar of the formation (*Bildung*) of "objects" as unities of validity (*Geltungseinheiten*), [the formation] of object-manifolds and infinities of valid (*geltende*) "worlds" for sense-bestowing subjects, and thereby, as a philosophy, it ascends from below into the heights.[117]

By the time we arrive at this point in Husserl's letter, it seems to me that he has already overtaken Lévy-Bruhl, which was perhaps the case from the very beginning.

Moran and Steinacher offer an insightful survey of the reception of Husserl's letter by his philosophical successors, focusing in particular on the interpretations of Maurice Merleau-Ponty, Jacques Derrida, and the Italian phenomenologist Enzo Paci (1911–1976). Another commentary is offered by Javier San Martín, who focuses particularly on the conflicting understandings of Merleau-Pointy and Derrida.[118] San Martín ends with a more sympathetic ear for Merleau-Ponty, though he ultimately arrives at the compromising position that "both opinions may draw the bow too taught."[119] My understanding concurs, however, with the conclusion of

Moran and Steinacher that "Derrida's appears to be the correct interpretation of Husserl's view of the relationship between the phenomenological investigation of essences and empirical fact."[120] For Derrida, the motif of *horizon* qualifies the eidetic sense of historicity as the Husserlian historical a priori.[121]

My concern in this chapter was to outline the methodological issues that, having their basis in the nature of the topic of the spatiality of the *reunião*, have determined the need for a turn to Husserl. The issues concern the status of the phenomenon of history, in light of the phenomenological and thus methodological priority of sense perception that I established at the end of the previous section. The issues and their resolution in my view are latent in Husserl's letter, which, although addressed to Lévy-Bruhl, seems to bypass him. Rather than consider the relationship between Husserl and Lévy-Bruhl, therefore, I propose to follow the lead of Moran and Steinacher and build on the interpretation of Paci.

Before turning to Paci, at least two aspects of the fragment quoted above should be highlighted in order to trace out in a preliminary way the relation between sense perception and the phenomenological possibility of history in Husserl's thought: the first with regard to the "ABCs and the elementary grammar of the formation [...] of 'objects'," and the second pertaining to "infinities of valid [...] 'worlds' for sense-bestowing subjects."[122] Husserl's image of "ABCs" is no exaggeration; indeed, it is even an understatement. In his lecture course at the University of Göttingen in 1907, published posthumously as *Thing and Space*, he begins with an elementary description of concrete sense perception, using the example of a house seen from a distance.[123] A fundamental motif is the *one-sidedness* of perception: "many perceptions [...] are and can be perceptions of one and the same object, e.g. a house [...] each displays the object only from one 'side', and each displays it from a 'different side.'"[124] Without yet considering the phenomenon of movement—the topic that is at the core of these lectures—Husserl clarifies the *how*, the manner in which spatiality and temporality are intertwined in sense perception and—here I project beyond this text to his later works—in such a way that the situation inheres "in" those present together as a *habitus*, as a shared comportment.[125] In principle, therefore, the sense perceptual basis that characterises mutual presence to the actual occurrence of the *reunião* cannot be qualified as a mere apprehension of "thingly" presence. Even at the elementary level of the perception of a "thing," the sense of the event inheres temporally, which means that there is no "elementary level" as such.

With regard to the second aspect of the quote, the matter is more difficult to treat as a rough outline. What Husserl's statement points to is the complex problem of the relative truths of cultural traditions. In this light, Paci asks:

> We must meet ourselves—for (?) the sense of concordance (?) of our life—and (but?) we have forgotten ourselves, this and that time of our

life and of our history. Thus mankind must find itself by feeling that it is also primitive mankind [...]. Did Husserl really think this way? I am reconstructing (it?) [...] But the problem is the very same one which in *Krisis* presents itself as the problem of the encounter between men of different eras (history, historiography).[126]

Paci here raises the theme of "primitive mankind" in relation to the "encounter between men of different eras." He is implying that the task of understanding an alien culture is "the very same one" as that of understanding one's own culture—for him European tradition—as it was lived in the historical past, and as this past reverberates in the present. I ask after Paci: "Did Husserl really think this way?"[127] We have already seen, through the critiques of Mudimbe and Fabian, that a framing of the matters in terms of the temporalities suggested by Paci's interpretation of Husserl's letter is problematic. Furthermore, Paci sets up the problem inappropriately, in that the ethical question pertains not to that of (European) self-understanding through the encounter with others, but of genuinely inhabiting the common situation together with others in intersubjective community:

> Over and above all differences between individuals, nations and ... traditions, stands things that are had in common, ... [stands] the common factual world, which is constituted in the exchange of experiences so that each can understand the other and each take recourse to what we all see.[128]

What Husserl's letter points us towards is the fundamental problem of understanding how, at the level of embodied perceptual experience, that is, at the level of *spatiality*, an intersubjective historical horizon is constituted. This is the problem that I take up in the following chapters.

Notes

1 Antonio Risério describes it as "Nosso mediterrâneo, com a sua cidade nascida no cimo do alto monte, de olhos postos nesse mesmo mar" (Our Mediterranean, with its city born atop the steep hill, looking onto that same sea). Antonio Risério, *Uma História da Cidade da Bahia* (Rio de Janeiro: Versal Editores, 2004), 20. All translations are my own, unless otherwise indicated.
2 Risério, *Uma História*, 48.
3 Risério, 21.
4 Eduardo Viveiros de Castro, *From the Enemy's Point of View: Humanity and Divinity in an Amazonian Society*, trans. Catherine V. Howard (Chicago, IL: University of Chicago Press, 1992), 24. The figure for population given by Viveiros de Castro extends beyond Brazil to include the Paraguayan basin. Rachel Harding gives an estimate of about 2.5 million for the indigenous population in Brazil. See Rachel E. Harding, *A Refuge in Thunder: Candomblé and Alternative Spaces of Blackness* (Bloomington: Indiana University Press, 2003), xiv.
5 Risério, 67.

6 Pedro de Almeida Vasconcelos, *Salvador: Transformações e permanências 1549–1999* (Ilhéus: Editus, 2002), 12; Boris Fausto, *A Concise History of Brazil* (Cambridge, UK: Cambridge University Press, 1999), 14.
 7 Risério, 89.
 8 Fausto, *A Concise History of Brazil*, 16–17.
 9 Stuart B. Schwartz, *Sugar Plantations in the Formation of Brazilian Society* (Cambridge, UK: Cambridge University Press, 1985), 245–63.
10 Harding, *A Refuge in Thunder*, 9.
11 Pierre Verger, *Trade Relations between the Bight of Benin and Bahia from the 17th to the 19th Centuries* (Ibadan: Ibadan University Press, 1976), 1.
12 Harding, *A Refuge in Thunder*, 38. See also Jim Wafer, *The Taste of Blood: Spirit Possession in Brazilian Candomblé* (Philadelphia: University of Pennsylvania Press, 1991), 199.
13 Harding, *A Refuge in Thunder*, 158.
14 Verger, *Trade Relations between the Bight of Benin and Bahia from the 17th to the 19th Centuries*, 1.
15 Luis Nicolau Parés, *The Formation of Candomblé: Vodun History and Ritual in Brazil*, trans. Richard Vernon (Chapel Hill, NC: University of North Carolina Press, 2013), 3.
16 Parés, *The Formation of Candomblé*, 3.
17 Parés, 7.
18 Parés, 67.
19 Harding, 12.
20 Harding, 15. Harding contrasts the interpretations of two scholars: Katia Mattoso emphasises the significance of economic and political prestige, while F.W.O. Morton stresses the importance of colour.
21 Harding, 74–76.
22 Harding, 69.
23 João José Reis, *Slave Rebellion in Brazil*, trans. Arthur Brakel (Baltimore, MD: John Hopkins University Press, 1993), 41. On maroon communities in Brazil see Richard Price, ed., *Maroon Societies: Rebel Slave Communities in the Americas* (Baltimore, MD: John Hopkins University Press, 1996), 169–226.
24 Vicente del Rio and William Siembieda, *Contemporary Urbanism in Brazil* (Gainesville: University Press of Florida, 2009), 1.
25 Ana Fernandes and Marco A. A. de Filgueiras Gomes, "Revisiting the Pelourinho: Preservation, Cultural Heritage, and Place Marketing in Salvador, Bahia," in del Rio and Siembieda, *Contemporary Urbanism in Brazil*, 147–48. On the population and make up of modern Salvador, see Pedro de Almeida Vasconcelos, "Metropolização: Acessibilidade e americanização (1970–1999)," in *Salvador: Transformações e permanências*, 343–77.
26 James Holston, *Insurgent Citizenship: Disjunctions of Democracy and Modernity in Brazil* (Princeton, NJ: Princeton University Press, 2008), 146.
27 Marcio Goldman, "An Ethnographic Theory of Democracy: Politics from the Viewpoint of Ilhéus's Black Movement (Bahia, Brazil)," *Ethnos* 66, no. 2 (2001): 177, note 4. For consistency I have capitalised "Candomblé" in Goldman's text to refer to the religious institution.
28 See Michel Agier, "Between Affliction and Politics: A Case Study of Bahian Candomblé," in *Afro-Brazilian Culture and Politics: Bahia, 1970s to 1990s*, ed. Hendrik Kraayb (Armonk, NY: M. E. Sharpe, 1990), 136.
29 See, for example, Maria Stella de Azevedo Santos, *Meu Tempo é Agora* (Curitiba: Projeto Centrhu 1995); idem., "*Iansã* Is Not Saint Barbara," in *The Brazil Reader*, ed. Robert M. Levine and John J. Crocitti (London: Latin American Bureau 1999), 408–10; and Juana Elbein dos Santos and Deoscóredes M.

44 *Phenomenon and method*

dos Santos, "O culto dos ancestrais na Bahia: O culto dos égun," in *Olóòriṣa: Escritos sobre a religião dos orixás*, ed. Carlos E. M. de Moura (São Paulo: Agora, 1981), 153–88. For a wider discussion see J. Lorand Matory, "Gendered Agendas: The Secrets Scholars Keep about Yorùbá-Atlantic Religion," *Gender & History* 15, no. 3 (November 2003): 409–439.

30 Gisèle Binon Cossard, "Contribution a l'étude des Candomblés au Brésil: Le Candomblé Angola" (PhD diss., University of Paris, 1970), 226–27. I use the translation as quoted in Marcio Goldman, "How to Learn in an Afro-Brazilian Spirit Possession Religion: Ontology and Multiplicity in Candomblé," in *Learning Religion: Anthropological Approaches*, ed. Ramón Sarró and David Berliner (Oxford: Berghahn, 2007), 108.

31 Rachel Harding interprets the social factors as having to do with the instrumental role of Candomblé in facilitating refuge and acts of resistance, while Luis Nicolau Parés sees it also as "the consequence or effect of the intra-African encounter, relatively autonomous in relation to society at large, and resulting from its own *internal dynamic*." Parés, *The Formation of Candomblé*, 89. See Harding, *A Refuge in Thunder*, 104–46.

32 Lisa Earl Castillo, "The 'Ketu Nation' of Brazilian Candomblé in Historical Context," *History in Africa*, Vol. 0 (2021), 3. For the dates of foundation see Renato da Silveira, *O Candomblé da Barroquinha: Processo de constituição do primeiro terreiro baiano da keto* (Salvador: Edições Maianga, 2006), 374.

33 Silveira, *O Candomblé da Barroquinha*, 378. I follow the conventions of both Harding and Parés and use "Candomblé" (capitalised) with reference to the religious institution and practice and "*candomblé*" (italicised) to refer to specific religious communities. See Harding, *A Refuge in Thunder*, xix, and Parés, *The Formation of Candomblé*, 301, note 1.

34 Silveira, *O Candomblé da Barroquinha*, 378; for the terms in brackets see Roger Bastide, *O Candomblé da Bahia*, trans. Maria Isaura Pereira de Queiroz (São Paulo: Compahnia das Letras, 2005), 313, 103.

35 See, for example, the discussion in Goldman, "How to Learn in an Afro-Brazilian Spirit Possession Religion: Ontology and Multiplicity in Candomblé," 110–18.

36 I use the word *praxis* in its basic Aristotelian sense as a "doing" related to life: "life is πρᾶξις, not ποίησις." See Nicholas Lobkowicz, *Theory and Practice: History of a Concept from Aristotle to Marx* (Notre Dame: University of Notre Dame Press, 1967), 10.

37 Silveira, 389.
38 Parés, *The Formation of Candomble*, 124–33.
39 Parés, xvi.
40 Parés, xiii.
41 Castillo, "The 'Ketu Nation'," 1–44.
42 Parés, *The Formation of Candomblé*, 242.
43 See Rafael Soares de Oliveira, "Feitiço de Oxum: Um estudo sobre o Ilê Axé Iyá Nassô Oká e suas relações em rede com outros terreiros" (PhD diss., Federal University of Bahia, 2005).
44 Pedro McGregor, *A Moon and Two Mountains: The Myths, Ritual and Magic of Brazilian Spiritism* (London, Souvenir Press 1996), 71.
45 Ruth Landes, *The City of Women* (Albuquerque: University of New Mexico Press, 1994), first published in 1947. On Landes's study see Matory, "Gendered Agendas: The Secrets Scholars Keep about Yorùbá-Atlantic Religion," 411–13.
46 Parés, *The Formation of Candomble*, 94–100. See also Harding, "The Nineteenth-Century Development of Candomble," in *A Refuge in Thunder*, 68–76.
47 See, for example, the description of Ilé Axé Iya Nassô Oká (Casa Branca) in Edison Carneiro, *Candomblés da Bahia* (Bahia: Brasileira de Ouro, 1948), 39–41.

48 Jocélio Teles dos Santos, "Os Candomblés da Bahia no século XXI," *Mapeamento dos terreiros de Salvador* (Salvador: Centro de Estudos Afro-Orientais, 2007), 5, http://www.terreiros.ceao.ufba.br/pdf/Os_candombles_no_seculo_XXI.pdf.
49 I conducted fieldwork in Salvador in March of 2008, and then again for four months in 2010.
50 Raymundo Nina Rodrigues, *L'Animisme fétichiste des Nègres de Bahia* (Bahia: Reis, 1900), 34.
51 Roger Bastide, *The African Religions of Brazil: Toward a Sociology of the Interpenetration of Civilizations*, trans. Helen Sebba (Baltimore, MD: John Hopkins University Press, 1978), 19. Nina Rodrigues, *L'Animisme fétichiste des Nègres de Bahia*.
52 Bastide, *The African Religions of Brazil*, 390–91.
53 Roger Bastide, *The African Religions of Brazil*, 10–12. Bastide gets the model of "depth sociology" from Georges Gurvitch. On the notion of Candomblé epistemology, see Bastide, *O Candomblé da Bahia*, 251–63.
54 Paul Ricoeur, *Memory, History, Forgetting*, trans. Kathleen Blamey and David Pellauer (Chicago, IL: University of Chicago Press, 2006), 188–200.
55 Bastide, *The African Religions of Brazil*, 395. On the concept of "collective representations" in Lévy-Bruhl, see E. E. Evans-Pritchard, "Lévy-Bruhl's Theory of Primitive Mentality," *Bulletin of the Faculty of Arts of the Egyptian University* 2 (1934): 1–36; see also Lucien Lévy-Bruhl, "A Letter to E. E. Evans-Pritchard," *British Journal of Sociology* 3, no. 2 (June 1952): 117–23.
56 Goldman, "How to Learn in an Afro-Brazilian Spirit Possession Religion: Ontology and Multiplicity in Candomblé," 116.
57 Goldman, "How to Learn," 116.
58 Goldman, "How to Learn," 117.
59 Goldman, "How to Learn," 118
60 V. Y. Mudimbe, *The Invention of Africa: Gnosis, Philosophy, and the Order of Knowledge* (Bloomington: Indiana University Press, 1988).
61 Mudimbe, *The Invention of Africa*, ix.
62 Mudimbe, 183.
63 Mudimbe notes his debt to the work of Johannes Fabian in developing his concept of "African *gnosis*." See V. Y. Mudimbe, *The Invention of Africa*, ix. and Johannes Fabian, "An African Gnosis: For a Reconstruction of an Authoritative Definition," *History of Religions* 9, no. 1 (August 1969): 42–58.
64 For a history of the idea in antiquity, see Hans Jonas, *The Gnostic Religion: The Message of the Alien God and the Beginnings of Christianity* (London: Routledge, 1992).
65 Lobkowicz, *Theory and Practice*, 53.
66 Mudimbe, ix–xii.
67 Mudimbe, x. According to Ricoeur, this is the critique levelled against Foucault by Michel de Certeau. See Ricoeur, *Memory, History, Forgetting*, 204.
68 Mudimbe, xi. For a discussion on Wilhelm Dilthey's influence on the concept of "world-view," see Hans-Georg Gadamer, *Truth and Method*, trans. Joel Weinsheimer and Donald G. Marshall (New York: Continuum, 2000), 218–42.
69 Mudimbe, 135–36.
70 Mudimbe, 154–61.
71 Mudimbe, 186.
72 Mudimbe, 186.
73 Mudimbe, 145.
74 See, for example, Dan Zahavi's discussion of the term as used by early phenomenologists in Zahavi, "Intersubjectivity, Sociality, Community: The Contribution of the Early Phenomenologists," in *The Oxford Handbook of the History of Phenomenology*, ed. Dan Zahavi (Oxford: Oxford University

46 Phenomenon and method

Press, 2018), 734–52; and Dermot Moran on the work of Edith Stein in Moran, "Edith Stein's Encounter with Edmund Husserl and Her Phenomenology of the Person," in *Empathy, Sociality, and Personhood: Essays on Edith Stein's Phenomenological Investigations*, ed. Elisa Magrì and Dermot Moran (Cham, Switzerland: Springer, 2017), 31–47.
75 Mudimbe, 183.
76 Paul Ricoeur, *From Text to Action: Essays in Hermeneutics, II*, trans. Kathleen Blamey and John B. Thompson (Evanston, IL: Northwestern University Press, 1991), 299.
77 Ricoeur, *From Text to Action*, 300.
78 Ricoeur is effectively attempting to arbitrate the positions of Jürgen Habermas and Gadamer.
79 Ricoeur, *From Text to Action*, 300.
80 Ricoeur, *From Text to Action*, 300.
81 Ricoeur, *From Text to Action*, 300.
82 Hans-Georg Gadamer, *The Relevance of the Beautiful and Other Essays*, ed. Robert Bernasconi (Cambridge, UK: Cambridge University Press, 2002), 126.
83 Gadamer, *Truth and Method*, 104. Gadamer's reference is to the classic text on the concept of play in Johan Huizinga, *Homo Ludens* (London: Routledge, 1980). Not even Huizinga himself makes ritual into an explicit theme for detailed consideration; although brief mention is made in a few places in the text, ritual is not given the status of "law," "war," "poetry," etc.
84 Gadamer, *Relevance of the Beautiful*, 145.
85 Gadamer, *Truth and Method*, 107.
86 Gadamer, *Truth and Method*, 107.
87 Gadamer, *Truth and Method*, 108.
88 Gadamer, *Truth and Method*, 110. Gadamer notes that "the mediation that communicates the work of art is, in principle, total." See *Truth and Method*, 120.
89 Gadamer himself warns us of the error of thematising the question of the relation between aesthetic and religious experience abstractly and ahistorically. See Gadamer, *Relevance of the Beautiful*, 140.
90 Mudimbe, 186.
91 I thank Viviani for facilitating this introduction.
92 Marcio Goldman, email correspondence to author, March 25, 2011.
93 Jocélio Teles dos Santos, *O Dono da Terra: O Caboclo nos Candomblés da Bahia* (Salvador: SarahLetras, 1995).
94 Santos, *O Dono da Terra*, 119–22.
95 Santos, *O Dono da Terra*, 91–115. For Jim Wafer's ethnography, see Wafer, *The Taste of Blood*, 68–83.
96 The public festivals for the African gods, and specifically the Yorùbá *orixás*, have been the topic of many anthropological monographs, as far back as the original work in 1900 of Nina Rodrigues. I refer to some of the classic and more recent ethnographic works in Chapter 4.
97 *O Dono da Terra*, 122.
98 Mudimbe, 186.
99 As an appendix, Mudimbe gives examples of an indigenous Ethiopic literary tradition and its Christian and Islamic inheritances. Mudimbe, 201–3.
100 In the Caribbean context Sylvia Wynter notes, in reference to Édouard Glissant's thought, that

> with respect to the uniqueness of both the Antillean and the New World black situation, [...] because Antillean societies 'did not pre-exist the colonial act, but were literally the creation of that act,' one cannot 'speak

of structures disturbed by colonialism, of traditions that have been uprooted.'

Stuart Hall states provocatively that "though time has been called on colonialism's earlier forms [...] the so-called colonial world is still unfolding—more accurately unravelling—*inside* the post-colonial, in the wake, in the devastating aftermath, of an untranscended colonialism." Sylvia Wynter, "Beyond the Word of Man: Glissant and the New Discourse of the Antilles," *World Literature Today* 63, no. 4 (Autumn 1989): 643; Stuart Hall, *Familiar Stranger*, ed. Bill Schwarz (Durham, NC: Duke University Press, 2017), 24; my emphasis.

101 Mudimbe, 186. In this quote, Mudimbe very much blurs the distinction between (Africanist) anthropology and African *gnosis*. I have emphasised anthropology.
102 Fabian's study is of a movement called the Jamaa, which was established by a Belgian missionary, Placide Tempels. Tempels was the author of a controversial book, *La Philosophie bantoue* (Paris: Présence Africaine, 1949), which in many ways served to institute a discourse on the "epistemology" and "ontology" of so-called "traditional" societies. See Fabian, "An African Gnosis," 46.
103 Johannes Fabian, *Time and the Other: How Anthropology Makes Its Object* (New York: Columbia University Press, 2002).
104 Matti Bunzl, "Forward to Johannes Fabian's *Time and the Other*: Syntheses of a Critical Anthropology," in Fabian, *Time and the Other*," xxix, endnote 1.
105 Fabian, *Time and the Other*, 156.
106 Fabian, *Time and the Other*, 32.
107 Fabian, *Time and the Other*, 162.
108 *Time and the Other*, 170, note 22.
109 Dan Zahavi, *Husserl and Transcendental Intersubjectivity: A Response to the Linguistic-Pragmatic Critique*, trans. Elizabeth A. Behnke (Athens: Ohio University Press, 2001), 68.
110 Edmund Husserl, *The Crisis of European Sciences and Transcendental Phenomenology: An Introduction to Phenomenological Philosophy*, trans. David Carr (Evanston, IL: Northwestern University Press, 1970).
111 Edmund Husserl, "Edmund Husserl's Letter to Lucien Lévy-Bruhl," trans. Lukas Steinacher and Dermot Moran, *The New Yearbook for Phenomenology and Phenomenological Philosophy* 8 (2008): 349–54.
112 Bastide, *African Religions of Brazil*, 391.
113 Mudimbe, 189–90.
114 Husserl, "Letter to Lucien Lévy-Bruhl," 353. Moran and Steinacher note that "Husserl had regarded 'anthropologism' as a particular form of relativism ... he now addressed it as part of a general kind of historicism." See Dermot Moran and Lukas Steinacher, "Husserl's Letter to Lévy-Bruhl: Introduction," *New Yearbook for Phenomenology and Phenomenological Philosophy* 8 (2008): 333–34. Text in brackets indicates Moran and Steinacher's insertion of German terms.
115 Husserl, "Letter to Lucien Lévy-Bruhl," 353.
116 Of Husserl's letter, Moran and Steinacher note that "Lévy-Bruhl remarked to Aron Gurwitsch: 'explain it to me; I understand nothing of it.'" Moran and Steinacher, "Husserl's Letter to Lévy-Bruhl," 325.
117 Husserl, "Letter to Lucien Lévy-Bruhl," 353.
118 Javier San Martin, "Husserl and Cultural Anthropology, Commentary on Husserl's Letter to Lévy-Bruhl," *Recherches husserliennes* 7 (1997): 87–115.
119 San Martin, "Husserl and Cultural Anthropology," 115.

120 Moran and Steinacher, 344.
121 Jacques Derrida, *Edmund Husserl's Origin of Geometry: An Introduction*, trans. John P. Leavey (Lincoln: University of Nebraska Press, 1989), 111–17.
122 See passage cited above, note 117.
123 Edmund Husserl, *Thing and Space: Lectures of 1907*, trans. Richard Rojecwicz (Dordrecht: Kluwer, 2010), 8.
124 Husserl, *Thing and Space*, 38.
125 I elaborate on Husserl's phenomenology of space constitution and problems of habituality in detail in Chapter 2.
126 Moran and Steinacher "Husserl's Letter to Lévy-Bruhl," 347. See also Paci's diary entry for May 25, 1957, http://www.yorku.ca/lbianchi/paci/dairy_ver_02.html.
127 On the question of the significance of the motif of "Europe" in Husserl's late writings, such as his "Vienna Lecture" and *Kaizo* articles, see David Carr, "The Project of Transcendental Philosophy," in *Phenomenology and the Problem of History: A Study of Husserl's Transcendental Philosophy* (Evanston, IL: Northwestern University Press, 1974), 260–77; and Donn Welton, "Husserl and the Japanese," in *The Other Husserl: The Horizons of Transcendental Phenomenology* (Bloomington: Indiana University Press, 2000), 306–27. Regarding the *Kaizo* articles, Welton makes the salient point that:

> What Husserl deals with for the first time in these articles is the fact that systems of knowledge are wedded to culture, that they can even have a social consensus as to what counts as veridical, but that they can be mistaken, they can enchain rather than liberate. Keep in mind that Husserl clearly distinguished between European scientific culture and European civilization, and that science opens to scrutiny not just mythic-religious societies but the "imperialism" and the accepted ideas of his own society. What he means by scientific inquiry, to put it negatively, is a strategy for dismantling an *edifice* of beliefs. In these texts Husserl realizes […] that the problem is not with particular claims or judgements but with the *context* of knowledge.
>
> The Other Husserl, 322

For a comprehensive treatment of the topic, see Timo Miettinen, *Husserl and the Idea of Europe* (Evanston, IL: Northwestern University Press, 2020).
128 Edmund Husserl, *Aufsätze und Vorträge (1922-1937)*, Husserliana, vol. 27, ed. Thomas Nenon and Hans Rainer Sepp (Dordrecht: Kluwer, 1989), 3, quoted in Welton, *The Other Husserl*, 322. It cannot be emphasized enough, the importance of approaching Husserl's late works with an understanding of the concrete historical conditions within which he was writing, so as not to misconstrue his intentions through hasty or cursory readings. Dermot Moran lucidly presents the context and genuine philosophical and *ethical* concerns of Husserl in "'Even the Papuan is a Man and not a Beast': Husserl on Universalism and the Relativity of Cultures," *Journal of the History of Philosophy* 49, no. 4 (October 2011): 463–494. Here Moran notes:

> The National Socialist promulgation of a particularist and race-based "worldview" (*Weltanschauung*) with its race-based relativism contextualizes and gives new pathos to Husserl's struggle to defend the universalist, rationalist, non-relativist core of "European" and, thereby, world culture. Husserl's supposed Eurocentrism is actually a trenchant defense of the philosophical vision of universal humanity against one-sided forms of racial particularism. […] Husserl emphasizes that the current crisis is a crisis of *reason*: "European crisis has its roots in a misguided rationalism." (476)

2 Corporeity and spatiality

In this chapter, I explore the relationship between space and embodiment in Husserl's thought. I draw on Ulrich Claesges's seminal study of Husserl's theory of the constitution of space, and introduce aspects of Candomblé ritual, in a sustained way as examples, in developing increasingly detailed phenomenological descriptions of space. The chapter investigates certain structural features of spatial experience, including the modes of givenness of the sensible, perceived and apperceived in structures of perspectivity, positionality, and horizonality; the peculiar mode of self-givenness of the perceiving subject as embodied, that is, the kinaesthetic structure and corporeity of the body as what Husserl terms the "lived body" (*Leib*); the integral relation between the "spontaneity" and "receptivity" of the lived body as a motivational structure tied to the *affectivity* of space; and the temporality of spatial experience as characterised by the accruing and sedimentation of sense in the form of lived bodily acquisitions and habitualities. Husserl's systematic descriptions of space constitution from the point of view of an experiencing, embodied subject for and through whom sense accrues as *habitus* imply intersubjective experience. These structurally descriptive analyses of what I term "phantom spatiality"—space given in its mere sensibility—and lived bodily corporeity set the bases for more concrete investigations of space as intersubjectively constituted.

*

Husserl's research on space was the topic of Ulrich Claesges's dissertation of 1963, published a year later as *Edmund Husserls Theorie der Raumkonstitution* (Edmund Husserl's Theory of the Constitution of Space).[1] Claesges's has long been one of the only book-length studies dedicated solely to the topic.[2] The sources for Claesges's study are Husserl's manuscripts on the constitution of spatiality, some of which are still unpublished, held at the Husserl Archives in Leuven. These include the group of manuscripts catalogued as group F I 13 that contain lecture notes delivered in 1907 at the University of Göttingen and referred to by Husserl as the "Thing Lectures" (*Dingvorlesungen*). The lectures were first published posthumously in 1973

DOI: 10.4324/9781351116145-3

as volume 16 of Husserliana—Husserl's complete works—under the title *Ding und Raum: Vorlesungen 1907 (Thing and Space: Lectures of 1907)* and are an important source for my study.[3] The primary source material for Claesges was the so-called group D manuscripts, a series of manuscripts dating between 1907 and 1934, catalogued at the Husserl Archives under the title "*Primordiale Konstitution ('Urkonstitution')*" (Primordial constitution ['originary-constitution']).[4] The manuscripts were an important source, directly and indirectly, for the development of a phenomenology of spatial experience for later phenomenologists, and specifically Maurice Merleau-Ponty who consulted the manuscripts between 1938 and 1940.[5] Herman Leo Van Breda, the Franciscan priest who established the Husserl Archives, describes the content of the manuscripts as follows:

> The group D manuscripts largely concern what Husserl called "primordial constitution" [*primordial* [sic] *Konstitution, Urkonstitution*]. Above all, they contain elaborations of the idea of the intentional genesis of the most original layers of consciousness of things, and a doctrine of the transcendental aesthetic, understood in Husserl's own terms.[6]

In his review of Claesges's book, Robert Sokolowski outlines the overall structure of the author's approach to interpreting Husserl's phenomenology of spatiality and is significant as a point of entry into the problem.[7] Sokolowski notes that "the texts of Husserl already contain many ideas about lived space which are commonly thought to be discoveries of later phenomenologists."[8] These aspects concern questions about the nature of visual space, bodily motility and tactility, spontaneity and receptivity of perceptions and sensations, and the temporality of spatial experience. The role of bodily tactility and motility in spatial perception and experience is shown to be of particular significance for Husserl. Claesges's study roughly follows the outline of Husserl's 1907 "Thing Lectures," beginning with visual perception of things as "phantom" bodies or mere sensuous schema, extending the analyses to tactile space and developing detailed descriptions of the aesthetic and kinaesthetic structures and capacities of the living body in its full corporeity and spatiality. Although Claesges, in the concluding section of his study, hints at the difficult problem of relating Husserl's theory of the constitution of space to his overall transcendental phenomenological philosophy, he does not extend his analyses to address questions of the relationship between the constitution of spatiality and problems of intersubjectivity, generativity, and historicity. In this chapter, I explore Husserl's descriptions and analyses of the constitution of space, as these are to be found in the "Thing Lectures" and other related works. These investigations are preparatory, directed towards the more expansive enquiry into the significance of corporeity and spatiality for empathic, intersubjective, and historical experience, which are taken up in Chapter 3. In developing my analyses I trace the contours of aspects of the Candomblé ritual—the *caboclo reunião*—descriptively as examples. To approach the problem of the constitution of space, the sense of the concept of "constitution" in Husserl must first be sketched out.

Constitution and experience

In Husserl's descriptive analyses, certain concepts function "operatively," that is, they are clarified in the process of analysis itself. Sokolowski thus points out that

> when he introduces a concept Husserl rarely gives an explicit and precise definition. The meaning he attributes to it is often determined more by the use he makes of a term than by what he expressly says about it, and therefore the context into which it is introduced, the manner in which it is treated, and the problems it is supposed to solve, all must be considered if we are to recover the meaning of his term.[9]

This manner of employing terms as working or operative concepts is of methodological significance for Husserl, as he himself notes of his "zigzag" (*Zickzack*) manner of enquiry:

> We search, as it were, in zig-zag fashion, a metaphor all the more apt since the close interdependence of our various epistemological concepts leads us back again and again to our original analyses, where the new confirms the old, and the old the new.[10]

Dermot Moran and Joseph Cohen situate the concept of "constitution" in the neo-Kantian tradition, according to which "objects do not exist simply on their own but receive their particular intelligible structure from the activity of the conscious subject apprehending them."[11] Husserl is considered to have taken up the term from the neo-Kantians, and over the course of the development of his philosophy to have radically transformed its sense.[12] Here, it is important to note that Husserl used terms current to the philosophical and scientific culture of his time but often imbued them with new meanings whose significance can only be properly grasped relative to the corpus and development of his philosophy.[13] Husserl's concept of constitution speaks to the nature of the appearance of the world experienced as objective to a perceiving subject, in a broad sense. In terms of this study's interest in space, the issue pertains to the appearance of the physical world, which includes the appearance to the subject of her own bodily presence. From this spatial perspective, the root of the problem does not concern questions of explicit knowledge or judgement, but rather the sense in which the "thingly" character of the surrounding world appears in prepredicative experience. By the concept of "constitution," therefore, Husserl is not implying an act of spatial "construction" or "representation," rather, the implication is that one's corporeal experience of space is an encounter through which spatiality "manifests itself" (*sich bekunden*) in its perceptual sensibility, visibility, and physicality.[14] It implies a "coming-to-be" in appearance of phenomena to an experiencing or perceiving subject.[15] Husserl's description of the structure of this appearance of the material world through experience and to perception is what I analyse in this chapter.

The concept of constitution is closely related to that of "experience" in Husserl's thought. The German terms typically translated as "experience" in his work are *Erlebnis* and *Erfahrung*.[16] Among the English expressions used to render the meaning of *Erlebnis* we find "experience," "lived experience," "subjective mental process," "mental process," and at times simply "process."[17] Dorion Cairns suggests "mental process" for *Erlebnis* and recommends that "so far as possible save 'experience' for 'Erfahrung.'"[18] Sokolowski, on the other hand, suggests "experience" for *Erlebnis* and the more literal sense of "encounter" for the everyday German word *Erfahrung*.[19] Husserl's use of *Erlebnis* is aimed at describing the experienc*ing* of the subject, which is why the verbal sense of a *process* is emphasised. The tension in the understanding of the relation between *Erlebnis* and *Erfahrung* as both indicating modes of experience can perhaps be shown from the point of view of spatial experience, in terms of a consideration of what Husserl terms the "double sensation" (*Doppelempfindung*) of touch.[20] Sokolowski describes this in the following way:

> The part of the body that organizes tactile space can also be perceived as something in tactile space, and the part of the body that is in tactile space can also be perceived as the organizer of the same space. Such reciprocity is not possible in visual space. I never *see* my organizing parts as mere objects within visual space. My organs of vision can only function as organizers, never as objects constituted in visual space. My organs of vision are only visual constitutors; they are never visually constituted as objects as well. I cannot see my seeing eye, although I can touch my touching hand (with my leg). One reason for this is that as a sense of distance, vision never enjoys the immediate contact with its object that touch has; the immediate contact is what allows the reciprocity between the part touched and the touching part.[21]

In Sokolowski's description, the touching hand experiences the touch sensation as both a spontaneous *activity* in the form of the touch*ing*, and a receptive *passivity* in its being touch*ed*, in the example, by one's own leg. The concept of constitution implies both these possibilities as senses of "experience." The case of touching one's own body, however, is a special one, very different, for example, from touching an object like the surface of a table. In the touching of the table one's experience—in the sense of *Erfahrung*—is precisely that: "touching the table's surface," and it is in this touching that the table discloses itself as, for example, a "smooth, warm, timber surface" as one passes one's hand over it for a time. In the touching, the table is "constituted" in its self-showing. The *process* of the touching that is "aimed" at the table can be said to be "lost" or "hidden" in the appearance of the table to the touching hand—insofar as the table cannot be said to be capable of "touch" in the same way—and it is this process that is described technically by Husserl as "experience" in the sense of *Erlebnis*. This touch*ing* experience (*Erlebnis*) is also integral to the "constitution" of the table's surface, that is, the manner in which the table reveals itself *as* a "smooth, warm timber surface" to my hand. The appearance of the table is at the same time an "accomplishment" of my touching hand, so that in this way, constitution can thus be said to be a "sense giving" at the level of corporeal, spatial experience. In principle, the "sense giving" need not relate to an actual object. One can, for example, imagine in phantasy or recollection touching or having touched a table. Here, however, the *Erlebnis* is the imagin*ing* as a quasi-perceiving. It is important to point out that what is at issue with these terms is not a matter of mere empirical, causal relationships, such as, in our example, between the physicality of my hand and the material composition of the table. The sense "smoothness" or "warmth" resides neither in the table nor in my hand; rather, it is a corporeal experience of *meaning* at the pre-predicative level of sense perception.

It is to emphasise the *processual* sense of "living through" one's engagement with things that *Erlebnis* is rendered as "lived experience." The idea of an experiential living through perception, memory, phantasy, and so forth also points to the accrual of sense over time. David Carr notes that "*Erfahrung* is the experience of objects in the world."[22] In the example of the touch sensation—the hand touching the table—we see that *Erlebnis* and *Erfahrung* implicate each other in the sense that lived experience (*Erlebnis*) is for the most part the experience (*Erfahrung*) of something, although the latter need not be an actual object of perception, for example experiencing a memory. As Carr notes, however, "certain kinds of sensations or feelings [...] are related to no object; I just have them. But they are experiences in the sense that I live through them."[23] In the following, I will use "experience" to suggest *both* the active processual sense of *Erlebnis* and the receptive letting-something-manifest that is implied in the everyday sense of *Erfahrung*. This is because in dealing with sense perceptual experience, something is always given. Where it is critical for clarification, I follow the convention of "lived experience" for *Erlebnis* or indicate the precise sense of the German term in parentheses. Both senses of experience are implied in the term "constitution," for example, the touch sensation experienced as smooth by the hand is at the same time experienced as the smoothness of the table. In this way, the surface of the table is given to experience or constituted as "smooth."

Visual space

Husserl speaks of space using the concept of the spatial "phantom" (*Phantom*) in his "Thing Lectures," which he characterises in a critical remark as "the lowest stratum of the thing (phantom)."[24] Husserl's use of the word "phantom" can be considered itself an indication of the type of phenomenon he is attempting to foreground, a kind of "appearance" that is the sense perceptually experienced object whose givenness to an experiencing subject is understood purely in terms of its merely sensual qualities. We are therefore not yet dealing with the concrete object—which, for example, has its typical name, its function, its value, and so forth—but rather with the mere appearance of the sensibility of the "thing."[25] Following the implied structure of Husserl's research manuscripts—specifically D 13—Claesges presents his interpretation of the development of Husserl's theme of the constitution of spatiality in the second part of his study, titled *"Die Entfaltung der konstitutiven Theorie des Raumes"* (The development of the constitutive theory of space).[26] The primary concern in this part is with the relationship between the visual and tactual modes of spatial experience in terms of the spatiality, receptivity, and kinaesthetic capabilities of the living body. The spatiality of sound is admittedly neglected in Claesges's study. Husserl, however, was not unaware of this problem; for example, in a manuscript fragment from the group F manuscripts titled "Time in Perception" dating from 1906/1907 and thus contemporaneous with his "Thing Lectures," Husserl enquires into the structure of the experience of a mere sound sensation as the "appearing-of-the-tone," what can be considered a mere aural phantom.[27] Although Husserl here is primarily concerned with the temporality of aural constitution, as opposed to the particular mode of spatial extension characteristic of the experience of sound, he traces the more general implications for understanding any mode of spatial experience as inherently *temporal*.[28] Claesges begins with the problem of the constitution of visual space. It should be noted in advance that Husserl recognises the intertwined nature of sensory experience, and by implication "synesthetic" perceptions, in terms of the kinaestheses of the living body.[29] At the same time, however, sensory perceptions are not homogeneous, and individual senses disclose spatial situations in unique ways, as Filip Mattens points out:

> The tendency to elide the differences between the senses [...] can be remedied by starting from the spatial nature of the senses themselves, for the bodily embedment of our senses indicates their respective roles in the organism's vital relation to a *material* environment, and these in turn suggest that different senses may have different *spatial* proficiencies.[30]

The working concept of the phantom functions methodologically for Husserl. John Drummond describes it as an "abstract moment" of the "thing" in its concreteness.[31] The phantom as an operative concept is a methodological abstraction, but its sense as such is mereological, that is, it is a nonindependent part of a whole.[32] Take, for example, the white colour of the partially embroidered cloth covering the table (Figure 2.1). The whiteness of the cloth is one of its "moments" or "parts," inseparable from it as a surface

Corporeity and spatiality 55

Figure 2.1 View towards the table in the room where the Candomblé ritual—the *caboclo reunião*—takes place. Photo by the author

spread across the table, unlike, for example, the embroidered linear strip, which one could cut out. Not even in phantasy could one imagine the whiteness of the cloth as such; its colour is inseparable from its spatial nature as spread out on the table, folded, and so forth. The colour sensation is typically "lost" or "hidden" in the perception of the thing—"white cloth"—unless, for example, one were to assume the attitude or stance of a painter whose interest aims at the cloth in terms of its colour; but even here the whiteness for the painter is a function of her painterly "reflection" *after* which the "white cloth" has already appeared for her in the immediacy of the seeing.[33] The perception of the white cloth in the concreteness of the ritual event shown in the photograph is more complex and historically layered than merely seeing the fabric as a material "thing," such that even the sense "white cloth" is also a "moment" of the actuality of the situation. However, we will not yet explore the ethnographic situation; rather, we continue to tarry with the problem of the white spread surface as visual phantom. Through the concept of *Erlebnis*, Husserl is characterising the sense, for example, in which the colour sensation is part of our perceptual experience (*Erfahrung*) of the "white cloth," but the colour sensation as such is not perceived; what we perceive is precisely the thing—"white cloth"—whereas the colour sensation is experienced (*erlebt*) in the see*ing*. Husserl shows, therefore, that even at the level of mere visual phantoms—such as colour sensations—spatiality is constituted in its appearance, and that this happens as a function of a mode of experience (*Erlebnis*) that is more fundamental than sense perception, although inseparable from it. As Mattens notes,

> Husserl starts from the most elementary conscious phenomena in external perception, namely various sorts of sensations (visual, tactile, olfactory...). Such sensory material is not perceived, but sensed—or "lived" (*erlebt*). In a first step, Husserl relies on [Carl] Stumpf's observation that one cannot present to oneself a specific color or texture without picturing it as spread out over a certain expanse.[34]

In our example, the spread of colour that qualifies the visual texture of the cloth is further differentiated: there are areas of shadow, of higher or lower intensity of light that affect the appearance of the vibrancy of the colour, the flicker of the candles' flames producing "moving" shadows on the surface, and so forth. Like the touch sensation of the table in our earlier example—of "smoothness"—the colour sensation in its perceptual visibility resides neither in the cloth nor in my eyes as organs of vision; the flux of the shadows and light intensities that are themselves inseparable from the appearance of the cloth's visual texture as white surface are not inherent in the fabric itself, and they are also not immanent to my eyes as organs. Rather, they are constitutive of a form of temporality. Let us shift our attention away from the spatiality of the visual spread of colour to some of the objects on the table and regard them in terms of their "shape."

Corporeity and spatiality 57

Figure 2.2 Detail of the *caboclo* "figurine." Photo by the author

Resting at the centre of the table is a figurine, whose full description and that of the setting in general we will take up in a later chapter. In the photograph, the specific features of the figurine are not clearly discernible, but viewed from another aspect, we see that it has a "face," and therefore a "front" and a "back" (Figure 2.2). "Behind" it to the left we can vaguely discern the leaves of a plant, and to the right "in front" of it a wide dish with vaguely recognisable things in it. The appearance is characterised by a radical perceptual inadequacy. If, for example, we were to continue

58 *Corporeity and spatiality*

Figure 2.3 View towards the table. Photo by the author

our engagement with the object on the table and walk around to another side, we come "face to face" with the figurine from the "front" and its features appear in greater distinctness and clarity, as does the dish with things wrapped in leaves in "front" of it and the leaves of the plant in the vase "behind" (Figure 2.3). Each aspect through which the things on the table and the table as a whole appear to our view clarifies their spatial relations and material articulations—for example, we see that the white cloth extends to the "far end" where there is another strip of embroidered fabric—and

Corporeity and spatiality 59

this happens in terms of relative positions and locations: "front," "back," "behind," "in front," "right," "left," "side," and so forth. In the concreteness of visual appearances there are what Husserl terms "proper" and "improper" appearances, for example, we see the "front" of the figurine—the side that faces us—but we do not actually see the back; the meaning of this is precisely that we *see* the object as *having* inherent to it a "back side," even though we do not actually see that side; rather, we *apperceive* the back as integral to our direct perception of the front. In walking around the table—or perhaps lifting the object and turning it around—we see the other side in its actuality, such that it "faces" us now as the "front." The structure of this appearing of the object to visual perception can thus be described as a givenness through proper-improper aspectual presentations; it is such that the "thing" reveals itself to be perceptually inexhaustible and always "coming-to-be." Husserl characterises this aspectual structure of the manifestation of the concrete "thing" in the following way:

> The one-sidedness of outer perception, the circumstance that it brings the thing to a proper presentation in only one of its sides, that the thing is given to perception only through the medium of appearance in relief, is a radical incompleteness; and this pertains to the essence of all those perceptions we include under the title of perceptions of physical things, or outer perceptions.[35]

The "one-sidedness of outer perception" is a function of the aspectual structure of the thing in its self-showing. The relationship between the apperception (*Apperzeption*) of the "back side" as inherent to the direct perception of the "front side" of the thing indicates other moments in the spatiality of the thing: its positional and horizonal structure.[36] The positionality and horizonality of the thing are intimately related. Claesges first describes the "horizon-structure" (*Horizontstruktur*) of the thing in terms of what Husserl calls its "internal horizon."[37] In our walking around the table to see the "face" of the figurine from its "front," its aspectual appearance from the "side" does not simply disappear; we experience the front as continuous with the side in the concreteness of the appearance of "the figurine" as a volumetric, material thing—what we have called its "phantom body" insofar as we are concerned with its merely sensible manifestation. But even as a mere phantom, its coming to proper appearance one-sidedly in aspects that inherently indicated the sides not actually seen is a structural feature of our experience of the thing. This is its inner horizonality.[38] It implies that—in terms of the spatiality apparent to vision—the thing can never be directly perceived in "proper" givenness from all of its sides at once. In this sense, the material object transcends possibilities of complete visual constitution; there are always "sides" that are "hidden" from vision.[39] This is not a defect of visual perception; it is rather what makes visual perception what it is.

60 *Corporeity and spatiality*

The aspectual structure of the appearance of the thing is also an indication of its positionality, in a spatial sense. Claesges notes that

> position is first thematized by Husserl as "distance" (*Entfernung*). With the concept of distance, the perceiving subject himself is brought into view in such a way, that the moment of position applies to the perceiving subject, that he himself is localized in relation to the phantom.[40]

Implicated, therefore, in the aspectual appearance of the thing is not merely its sensibility but its inherent positional structure as being "there," in some relation of distance from the perceiving subject. Although Claesges's subject has a gendered grammatical sense as "the [male] perceiver" (*der Wahrnehmende*), in principle the perceiver, at the level of descriptions of the *structures* of phantom spatiality, is a generalised subjectivity. As the descriptions become more concrete and take on an ethnographic texture, I address the question of the perceiving subject in its specificity and embodiment. Claesges notes further that there is an inherent structural relationship between the aspectual appearance of the thing and its positionality in terms of the distance from the perceiver: if we move to the other side of the table, the aspectual appearance of the figurine necessarily changes correlative to our movement (Figure 2.4).[41] It is not merely that we see the figurine from its other "side"; not only has the particular aspectual appearance of the figurine changed, but the appearance of the entire spatial condition has changed inherently and continuously with it—the wide dish "in front," the leaves of the plant in the vase "behind," the table covered by the white cloth, and so forth all now appear in harmonious continuity with the figurine from the other "side." The spatial condition as a whole manifests as having an aspectual and positional structure. Dan Zahavi describes this aspectual structure of the givenness of things as their "perspectivity."[42] This perspectivity has a horizonal structure in a wider sense than the individual thing's "inner horizon"; Husserl alludes to this wider horizonality in terms of its environmental sense:

> We acted in a certain sense as if the object perceived at any time were alone in the world, *note bene* in the perceived world. But a perceived thing is never there alone by itself; instead, it stands before our eyes in the midst of determinate, intuited environing things [*Dingumgebung*]. [...] The environing things are equally "perceived." As the words "amid" ["*inmitten*"] and "environment" ["*Umgebung*"] signify, this is a spatial nexus, which unifies the especially perceived thing with the other co-perceived things.[43]

As we have moved and continue to move around the figurine with our attention, for example, directed towards its "face," "environing things" appear always in the background—and by this is meant a perceptual background, such that in our attention to the face of the figurine, the candle

Corporeity and spatiality 61

Figure 2.4 Detail at the table. Photo by the author

62 Corporeity and spatiality

in "front" of it is perceptually part of the background; even aspects of the thing itself appear in the mode of a background, for example, the "torso," "arms," and "legs." Any of the environing things can be foregrounded, such that the figurine fades into the background environmentally as our gaze wonders—the embroidered pattern of the white cloth, the field of popcorn scattered on the cloth's surface, the dish filled with things wrapped in leaves, the glass of water through which the light of the flicker of the candle's flame is reflected and refracted, the candle in its holder, the sheet of paper with text written on its surface, the obscure object next to the box of cigars, the leaves in the vase, the shadows, and so forth. This environmental whole—which includes our apperception of what we do not see directly, such as the ground beneath the table and the white, fluttering strips of paper suspended and dispersed across the ceiling like the sky on a cloudy day—appears in its experiential perspectivity or aspectual-positional structure as a *spatial nexus*. This sense of spatiality as a perceived world of background environing things that appear in their perspectivity in continuity with the aspectual givenness of a foregrounded thing—the face of the figurine—can be understood as a moment of spatiality as horizon.[44] It is horizon understood in terms of space—actual and possible givenness of the "thing" with "environing things" in general to sense perception: "apperception implies a regional general: 'thing'-apperception; intrinsic to its sense is world-space [*Weltraum*] as universal horizon."[45] The structure of the appearance of the "thing" as a certain general "region" of being—the "phantom" as that which is experienceable in direct sense perception—can be described, therefore, in terms of its *aspectuality, positionality*, and *horizonality* given in relation to a perceiving subject (Figure 2.5).[46]

In our considerations thus far the spatial nexus in which the thing in its relation to environing things as a background horizon appears has been limited to the abstract moment of its visual givenness; keeping in mind the sense of the term "moment," this can be characterised, after Husserl, as the "visual field."[47] Husserl also speaks of other "sense-fields," for example, the "tactile field," "auditory field," "olfactory field," and the "field of thermal sensation," in which the visual and the tactile have primary significance for the corporeal givenness of spatiality.[48] The relationship between perceptual fields in concrete spatial experience will become clear as we approach problems of touch, movement, and the lived body.

The spatiality of the visual field, as we have seen, involves our apperception of the "back" of things, that is, yet to be realised but intrinsically prefigured possibilities for direct perception of the thing from different points of view. The implications of the aspectuality or perspectivity of the givenness of the thing and its horizonal spatial nexus of environing things are not limited to its positionality and horizonality. Its position as a function of its appearance as at a distance "near to" or "far from" the perceiving subject implies possibilities for movement, either of the thing or of the body of the perceiving subject. In its "nearness" or "farness," the thing can appear

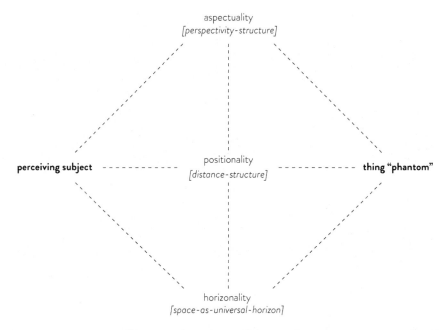

Figure 2.5 Diagram of the spatial structure of thing "phantom" perception. Sketch by the author, digitised by Gracie Meek.

more or less distinct. We continue our walking movement around the table until we are on the "other side," and we see the "back" of the figurine, no longer in apperceptive anticipation but in direct perception (Figure 2.6). The leaves in the vase now obscure our vision, as does the ribbed glass jug of water and the flickering flame of the candle. As we move around the room, not only does the aspectual givenness of the figurine correspondingly change, but inherent to this change is its continuity as a moment of the overall change in the aspectual givenness of the visual space as a whole. The continuity of the changing appearance of the visual space in its changing aspectual givenness is, however, not merely spatial. It implies a certain fulfilment of sense and clarification of our apprehension of the thing and the spatial horizon; for example, with the lights now turned off and the table illuminated purely by the glow of the candles' flames, the figurine appears in obscurity but not in the same sense as when we first encountered it (Figure 2.7). We see it obscurely, yet with a familiarity and physiognomic recognisability not available to us when we initially encountered it. Certain phenomenologically structural features of the constitution of visual space are at play here in addition to those we have already considered, and which indicate a sense of the temporality of visual perception. These have to do

Figure 2.6 Detail at the table, towards the vase and foliage. Photo by the author

with the perceiving subject's bodily kinaestheses. Claesges identifies the following passage in Husserl: "each aspectual appearance (*Aspekterscheinung*) of the phantom exists only in this relatedness to a kinaesthesis, to a kinaesthetic rest or to a kinaesthetic movement."[49] This inherent structural correlation between the bodily movement of the perceiving subject and the perspectivity of the appearance of visual space—things and their horizontal environment—is what Husserl describes in terms of the concept of *adumbration* (*Abschattung*).[50]

Corporeity and spatiality 65

Figure 2.7 View towards the table with the lights turned off. Photo by the author

Husserl sometimes describes this adumbrative structure as if it emerges independently from the thing, as if the thing were able to articulate itself affectively: "Draw closer, closer still; now fix your eyes on me, changing your place, changing the position of your eyes, etc. You will get to see even more of me that is new, ever new partial colorings, etc."[51] Implied in this suggestive description is precisely the kinaestheses of the perceiving subject in its relation to the perspectivity of the thing. In the focusing kinaesthesis of our eyes, which may be accompanied by subtle cephalomotor movements, we foreground one thing—the figurine—or part of it—its "face"—a moment that qualifies it—the partial colourations of its surface—or shifting our bodies slightly to one side the face appears no longer frontally but obliquely in profile. In all of these various aspectual appearances of the thing, we never lose sight of its horizonal significance as a whole—including what we do not directly perceive but apperceive, such as its "back" and the texture of the material beneath the colourings of the dark surface. In our perceptions and apperceptions of the aspectual-horizonal givenness of the thing, what we see before us is precisely the concrete thing, the "figurine." But we have only described moments of its "inner horizon"; the figurine rests on the table with the other environing things in their wider horizonality as a spatial nexus in which another thing—the vase of leaves—could be foregrounded in the shifting oculomotor movement.[52] As our gaze and our bodies move closer to or further away from the figurine with its always environing background, we develop over time a familiarity with its contours, its textures and colourations, its articulations, and so forth, in such a way that "certain appearances are privileged (*bevorzugt*) as normal."[53] The perceptual, experiential sense of normality is framed by Anthony Steinbock in terms of Husserl's characterisation of the optimal: "If the lived-body is intermeshed in a network of phenomena [...] then there will be a perspective or a situation that will be *preferred* as *better* or *best* for experiencing."[54]

In describing the figurine thus far as an example, I have not yet attended to it in its ethnographic concreteness. Although methodologically we are starting with a structural enquiry into the constitution of visual space—as if there were no history—this does not mean that static spatiality is primary. Already with the theme of optimality as a structural feature of aspectuality, we see that the experience of spatiality involves a certain kind of preferentiality and differentiation at the level of sense perception. It would suggest, for example, that the aspectual clarity of the figurine when viewed with the lights on and unobscured by other environing things is optimal and thus "normal" (Figure 2.3), as against its obscurity with the lights off and visibility a function of the glow of the candles' flames (Figure 2.7). However, in the concreteness of the situation of the ritual, the relation between normality and optimality is not straightforward, but we can still point out that even in the case of candlelight alone, oculomotion performs its clarifying function at the level of sense perception. We will not approach the ethnographic situation so quickly; rather, we continue in a meandering way and linger with the problem of spatiality.

The fact that the aspectual-positional-horizonal givenness of the thing is not experienced as a mere juxtaposition of fragments in a homogeneous "space," but rather in the adumbrative structure of experience the thing is given through aspectual syntheses as a continuously appearing spatiotemporal unity in which there are *preferred* appearances as optimal, is already an indication that spatiality is *qualitative*. The sense perceptually experienced optimal functions as an originary orienting "belief," what Husserl calls "primal belief" ("*Urglaube*") or "protodoxa" ("*Urdoxa*").[55] When we first enter the room and encounter the table laid with things, this setting—"table laid with things"—stands out against a wider environing background: the tiled floor, white walls with wide, windowless openings through which our view extends to the rustling leaves of the large tree whose branches sway in the wind, and towards the night sky, the stars, and so forth. As we approach the table the figurine stands out in its peculiarity and unfamiliarity in relief against its environing things on the table; we see it first obliquely from the side in profile, and we are drawn towards it until we are able to clearly discern the features of its "face," foregrounded against the background "inner" horizon of its "body," and the wider background of the environing spatial nexus that may even reach the stars. At certain moments in our approaching the figurine—even if this approaching is merely oculomotor and we focus our gaze on its "eyes" as we are too shy to reach over the table to face it closely—we have the sense that we have seen it clearly, and in this perceptual manner it acquires the character of the "familiar" (assuming, of course, that "we" have not been here before). It is a spatial familiarity in that our gaze has moved around the thing from many sides until we have a familiar situation: "figurine" resting on the table amid other environing things, "facing" this direction with this or that "behind" and "in front of" it, to the "side," in this light, and so forth. At any opportune moment if we want the figurine to appear in its visual clarity again, we can move to where we once were at "that side of the table." As I noted, this means that we are dealing with spatiality as qualified, differentiated, and oriented in terms of preferences. The familiar situation in which the figurine in its environmental horizon is clearest is intrinsically correlated to our kinaesthetic situation, standing and looking from that side of the table.[56] But there is implied here a certain spatial play, for example, if we wanted instead to see the "back" of the figurine clearly and distinctly we could move to the other side—now, here on "this side of the table" the figurine appears optimally for our interest in its "back," and from this perspective we also see in an optimal way the environing things "behind" it, and the entire spatial situation from this point of view. In a certain generalised way, therefore, our kinaesthetic possibilities are at the same time possibilities for multifarious spatial appearances.

Insofar as any of the environing things can be foregrounded, even moments "internal" to a thing—the veins on the leaves of the plants in the vase—or "things" that appear as "concrete" phantoms in that their "bodies" elude our kinaestheses—the moonlit glow of the night sky[57]—the possibilities for qualitative transformations and reorientations of visual space are *open* in terms of the "space-of-potential" or "leeway" (*Spielraum*) of the environmental horizon.[58] From certain kinaesthetic situations—across from one of the windowless openings in the wall—we can foreground a heavenly constellation, letting the figurine on the table with its environing things fade into the background. In the actual and possible enactment of manifold bodily kinaestheses spontaneously, we accomplish in their actuality and anticipate in their potentiality differentiated spatial experiences. That our bodily motility foreshadows continuous aspectual appearances of the spatiality of things in a process whereby our surroundings become familiar over time and do not readily lose their acquired sense of "having become familiar" such that our experiences take on the character of "truth"—the figurine is actually there on the table—points to the problem of *time* in perception (*Wahrnehmung*).[59] Alienation presupposes the prior acquisition of a level of familiarity. The sense in which Husserl characterises sense perception as originary "belief" (*Urdoxa*) pertains to its particular temporal structure. The ethical implications of the temporality of perception are far-reaching and pertain directly to the problems of empathy (*Einfühlung*) and coevalness, as theorised in the works of Mudimbe and Fabian that were introduced in the first chapter. I explore the phenomenological significance of this in Chapter 3.

The spatial phantom and time

Thus far the objects of description—the "figurine," for example—have functioned as examples through which to characterise Husserl's concept of things as "phantoms." We are not yet enquiring into their historically situated concreteness, for example, as related to the *caboclo*.[60] For us it is a phantom body as mere sensual "thing," a visual phantom, discreet in its general physiognomic appearance—*this* shape, colouring, surface texture, and so forth, versus *that* other environing thing—the "candle" as a differently appearing phantom body. The figurine appears in *its* particular way; a mode of appearing that incorporates and is continuous with the candle as one of its horizonal environing things—one side is more illuminated than the other, for example, and the colouration of its surface varies with the flickering flame as the wax melts. In these changing states of illumination we continuously see the identical thing—the "figurine"—*through* its continuously changing appearances as the glow of the flame varies. Similarly we see the identical thing—"lit candle"—until the wax melts completely. Perhaps if we were close enough to the figurine, so that we touch it with our hands in proximity to the candle, we could "feel" its changing colouration in terms of a proximal field of thermal sensation—the descending flame of the candle. But we continue with visual space. In seeing the figurine, it is *it* that my view "aims" at in its changing appearance—its subtle but ever-changing colouration as the candle burns and the changing luminosity of the candle itself in its melting as a background, and so forth. But I do not "aim" at my *seeing* in its kinaestheses—the focusing of oculomotion following the descending shimmer of the "back" of the figurine, subtle turning of the head, perhaps my body gestures slightly forward, and so forth. Our own movements do not themselves become available to our perceptions in the perceiving; they are themselves "invisible"; they function, rather, towards that which is perceived and in attunement with the coming to visibility of the spatiality of the thing. The intertwining of our kinaestheses with the coming to visibility of the thing has a peculiar temporal structure, which Husserl describes in terms of the continuity of "running-off phenomena" (*Ablaufsphänomene*), an expression indicating the structure of time in perception, which I take up further along.[61]

Husserl's analyses typically use the example of the experience of temporal objects, such as a tone or melody.[62] The fundamental problematic that Husserl aims to clarify, however, is what he terms "internal time-consciousness" (*inneres Zeitbewusstsein*). The analyses concerning the consciousness of internal time are perhaps the most complex problems of Husserl's philosophy, "the most difficult of all phenomenological problems."[63] They were first published in 1928 and then posthumously as volume 10 of Husserliana, in English translation as *On the Phenomenology of the Consciousness of Internal Time (1893–1917)*.[64] I draw on sections of these analyses that explicitly address the problem of the experience of the duration of spatial objects and, following Claesges, on sections of manuscript D 8 in the unpublished group D manuscripts.

Claesges points out that Husserl's approach to the problem of space is to start with concrete perceptual experience, rather than as if space were first encountered whereby one "thinks-away all things."[65] Thus, space is fundamentally experienced as a givenness beforehand (*Vorgegebenheit*) in terms of the "discoverability" (*Vorfindlichkeit*) of things; it enables things to be encountered in their particular modes of appearing.[66] In sense perception—as opposed, for example, to recollection—the thing is present before us in the "here" and "now." The apparent availability of the thing in its physical presence "now"—we can reach and touch the figurine, or look out at the stars in the night sky—is a function not of its mere presence; rather, its presence to perception is such in relation to its "having just been present" and its anticipatory "continuing to be present."[67] We must keep in mind that we are speaking of the thing in its manner of appearing to a perceiving subject which, as we have seen, involves its adumbrative horizonal structure as intertwined with our kinaestheses. Our perception of the thing is implicated in its "duration."[68]

Approaching the problem of space in terms of its sense perceptual apprehension means that from the start the perceiving subject is already and in advance within surroundings, in the presence of environing things, even if these are stars in the night sky. Prior to our perceptual acts lie already given surroundings in their structure of discoverability. Husserl begins with these surroundings described in terms of their "apartness," their givenness as "explicated" in the sense of the appearance of manifold things besides or "outside one another" in "mutual externality" (*Außereinander*).[69] There is thus a sense of the possibility of things not only as related to the kinaestheses of the perceiving subject, but as pertaining to the positional relationships between things themselves. This spatial figure (*Raumgestalt*) experienced in the "besides each other" locality of things displays a temporal characteristic of "simultaneity" (*Gleichzeitigkeit*).[70] This "coexistence" of explicated space in its simultaneity of appearance is described by Husserl as "having grown together" (*zusammengewachsen*) in the temporal continuity of their perception.[71] This "having grown together" is not to be understood as if things in their side-by-side appearance have synchronous but distinct times in parallel; rather, the simultaneity pertains to *coexistence*: "[the process of] having grown together is simply coexistence. And it [coexistence] has grown together in spatial contiguity of continually mediated spatial fullness."[72] I have described this spatial coexistence in terms of the concept of horizon—the figurine is never "alone," it is always given amid environing things: candles, the vase with foliage, white cloth, rustling leaves outside, the night sky, and so forth—and have alluded to the temporality of this "having grown together" of things in terms of the structures of aspectuality and adumbration. Husserl sometimes refers to the particular adumbrative aspect of the appearance of the thing in its horizonal spatiality as an "image" (*Bild*).[73] As Husserl explicitly notes, this is "a concept of image which naturally has nothing to do with illustration"; the aspect is thus not a "picture" or "representation" in a derivative or illustrative sense but an *appearance* of the thing itself in its immediacy to perception—"how it presents itself to us."[74]

Husserl's description of the coexistence of things in their perceptual encounter as "having grown together" suggests a kind of structural, developmental "kinship" between things as perceived. He characterises the duration of their visibility in terms of "image-phases." In their simultaneous coexistence, images grow together in succession as a visual field in temporal phases.[75] Breaks in this duration can arise, for example, if the "images" appear for the most part still, but then suddenly an image in this visual field of images appears to move "now"—the melting wax flows along the side of the candle, which draws one's gaze away from the face of the figurine in a simultaneous turn of the head. The candle appears in a new "now" as "melting wax"—the same "species" of phantom body, but now one in motion—while its environing things remain given as phantom bodies at rest.[76] The melting wax has ruptured the kinship of growing together, and its duration stands out as "changing." Yet, the new "now" in which the melting wax came to visibility to our gaze is also the "now" of its environing things. The figurine, vase, white cloth, and so forth continue to appear as "at rest," however, in a modified form as "at rest as the wax melts." But the new "now" is already a "just now," fading away into a "having been" even as it anticipates a "will immediately come to be," such that in the "having melted" the wax is experienced in an anticipatory way as "melting."

Corporeity and spatiality 71

Figure 2.8 View towards the ceiling. Photo by the author

As the flame of the candle slowly descends, so does the shimmer of its glowing reflections on the surface of the figurine. The changing appearance of the "image" of the colouration of the figurine to my perception is inseparable from my kinaesthesis—oculomotion at the least, but perhaps I move my head slightly, and so forth. I do not merely see the descending glow of the flame "now" shimmering along the head of the figurine, "now" glistening along its back, as if two juxtaposed pieces of time; rather, I see the shimmer of the back in a "now" that *stretches back* to the halo of light "just now" illuminating the head, and that *reaches forward* towards the flame's descent in a "thickening" of time.[77] The "just now" of the figurine's glowing face was also the "just now" of the "having grown together" in coexistence of the entire background of environing things in their appearance "at rest"—the vase, table, the foliage outside, the night sky, stars, and so forth. The entire spatial situation in its "running-off" *continuity* "away" from the "now" in its anticipatory fading into the "just now" and the "coming now" is implicated in the perception of the candle's descending glow. This means that even if my attention were to be drawn away from the candle's glow—a gentle wind blows and I hear a rustling sound above, I lean back and tilt my head up to look at the fluttering paper strips of the ceiling (Figure 2.8)—my perception of the entire room has been infused with the "just now" of the figurine's glow, and although the latter is no longer given in direct perception, it remains within my perceptual horizon as a possibility of my kinaestheses.

Tactual space, motility, and the lived body

In our consideration of visual space we have not yet touched anything, but we have moved, for example, the focusing eyes and turning head, or the walking body as we look at things on the table from this or that angle. We characterised one of the structural features of the experience of visual space as the distance (*Entfernung*) of objects that appear in the visual field—the perceiving subject experiences these as located "there" in relation to her "here." This "here" as the indexical position of the subject has the sense: "here, where my body is." Husserl describes the peculiar structure of this subjectively experiencing body in terms of the concept of the "lived body" (*Leib*).[78] Husserl's analyses of lived bodily spatiality are not derivative of, but rather are integral to, the sense of "subjectivity" when describing the perceiving subject's experience of space, as Dan Zahavi notes:

> Husserl claims that spatial objects can only appear for and be constituted by *embodied subjects*. Thus the body is characterized by being present in any experience as the zero point, the absolute "here", in relation to which every experienced object is oriented. In our immediate experience of space [...] our body possesses a unique position, as the center around which and in relation to which space unfolds itself. Every spatial orientation and every experience of objects in space thus refers to the indexical "here" connected with our embodiment.[79]

To grasp more comprehensively the implications of Husserl's concept of the lived body, we need to consider the constitution of visual space in relation to his descriptions and analyses of lived bodily motility and the experiential structures of tactile space. In approaching the concept of the lived body—which has already been implied in our provisional description of the kinaestheses involved in the constitution of visual space—I follow Claesges in elaborating the function of bodily motility and the constitution of tactile space.

The tactual sphere exhibits certain unique structures in terms of which the lived body can be essentially described. As an essential structure, it is important to note in advance that the concept of the lived body in Husserl does not fundamentally assume any particular empirical or anthropological type, for, as Zahavi emphasises, "the analysis of the body's function as a condition of possibility for the experience of objects is as well an analysis of the body's function as a condition of possibility for objects of experience."[80] In its concreteness as lived body of this or that particular perceiving subject—human or non-human—certain objects (in a wide sense, not limited to physical things) may be experienceable for it or not, or in different ways that are circumscribed as lived bodily possibilities. We will come to these more complex problems as we approach the ethnographic situation, for example, in relation to the physiognomic and apparent gender, race, vocational, generational, and so forth transformations that occur during the Candomblé *caboclo* ritual. That in the descriptions thus far the perceiving subject is characteristically human—focusing eyes, turning head, walking body, and so forth—should not be mistaken for a philosophical anthropological thesis; Husserl's phenomenology is not a philosophical anthropology.[81] In describing the experience of the perceiving subject, its spatiality as that constituted by a human subject is to be understood as exemplary of perceiving subjectivity in a certain generalised sense, at least with regard to an analysis that limits itself to the constitution of spatial phantoms.[82]

I noted the principle of distance (*Entfernung*) regarding the constitution of visual space, in which spatiality is first experientially disclosed in terms of the adumbrative appearance of things over "there" in my field of vision. This sense of distance includes the relative proximity of things in my visual field to my lived body as absolute indexical "here," which, as Filip Mattens notes, "is further articulated into a near-space—in which I can haptically intervene—and a far-space."[83] The scope or optic leeway (*Spielraum*) of the visual field ranges between optimal visibility and disappearance or, in the case of objects too close, blurring. The tactual field, however, is articulated through touch as a *near-sense* (*Nahsinn*): "The tactual phantom is either optimally near if it is actually felt, or it is tactually completely absent."[84] This does not mean, however, that the structure of positionality does not pertain; on the contrary, bodily motility in the tactual sphere has a pre-eminent function in the constitution of spatiality:

> We find now a striking difference between the sphere of the visual and that of the tactual. In the tactual realm we have the *external Object*, tactually constituted, and a second Object, the *Body* [*Leib*], likewise tactually constituted, e.g. the touching finger, and, in addition, there are fingers touching fingers. So here we have a double apprehension: the same touch-sensation is apprehended as a feature of the "external" Object and is apprehended as a sensation of the Body as Object [*Leib-Objekts*]. And in the case in which a part of the Body [*Leibesteil*] becomes equally an external Object of an other part, we have the double sensation [...] and the double apprehension as feature of the one or of the other Body part as a physical [O]bject. But in the case of an *Object constituted purely visually* we have *nothing* comparable.[85]

With this extended passage from Husserl's analyses of the tactile sphere of the lived body—taken from the Second Book of *Ideas*, a work that Husserl began in 1912 and continually revised for almost two decades—I take up anew the provisional sketch of the "double sensation" (*Doppelempfindung*) of touch outlined by Sokolowski.[86] I have for the most part been describing the sense perceptual apprehension of things as spatial phantoms. In oculomotion, things reveal themselves in their structures of discoverability. The lived body of the seeing subject itself, however, cannot be encountered in the same way—I cannot see my seeing eyes. In principle, I can walk around the thing, or depending on its size lift it and turn it around to scan it from multiple aspects in continuous motion, of my own or that of the thing. My perceiving body, however, is not discoverable to me visually in this way; I can neither scan nor move around my own body to experience its multiple sides as with a thing—my face, the back of my head, my neck, and so forth are not accessible to my direct visual perception in the way, for example, the figurine or the table is.[87] It is important to note that even in the case of one's own body, the question of "constitution" pertains to the manner in which one experiences one's body in its immediate givenness, which necessarily implies a certain reflexivity. In visual perception, for example, my hand can come to givenness according to the structures of appearing that pertain to things, for example, aspectually in adumbrations. But even in the case of my hand, I cannot survey it in quite the same way as with a thing, because I experience its visual givenness as incorporated into the kinaestheses of my body as a whole—I move my hands to see first the palm and then the back, but this is not the same sense of "movement" as when I "move" a thing.[88] I experience movement of my body—oculomotion, cephalomotion, locomotion, and so forth—in its immediacy as if by fiat—"I move," rather than "my body moves." As Claesges notes, "the original kinaesthesis of 'walking' does not yet have the character of moving my body in space."[89]

The role of lived bodily movement in the constitution of spatiality is not incidental, but rather is of essential necessity: "All spatiality is constituted, i.e. comes to givenness, in movement, in the movement of the Object itself and in the movement of the 'Ego' [*Ich*], along with the change in orientation that is given thereby."[90] Here, "the movement of the 'Ego'" is the movement of one's own body as "self-movement" and is privileged in such a way that it is precisely this facility for self-movement that determines the perceiving body as a lived body over against the sense of the "body" of inanimate things, which Husserl qualifies by the German "*Körper*."[91] This sense of self-movement is not merely mechanical and should not be confused with movement attributable to automation and so forth. The lived body is not a mechanism, but an "animate organism" in its facility for spontaneous movement.[92] Our consideration of sense perceptual apprehension has been limited thus far to the appearance of things as spatial phantoms in the visual or tactual fields of the perceiving subject in the constitution of space. Movement of objects in my visual field—the melting wax of the candle and its flickering flame—is given in terms of my own sensations of bodily movement—in the movement of my eyes, for example. The visual field, therefore, corresponds to actual and possible kinaestheses. As suggested in the example of seeing my own hand, my body itself can manifest or come to givenness as part of my field of visual sensations, and thereby constituted in the kinaestheses of oculomotion; however, as Claesges notes: "The visually appearing lived body differs from all other phantoms thus, in that it has a set constant position at the orientation centre of visual space."[93]

Prior to any perceptual experience of my body as a spatial phantom among others are my kinaesthetic experiences. Through my kinaestheses I experience and thus "constitute" my own living body as a spatial body. Tactile sensations that "clothe" my body facilitating my experience of a tactual field in the constitution of tactual space function pre-eminently for my actual and possible kinaestheses in such a way that kinaesthetic sensations are "inserted" into my body and localised as tactile sensations. This is not the case with vision. Although the visually appearing thing in its environmental horizontality is perceived in a temporal continuity of adumbrations in correlation with oculomotion—the subtle movements of my eyes follow laterally the shimmer of the candle's light in its descent along the back of the figurine as the wax melts, or in sudden darkness, or an intense glare my eyes adjust—none of these visual sensations are localised in my eye. I can, of course, touch my eyes, and in *this* sense, as Husserl notes, "the eye, *too*, is a field of localization but *only for touch sensations*."[94] My eyes as organs of vision are never themselves experienced as visual sensations in my visual field and thus constituted within visual space. My body as a tactual field, however, is experienced as both constituting tactual space—in the kinaesthesis of touch, objects come to givenness—and as a part of tactual space: "To be sure, in seeing, I do not localize the visual appearances, as appearances, in my body, although I do indeed so localize the tactile sensations and the others interwoven with them, including the sensations of movement."[95]

Building on Husserl's analyses and stressing the material nature of the body's surface, Filip Mattens emphasises this difference between visual and tactile perception:

> The perceptual appearance of extended surfaces thus seems reserved to sight and touch. However, the embedment of touch-receptors throughout the skin at different depths indicates that tactile perception is not exclusively a matter of exploiting the interplay between sense-impressions and *lateral* movements. The cutaneous surface is not merely a perceptual field in which phenomenal events take place, but also a physical sentient surface. [...] when an object in contact with the skin expands and rotates, we do not only perceive rotation and expansion but also experience a mechanical effect on the skin: as we sense friction, tickling, torsion…, we experience what our skin physically undergoes. [...] the skin itself however is also a real, sentient integumentary mass, and *in that capacity* it enables us to understand what our body undergoes and to probe the material nature of things.[96]

It is thus the body's facility for kinaesthetic experience, by means of which a tactual field is given and thus the givenness of objects through tactile

76 Corporeity and spatiality

sensations, that makes spatial experience possible.[97] Kinaesthetic sensations, however, are not experienced as "presentational" in the sense that they themselves do not come to givenness in the manner of the appearance of things. The kinaestheses themselves are not spatial in this sense, but they are essential for the experience of things in their adumbrative horizonal givenness, and thus for the constitution of spatiality.[98] This is thus not space experienced as unqualified, but rather always as an actual or possible kinaesthetic situation through which a perceptual field—necessarily tactual and determined by localised sensations—is constituted. Still, however, although not in terms of adumbrative appearance as with spatial objects, kinaesthetic sensations are also constituted, that is, they also come to givenness to an experiencing subject.

In setting the table, after placing a few objects—the dish with things wrapped in leaves, the vase with foliage, popcorn—I pass my hand across some areas of the surface of the white cloth to smoothen it (Figure 2.9). In an analogous way to the movement of my gaze as the shimmer of the candle's light descends and fades, the movement of my hand along the surface of the cloth stretches out temporally. The tactile sensation of "softness" that spreads and fills the surface of my palm is experienced as a quality of the fabric itself; in my tactile field the cloth appears to me in its aspect as "soft," "smooth," and so forth, at this or that moment corresponding to the movement of my hand, and I can distinguish clearly the softness of the cloth against the hardness of the table it covers as a tactual background—analogous to the variation in colouration of its whiteness, for instance in shadow or not, and the environing horizon that I have in visual perception. In touch, however, as Mattens has noted, my skin itself experiences its own sensing activity as inherent to its tactual field, in such a way that it takes on the quality "softness" as if this quality belonged to it as much as to the fabric. The material quality of the fabric is, of course, not really present in the touch sensation of my skin; rather, the cloth is experienced by me in the localised tactile sensation of my hand as "soft." There is in the experience of touch a peculiar identification that takes place at the localised level of the tactile sensation. Claesges describes this in the following way:

> Each sensation in the tactual sphere that brings a phantom to givenness, brings at the same time the sensing lived body to givenness with it, because the localizations through which the phantom is given belong to the lived body as aspectual [givenness of the phantom]. Thus in the tactual sphere every sensation is "sensation of oneself," whereby sensations [*Empfindungen*] thus have the character of localized lived bodily sensations [*Empfindnissen*]. Thus the lived body and outer world are given equally originaliter.[99]

Claesges here is referencing Husserl's description of the unique character of tactile sensations as among a "certain group of '*sensations*'" that the lived

Corporeity and spatiality 77

Figure 2.9 The table partially set. Photo by the author

body "carries" on and in it, "spread out over it, existing in it, in short, as localized," and intertwined with kinaesthetic sensations, which are also in this "group" of localised lived bodily sensations (*Empfindnissen*).[100] The kinaesthetic nature of tactual experience results in a givenness of one's own body in the immediacy of the touch sensation through which a spatial object is given, and this is what Claesges means when he says that every tactile sensation of a thing is at the same time a "sensation of oneself" that is given "*originaliter.*" A traditional subject-object dichotomy cannot account for this experienced identity between touch sensation and quality of the touched thing. The implication, therefore, is that at the level of localised lived bodily touch sensations, the body and the thing are experienced as interlaced in the duration of the touching activity.[101] The issue is not simply physiological, for, as Dermot Moran notes, "in grasping the object we take-up and interpret the sensations, performing a sense-interpreting act which yields an interpreted sense, *Auffassungssinn*."[102] The cloth, for example, is experienced in touch *as* "soft" and continuously so in modified ways as my palm moves across its surface—"just now" experienced as "soft and smooth," but "now" as "soft and wrinkled having been just soft and smooth"—the two moments of the touch sensation do not stand side by side, but the past sense is enfolded in the present "now" in such a way that the present moment is experienced in terms of the past and vice versa. This tactual experience of the spatiality of the thing necessarily has the character of a temporal spread, not as a quantitative measure but *originaliter* (*ursprünglich*) in the sensing, as past qualities are "retained" in present sensations.[103] This "retention" has the character of a modification of the past sensation—"soft and smooth *then*"—and the modificational structure is continuous—continuity of continuous modification—until I lift my hand off the surface.[104] The temporal structure of the givenness of the thing indexes the temporal structure of the apprehending kinaesthesis, which, in turn, functions as a clue to the structure of the temporality of the perceiving subject. I have provisionally traced out this structure of temporality in the above example of tactual experience and earlier in relation to visual space; its essential nature and implications will become clearer through further investigation of kinaesthetic experience.

Corporeity and time

Let us return to the figurine, as a "simple" example of a thing given as unchanging in manifold perspectives versus, for example, the candle and its flickering flame constantly appearing in motion as we also feel the blowing wind and see its changing "state" and "shape" as the wax melts. In oculomotion or by reaching out, we can see or touch the figurine. Husserl emphasises that movement as such—the focusing eyes or arms reaching out—is a type of sensation different from the visual or touch sensation, even though it is integral to seeing and touching; kinaesthetic sensations are "interwoven" with visual and tactual sensations, although "they still cannot blend with them in the sense of exchanging functions with them."[105] The seeing and the touching bring the thing—the figurine, for example—to presentation or givenness, visually or tactually, but, as described above, my bodily movements through which the figurine is seen or touched are themselves not experienced as seen or touched in the same way. The kinaesthetic sensations interwoven with touch are "inserted" into my living body.[106] I described this with reference to the touch sensation in its localisation, in relation to which Husserl also includes senses of warmth, olfactory, taste, but also pain, pleasure, and so forth.[107] As distinct from vision, in which the sense field is structured primarily in terms of the presentational facility of the kinaesthesis of the eye movements for the givenness of things "distanced" from my lived body, Husserl characterises the kinaestheses themselves, the tactual sensations, and so forth as "subjective" determinations of the lived body. Edith Stein—Husserl's student and assistant from 1916 to 1918—would include among these "subjective" sensations—in which the lived body is experienced "as sensing, as the bearer of these and those sensations"[108]—sensations of "feelings." It is useful to quote Stein at length as she sketches relations between the narrower sense of localised lived bodily sensations (*Empfindnissen*) in Husserl strictly pertaining to the founding sensations of sense perceptual experience, and a wider scope of sensible and sensual "feelings" (*Gefühle*):

> Sensations of feelings [*Gefühlsempfindungen*] or sensual feelings [*sinnlichen Gefühle*] are inseparable from their founding sensations. The pleasantness of a savory dish, the agony of a sensual pain, the comfort of a soft garment are noticed where food is tasted, where pain pierces, where the garment clings to the body's surface. However, sensual feelings not only are there but at the same time also in me; they issue from my "I." General feelings [*Gemeingefühle*] have a hybrid position similar to sensual feelings. Not only the "I" feels vigorous or sluggish, but I "notice this in all my limbs." Every mental act, every joy, every pain [...] every movement I make is sluggish and colorless when "I" feel sluggish. [...] Moods [*Stimmungen*] are "general feelings" of a non-somatic nature [...] But this does not imply that psychic and bodily general feelings run beside one another undisturbed. Rather, one seems to have a reciprocal "influence" on the other. [...] While looking at a view, I feel that a cheerful mood wants to take possession of me, but cannot prevail because I feel sluggish and tired. "I shall be cheerful here as soon as I have rested up," I say to myself. I may know this from "previous experience," yet its foundation is always in the phenomenon of the reciprocal action of psychic and somatic experiences.[109]

In a preliminary remark in *Thing and Space* that anticipates his wider analyses of the lived body in *Ideas II*—the manuscript of which was initially transcribed and redacted by Stein while she was Husserl's assistant—Husserl alludes to the more concrete and complex problem of the givenness of the body of other perceiving subjects in the immediacy of sense perceptual experience—and thus originarily—as "animate Bodies" (*beseelte Leiber*).[110] Here, in relation to the peculiar givenness of one's own lived body to oneself "in" kinaesthetic sensations, tactual sensations, and other "subjective" determinations, Husserl raises the problem of the experience of other subjects as lived bodies. Thus far, we have been considering the constitution of spatiality as an "accomplishment" (*Leistung*) of a perceiving subject in terms of the adumbrative horizonal and temporal structures of the givenness of things, understood in their structures of discoverability (*Vorfindlichkeit*) as sensible "phantoms."[111] In relation to this, the lived body itself came to givenness in terms of the peculiar intertwining of the tactual field—the surface of the skin—and the aspectual, haptic qualities of the touched thing, in the kinaesthesis of the localised touch sensation. This experience was radicalised in the moments where one surface of the body touched another. With the problem of the localised lived bodily sensations in view—kinaesthetic and tactual in particular—we can shift the emphasis from the constitution of the spatial thing to the constitution of the lived body, its peculiar mode of self-givenness. Zahavi makes the extraordinary observation in this light that "giving constitutive priority to this kind of experience rather than to the experience of material spatio-temporal objects has decisive consequences for any account of the experience of another embodied subject."[112] As we saw, the constitution of the thing is revealed as having a temporal structure that refers back to the experiencing subject. In the kinaesthesis of tactual experience, the perceiving subject constitutes—brings to givenness in touch sensations—its own lived body, and reflexively so in the case of touching one's own body. This peculiar self-affection also has a temporal structure. Its investigation, and the entire problem of spatial constitution, would gradually be described and analysed by Husserl in terms of a "genetic" method. The word "genetic" here is not a reference to empirical or biological sciences. The issue, rather, pertains to problems of the temporality of subjectivity and, specifically, the way in which sense is built up or "sedimented" over time.[113] The implications of these genetic analyses are far-reaching and extend to the problem of the *intersubjective* constitution of spatiality, or, put differently, the perceiving subject's experience of spatiality as intersubjective. It indicates further levels of problems, such as those of the linguality of tradition and historicity, as explored, for example, in Jacques Derrida's "Introduction" to Husserl's well-known essay of 1936, "The Origin of Geometry."[114] At the basic level of sense perception, Husserl starts with the problem of "passive genesis" in terms of the structures of "receptivity" and "spontaneity," that is, the problem of how the phantom engenders an "affection" (*Affektion*) from the perceiving subject in the first place.[115]

Claesges does not address explicitly the significance of Husserl's analyses of what he terms "passive genesis" for the constitution of space, but the problem is implied in his consideration of the "receptivity" and "spontaneity" of lived bodily kinaesthesis.[116] Husserl's analyses of "passive synthesis" involve extremely detailed descriptions of perceptual experience *originaliter* and its varying modalities. Donn Welton has explored their significance for Husserl in the development and "systematization" of his transcendental phenomenological philosophy as a whole, and I draw on Welton's study in approaching the question of "genetic spatiality" in Chapter 3.[117] Husserl initially developed these analyses in a series of lectures between 1920 and 1926, after his

"Thing Lectures" but contemporaneous with and prior to some of the D manuscripts on space. The lectures were published in part as Husserliana volume 11 (1966), as *Analysen zur passiven Synthesis* (Analyses concerning passive synthesis); the English translation—*Analyses Concerning Passive and Active Synthesis*—expands on the Husserliana volume, incorporating material from other sources.[118] They pertain specifically to Husserl's development of a "transcendental logic." The scope of the problem extends beyond this study's particular concern with space; but in relation to this we can work with John Drummond's characterisation of the kind of analyses that function in a preparatory and fundamental way for Husserl's transcendental logic: "These analyses include the analysis of the *pre-predicative* experiences underlying acts of judging, including the *passive syntheses* and *passive genesis* involved in the formation of those judgements."[119] These analyses involve the phenomenology of sense perception and memory, and thus by implication a phenomenology of spatiality, but now with a view to the "facticity" (*Faktizität*) of the perceiving subject.[120] Although they concern analyses of perception as among originary or "primordial modes of constitution" (*Urkonstitutionen*), Husserl's investigations function in part as a critique of "logic" and "reason," "tracing the accomplishments of thinking to their genetic origins in *passive*, pre-cognitive syntheses."[121] Thus, as Steinbock suggests, Husserl's *Formal and Transcendental Logic* (*Formale und transzendentale Logik*, 1929), published during his lifetime, could also be seen as preparatory in a different sense, that is, as an enquiry back (*Rückfrage*) from already sedimented, traditional meanings regarding logic, predicative judgement, and so forth.[122] *Experience and Judgment* (*Erfahrung und Urteil*), first published in 1938, the year of Husserl's death, belongs to this project, and contains genetic analyses of passivity and receptivity to which I will also refer.[123] What is important for the purposes of this study is that in these works Husserl's treatment of sense perception is not only concerned with "static" structures—for example, the perspectivity of the thing in adumbrative givenness—but also with the "genesis," accrual, and "sedimentation" of the sense of that which is given. In this way, these texts establish a relation between static and genetic methods. This distinction, as Anthony Steinbock has noted, was latent in and internal to the development of Husserl's phenomenology and is already implied, for example, in his analyses of the lived body.[124] My aim in drawing on these analyses is limited to the problem of spatiality, and specifically the role of lived body kinaesthesis in the passive genesis and sedimentation of the *sense* of spatial experience.

Let us return to that moment when the rustling sound drew our attention to the paper strips on the ceiling, swaying with the wind, and thus to the wind in coexistence. Perhaps with the subtle force of the wind as against our skin we also feel a slight chill. The skin experiences the tactile sensation of the "touching" wind and the thermal sensation of coolness. The rustling sound in some mixture with the "touch" of the wind and the cool sensation has affected me in such a manner that I potentially turn

82 Corporeity and spatiality

away from the reflective glow of the candle's light on the surface of the figurine, towards the ceiling. Perhaps I do not turn, but rather keep my gaze steadfastly on the figurine "in spite of" the affection of the rustling sound and cool touch sensation, or perhaps I turn for a fleeting moment with the sense, "it's just the wind blowing these paper strips," and then turn back to the figurine, now with a slightly changed glow. Claesges describes the potentiality of a "turning towards" in terms of the concept of "receptivity," that is, "receptivity in the sense of affection," which implies the kinaestheses of the lived body.[125] In the *Analyses* Husserl analyses the structure of "affection" as that through which spatiality comes to givenness for the perceiving subject, in painstakingly intricate detail, so that at best its contours can only be sketched in outline. In this work—which we must keep in mind is a compendium of lectures—Husserl's emphasis is not on space per se, but on pre-predicative experience. Insofar as pre-predicative experience necessarily implies sense perceptual experience, but is not limited to this—for example, as we saw with Edith Stein, there are also "sensual feelings," "moods," one's axiological relations and practical engagement with things, and so forth—and spatiality is given to perception as one of its foundational "moments," Husserl's analyses are inherently spatial. The well-known dispute with Heidegger regarding the question of the ontological priority of our practical engagement in circumspection with things in their equipmentality given as "ready-to-hand" is implicated here. It is also well-known that Heidegger in *Being and Time* does not address the problem of embodiment.[126] Husserl is careful in outlining the methodological significance of beginning his enquiry into space from the manner in which things are given as spatial phantoms, and indicates that one's apprehension even at the level of sense perception is already a mode of "interpretative" involvement with things.[127] The temporality of the lived experience of the sensation—as visual, tactual, "feelings," "moods," and so forth—*coincides* with the sensation; as Sokolowski elaborates:

> Husserl's argument can be rephrased in two ways. (1) There is not an X, an object of some sort, behind my sensations which is revealed to me through them and which I call "pain." My sensations themselves are the pain. (2) There is no consciousness outside the sensations which is directed towards them and acknowledges them as pain. All there is in consciousness is the row of successive instants during which I am in pain. Everything transpires within the same flow of consciousness, and with this flow there is only a sensation-state which we call pain. The sensation thus bears consciousness within itself; pain, to exist, must be conscious pain.
>
> What is true of pain is likewise true of other sensations. If I have a "red" sensation, a "soft" sensation, or a "loud" sensation, they must all be conscious if they are to exist as immanent objects in my subjectivity.[128]

For Husserl, in the path towards phenomenological analyses of the concreteness of lived experience, the givenness of spatial "things" to the lived body functions as a "leading clue" (*Leitfaden*).[129]

I begin with the theme of "affection," as it suggests a potentiality on the part of things, which means as well the environing horizon. The rustling sound of the paper strips stands in contrast to a given ambience, for example one of relative quiet. For the moment, I do not enquire into the particular relation of the givenness of sound for the constitution of space, but only notice that the sound potentially draws us away from the givenness of things in our current visual field.[130] The sound entices us to turn our gaze, and through it the ceiling attracts us; it has a certain affective "allure" (*Reiz*).[131] But so too does the figurine, which continues to stand out, capturing our interest as we trace the movement of its reflective glow which, for example, continually demands the focusing movement of our eyes and bodily gesture as "not turning away." The glow traced out on the figurine was continuously enticing us to "keep looking"; at moments perhaps the candle's flame would move more vigorously with the wind, inviting us to move our eyes along this new path, with the figurine still in view, now slightly "blurred," but not to "turn away" completely—which means more exaggerated bodily kinaestheses, for example, the head turns with the torso, arms, and so forth—such that we no longer see it directly. In all of this, the environing things remain given in the background. The vase with foliage, the white cloth covering the table, the arched openings in the wall, the stars in the night sky—any one of them can entice our gaze; a draught outs the flame of a candle across the table, increasing its affective allure. Insofar as the lived body is always in some kinaesthetic relation to things, which implies their environing horizon, affectivity is intrinsic to space.

I noted earlier that Husserl begins with the enquiry into spatiality in terms of the givenness beforehand (*Vorgegebenheit*) of things and their structures of discoverability (*Vorfindlichkeit*).[132] We are somewhere—in a room in a house in the city of Salvador in the northeast of Brazil, this is true, but in the immediacy of our experience we are simply face to face with the figurine and its environing things; our situation is an example of a givenness of things beforehand somewhere, and we will gradually unfold its temporality, intersubjectivity, and historicity. That this or that phantom appears in a sense field and mixture of sense fields in terms of the peculiar auto-affection and kinaesthesis through which my own body is given, in such a manner that some things are always given more distinctly than others in a foreground-background structure, points to the problem of "origin" or "genesis." Here the question is posed simply in terms of sense fields: why *this* is given more distinctly at one moment, but then becomes clouded as *that* emerges from the background. The thingly character of the spatial environment is qualitatively *affective*; it has its own varying levels of "affective vivacity."[133] The affectivity of space points to the receptivity of the perceiving subject, at the level of sense perception and lived bodily kinaestheses. The phenomenon of the affective vivacity of space is a clue to the phenomenon of "the" world. This sense of "world" in Husserl is the most basic; as a structure of phantom spatiality "the" world appears to perceiving subjectivity—human or non-human—in its corporeity in the fundamental mode of self-affection, as the basis of world-affection.[134]

A forceful wind blows. It sways the flame of the candle near to us, at the same time having outed the glow of the candle to the far end of the table, as the leaves of the tree outside whisper in apparent symphony with the rustling of the paper strips of the ceiling, and I feel a chill as the draught brushes against my skin. All of this happens "now," in what Husserl terms the "living present" as that moment in which I am perceiving the thing as given to me in the flesh.[135] The "now" undergoes a "thickening," to use a term from Merleau-Ponty, and we have already considered its structure as a modificational "double continuity"—the previous moment tarries with the "now" like the tail of a comet, and we experience the present and immediate past in terms of each other as they *continuously* modify each other in the continuous "running off" flow of the temporality of perceiving.[136] Husserl qualifies this stretching out of the "now" as a temporal horizon, by referring to the inherence of the past as the perception happens *originaliter*, in the flesh, as "retention"; every "now" becomes a retention in a continuous temporal movement away from an original perceptual moment, as a continuous modification that fades—a retention becomes a retention of a retention, and so forth continuously—towards emptiness. Husserl notes, however, that this "does not lead to a simple infinite regress, since each retention is in itself continuous modification that carries within, so to speak, the heritage of the past in the form of a series of adumbrations."[137] The structure, therefore, is also *anticipatory*; the perception as an acquired "heritage" becomes "habitual" in its immanence and immediacy so that I anticipate its continuity—that the candle's flame continues to flicker, the shimmer on the surface of the figurine remains, the cloth maintains its white colouration. The *futural* horizon of the living present is "an expectational horizon [...] immediately there along with it; a progressive process of becoming analogous to the previous becoming, expected according to the same continual *style* of the course."[138] The retention-protention structure of the living present is intrinsic to spatial experience as a subjective "style," a style that pertains to lived bodily kinaestheses in a process of sedimentation as "habit."[139]

In spite of all of the contrasts around me that entice me to look away as the wind blows, the allure of the illuminated surface of the figurine still holds my gaze. As the glow slowly descends, its specific location at the figurine's "face" recedes in my current perception but is not totally "forgotten"; it is still with me in the living present as the light flickers, but as a background increasingly vague and fusing in indistinctiveness with the background of environing things *then*. As my gaze continues there is a sudden gust and the flame near the figurine is outed, rupturing my experience, which by then is already a habit, a style of oculomotor tracing the contours

Corporeity and spatiality 85

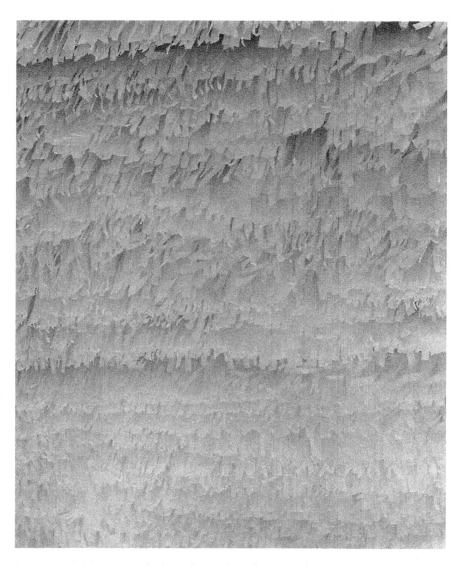

Figure 2.10 View towards the ceiling. Photo by the author

86 *Corporeity and spatiality*

of the figurine. Or instead, the allure of the rustling ceiling entices me away from the figurine and I tilt my head upward, and in this moment my gaze is transfixed by the whiteness of the ceiling like a cloudy sky on a windy day (Figure 2.10). But "transfixed" here pertains to my interest generally; as my lived body I am moved in a new way as the ceiling shows itself in all manner of subtle and more vigorous undulations—the ceiling as a field of white fluttering strips appears this way with the kinaesthesis of my eyes, which have developed an oculomotor style attuned to the variability of the wave-like movement of the "sky" above me. It will become for me an abiding oculomotor style, a kinaesthetic habit of my eyes motivating my tendency to see *this* ceiling—and ceilings like it—whose givenness comes actually or anticipatorily with the wind.

But let us go back to the moment of the gust of wind and try to tarry with the living present. The affective allure of space exists in degrees of relative enticement, as does my receptivity in degrees of correlative desire or tendency towards this or that allure. In this sense, spatiality is characterised by a certain "sensuality" and potential to "enchant." Space is thoroughly saturated with varying levels of affective vivacity and possibility:

> But that something should gain an affective force at all where nothing of the sort was available; that something which was not there at all for the ego [*Ich*]—a pure affective nothing—should become an active something for the first time, precisely that is incomprehensible.[140]

At the moment of the gust our gaze is still held by the figurine, but the rustle of the ceiling, the chill, the flame flickering violently, the leaves whispering outside, perhaps the cloth on the table fluttering, or myriad other enticing possibilities begin to emerge from the background. These are open possibilities, but they are still motivated by our lived bodily kinaestheses and thus possibilities *for us*—the whispering leaves of the tree outside, for example, could entice us to look out through the large arched opening in the wall, or even to walk over to see more closely the source of the sound, but could not entice us to fly and perch ourselves on the branches of the tree.[141]

I described earlier in this chapter the horizontal structure of things—their "inner horizon" and horizon of environing things as always given in the experience of space. The affectivity of space that is motivated by our receptivity in terms of lived bodily kinaesthetic possibilities is also horizontal. This horizon is a horizon of kinaesthetic motivation. Claesges outlines certain structural features of lived bodily motility or "kinaesthetic consciousness," the primary being its temporality, that is, the retention-protention structure of the living present as a structure of kinaesthetic corporeity.[142]

At the moment the wind blows, in the living "now" of possibilities opened up by the competing affections of the environing space, I keep my gaze steady on the figurine, or glance towards the outed candle, or tilt my head up to spy the ceiling, or I shiver in the chill and brush my arms for warmth, or I rise and walk towards the side window to close it, or I do a mixture of these, or something else within the scope (*Spielraum*) of spatial affectivity and my receptivity. The anticipation of this or that possibility is at the same time an anticipation of movement that has the sense: "I can," that is, the sense of "spontaneity." The "I can" of spontaneity is not to be understood in a merely empirical sense; rather, it indicates my facility—what I am actually and potentially able to do—which includes disability as situationally embodied, as well as the temporality of "moods" and "feelings," as we noted earlier with Edith Stein. The sense of the "I can" of "spontaneity" indicates the temporal structure of motivation, but this is not merely a "static" structure; rather, it pertains to my facticity. It is, as Merleau-Ponty notes, "a power, not a thing known (*ein Können, kein Kennen*)."[143] This sense of kinaesthetic facility as anticipatorily motivational is *prior* to the physiological make-up of my body, which I only grasp through a certain mode of objectification as "thing-like," for example in the auto-affection of touch or as mediated through the gaze of another. The priority is not a "before" in "objective" time—I am already looking at the illuminated surface of the figurine and continue in this "style" of oculomotion and in this way "I can" continue to look, because I remain enchanted by the current spatial situation "in spite of" the gust; or I feel the chill of the draught and do not brush my exposed arms "in spite of" the coolness because it provokes a pleasant memory. The kinaesthetic motivation has the character "because thus," which Husserl describes as "a nexus founded in the relevant acts themselves."[144]

If I surrender to the enticement of the rustling paper above and glance towards the ceiling, trailing behind my new perception is the horizon of my "having just been transfixed by the figurine" but now following the waves of the ceiling. The perceptions form a nexus of experiences lived through in their spatiality as a nexus of kinaestheses. The genesis of this movement is not physiological: "But the physiological processes in the sense organs, in the nerve cells and in the ganglia, do not motivate me even if they condition, in my consciousness, psychophysically, the appearance of sense data, apprehensions, and psychic lived experiences."[145] My living present, having just turned away from the figurine, is a new kinaesthetic situation through which the fluttering ceiling is given; I no longer perceive the figurine, but it still trails behind my current perception as a horizon of meaning. A new motivation is embodied in my movement—because I had not noticed the wave-like rhythm of the ceiling before, and because the figurine in its setting has become familiar, I realise a new desire and look at the rustling paper "sky." In this way the figurine and its environing things are not "lost," but rather recede as having become familiar, now veiled and implicit to my current perception as a horizon of memory in which past experiences blend together, lacking explicit perceptual articulation and differentiation.[146] This implicit horizon of past experiences is a horizon of past kinaestheses, and as such a sedimentation of kinaesthetic motivations as habitualities, or a lived bodily

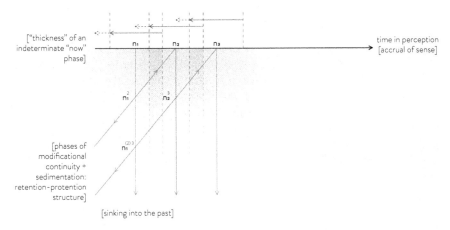

Figure 2.11 Diagram of the retention-protention structure of the temporality of perception after Husserl. Sketch by the author, digitised by Gracie Meek.

style of constituting space—of being receptive to the affectivity and sensuality of the allure of spatiality by realising perceptual desire in the living present through the corporeity of movement. Memory is sedimented in the motivational kinaestheses of the lived body as a reservoir of past lived experiences through which spatiality continuously came to givenness as living "institution" (*Stiftung*).[147] The living present "institutes" new experiences in the genesis of familiarity, and in the "running off" of temporality the "now" as superseded also sediments in the formation of the horizon of the past (Figure 2.11).[148] The gust has faded and the rustling of the paper "sky" has subsided; in the calm, I glance back at the figurine—it is still there, only now I look at it with the ease of familiarity, yet something has changed, and the change awakens a memory: as I look at the figurine adjusting my eyes to see it more distinctly—now that the candle's flame has blown out—I "see" it at the same time in memory as "having just been illuminated," and with the memory of the figurine "just before I turned my gaze to the ceiling" is also my former kinaesthesis "as if" I were still there *then*; the situation now has the sense: "the wind must have blown out the flame."

We have, over the course of these descriptions and analyses, acquired some familiarity with the ethnographic context. We felt the softness of the white cloth against the palm of our hands through the rigidity of the table's covered surface. But that past moment, which was once a living present before we awakened it again in memory, receded after the touch sensation ceased. Even during the living present of the touch—as we actually pass our palms along the cloth's surface—the sensation in the touching appears in the mode "more and more past" as the sensation "now" in its running off with its "just now" trailing along and in the process the touch "then" and "just before then" becomes more and more obscure in the "clouding over" of a hazy retentional fog. The moment we lift our hands, the horizon of the living present—at least for the touch sensation, as we probably continue to perceive the cloth visually—empties out and is completely blurred, now a style of appearance sedimented in the kinaestheses of our hand in such a way that at any future point we expect the same sensation when we touch the cloth again. This experience, and the others that are in a similar way blended in the misty haze of memory—the visual sensation of the table, the givenness of the figurine and its environing things now from this side, then "face to face," seen from the "back," then in obscurity as the lights were turned off (Figures 2.1–2.4, 2.6, 2.7)—are with us habitually, such that we anticipate that this is what the room will look and "feel" like if we are invited here again. We have grown familiar with the environing space as a lived bodily past and potential future horizon of our kinaestheses—when we visit the next time, the gust of wind, the rustle of the undulating "sky," the whispering of the leaves outside will be felt with a familiarity in the living present as an awakening of our corporeity, such that "individualized, especially strong sense-moments of the distant present in question will come into relief in the emptiness, just like rough contours in a dimly illuminated fog."[149] We have been in a sense "initiated" into the spatial style of the ritual, not merely as a spectacle as if viewed by a disembodied eye; rather, it is our living bodies that are in kinaestheses of desire with the affective allure of the space, manifesting this or that aspect in this or that way—perhaps the figurine then, another moment the ceiling, or the stars in the sky through the arched opening in the wall, and so forth. And insofar as spatiality is affectively saturated, we have necessarily instituted a style of experience as the genesis of a *habitus*, not yet as a social condition, but a mode of familiarity inherent in one's corporeity as lived body:

> This lived experience itself, and the objective moment constituted in it, may become "forgotten"; but for all this, it in no way disappears without a trace; it has merely become latent. With regard to what has been constituted in it, it is a *possession in the form of a habitus*.[150]

*

The experience of the room has been characterised by a certain abstraction through my descriptions and analyses, our comportment approximating lived experience in an originary sphere of visual and tactual perceptual givenness, alone in the room with spatial phantoms—the figurine, candles, fluttering ceiling, rustling foliage, the night sky, and so forth. Its space is seen and felt as if in slow motion, like the closing scenes of the film *Nostalghia* by Andrei Tarkovsky with the candle as protagonist, echoed in the stillness of Franketienne and Charles Najman's images of slow movement filmed in the ruined cathedral of Port-au-Prince in Haiti.[151] Through my descriptions we have been following Husserl's analyses, starting with the

90 Corporeity and spatiality

givenness of phantoms as a leading clue to spatiality. I propose that there is not only a phenomenological appropriateness to this path, but also an ethnographic one. To get to the ethnographic situation in its concreteness, we have to widen the phenomenologically descriptive horizon and attend to the presence of others—our host, the *mãe-de-santo* (mother-of-saint), and her family of persons and "saints." Our enquiry into spatial experience therefore must expand beyond the single perceiving subject and address the problems of "empathy" (*Einfühlung*) and intersubjectivity, generativity, and historicity. But this does not necessarily mean that the problem of spatiality in terms of the corporeity of the perceiving subject will be superseded when viewed from the perspective of this more expansive horizon. Dan Zahavi, quoting Husserl, traces out this problematic in advance:

> *As mundane experience, my experience (thus already each of my perceptions) not only includes others as mundane objects, but constantly includes them, in existential co-validity, as co-subjects, as co-constituting—and both are inseparably intertwined.*[152]

Notes

1 Ulrich Claesges, *Edmund Husserls Theorie der Raumkonstitution* (The Hague: Martinus Nijhoff, 1964) (hereafter cited as *Raumkonstitution*).
2 Fred Kersten's doctoral dissertation of 1964 also investigated Husserl's theory of space. See Frederick Irving Kersten, "Husserl's Investigations Toward a Phenomenology of Space" (PhD diss., New School for Social Research, 1964).
3 Edmund Husserl, *Thing and Space: Lectures of 1907*, trans. Richard Rojcewicz (Dordrecht: Kluwer Academic Publishers, 1997). Hereafter cited as *Thing and Space*, followed by the page number of the English translation and, where intended, pagination of the corresponding Husserliana volume in brackets; idem., *Ding und Raum: Vorlesungen 1907*, Husserliana, vol. 16, ed. Ulrich Claesges (The Hague: Martinus Nijhoff, 1973). On the history of the manuscripts see Ulrich Claesges's introduction to *Thing and Space*, xiii–xxix.
4 Claesges, *Raumkonstitution*, 4. This is according to Husserl's own classification system. Claesges also consulted a third group of manuscripts, catalogued as M III 3 V, dating from 1916, titled "Systematische Raumkonstitution" (systematic constitution of space) and described as "an elaboration by Edith Stein of the last part of the 'Thing Lectures'" (eine von Edith Stein hergestellte Ausarbeitung des letzten Teiles der 'Dingvorlesung'). See Claesges, 146. I was a Visiting Scholar at the Institute of Philosophy at KU Leuven in 2019, where I consulted some of the texts of the D manuscripts at the Husserl Archives. I thank Professor Julia Jansen, the Director of the Husserl Archives, and Head Archivists Emanuele Caminada and Thomas Vongehr for facilitating my visit and for their kind assistance.
5 See H. L. Van Breda, "Merleau-Ponty and the Husserl Archives at Louvain," in Maurice Merleau-Ponty, *Texts and Dialogues on Philosophy, Politics, and Culture*, ed. Hugh J. Silverman and James Barry Jr. (New York: Humanities Books, 1992), 152–53.

6 Van Breda, "Merleau-Ponty and the Husserl Archives at Louvain," 152–53; text in brackets given in the passage quoted.
7 Robert Sokolowski, "Review of *Edmund Husserls Theorie der Raumkonstitution*, by Ulrich Claesges," *Journal of the History of Philosophy* 6, no. 3 (July 1968): 305–7.
8 Sokolowski, "Review," 305.
9 Robert Sokolowski, *The Formation of Husserl's Concept of Constitution* (The Hague: Martinus Nijhoff, 1970), 41.
10 Edmund Husserl, *Logical Investigations*, vol. 1, trans. J. M. Findlay (London: New York, 2008), 175. On the notion of "operative concepts" in Husserl see Eugen Fink, "Operative Concepts in Husserl's Phenomenology," in *Apriori and World: European Contributions to Husserlian Phenomenology*, ed. William McKenna, Robert M. Harlan, and Laurence E. Winters (The Hague: Martinus Nijhoff, 1981), 56–70.
11 Dermot Moran and Joseph Cohen, *The Husserl Dictionary* (London: Continuum, 2012), 71.
12 Sokolowski, *Formation*, 214–17. Sokolowski notes that Husserl from the start used the term with a transformed sense:

> His method of looking for an explanation for objectivity in subjective structure and process bears much similarity with the general project of the neo-Kantians. There is an important difference, however, for the Kantian tradition maintained the idea of fixed subjective categories that are imposed upon sensation, while Husserl never accepted this.

Sokolowski notes further, commenting on Iso Kern's *Husserl und Kant*, that: "Besides this external influence [of Paul Natorp], however, we feel that the internal development of Husserl's thought led to the theory of genetic constitution." *Formation*, 216.
13 Anthony Steinbock, for example, makes the point that "it was not uncommon for Husserl to appropriate terms from other contexts and give to them a new phenomenological sense" and that "Husserl was still in the process of inventing phenomenological language by borrowing from the resources of 'natural language,' which is at root not bothered with 'phenomenological distinctions'." See Anthony J. Steinbock, introduction to Husserl, *Analyses Concerning Passive and Active Synthesis: Lectures on Transcendental Logic*, trans. Anthony J. Steinbock (Dordrecht: Kluwer, 2001), xliv, lxiv. Hereafter cited as *Analyses*, followed by the page number of the English translation and then the pagination of the corresponding Husserliana volume in brackets. Edmund Husserl, *Analysen zur passiven Synthesis. Aus Vorlesungs- und Forschungsmanuskripten*, Husserliana, vol. 11, ed. Margot Fleischer (The Hague: Martinus Nijhoff, 1966).
14 Sokolowski notes that the expression "to manifest itself" is "used by Husserl as a synonym for constitution and connotes at least the fact that reality brings something to consciousness." Sokolowski, *Formation*, 217.
15 Sokolowski, *Formation*, 217:

> In order to paraphrase the constitution of meaning and objects, it seems that a neutral term like the "coming-to-be" of such objects and senses would be best. It must be understood that they cannot "come into being" without the presence and concurrence of consciousness, which is the necessary condition for becoming real [...] However, consciousness is not the sufficient cause of all that transpires in constitution. There is a facticity and givenness in the actual content found in objects and senses when they come to be.

92 Corporeity and spatiality

16 Gadamer critiques the *epistemological* function of the concept of *Erlebnis* for the subjectivisation of aesthetics in the neo-Kantian tradition, resulting in a severing of the work of art from its traditionality. See Hans-Georg Gadamer, "The Subjectivization of Aesthetics through the Kantian Critique," in *Truth and Method*, trans. Joel Weinsheimer and Donald G. Marshall (New York: Continuum, 2000), 42–80. Gadamer's position regarding the meaning of "constitution" and its relation to the concept of "experience" in Husserl is, however, ambiguous. See Walter Lammi, "Gadamer's Debt to Husserl," in *Passions of the Earth in Human Existence, Creativity, and Literature*, ed. A. T. Tymieniecka (Dordrecht: Kluwer Academic Publishers, 2001), 167–79; see also David Vessey, "Who Was Gadamer's Husserl?" *New Yearbook for Phenomenology and Phenomenological Philosophy* 7 (2007): 1–23.
17 Compare, for example, renderings of *"Erlebnis"* in translations of Husserl's works by Dorion Cairns (*Cartesian Meditations*), Fred Kersten (*Ideas I*), and J. N. Findlay (*Logical Investigations*).
18 Dorian Cairns, *Guide for Translating Husserl* (The Hague: Martinus Nijhoff, 1973), 46.
19 Solokowski, *Formation*, 4:

> We [...] use the term "experience" exclusively as the correlate for *Erlebnis*, to express our consciousness of what is immanent to subjectivity, while the term "encounter" will be used exclusively as correlate for *Erfahrung*, to name our consciousness of what is transcendent to subjectivity. [...] As we use it, "encounter" means our awareness of anything in the world [...] outside of our own subjectivity. Its scope of application is as wide as that of the German term *Erfahrung*.

20 Claesges, 106.
21 Sokolowski, "Review," 306.
22 David Carr, "Husserl: Subjectivity and Intentionality," in *The Paradox of Subjectivity: The Self in the Transcendental Tradition* (Oxford: Oxford University Press, 1999), 70.
23 Carr, "Husserl: Subjectivity and Intentionality," 70.
24 Husserl, *Thing and Space*, 293.
25 John J. Drummond describes the "phantom" as follows:

> Our experience of objects in the world grasps them in their full materiality and substantiality as having causal and functional properties along with their value attributes. The experience of the object as having these properties is rooted, however, in our grasp of the purely descriptive and sensible properties of the thing. The object considered purely with respect to its sensible properties is the phantom.

John J. Drummond, *Historical Dictionary of Husserl's Philosophy* (Lanham, MD: Scarecrow Press, 2008), 156.
26 Claesges, 55–115.
27 Edmund Husserl, "Time in Perception," in *On the Phenomenology of the Consciousness of Internal Time (1893–1917)*, trans. John Barnett Brough (Dordrecht: Kluwer Academic Publishers, 1991), 281. Hereafter cited as *Consciousness of Internal Time*, followed by the page number of the English translation and, where intended, pagination of the corresponding Husserliana volume in brackets; idem., *Zur Phänomenologie des inneren Zeitbewusstseins (1893–1917)*, Husserliana, vol. 10, ed. Rudolf Boehm (The Hague: Martinus Nijhoff, 1966).
28 See, for example, the fragment from Husserl's manuscripts on internal time consciousness from 1908, titled "The Modification Proper to Primary

Corporeity and spatiality 93

Memory," where Husserl outlines the protentional-retentional structure of perception in terms of the modificational continuity of temporal phases. Husserl, *Consciousness of Internal Time*, 337–46. Merleau-Ponty would build on Husserl's analysis for his studies on temporality, even drawing on Husserl's diagrams; see Merleau-Ponty's chapter on "Temporality" in Maurice Merleau-Ponty, *Phenomenology of Perception*, trans. Colin Smith (London: Routledge, 1989), 410–33, specifically 415–17.

29 For example, Husserl states that *"every* sense field and every essentially closed sensation group acquires a realizing connection to the animate organism [*Leib*], showing different sides of its real sensitivity and making up different strata of sensation contexts belonging really to it." Edmund Husserl, *Phenomenology and the Foundations of the Sciences: Ideas Pertaining to a Pure Phenomenology and to a Phenomenological Philosophy: Third Book*, trans. Ted E. Klein and William E. Pohl (The Hague: Martinus Nijhoff, 1980), 5. Hereafter cited as *Ideas III*, followed by the page number of the English translation and, where intended, pagination of the corresponding Husserliana volume in brackets; idem., *Ideen zu einer reinen Phänomenologie und phänomenologischen Philosophie. Drittes Buch: Die Phänomenologie und die Fundamente der Wissenschaften*, Husserliana, vol. 5, ed. Marly Biemel (The Hague: Martinus Nijhoff, 1952, rpt. 1971). Klein and Pohl render *Leib* as "animate organism," but the term is also typically translated as "living body" or "lived body." On *Leib* see, for example, Moran and Cohen, *The Husserl Dictionary*, 193–95.

30 Filip Mattens, "Spatial Phenomena in Material Places: Reflections on Sensory Substitution, Shape Perception, and the External Nature of the Senses," *Phenomenology and the Cognitive Sciences* 18 (2019): 835. Mattens in this article explicitly addresses the question of spatial experience from the perspective of auditory sense.

31 Drummond, *Historical Dictionary of Husserl's Philosophy*, 156.

32 Drummond defines Husserl's concept of a "moment" as "any part that is non-independent relative to the whole of which it is a part. A moment, in other words, is an abstract part or abstract content that cannot exist apart from other parts with which it forms a concrete whole." Drummond, 136.

33 I use photography in this and the following chapters to supplement the written description. I do not thematise the mediating role of the photographic image itself, or the role of imagination in relating us to the perceptual situation in this and the following chapter. I outline the contours of this problem at the start of Chapter 4, and I note in advance that the phenomenological analysis of imagination is beyond the scope of this study. On the question of "picture" or "image consciousness," which would pertain to the status of photography, see, for example, Javier Carreño, "On the Temporality of Images according to Husserl," *New Yearbook for Phenomenology and Phenomenological Philosophy* 8 (2008): 73–92, and on imagination more broadly see Julia Jansen, "Imagination De-Naturalized: Phantasy, the Imaginary, and Imaginative Ontology," in *The Oxford Handbook of the History of Phenomenology*, ed. Dan Zahavi (Oxford: Oxford University Press, 2018), 676–95.

34 Filip Mattens, "From the Origin of Spatiality to a Variety of Spaces," in Zahavi, *Oxford Handbook*, 561. Sokolowski notes similarly that "Husserl prefers to say that sensory data are experienced (*erlebt*), whereas objects are perceived or appear." See Sokolowski, *Formation*, 52. See also, for example, Husserl, *Thing and Space*: "The red-moment, with such and such brilliance and saturation, is what it is only as the fullness of a certain extension; the red-moment expands" (135).

35 Husserl, *Thing and Space*, 44.

36 The enquiry here is limited to the sense perceptual constitution of space in terms of a structural or "static" description, so that "apperception" in this

94 *Corporeity and spatiality*

instance has a narrow sense, along the line of Moran and Cohen's characterisation: "In all perception of a physical object, direct perception is of the facing side of the object, the hidden sides of the object are *apperceived* or *appresented* in an empty manner" See (39).

37 Claesges, 60. For Husserl's discussion of the "internal horizon" of the thing, see, for example, Edmund Husserl, "The Horizon-Structure of Experience. The Typical Precognition [Vorbekanntheit] of Every Individual Object of Experience," in *Experience and Judgement*, ed. Ludwig Landgrebe, trans. James S. Churchill and Karl Ameriks (Evanston, IL: Northwestern University Press, 1973), 31–39; also Husserl, "Original Consciousness and the Perspectival Adumbration of Spatial Objects," in *Analyses*, 39–43.

38 Claesges, 60: "Die in einem Aspekt erscheinende Seite hat nun in sich eine Horizontstruktur, indem sie auf die Apparenz und das in ihr gegebene Phantom verweist." (The side that appears in one aspect has a horizon-structure in itself, in that it, by referring to the appearance, refers to the phantom given in that appearance.)

39 Mirrors do not solve the problem, as then what we encounter are reflections. Zahavi makes this point; see Dan Zahavi, *Husserl and Transcendental Intersubjectivity*, trans. Elizabeth A. Behnke (Athens, Ohio: Ohio University Press, 2001), 220, note 18.

40 Claesges, 61:

> Lage wird von Husserl zunächst als "Entfernung" thematisiert. Mit dem Begriff der Entfernung kommt der Wahrnehmende selbst in der Weise mit in den Blick, dass für ihn selbst das Moment der Lage zutrifft, dass er selbst in Bezug auf das Phantom lokalisiert ist.

41 Claesges, 61: "Insofern nun die Entfernung wechseln kann, die Entfernung nimmt ab oder zu, bedingt dies zugleich einen Wechsel der Aspekte." (Insofar as the distance can now change—the distance either decreases or increases—this change at the same time implies a change of the aspects.)

42 Zahavi notes: "One cannot trace the perspectivity of the givenness of things back to the finite character of our structure of consciousness; rather, the thing's perspectival mode of appearance is determined by its own regional essence." Zahavi, *Husserl and Transcendental Intersubjectivity*, 221, note. 32. On the sense of the "perspectivity" of appearance, Burt Hopkins notes that

> since what is at issue here is the invariant character running through a manifold of appearing of an outer percept [...] the transcendental status of the outer perceptual object's appearance concerns its meaning (*Sinn*) as a phenomenon, and not its extra-perceptual being or reality.

Burt C. Hopkins, *Intentionality in Husserl and Heidegger: The Problem of the Original Method and Phenomenon of Phenomenology* (Dordrecht: Kluwer, 1993), 23.

43 Husserl, *Thing and Space*, 66 [80].

44 Here, the idea of a horizonal "moment" has a wider mereological implication, not limited to the sense of non-independent, relative "parts" of material objects; its meaning for sense perception alone does not capture the full significance of the concept of horizon in Husserl.

45 "Ein regionales Allgemeines liegt in der Apperzeption, sie ist 'Ding'-Apperzeption; sie hat im Sinne schon den Weltraum als universalen Horizont." Edmund Husserl, *Zur Phänomenologie der Intersubjektivität. Text aus dem Nachlass. Dritter Teil: 1929-1935*, Husserliana, vol. 15, ed. Iso Kern (The Hague: Martinus Nijhoff, 1973), 266.

46 I use the term "aspect" (*Aspekt*) along the lines of Zahavi's use of "perspective,", in reference to Husserl's way of characterising the one-sided givenness of the thing. See note 42 above.
47 Husserl, *Thing and Space*, 68: "The presentational contents of the total visual appearance form a continuous nexus: we call it the visual field." See also Husserl, "The Field of Passive Data and Its Associative Structure," in *Experience and Judgement*, 72–76. Claesges describes the visual field in its formal generality (*das Formal-Allgemeine des visuellen Feldes*) in terms of its structures of "center-periphery," "right-left," "top-bottom," "intersection," etc.; see Claesges, 69–70.
48 Husserl, *Thing and Space*, 68.
49 Claesges, 65: "jede Aspekterscheinung vom Phantom nur ist in dieser Bezogenheit zu einer Kinästhese, zu einer kinästhetischen Ruhe oder zu einer kinästhetischen Bewegung." Quoted in Claesges from Husserl's manuscript D 13 I (1921), 6.
50 Husserl notes:

> A kinaesthetic field is variable immediately and freely, and what is dependent on the free variation of the kinaesthetic data that enter into the apperception of a body is the variation of the sense-data, which, in this apperception, perform the necessary constitutive function of adumbrations. The content of the perception of a body implies the coordination, in virtue of this apperception, between a sense-datum and a kinaesthetic complex.
> Husserl, *Thing and Space*, 258.

51 Husserl, *Analyses*, 43.
52 See, for example, "Sense-Fields and Kinaesthetic Systems," in *Thing and Space*, 257–66.
53 Claesges, 63; Claesges quotes from Husserl's manuscript D13 I (1921), 8: "gewisse Apparenzen bevorzugt sind als normale."
54 Anthony J. Steinbock, *Home and Beyond: Generative Phenomenology after Husserl* (Evanston, IL: Northwestern University Press), 138.
55 Edmund Husserl, *Ideas Pertaining to a Pure Phenomenology and to a Phenomenological Philosophy: First Book*, trans. F. Kersten (The Hague: Martinus Nijhoff Publishers, 1983), 252 [241]. Hereafter cited as *Ideas I*, followed by the page number of the English translation and, where intended, pagination of the corresponding Husserliana volume in brackets; idem., *Ideen zu einer reinen Phänomenologie und phänomenologischen Philosophie. Erstes Buch. Allgemeine Einführung in die reine Phänomenologie*, Husserliana, vol. 3, ed. Karl Schuhmann (The Hauge: Martinus Nijhoff, 1976). It is from this Husserlian motif that Merleau-Ponty derives his notion of "perceptual faith" (*la foi perceptive*). See Maurice Merleau-Ponty, "La foi perceptive et son obscurité," in Merleau-Ponty, *Le visible et l'invisible* (Paris: Gallimard, 1964), 17–30.
56 On the concept of "kinaesthetic situation," Claesges notes, "Das kinästhetische System ist ein System der Vermöglichkeit, das jeweils aktualisiert ist in einer 'kinästhetischen Situation.'" (The kinaesthetic system is a system of facultative possibility, which is actualized in each respective "kinaesthetic situation.") (72). And on the "kinaesthetic system" generally: "Der *Raum* als '*Form*' dieser meiner anschaulichen Welt ist so das *Korrelat* meines *kinästhetischen Gesamtsystems* und seine Horizontstruktur, seine Struktur der Bekanntheit und Unbekanntheit, in einsichtiger Weise auf die Struktur des kinästhetischen Systems bezogen." (*Space as "form"* of my intuitive world is as such the *correlate* of my *kinaesthetic total-system* and its horizon-structure, its structure of familiarity and unfamiliarity is related to the structure of the kinaesthetic

96 Corporeity and spatiality

system in an understandable way.) Claesges, 84. Cairns renders "Vermöglichkeit" as "facultative possibility, ability, power"; what Husserl is pointing to is the sense of the *capacity* of the lived body in its *potentiality*, so that even if, for example, I were restrained in a straitjacket, this does not negate my capacity in terms of my *potential* for movement. See Cairns, *Guide for Translating Husserl*, 125.

57 John Drummond notes that "Husserl thinks that there are concrete existing phantoms—rainbows, the blue sky, the sun, stars and planets in the night sky—but these examples are themselves troublesome and the experience of concrete phantoms is rare." Drummond, 156–57.

58 Claesges, 75:

> Das aktuelle Bewußtsein einer Apparenz, das auf die es konstituierenden noetisch-noematischen Mannigfaltigkeiten hin befragt werden kann, erweist sich so als eingeordnet in ein umgreifendes Bewußtsein, das nun aber nicht aktuelles Bewußtsein, sondern Bewußtsein im Modus der Potentialität ist. Dies aber ist das Bewußtsein eines 'Spielraumes' als der Korrelation von Vermöglichkeit und Horizont.
>
> (The current consciousness of an appearance, which can be examined regarding its constitutive noetic-noematic diversity, turns out to be integrated into an all-encompassing consciousness that is, however, not current consciousness, but rather consciousness in the mode of potentiality. This, however, is the consciousness of a "space-of-potential" as the correlation of facultative possibility and horizon.)

I follow Steinbock's rendering of *Spielraum* as "leeway"; see Husserl, *Analyses*, 87 note 47. See also Merleau-Ponty, *Phenomenology of Perception*, 286: "Sometimes between myself and the events there is a certain amount of play (*Spielraum*), which ensures that my freedom is preserved while the events do not cease to concern me."

59 Husserl notes: "Perception [*Wahrnehmung*] in the full sense includes *heedfulness of* ..., therefore more than mere perception [*Perzeption*], which can be connected with other attentional modes. (The word for perception = "*Wahrnehmung*" = "*Wahr*"-*nehmung* = "truly" grasping.)." Husserl, *Consciousness of Internal Time*, 283; text in square brackets given in the original passage.

60 See my discussion in Chapter 1 on the ethnographic context of this study.

61 Husserl, *Consciousness of Internal Time*, 375 [364].

62 Rudolf Bernet, Iso Kern, and Edward Marbach, *An Introduction to Husserlian Phenomenology* (Evanston, IL: Northwestern University Press), 101.

63 *Consciousness of Internal Time*, xviii.

64 *Consciousness of Internal Time*, xviii. On the history of the publication, including the editorial involvement of Edith Stein and Martin Heidegger, see the presentation by John Barnett Brough in, *Consciousness of Internal Time*, xi–xviii.

65 Claesges, 36:

> Die Vorgegebenheit von Raum und Zeit ist also nie eine unmittelbare, sondern—und das ist für den Husserlschen Ansatz der Raumproblematik charakteristisch—ihre Vorgegebenheit ist durch ein Substrat (das Ding) vermittelt. Das Wesen von Raum und Zeit ist deshalb nicht einfach durch 'Abstraktion' zu gewinnen, indem man alle Dinge aus Raum und Zeit wegdenkt, sondern nur in der Weise, daß man herausstellt, wie Raum und Zeit die erscheinenden Dinge a priori bestimmen.
>
> (The givenness beforehand of space and time is never unmediated, rather—and this is characteristic of the Husserlian approach to the problematic

of space—its givenness beforehand is mediated through a substrate [the thing]. The essence of space and time is therefore not achievable simply through "abstraction," whereby one thinks-away all things from space and time, but rather only in the way that one brings out how space and time determine the appearing things a priori.)

66 Claesges, 36: "Die spezifische Vorgegebenheit der Dinge fassen wir terminologisch als 'Vorfindlichkeit.' Raum und Zeit sollen zunächst daraufhin betrachtet werden, inwiefern sie es gerade sind, die die Vorfindlichkeit von Dingen ermöglichen." (The specific givenness beforehand of things we grasp terminologically as "discoverability." Space and time should be firstly considered with respect to the way they are precisely that which makes possible the "discoverability" of things.)

67 Husserl uses the perception of a star, for example, to demonstrate the point that the temporality of the thing in its givenness presents unique problems for the analysis of the temporality of spatial constitution. That the star "no longer exists" is a different and derived problem from its appearance in the night sky to a perceiving subject. See Husserl, "Appendix V: Simultaneity of Perception and the Perceived," in *Consciousness of Internal Time*, 114–15.

68 *Consciousness of Internal Time*, 114–15. Husserl describes here the retentional-protentional structure of the temporality of perception, or the temporal "thickness" of the instant of perception, to use Merleau-Ponty's expression:

> But one can say that the perceived object is the correlate of a possible continuous perception that follows it from the beginning to the end of its duration. A phase of the perception then corresponds to each phase of the object's duration. But that is not to say that the point at which the object's duration begins and the point at which the perception begins must coincide [...] in the moment in which the apprehension begins, a part of the datum of sensation has already elapsed and is preserved only in retention. The apprehension then animates not only the phase of primal sensation actual at the moment but the entire datum of sensation, including that portion of it that has elapsed.

69 Claesges, 37. Husserl's description in the D 8 manuscript reads: "Es liegt also das Charakteristische im 'Außereinander.' Zeitliche und räumliche Wesen liegen außereinander, sie bilden ein System der Äußerlichkeit." (The characteristic thus lies in "mutual externality." Temporal and spatial entities lie outside one another, they form a system of externality.) Husserl manuscript D 8 (1918): 60b. Cairns suggests "entities (*or* phases *or* objects) outside one another" or "mutual externality" as ways of rendering the German *"Außereinander"*; see Cairns, *Guide for Translating Husserl*, 14. I thank Emanuele Caminada, Head Archivist at the Husserl Archives, for permission to quote from the unpublished manuscripts.

70 Husserl manuscript D 8 (1918): 60b; see Cairns, *Guide for Translating Husserl*, 66.

71 Husserl manuscript D 8 (1918): 61b; see also Husserl, *Analyses*, 213:

> What belongs to one and the same object being constituted in the unity of a momentary phase [...] must have some kind of integrally cohesive unity opposing it to what constitutively belongs to another object in the same point of time. The content of one momentary now and of another momentary now must, in the transition from one moment to the next, be connected in an integral togetherness.

72 Husserl manuscript D 8 (1918): 60b: "Zusammengewachsen ist nur Koexistentes." Husserl manuscript D 8 (1918): 61b: "Und es ist zusammengewachsen

98 Corporeity and spatiality

in räumlicher Angrenzung kontinuierlich vermittelter Raumfüllen." Similarly, Husserl notes in the *Analyses*: "What is constituted universally through these syntheses is known under the rubric of coexistence and succession of all immanent objects in relation to one another" (172). See also Husserl, "The Passive (Temporal) Unity of Perception," in *Experience and Judgement*, 157–59.

73 For example, Husserl in *Thing and Space* states: "If a materially filled space is to appear Objectively, then it must present itself in a field of sensations, in a predication of sensation, in an image, as it were"; and in a critical note: "Since the sensuous 'image,' the adumbration as such, is constituted in terms of, and thus is related to, the kinaesthetic system and its position, the Object is then given in a determinate orientation" (135, 258). See also Claesges, 68–69: "Wir haben früher den Aspekt als eine erste Gegebenheit der visuellen Sphäre eingeführt [...] Jeder Aspekt kann als ein, 'Bild' angesehen werden, und so ergibt sich als die erste Gegebenheit das visuelle Feld von Bildern." (Earlier we introduced the aspect as a first givenness of the visual sphere [...] Each aspect can be viewed as an "image," and as such, results in the visual field of images as the first givenness.)

74 Husserl, *Experience and Judgement*, 83.

75 On the syntheses of time-consciousness, Steinbock notes: "These syntheses give a necessary temporal unity to all potentially disparate objectlike formations according to the universal forms of connection: coexistence and succession." See Husserl, *Analyses*, xliv.

76 In a somewhat enigmatic passage Husserl states:

> Die Lage-Figur ist eigentlich kein Moment, wie die Dauer kein Moment ist, in dem Sinn wie Farbe etc. es ist. Oder wie sollen wir sonst sagen? Moment ist das 'wiederholt' Auftretende, das Gleiche, dem eine Spezies entspricht. Die Dauer, die Figur sind Momente, die Lage nicht. Lagenunterschiede sind nicht Unterschiede der Momente, wie sie nicht Unterschiede der Spezies sind. Aber ohne Lage keine Spezies und kein Moment.
>
> (The position-figure is actually not a moment, just as duration is not a moment in the way that colour, etc., is. Or how can we put it another way? Moment is that which "repeatedly" appears, the same, that corresponds to species. Duration, figure are moments, position is not. Differences of position are not differences of moments, just as they are not differences of species. But, without position, no species and no moment.)

Husserl manuscript D 8 (1918): 61b. See the discussion in Burt Hopkins, "Categorial Intuition," in *The Philosophy of Husserl* (Durham, UK: Acumen, 2011), 102–5.

77 Husserl characterises this structure of the continuous modification of the continuity of temporal phases in the perception of the temporality of the thing as the "double continuity of running-off modes"; see Husserl, *Consciousness of Internal Time*, 377. On the time of spatial objects see, for example, Husserl, "Analogy for Spatial Things, for the Appearance of Space and for the Consciousness of Space," in *Consciousness of Internal Time*, 373–79. Merleau-Ponty, drawing on Husserl's analyses of temporality, speaks of the "thickening" of time. See Merleau-Ponty, *Phenomenology of Perception*, 115–17.

78 Cairns recommends "(animate) organism" and Heinämaa uses "living body" to render Husserl's use of the German *Leib*. See Cairns, *Guide for Translating Husserl*, 79 and Sara Heinämaa, *Toward a Phenomenology of Sexual Difference: Husserl, Merleau-Ponty, Beauvoir* (Lanham, MD: Rowman & Littlefield, 2003), 26 et passim. I follow what can be considered the convention of rendering *Leib* as "lived body"; see Moran and Cohen, 193. Merleau-Ponty would go on to develop these themes in his phenomenological analyses of the body, see, for example, Merleau-Ponty, "The Spatiality of One's Own Body

and Motility," in Merleau-Ponty, *Phenomenology of Perception*, 98–147. See also Merleau-Ponty's rendering of *Leib* in French as "*la chair*," typically translated as "flesh," for example, Merleau-Ponty, "L'entrelaces—le chiasme," in *Le visible et l'invisible* (Paris: Gallimard, 1964), 170–201; English translation, Merleau-Ponty, "The Intertwining—The Chiasm," in *The Visible and the Invisible*, trans. Alphonso Lingis (Evanston, IL: Northwestern University Press, 1968), 130–55. For a concise account of Merleau-Ponty's consultation of Husserl's manuscripts, see H. L. Van Breda, "Merleau-Ponty and the Husserl Archives at Louvain," 150–61.

79 Dan Zahavi, "Husserl's Phenomenology of the Body," *Études Phénoménologiques* 19 (1994): 65–66.

80 Zahavi, "Husserl's Phenomenology of the Body," 64.

81 Husserl addressed this question explicitly at a lecture delivered in Berlin in 1931. See Edmund Husserl "Phenomenology and Anthropology," in Husserl, *Psychological and Transcendental Phenomenology and the Confrontation with Heidegger (1927–1931)*, ed. and trans. Thomas Sheehan and Richard E. Palmer (Dordrecht: Kluwer 1997), 485–500. See also John Scanlon, "A Transcendentalist's Manifesto: Introduction to 'Phenomenology and Anthropology'," in *Husserl, Shorter Works*, ed. and trans. Frederick Elliston and Peter McCormick (Notre Dame, IN: University of Notre Dame Press, 1981), 311–14. The issue in some ways lies at the heart of Husserl's *critical* project of transcendental phenomenology. Heidegger seems to evade the question through his hermeneutics of *Dasein* as facticity, but, as Jan Patočka observed on his notion of existence: "Isn't this transcendental philosophy trying to step over its own shadow?" See Jan Patočka, *Body, Community, Language, World*, ed. James Dodd (Chicago: Open Court, 1998), 101, quoted in Steven Crowell, "'Idealities of Nature': Jan Patočka on Reflection and the Three Movements of Human Life," in *Jan Patočka and the Heritage of Phenomenology: Centenary Papers*, eds. Ivan Chvatik and Erika Abrams (Dordrecht: Springer, 2011), 13. On Heidegger's "hermeneutics of facticity" see Hans-Georg Gadamer, *Reason in the Age of Science*, trans. Frederick G. Lawrence (Cambridge, MA.: The MIT Press, 2001), 40–41. On Husserl and Heidegger see Steven Crowell, "Does the Husserl/Heidegger Feud Rest on a Mistake? An Essay on Psychological and Transcendental Phenomenology," *Husserl Studies* 18, no. 2 (2002): 123–140.

82 Zahavi summarizes the issue as follows:

> To what degree does [a transcendental-philosophical investigation of the body] imply an anthropomorphisme [sic]? Is reality suddenly viewed as being dependent upon the human organism—in which case the consequence would be an anthropological relativism? To answer these questions one should bear in mind what aspects of the body Husserl regards as being of transcendental importance. Husserl is obviously concerned with certain formal attributes such as spatiality, mobility and the faculty of articulation, and not with the specific number or composition of arms, heads or eyes.

See Zahavi, "Husserl's Phenomenology of the Body," 75, note 16.

83 Mattens, "From the Origin of Spatiality to a Variety of Spaces," 564.

84 Claesges, 92: "Das Tastphantom ist entweder in einer optimalen Nähe, sofern es tatsächlich getastet ist, oder es ist taktuell völlig abwesend."

85 Edmund Husserl, *Ideas Pertaining to a Pure Phenomenology and to a Phenomenological Philosophy: Second Book*, trans. R. Rojcewicz and A. Schuwer (Dordrecht: Kluwer, 1989), 155 [147]. Hereafter cited as *Ideas II*, followed by the page number of the English translation and then pagination of the corresponding Husserliana volume in brackets; idem., *Ideen zu einer*

100   *Corporeity and spatiality*

reinen Phänomenologie und phänomenologischen Philosophie: Zweites Buch: Phänomenologische Untersuchungen zur Konstitution, Husserliana, vol. 4, ed. Marly Biemel (The Hague: Martinus Nijhoff, 1976). Merleau-Ponty employs this example, acknowledging his consultation of Husserl's then-unpublished *Ideas II* in a note. See Merleau-Ponty, *Phenomenology of Perception*, 92.

86 See my reference to Sokolowski earlier in this chapter. On the history of *Ideas II*, see the introduction by Rojcewicz and Schuwer in Husserl, *Ideas II*, xi–xvi.
87 As noted previously, my reflection in the mirror is precisely that, a *reflection*.
88 Claesges, 113:

> Zugleich aber ist die Bewegung der Hand als kontinuierliche Veränderung innerhalb des taktuellen Systems bewußt. Indem zum Sehen der Hand das Bewußtsein gehört, daß ihre Bewegung meiner Verfügbarkeit unterliegt, gehört die gesehene Hand zu meinem Leibe, was natürlich die haptische Konstitution der Hand bereits voraussetzt.
>
> (But at the same time the movement of the hand as continuous change within the tactual system is conscious [movement]. In that since seeing the hand belongs to consciousness, that its movement is subject to my availability, the seen hand belongs to my lived body, which naturally the haptic constitution of the hand already presupposes.)

89 Claesges, 103: "die ursprüngliche Kinästhese des 'Gehens' noch nicht den Charakter der Bewegung meines Leibkörpers im Raume hat." This statement can become clearer if, for example, we think of when we misjudge a distance or material surface and stumble or trip, in the tripping I become aware that "my body moves."
90 Husserl, *Thing and Space*, 131 [154].
91 Husserl, *Thing and Space*, 134 [158]: "What matters above all, then, is 'self-movement,' and that manifests itself in kinaesthetic sensations." On the difference between the German terms *Leib* and *Körper*, Moran and Cohen note, "The lived or animate body (*Leib*), i.e. the body as organism, is distinguished by Husserl from the body (*Körper*) understood as a piece of physical nature." See Moran and Cohen, *The Husserl Dictionary*, 193.
92 Drummond notes, "Husserl uses the term *Leib* to denote the body of an animate organism. On his understanding, the body is that which is involved in our consciousness of the world as the perceptual organ of the experiencing subject" (46).
93 Claesges, 104: "Der visuell erscheinende Leib unterscheidet sich von allen anderen Phantomen dadurch, daß er eine bestimmte konstante Lage zum Orientierungszentrum des visuellen Raumes hat."
94 Husserl, *Ideas II*, 156.
95 Husserl, *Thing and Space*, 137.
96 Mattens, "Spatial Phenomena in Material Places," 840–41.
97 As Dan Zahavi notes, Husserl "claims that the perception of spatial objects presupposes and depends upon our kinesthetic experience—that is, our experience of the movements, positions and muscle-tensions of the bodily parts." See Zahavi, "Husserl's Phenomenology of the Body," 67.
98 Of the kinaesthetic experiences, Husserl notes that they

> play an essential role in the apprehension of every external thing, but they are not themselves apprehended in such a way that they make representable either a proper or an improper matter [...] Nothing qualitative corresponds to them in the thing, nor do they adumbrate bodies or present them by way of projection. And yet without their cooperation there is no body there, no thing.

99 Claesges, 112:

> Jedes Empfinden im taktuellen Bereich, das ein Phantom zur Gegebenheit bringt, bringt zugleich auch den empfindenden Leib mit zur Gegebenheit, weil die Stellungsdaten, durch die das Phantom gegeben ist, als Aspektdaten dem Leibe zugehören. Somit ist im taktuellen Bereich jedes Empfinden ein 'Sich-selbst-empfinden', wodurch Empfindungen dann den Charakter von Empfindnissen annehmen. Damit ergibt sich eine gleichursprüngliche Gegebenheit von Leib und Außenwelt.

Cairns suggests "feeling" or "sentiment" for the German *Empfindnis*, and the term is also rendered as "feelings" by Klein and Pohl. The meaning, however, is clearly given by Husserl in *Ideas III*, specifically in Supplement I, §4 a) "The animate organism as localization-field of the senses," for example where Husserl says: "We shall speak of 'feelings,' [*Empfindnissen*], in order to distinguish the groups of sensations [*Empfindungsgruppen*] that have aforementioned 'localization' on or in the animate organism [*Leib*]." See Husserl, *Ideas III*, 105 [118].

100 Husserl, *Ideas III*, 105 [118]. Husserl also includes in this "group" "temperature-, smell-, taste- sensations."

101 Husserl speaks of "the intertwining, in a remarkable correlation, of the constitution of the physical thing with the constitution of an Ego-Body" in *Thing and Space*, 137. Merleau-Ponty's concept of "the chiasm" (*le chiasme*) that he introduced in *The Visible and the Invisible* is indebted to these fundamental analyses of Husserl of the experience of the intertwining (*Verflechtung*) of the lived body and the physical thing. See Dermot Moran, "The Phenomenology of Embodiment: Intertwining and Reflexivity," in *The Phenomenology of Embodied Subjectivity*, ed. Rasmus Thybo Jensen and Dermot Moran (Dordrecht: Springer 2013), 285–303.

102 Dermot Moran, "Heidegger's Critique of Husserl's and Brentano's Accounts of Intentionality," *Inquiry* 43, no.1, (March 2000): 52.

103 On the sense of the term "*originaliter*" or "originally" Husserl notes, "'originally' [*ursprünglich*] is not used here in a temporal-causal sense; it has to do with a primal group [*Urgruppe*] of Objects constituted directly in intuition." Cairns recommends "originally," "in an original (*or* originary) manner," and "originaliter" as possible renderings of *ursprünglich*; I follow Steinbock in his use of "*originaliter*" in Husserl's *Analyses*, which serves to avoid confusion with the empirical or "objective" sense of time. See Husserl, *Ideas II*, 156 [148] and Cairns, *Guide for Translating Husserl*, 118.

104 Merleau-Ponty both appropriates and critiques Husserl's supposed notion of the "*Präsenzfeld*" in developing his concept of the "thickness" of the "now," but, as Patrick Burke has argued, it seems that Merleau-Ponty is actually critiquing his own misappropriation of a concept using a term that, apparently, Husserl himself did not use. See Patrick Burke "Merleau-Ponty's Appropriation of Husserl's Notion of '*Präsenzfeld*'," in *Husserl in Contemporary Context*, ed. Burt C. Hopkins (Dordrecht: Springer, 1997), 37–58. I address in greater detail below the implications for space of Husserl's analyses of subjective or "internal time," but see, for example, on the analysis of the "double continuity" of temporal modes, "Analogy for Spatial Things, for the Appearance of Space, and for the Constitution of Space," in Husserl, *Consciousness of Internal Time*, 373–79.

105 Husserl, *Thing and Space*, 136.

106 *Thing and Space*, 137.

102 Corporeity and spatiality

107 See, for example, Husserl, *Ideas III*, 105; *Thing and Space*, 138.
108 *Thing and Space*, 138.
109 Edith Stein, *On the Problem of Empathy*, trans. Waltraut Stein (Washington, DC: ICS, 1989), 48–49; Edith Stein, *Zum Problem der Einfühlung* (e-artnow, 2018), 54.
110 *Thing and Space*, 138 [163].
111 Husserl's describes the constitutive process as an "accomplishment of consciousness" (*Bewußtseinsleistung*):

> This accomplishment does not simply consist in bringing to intuition something new in a fixed pregiven sense, as if the sense would already be prefigured in a finished manner from the very beginning; rather in the process of perceiving, the sense itself is continually cultivated and is genuinely so in steady transformation, constantly leaving open the possibility of new transformations.
> *Analyses*, 57 [19].

112 Zahavi, "Husserl's Phenomenology of the Body," 73, note 14.
113 For a compact "definition" see Drummond: "Genetic phenomenology analyzes the coming-to-be (the 'becoming' or genesis) of [...] fully constituted objectivities with their significance" and "is concerned to uncover the 'origins' of the layers of sedimented sense that characterize that objectivity and the transformations of sense over time" (86–87). Moran and Cohen emphasise the significance of genetic phenomenology for grasping "the constitution of a living ego which is a concrete person evolving and developing in time, with a personal history" (137). For detailed discussions see Donn Welton, "The Systematicity of Husserl's Transcendental Philosophy: From Static to Genetic Method," in *The New Husserl: A Critical Reader*, ed. Donn Welton (Bloomington: Indiana University Press, 2003), 255–88; Janet Donohoe, "On the Distinction Between Static and Genetic Phenomenologies," in *Husserl on Ethics and Intersubjectivity: From Static to Genetic Phenomenology* (Toronto: University of Toronto Press, 2016), 19–42, and Mary Jeanne Larrabee, "Husserl's Static and Genetic Phenomenology," *Man and World* 9 (June 1976): 163–74.
114 Jacques Derrida, *Edmund Husserl's Origin of Geometry: An Introduction*, trans. John P. Leavey (Lincoln: University of Nebraska Press).
115 See, for example, Husserl, "The General Structures of Receptivity," in *Experience and Judgement*, 71–101.
116 This is perhaps due to the fact that Claesges's work primarily studies Husserl's manuscripts that dealt expressly with the problem of space constitution, specifically the D manuscripts; of these Claesges identifies, but does not refer to explicitly in the text, D 12 I (1931) "Assoziative Passivität und Ichaktivität in der untersten Stufe; Kinästhese in der praktischen und nicht praktischen Funktion" (Associative passivity and ego-activity in the lowest level: The practical and non-practical function of kinaesthesis). See Claesges, 146.
117 Don Welton, "Part I. Contours: The Emergence of Husserl's Systematic Phenomenology," in *The Other Husserl: The Horizons of Transcendental Phenomenology* (Indianapolis: Indiana University Press), 11–256. See also Donohoe, "On the Question of Intersubjectivity," in *Husserl on Ethics and Intersubjectivity*, 71–118, and the extremely informative introduction by Iso Kern in Edmund Husserl, *Zur Phänomenologie der Intersubjektivität. Texte aus dem Nachlass. Dritter Teil: 1929–1928*, Husserliana, vol. 15, ed. Iso Kern (The Hague: Martinus Nijhoff, 1973), xv–lxx (hereafter cited as *Intersubjektivität III*).
118 Previously cited as *Analyses*.
119 Drummond, 206, my emphasis. In the passage cited, Drummond defines transcendental logic as the "phenomenological reflection upon and investigation

of the subjective achievements at work in the constitution of the categorial formations and fundamental concepts proper to the *mathesis universalis*."

120 Steinbock describes the phenomenology of genesis as "the phenomenology of the primordial becoming in time, of the genesis of one shape of consciousness emerging from another, acquiring temporal depth. In short, it is a phenomenology of what Husserl calls at this time, 'facticity.'" See Husserl, *Analyses*, xxxii.

121 Steinbock's introduction to *Analyses*, xvii, xxii.

122 Steinbock's introduction to *Analyses*, xvii–xxiv. For example, on the sense of pre-predicative experience as already a mode of judgement, Husserl notes,

> The lowest level reached by tracing back the clue of sense-genesis brings us [...] to *judgements about individuals* [...] These are the pure and simple *experiential judgements* [...] which give norms for the correctness of categorical judicial meanings at the lowest level concerning individuals.

Edmund Husserl, *Formal and Transcendental Logic*, trans. Dorion Cairns (The Hague: Martinus Nijhoff, 1969), 208–9.

123 The text was edited and published after Husserl's death by his assistant, Ludwig Landgrebe. For a summary of the relation between these texts—*Analysen zur passiven Synthesis, Formale und transzendentale Logik* and *Erfahrung und Urteil*—see Welton, *The Other Husserl*, 442 note 27.

124 Steinbock draws our attention to the research of Tetsuya Sakakibara, who locates Husserl's development of a genetic phenomenology in terms of the ego's habitualities and the "constitution of the spiritual world" in *Ideas II*. *Analyses*, xxix–xxx, note 14. Husserl reflects on his own methods in reference to space constitution in this regard: "Phenomenological eidetic analyses of consciousness constituting a temporal objectlike formation already led to the beginnings of a lawful regularity of genesis prevailing in subjective life" (*Analyses*, 163).

125 Claesges, 129: "So ist Rezeptivität im Sinne der Affektion nur im kinästhetischen Bewußtsein möglich." (Thus receptivity in the sense of affection is only possible in kinaesthetic consciousness.)

126 See Zahavi, "Husserl's Phenomenology of the Body," 76, note 17. Heidegger states explicitly that "this 'bodily nature' hides a whole problematic of its own, though we shall not treat it here." Heidegger, *Being and Time*, trans. John Macquarrie and Edward Robinson (Oxford: Blackwell, 1962), 143; in Part One, Division One III of *Being and Time*, "The Worldhood of the World," Heidegger develops his theory of spatiality (*Räumlichkeit*). For an extended and detailed discussion of the difference in methodological approach to phenomenology between Husserl and Heidegger, see Burt C. Hopkins, *Intentionality in Husserl and Heidegger: The Problem of the Original Method and Phenomenon of Phenomenology* (Dordrecht: Kluwer, 1993).

127 This can be seen as early as the *Logical Investigations*, where Husserl speaks of perception in terms of a threefold interpretative structure of "form-matter-content," which, as Sokolowski notes, does not address the problem of the origin of sensations. See Husserl's "Fifth Logical Investigation," specifically §27, in Edmund Husserl, *Logical Investigations*, vol. 2, trans. J. N. Findlay (London: Routledge, 2006), 244–45. See also Sokolowski, *Formation*, 59–60.

128 Sokolowski, *Formation*, 96–97.

129 See Steinbock's discussion in his introduction to the *Analyses* of the methodological significance of the "leading clue" in Husserl's movement between static and genetic phenomenology. *Analyses*, xxxii–xxxvi.

130 Filip Mattens has explored the phenomenology of sound. See, for example, Mattens, "Spatial Phenomena in Material Places," 850–54.

131 Steinbock notes that Husserl appropriates the term "*Reiz*" from physiology and psychology, giving the term a "new phenomenological sense." *Analyses*, xliv–xlv.
132 Claesges, 36. See my discussion above, "The spatial phantom and time."
133 *Analyses*, 214.
134 *Analyses*, 214: "For us the universal synthesis of harmonizing intentional syntheses corresponds to 'the' world, and belonging to it is a universal belief-certainty."
135 *Analyses*, 204 [156].
136 Husserl describes the retentional "running off" modes of the "now" using the metaphor of the "comet's tail": "This now-apprehension is, as it were, the head attached to the comet's tail of retentions relating to the earlier now-points of the motion" (*Consciousness of Internal Time*, 32). Drawing on Husserl's analyses, Merleau-Ponty describes how the layer of time between "the retention of a retention" and the living present "thickens." Merleau-Ponty, *Phenomenology of Perception*, 417. Merleau-Ponty would use the image of the comet's tail to describe the continuity of the living body: "If I stand in front of my desk and lean on it with both hands, only my hands are stressed and the whole of my body trails behind them like the tail of a comet" (*Phenomenology of Perception*, 100). The metaphor of the comet's tail points to the phenomenological relationship between the lived body and "internal" or lived temporality. In "Signs and the Blink of an Eye," Jacques Derrida points to Husserl's metaphor of the comet in his critical interpretation of Husserl's concept of the "living present." See Derrida, *Speech and Phenomena: And Other Essays on Husserl's Theory of Signs*, trans. David B. Allison (Evanston, IL: Northwestern University Press, 1973), 62. Janet Donohoe has argued that Derrida's presentation is a misconception; see Janet Donohoe, "The Nonpresence of the Living Present," *Southern Journal of Philosophy* 38 (2000): 221–30.
137 Husserl, *Consciousness of Internal Time*, 31.
138 *Analyses*, 236, my emphasis. For a detailed study of the concept and phenomenon of time-consciousness in Husserl, see Toine Kortooms, *Phenomenology of Time: Edmund Husserl's Analysis of Time-Consciousness* (Dordrecht: Springer, 2002).
139 In terms of the habituality of the living present, Husserl speaks of "doxic habit," and even of a "habitual style." See *Ideas II*, 268 and 260, note 1 respectively. Similar discussions of "habit" and "style" are found in Merleau-Ponty. See, for example, *Phenomenology of Perception*, 137ff. and 327ff.
140 *Analyses*, 211 [163].
141 It could entice us to imagine our own lived bodily kinaestheses *as if* we were birds, but this is a problem of "empathy" that I have not yet considered. Perhaps an ontological "becoming-bird" is possible, but the ritual must indicate this to us; in any event, as we will see, "transfiguration" seems to require its own processes according to its own temporality.
142 Claesges outlines six features, briefly: temporality (*Zeitbewußtsein*), spatiality (*Raumbewußtsein*), horizonality (*Horizontbewußtsein*), "world-consciousness" (*Weltbewußtsein*), corporeity (*Leibbewußtsein*), and "self-consciousness" (*Selbstbewußtsein*); see "Der Begriff des kinästhetischen Bewußtseins" (The concept of kinaesthetic consciousness) in Claesges, 119–24. All of these I propose are based on the intertwining of the structures of temporality and corporeity.
143 Merleau-Ponty, *Phenomenology of Perception*, 138, note 2, quoting Hugo Liepmann. See also the discussion of "complex embodiment" and disability in Tobin Siebers, *Disability Theory* (Ann Arbor, MI: University of Michigan Press, 2008), 22–33.
144 Husserl, *Ideas II*, 241.
145 *Ideas II*, 243. Merleau-Ponty develops the concept of motivation as found in his readings of Husserl. See, for example, *Phenomenology of Perception*, 48–51, specifically 49, note 1 for reference to Husserl.

146 *Analyses*, 223:

> But this [affective force] ultimately dries up, the retentional modification leads to an empty identity that has lost its particular differentiation [...] And yet, in the continuity of this process, the sense remains identical, it has only become veiled, it has shifted from an explicit sense to an implicit one.

147 *Analyses*, 226–27 [177]: "But this retentional modification leads further and further into the one nil. What does this nil mean? It is the constant reservoir of objects that have achieved living institution [*Stiftung*] in the process of the living present." See Merleau-Ponty's discussion of the concept of "institution" in Husserl in terms of the structure: "*Urstiftung* <'primal institution'> calling forth *Nachstiftung* and *Endstiftung* <'reinstitution and final institution'>," in Maurice Merleau-Ponty, *Husserl at the Limits of Phenomenology: Including Texts by Edmund Husserl*, eds. Leonard Lawlor with Bettina Bergo (Evanston, IL: Northwestern University Press, 2002), 19.

148 Figure 2.11 draws on Husserl's diagram in *Consciousness of Internal Time*, 238 [230]. Husserl made multiple diagrams to illustrate his analyses of the retention-protention structure of the temporality of perception, which are interspersed in the aforementioned volume. Merleau-Ponty cites Husserl as the source of his time diagram in *Phenomenology of Perception*. See Maurice Merleau-Ponty, *Phenomenology of Perception*, trans. Donald A. Landes (London: Routledge, 2014), 560 note 12.

149 Husserl, *Analyses*, 232. Husserl uses the atmospheric metaphor of the "clouding over" of retentional modification and the awakening of "reproductive intuition" or memory as the emerging from a "fog" of the past in various moments in the *Analyses*; see for example, 159–61, 217, 220, 474. It is interesting to compare this to the following quote from Gadamer on the question of "truth" in Heidegger noted by Walter Lammi:

> The sentence, 'life is hazy (*diesig*),' is given to us by Heidegger in his earliest lectures. *Hazy* has nothing to do with the 'this' (Dies); rather it means misty, foggy. Thus, the sentence means that it belongs to the essence of life that no complete enlightenment can be gained within self-consciousness; rather it is constantly being reenshadowed in a fog.

Lammi notes that "this insight of Heidegger's is not only Heideggerian. Gadamer points out that Husserl had already recognized an ineluctable limitation to the transparency of consciousness with his doctrine of 'anonymous intentionalities' that co-constitute the horizons of all human consciousness." See Walter Lammi, "Gadamer's Debt to Husserl," in *Analecta Husserliana LXXI: Passions of the Earth in Human Existence, Creativity and Literature*, ed. Anna-Teresa Tymieniecka (Dordrecht: Springer, 2001), 178, note 41 and 172 respectively.

150 Husserl, *Experience and Judgement*, 122. The more concrete sense of *habitus* pertaining to one's personal life as part of a community, etc. I explore in the next chapter. For a concise presentation of the concept of *habitus* in Husserl and his influence on and anticipation of formulations in later thinkers such as Merleau-Ponty, Jürgen Habermas and Pierre Bourdieu, see Dermot Moran, "Edmund Husserl's Phenomenology of Habituality and Habitus," *Journal of the British Society for Phenomenology* 42, no.1 (January 2011): 53–76.

151 Andrei Tarkovsky, dir., *Nostalghia* (Grange Communications, 1983); Charles Najman and Franketienne, dirs., *Une étrange cathédrale dans la graisse des ténèbres* (A strange cathedral in the fat of darkness) (La Huit Productions, 2011), https://www.youtube.com/watch?v=U8RbFX3G2t0. I thank Natalie Melas for the reference to the work of Franketienne and Najman.

152 Zahavi, *Husserl and Transcendental Intersubjectivity*, 58, emphasis in Zahavi.

3 Space and the other

The enquiry into space in the previous chapter began with the phenomena of differentiated sense fields—primarily the visual and the tactual, but also the aural—as constituted, or given through appearances, to a perceiving subject. The "subject" was described in terms of the structure of its corporeity, qualified as the "lived body" (*Leib*). Analyses of the lived body were concerned with certain structural features of its spatial experience, rather than, for example, the body as the being of this or that *person* in its individual uniqueness. The lived body was described as a somewhat generalised corporeity understood in terms of its relations to appearing spatial "things"—its own "think-like" appearance reflexively in self-affection included—and in this manner its characteristics were determined as those of *any* actual or possible lived body.[1] At a fundamental level, the lived body was shown to be a *tactual* body; vision was analysed and the significance of visuality as an index of space in terms of the phenomenon of "distance" (*Entfernung*) was fleshed out. The appearing thing was qualified as a visual or tactual "phantom," that is, the thing given in its "moment" as merely sensible. In this limited region of enquiry, I identified structural features of the constitution of space: the absolute "here" of the lived body and its experience of space in terms of the discoverability of things in their givenness beforehand, in their structures of aspectuality or perspectivity (their "one-sided" appearance in adumbrations), positionality (as "there" oriented in relation to lived bodily corporeity), and their horizonality ("inner" horizon and environing horizon). In this way, I developed what Husserl would term a "static" description of spatialty, in that the significance and transformation of the *sense* of things—for example, as ritual implement, symbol, ornament, or, in general, axiological or practical significance, and so forth—was provisionally put to the side. In the final section of the previous chapter, we took up questions of the *temporality* of the experience of things, and the relationship between this and the kinaestheses of the lived body. In a slow and tentative manner, things began to appear in their temporal depth, affectivity, sensuality, and sedimented meaning, and the analysis of spatiality proceeded not merely structurally but in its constitution as a kind of "heritage" in motivating our perceptions—the candles' flames flickered with the blowing wind as we felt

DOI: 10.4324/9781351116145-4

a chill and were drawn by the affective "allure" of the rustling ceiling before turning back towards the figurine in recognition of the loss of its illumination. In this way, our experience of the spatiality of the room became for us nascently "habitual," an acquisition as *habitus*.

This chapter continues and deepens the investigation of the temporal density of spatial experience in the genesis, accrual, sedimentation, and transformation of sense. I explore the methodological shift in Husserl's philosophy from "static" to "genetic" phenomenology—the latter term to be understood in a *phenomenological* sense concerned with *temporality*—and elaborate the spatial implications of Husserl's theory of the experience of another embodied subjectivity through what he terms "empathy" (*Einfühlung*). Husserl uses this term with a specific phenomenological meaning, and I analyse its significance for a description of the intersubjective constitution of space as a more concrete mode of spatial experience that I term "empathic spatiality." Drawing on Anthony Steinbock's "generative phenomenology" and with reference to the Candomblé ritual as exemplary, I propose and develop the concept of "generative space" as a mode of intersubjective, intergenerational, historical, and environmental (implying interspecific) experience that is inextricably intertwined with the spatiality and corporeity of the lived body. In elaborating these relations, I introduce and explore a *phenomenological* concept of "environmentality" (*Umweltlichkeit*), which speaks of the generativity and geo-historicity of space.

*

In the *Cartesian Meditations,* first published in French in 1931 based on lectures given in Paris in 1929, Husserl, in addressing the question of the experience of others, spoke of a methodological "reduction" to the "sphere of ownness" (*Eigenheitssphäre*).[2] The closing considerations in the previous chapter were developed in allusion to this mode of analysis. Although problems of the sense of "nature," "world," and intersubjective experience were recognised by Husserl very early on—for example, as Donn Welton has pointed out, in Husserl's lectures on intersubjectivity of 1910—*Cartesian Meditations* has tended to be seen as his principal presentation of the problem of intersubjectivity, in terms of the experience of empathy (*Einfülhung*).[3] In this chapter, we will meet our hosts—the *mãe-de-santo* ("mother-of-saint") and her "daughters-" and "sons-of-saint"— as we have not been invited to the *caboclo reunião* (the Candomblé ritual) merely to gaze at spatial phantoms in their envirolearning horizons; but even at this level, we gained some familiarity with these as "figurine," "candles," "fluttering paper ceiling," "whispering tree," "night sky," and so forth. In this way, we will follow Husserl in his movement from methodologically delimited solipsistic experiences *originalitier* of the perceiving lived body, to empathic experience of another person and the richness of problematics that this opens up.

Before taking up the theme of the "sphere of ownness"—which is at first, methodologically, a *spatial* sphere—and its significance for an enquiry into empathic experience, it is important to trace the trajectory of Husserl's thought on spatiality in relation to the development of his meditations on the problem of intersubjectivity. As explored in the previous chapter, Husserl's research on the problem of space constitution extended over a long period, exemplified in the D manuscripts (1907–1934), with the "Thing Lectures" marking a significant early phase. Of works published in Husserl's lifetime, *Formal and Transcendental Logic* (1929), *Cartesian Meditations* (1931), and *The Crisis of European Sciences and Transcendental Phenomenology* (1937) explicitly deal with problems of empathy, intersubjectivity, and Husserl's concept of the "life-world" (*Lebenswelt*).[4] It might appear, therefore, that Husserl came to the problem of intersubjectivity late in the development of his philosophy. This, however, is not the case. The development of the problem of intersubjectivity in Husserl's phenomenology is explored in depth by Dan Zahavi in *Husserl and Transcendental Intersubjectivity*.[5] Apart from the works mentioned above, Zahavi directs us to Husserl's extensive research manuscripts published in three volumes in Husserliana as *Zur Phänomenologie der Intersubjektivität* (On the phenomenology of intersubjectivity).[6] The introductions to each of these volumes by the editor, Iso Kern, provide a clear picture of the development of Husserl's treatment of intersubjectivity between the years 1905 and 1935. Of particular importance for an interest in the problem of spatiality is Husserl's treatment of the significance of sense perception and lived bodily corporeity for the experience of others in empathy. The period between 1905 and 1910/1911 stands out as being of particular significance in this regard, specifically, as Kern has noted, Husserl's lectures on the "Basic Problems of Phenomenology" (*Grundprobleme der Phänomenologie*).[7] By this time, Husserl had already developed detailed analyses of space constitution as exemplified in his "Thing Lectures" of 1907.

Donn Welton points to the significance of the 1910/11 lectures as anticipating problems latent in Husserl's "Fifth Meditation" in the *Cartesian Meditations*.[8] These relate to ambiguities in Husserl's concept of "primordiality" (*Primordinalität*) that have to do with the subtle but fundamental difference between the constitution of space in sense perception and spatial experience in the "sphere of ownness."[9] The difference can be seen as a conceptual threshold between a static phenomenological description of the structure of spatiality in the manner analysed in detail in the "Thing Lectures," and a genetic phenomenological analysis of the passive genesis, acquisition, and sedimentation of the *sense* of spatiality as explored in the *Analyses*. This is the moment where we left off at the end of the previous chapter. In the following I build on the analyses of passive genesis of the latter part of Chapter 2 in approaching Husserl's theme of the "sphere of ownness." This is interpreted as a spatial sphere; anticipating the problem of the empathic experience of others, it is what I provisionally term "genetic spatiality."

The genesis of space

Husserl begins his lectures in the winter semester of 1910/1911 on the "Basic Problems of Phenomenology" with the theme of the spatiality of the lived body.[10] Insofar as one's lived body is experienced in direct perception as part of a sense field or mixture of sense fields—I see and feel my hand touch my leg—my body appears in a peculiar "thing-like" manner, which was explored in depth in the previous chapter. Of this reflexive appearance of my own bodily corporeity to my perception, Husserl notes:

> The thing, which each I comes upon as *"its body"* is precisely distinguished from all other things as the *lived body it owns* [*Eigenleib*]. It is always and ineluctably there in the actual sphere of perceptions. And it is perceived in its own manner.[11]

The sphere of ownness (*Eigenheitssphäre*) should be understood as pertaining, first and foremost, to the sense in which the lived body is experienced in self-affection as one's *own*. Here, it is precisely the *lived body* (*Leib*), and not the body as a mere material object (*Körper*), that Husserl begins with, thus implying its structures of corporeity, temporality, motivation, kinaestheses and habitualities, and its spontaneity in the form "I can." But the lived body is necessarily an *experiencing* body, which is to say, it is situated in surroundings, it is *spatial*. Its kinaestheses are not mere motile facilities in the abstract; rather, it is through lived bodily kinaesthetic motivation that spatial surroundings come to givenness in terms of *their* structures of perspectivity, coexistence, simultaneity, succession, and horizontality. The spatiality of the lived body is also saturated with the affectivity of its surroundings, on varying levels—the wind blows and rustles the ceiling of white paper strips, and as they undulate whispering with the draught, I raise my head and trace in oculomotion the sinuous wave-like gestures. Swooned by the scene, my eye movements become synchronous with the rhythm of the fluttering ceiling, in the genesis and continuity of perceptual habit (Figure 2.10). We followed this emergence and unfolding of our perceptual constitution of the room in its thingly articulation, to the point at which we are able to experience the surroundings as "familiar." In this way, at the level of lived bodily motility in kinaesthetic motivation, the space acquires temporal depth in the form of individual, embodied memory, that is, bodily disposition as a habitual tendency—the candle's flicker becomes vigorous with the wind calling my gaze, but the allure of the ceiling is still strong even as the flickering candle emerges at the threshold of the background in my peripheral vision as my eye movements negotiate the conflicting motivations.

At the level of the peculiar "ownness" that characterises my experience of the spatiality of my lived body, the sense in which Husserl speaks of the sphere of ownness extends to any appearance in my perceptual field—the figurine, candles, fluttering paper ceiling, stars in the night sky through the arched openings—and the *temporality* in terms of which appearance is possible. As described in Chapter 2, this sense of time in perception is that of the temporality of the *living present*—its retentional-protentional structures in modes of continuity and continuous modification of "running off" temporal flow towards the "foggy haze" of the recent past and anticipatory horizon of the immediate future (Figure 2.11). Thus, the soft surface of the white cloth, the illuminated colouration of the figurine by the candle's flickering light, the cool draught and the fluttering ceiling, the whisper of rustling leaves outside, and the entire background horizon of environing things in their relation to this temporal flow of perception are inherent to my sphere of ownness. It includes, therefore, what I *had* perceived and can present to myself again through recollection. Husserl differentiates this mode of mediated "perception"—in which the thing is not present in the flesh to sense perception, such as memory or phantasy—from my immediate sense perceptual apprehension, by the term "presentification" (*Vergegenwärtigung*).[12] My memory of the table—with only the white cloth and a few things laid out, before the candles were lit and the wind blew—is also immanent to my sphere of ownness. In this way, my sphere of ownness can be layered (as I trace the waves of the fluttering paper ceiling in oculomotion I remember the illuminated surface of the figurine); I can presentify a past experience in my living present of actual perception, and then, in the receding of this living present—of perception and recollection in simultaneity—towards the cloudiness of the past, I can recollect my past experience of recollection, and so forth. All of this is immanent to my sphere of ownness. The givenness beforehand of the thingly quality of space, that is, space as an affective structure for the discoverability of things through the spontaneity of my lived bodily kinaesthetic motivations, Husserl characterises as having the sense "*mere Nature*."[13]

The natural world

Husserl's first lecture of 1910, on "The Basic Problems of Phenomenology," is given the title "The Natural Attitude and the 'Natural Concept of the World'" (*Die natürliche Einstellung und der 'natürliche Weltbegriff'*).[14] Kern states that Husserl appropriates the expression "natural concept of the world" (*der 'natürliche Weltbegriff'*) from the nineteenth-century positivist Richard Avenarius,[15] and David Carr notes that although the term was "clearly borrowed" from him, "Husserl had never used the term in the sense used by Avenarius for his positivistic purposes."[16] Husserl, of course, rejects Avenarius's naturalistic mechanistic conceptions but recognises certain non-dogmatic insights regarding the problem of a *description of experience* in which "I have to make a start with describing the world as it gives itself to me *immediately*, that is, I must describe experience with respect to what is experienced as such" and that this givenness is "the world that I have, that I have by way of experiencing before all theorizing."[17] It is important to note here that Husserl does not mean before "theory" as such, but before one engages in the *activity* of theorising, implying, for example, everydayness. As John Scanlon notes, therefore, the "natural concept of the world is tacitly identified with the concept of the pre-theoretical, experiential world."[18] It thus "takes the experienced world to be whatever is posited as found."[19] In this sense, the natural concept of the world is both spatial and intersubjective from the start: "I find myself with all my thoughts and feelings in the midst of an environment. That environment contains many components, among them other human beings."[20] Thus, in light of this peculiar sense of the use of the term "nature," what is at issue with regard to the sense "natural" is not a counter notion of the "unnatural" or the "supernatural"; rather, the conflict is between the "natural" as the experientially given and the "theoretical" as a particular manner of thematising the given conditions from which it itself emerges and which functions to obscure the experiential world.[21] This issue should therefore not be misconstrued, as if one were speaking about different historical cultures or epochs—the "modern" versus the "pre-modern," for example. The conception of the "natural" here pertains to perception; it points to *la foi perceptive*, to use Merleau-Ponty's expression, the "perceptual faith" that characterises pre-predicative experience.[22]

In a supplement to his lectures dated ca. 1915, Husserl clarifies that it is not a "concept" (*Begriff*) of the world in a predicative sense that is meant, but rather "the '*sense*' of the world" (*des "Sinnes" Welt*).[23] Husserl would thus speak simply of *the natural world* as that which is given in the immediacy of sense perceptual experience.[24] As Merleau-Ponty notes:

> It is a matter of unearthing a more original world *vor aller Thesis* <before any thesis>. [...] The life of consciousness presupposes the *vorgebende Erlebnisse* <pregiving experiences>, a *vortheoretische Konstituierung* <pretheoretical constitution>. The originary constitutive objects are given to us *leibhaft* <bodily>. That is to say, consciousness has a very strong intuition of the insurmountable character of the perceived. It is stuck, bogged down in the perceived thing, even though the *blosse Sachen* [mere things] form a thin universe. This pre-thetic universe is inscribed in the sense of the *blosse Sachen*, sedimented in them.[25]

Husserl is therefore using the terms "nature" and "world" as working or operative concepts in relation to the problem of a description of the structures of the experience of the givenness of phenomena. The term "nature," therefore, is not meant in the sense of the tradition of naturalism, and the sense of "world" does not at this level of description signify things existing independent of experiencing subjects, or products of culture, and so forth.[26] Rather, these terms point to the peculiar structures of *spatiality* that were analysed in depth in the previous chapter, that is, "nature" refers to the givenness beforehand of *blosse Sachen*, or "mere things" as thingly *phantoms* in their structures of aspectuality, positionality, and horizonality; and "world" as *phantom spatiality*, itself not given in the manner of "things," but rather, that which is experienced with reference to the discoverability of things. At this level, that of perceptual experience, "nature" is pregiven in terms of sense fields, and thus the "world," as a structure through which the spatiality of nature is discovered, is also pregiven through its sensibility, but not in the manner of the givenness of things. The givenness of the "world" can be described in terms of the structures of the *affectivity* of space, that is, an open, indeterminate sense of possibility that we can term *horizon*. Insofar as sense fields are indices of lived bodily corporeity in its spontaneity, kinaesthetic motivation, and orientation, the horizonality of space is an index of the horizon structure of the lived body. Dan Zahavi has shown that this interplay between the horizonality of space and the "horizon intentionality" of the lived body—what I have termed, after Claesges, its horizon structure—necessarily points to the *intersubjectivity* inherent in the givenness of space, which functions at the fundamental level of sense perception.[27] This means that the natural world—as a world of phantom spatiality—has an intersubjective sense.

Husserl refers to the "sphere of ownness" as the "primordial sphere" (*primordinale Sphäre*).[28] As has been noted, the concept is related to, but not coincident with, Husserl's characterisation of experience *originaliter*, that is, sense perception as an act of direct intuition and original consciousness in two ways: first, it "gives us the object as originarily present in person; second, in comparison with all other types of acts, it is the most original."[29] Husserl's use of the term "primordial," therefore, should not be misunderstood; it does not refer to an empirical "pre-history" or a "primitivism" or anything of that sort, this much should be clear. The concept of the natural world indicates this dimension of "primordiality," that is, the sense perceptual level of experience of what I have termed phantom spatiality. Before we can approach the concrete, exemplary context of the *reunião* (the Candomblé ritual) in which we are in the room together with others, it is important to clarify the intersubjectivity that is inherent in this level of experience, the direct intuition in sense perception of the *blosse Sache*, the thingly phantom. The importance of this step is to qualify in a non-dogmatic way how it is that the singularity of *the* world as the "natural" world is given over to intersubjective experience. The issue has to do with the claims to truth of the Other's world experience—and here meaning the ethnographic "Other"—as not merely that of a culturally relative "world view" (*Weltanschauung*), but ontologically a *world*. I had never experienced a *caboclo* "manifest" in such a setting before—the apparent physiognomic transformation of an Afro-Brazilian woman into an "other" described to me and appearing as masculine in speech and gesture, and in some way Amerindian, from another time and place—and was there in the flesh together with my hosts, who would become friends, in the room. To assume that the basis of this being together is the existence in itself of an inanimate material cosmos is to prejudice a conception of "space" that presupposes a methodological naturalism, which closes off in advance the ontological claims of my hosts that take the evident form of experiential truths. My interest as a researcher is in spatial experience, and the process of disclosure and understanding through which I approach a description of the spatiality of the *reunião* is one of negotiation, approximation, and, to borrow a term from Brazilian anthropologist Eduardo Viveiros de Castro, "equivocation."[30]

In the analyses of the constitution of space in the previous chapter, I followed the path laid out in Claesges's study of Husserl's manuscripts on spatiality. This approach began with the problem of the mere "thing," that is, the phantom given in terms of its structures of disclosure through a continuity of appearances. The object was said to be given "one-sidedly" in aspects or profiles—I see the front of the figurine directly and *with* this I apperceive its other sides not directly visible. That I cannot directly perceive all of the sides of the object in a single act of perception—not merely its surfaces, but also the texture of the material beneath the painted surface of the figurine, for example—points to the object's transcendence. But my perceptual act is not aimed at the aspect; rather, I perceive the thing itself—I am looking or touching the face *of the figurine*. Zahavi puts it as follows:

> Husserl often pointed out that in the perceptual performance, I do already have a consciousness of a complete thing. Although only a profile is there "in person" in the perception, I do not see and intend this profile, but rather the thing itself; I am directed through the profile toward the object.[31]

This peculiar characteristic of perception to grasp the identity of the thing *through* the partiality of its aspectual appearance, or profile—in which "hidden" sides are apperceived in a co-perception—was discussed in Chapter 2 in terms of the concept of "adumbration" and the structure of its temporality. It is not merely that in directly perceiving the face of the figurine I apperceive its hidden sides as surfaces; rather, the apperception and adumbration pertain to any conceivable moment of the object. The perception of what is directly seen or touched is at the same time a co-perception of the thing more or less indeterminately:

> without this horizon of what is co-intended, the transcendent perceptual object would not be thinkable, for it is the horizon of anticipations—a horizon that cannot be separated from the object—that gives the concept of transcendence its particular sense.[32]

At the level of mere sensibility, therefore, the phantom is transcendent. Thus, before even entering into the complex problems of describing the figurine in the concreteness of its ethnographic reality—which carries with it the historicity of ethnography as an epistemological and colonial project, traced out in Chapter 1 through the critiques of Valentine Mudimbe and Johannes Fabian—we are confronted with a givenness that is at the same time a holding back, a transcendence. Giving itself as a phantom appearance whose contours delineate in advance open possibilities for further appearance in the manner of a more or less indeterminate horizon is a first clue to the intersubjectivity inherent to the natural world as a sense perceptually *experienceable* world.

It is curious that Husserl used the term "*Phantom*" to describe the appearance of the *materiality* of the world, the analysis of which does not dogmatically assert an ontological thesis but rather reveals only that the perspectivity of its appearing is an essential structural moment inherent to its mode of being, and that this appearance is an index of a lived bodily corporeity for whom it appears; the latter in principle is an open subjectivity, human or non-human. In the ethnographic context, however, we encounter the problem of "spirits," that is, disembodied subjectivity in principle, although their "manifestation" means, precisely, embodiment.[33]

Zahavi's analyses, therefore, direct us to the subject's living bodily facility to perceive the phantom in an anticipatory way, that is, in terms of the relative indefiniteness of its "inner" horizon. Direct perception of the thing in the flesh is therefore also a *horizon perception* of the relatively indeterminate sense of the thing. As described in the previous chapter, the thing is always perceived in surroundings, that is, in relation to a background of environing things—candles, the white tablecloth, the fluttering ceiling, foliage outside, the stars in the night sky through the arched openings, and so forth. We spoke of the temporality of the relationship between thing and environing things as their "coexistence" in the continuity of perception "having grown together" (*zusammengewachsen*) in simultaneity.[34] The environing things are also characterised by a certain indeterminacy; they cannot be listed as such, but, as we saw, come to givenness in terms of levels of affectivity such that the perceiving subject turns towards this or that and foregrounds it through bodily kinaestheses—focuses the eyes or touches it, for example. It is in terms of affective force or allure that kinaestheses are motivated, and Husserl qualifies this as a *relational* structure, that is, things are not merely there, side by side, but are discoverable *in relation to* each other—the figurine comes to givenness as the candle's flame illuminates it; I feel the coolness of the draught in its relation to the sudden rustling of the paper strips of the ceiling and the whistle of the leaves outside.[35]

The manner in which the environing things are given in the background as horizonal cannot be described in the same way as the horizonality of the thing. At the level of phantoms, the sense of horizon is as a "moment" of the natural world, as I have described in terms of the experienceability *originaliter* of the world. Experience *originaliter* is sense perceptual, so that the world at this level is a structure of the coming to givenness of the sensible, that is, that which is able to be perceived. But the merely sensible thing, the phantom, is an index not only of the lived bodily corporeity of the perceiving subject but of the entire open, more or less indeterminate, structure of the *affectivity* of space. That space is affectively saturated points to the characteristic of the natural world as a *spatial* world. *Affectivity puts things into relation*:

> The relational determinations emerge *on the ground* of the pregiven; this unity itself does not become thematic, but only the object considered *according to the mode of relation* [my emphasis]. It is *about* the object [...] that we apprehend relative properties [...] the relative determinations [...] are never *in* the object but first come into being with the transition to the relative object, extending "tentacles" toward it, so to speak.[36]

We must not lose sight of our analyses of lived bodily corporeity and the structures of kinaesthetic motivation, through which the perceiving subject is more or less receptive to the allure of the affectivity of this or that object, and through which the relative object is foregrounded in a new relation—I turn away from the figurine towards the rustling ceiling. We can identify here a more or less indeterminate horizon of the relationality that qualifies my kinaesthetic situation in terms of the foregrounded object—in tracing the wave-like movement of the rustling ceiling I remain in surroundings in which this or that environing thing may draw my interest away from the flowing ceiling in terms of more or less prefigured yet still open possibilities: the wind blows more violently and the vigorous flicker of the candles' flames draws my attention back to the table… But here we are entering a genetic description, in which a familiar sense of space is emerging. We must take a step back and tarry with the phantom.

Zahavi points to the sense in which the indeterminate horizon of the thing—its "other sides"—indicates indeterminate *possible* perceptions:

> These possible perceptions must be compatible with my current actual perception, for they must be simultaneously actualizable with it; indeed, it is exactly from this circumstance that the absent but co-meant aspects of the thing provided by my horizonal appresentation are to obtain their character as *currently actually coexisting aspects*. [...] And it is precisely for this reason that it is impossible for the absent profile to be a correlate of *my* possible perception.[37]

The horizonality of the phantom thing experienced by the perceiving subject in the living present is an index not only of its "having grown together" in simultaneity and coexistence with the relational horizon of environing things, but also indicates the open temporality of originary *experienceability* in general.[38] In other words, my "horizon intentionality," or what I have referred to as the horizon structure of perception, is not to be characterised fundamentally by the kinaesthetic anticipation: "if I walk over there I will see the other side"; rather, in relation to the indeterminacy of the thing in the living present is the horizon structure of my perception as *indeterminate*. The sense of this indeterminacy points not to *my* subjectivity—that is, to my actual and possible perceptions—but rather to *indeterminate others*. Precisely as indeterminate, "others" has the sense here of *any possible* perceiving subject. The sense of indeterminate subjectivity is thus neither quantifiable nor merely anthropological. As Zahavi has noted,

> the explication of the horizon would seem to lead to *possible* others, and insofar as a single other alone is not sufficient, the explication ultimately leads to an *infinite plurality of possible others*, which Husserl occasionally characterizes as the *open intersubjectivity*.[39]

We can now attempt to relate Husserl's concept of "open intersubjectivity"—which points to the horizon structure of the perception of the natural world in terms of the constitution or coming to givenness of the horizonality of the phantom thing, and thus phantom spatiality—to the problem of the concrete experience of the other. We will have to take up where we left off, regarding the peculiar spatiality that qualifies the perceiving subject's sphere of owness, which was characterised in advance as "genetic spatiality."

Genetic spatiality

I have traced the contours of the sphere of owness or the "primordial sphere," in terms of the structures of lived bodily corporeity and the affectivity of space, which were described in detail in the previous chapter. With the theme of "genesis" in view, I analyse in this section the manner in which spatiality can be said to accrue and sediment as a lived bodily "heritage" (*Erbe*) or "sense history" (*Sinngeschichte*).[40] I thus introduce more sharply the distinction between "static" and "genetic" phenomenological descriptions.

Donn Welton, in the first part of *The Other Husserl*, examines the development and transformation of Husserl's phenomenological method, from his early "descriptive eidetics" to genetic phenomenology.[41] As noted in the previous chapter, this movement from static description of essential structures—such as the structures of lived bodily corporeity—to genetic analyses of the "temporal generation and coming-to-be" of sense was not a linear development, nor did one approach supersede the other. As Iso Kern notes:

> Not until the period of 1917 to 1921 does Husserl outline for the first time the idea of a properly genetic phenomenology. To be sure, this

phenomenology has nothing to do with empirical, causal explanation. Rather, it involves an *a priori* comprehension of the motivational complexes of transcendental consciousness. Nevertheless, Husserl's phenomenology is not from this moment on simply and exclusively genetic in its approach. Its first task continues to be a "static" analysis of immanent experiences and of the constitution of objects within consciousness. As a second step, however, a genetic analysis of constitution has to follow this "static" phenomenology.[42]

What Kern has characterised above as the "motivational complexes of transcendental consciousness" I have explored in terms of Husserl's qualification of subjectivity as *embodied*, that is, the lived body and its phenomenological structures as analysed in Chapter 2.[43] Welton provides a schematic outline of the emergence and development of Husserl's genetic phenomenology, summarising his interpretation of its systematic nature, in the section of his study titled "Systematic Phenomenology."[44] He identifies six stages, beginning with the first two volumes of Husserl's *Ideas*. Here, Welton points to the structural concept of intentionality for the phenomenological analyses of the relationship between categories of beings and modes of experience, for example, the ontological region of the spatial "thing" and its experience in sense perception in terms of perceptual fields. The "Thing Lectures" and early D manuscripts would correspond to this type of analysis, as explored in the previous chapter. In terms of a concern with space, these analyses retain their force and, as Zahavi has shown, point to the open intersubjectivity already implicated at the level of mere sensuous appearance, that is, phantom spatiality as the horizon of the natural world. Welton then identifies a second stage that is concerned with relationships of "depth" or vertical structures. Welton's analyses here are comparable to Robert Sokolowski's discussion of "genetic constitution." With regard to questions of space, the depth levels of perception are at issue, what Sokolowski terms "pre-predicative constitution."[45] It is in this context that we can begin to speak of a genesis of sense and of a history of sense.

Welton, for example, points to the "transformations by which everyday speech becomes propositional discourse."[46] Tracing this to lower levels of constitution, Sokolowski refers to "the pre-predicative encounter which was the basis for the first categorical formation."[47] But it is not merely that the pre-predicative is a singular horizontal plane, for there are depth levels to perception, and the intertwining of perception and discourse is complex. Welton characterises the relationship between "perceptual situations" and the "occasionality of speech" as that between "background" and "context"; this is evocative of architectural theorist Dalibor Vesely's elaboration of the relationship between the articulate levels of culture expressed in speech, writing, and other discursive modes including music, and its embodiment in architecture as a background or "latent world."[48] Our interest, however, tarries with the pre-predicative depth levels in the attempts to grasp the "magnitude" of the "lower levels of experience" through which spatiality is constituted.[49] Thus, speaking of pre-predicative experience, Sokolowski points out that "Husserl observes that even on this rudimentary level of consciousness, there is a history."[50]

Welton sees this second stage, in which constitutive problems are concerned with the genesis, transformation, and sedimentation of sense, as a bridge from static descriptions of structure to genetic analyses concerned with the *becoming* of sense. The latter define Husserl's genetic phenomenology proper in a third and fourth stage, in which the constitutive problems concerned with the *objects* of perception are understood as indices of the constitutive becoming of the *subject*, its temporality and historicity. Here we encounter problems of the lived bodily acquisition of habitualities, personhood, the life-world, empathy, and intersubjectivity.[51] Welton finally identifies a fifth and sixth stage at the limits of genetic phenomenology, in which Husserl directs his genetic approach towards problems of temporal and historical transformation, the genesis of community, intergenerationality—within which should be included problems of plant and animal generativity—the phenomenology of homeworld/alienworld and historicity in the development of a *generative* phenomenology.[52] Husserl's generative phenomenology has been studied in depth by Anthony Steinbock, and I will explore this in its relation to genetic spatiality in the last part of this chapter.[53] In the following, using Welton's staging, I focus on the second, third, and fourth stages, deepening the enquiry into the problem of the genesis of space in pre-predicative constitution.

Husserl thematises the relationship between his own methodological innovations in an essay from 1921, "Static and Genetic Phenomenological Method."[54] The essay dates to the period of Husserl's lectures on "passive synthesis" (1920–1926), which Welton identifies as the period of Husserl's attempt to systematise his philosophy.[55] The problem of "passive synthesis" concerns sense perception and its modifications, for example, recollection and expectation. What is extraordinary from the perspective of an interest in space is the priority Husserl places on the concepts of "apperception" and "association" for genetic analysis. Its significance lies in the role that apperception and association play in the experience of space, when one is there together in person with others, what I term "empathic spatiality." In my description of the open intersubjectivity that qualifies the horizonality of the natural world as phantom spatiality, we are not yet faced with an actual other subject, in person with us; there is as yet no "empathy," as Husserl develops this concept, for example, in the *Cartesian Meditations*. Thus, before we meet our hosts—the *mãe-de-santo* and others—we must explore more deeply the peculiar apperceptive and associative structures that engender and sustain the development of our spatial sense as an immanent habituality always in a process of becoming.

In the previous chapter I discussed apperception as a co-perception—I see directly the front of the figurine and in the same act I co-perceive or *apperceive* in the living present the sides not directly visible as inextricably *one* perceptual act; or I pass my palm along the surface of the tablecloth and with the touch sensation I apperceive a certain indefinite expanse of the surface as "smooth" expanse; or I hear the rustling of the leaves outside and apperceive a rhythmic phase. What this points to is the *temporality* of apperception, as a horizon or halo of indeterminate co-perception with what is directly perceived. I examined this temporality in its structures of retentional-protentional phases as a continuity of continuous modification of "running off" phases of the living present in Chapter 2 (Figure 2.11). We must keep in mind that the "living present" is not a "point" in numerically measured time—I do not hear a juxtaposition one after another of individual "rustle sounds"; rather, I hear the *rustling of the leaves*.[56] In a genetic analysis, Husserl goes further and makes explicit what is implicit in his earlier analyses of the retentional-protentional structure of the living present:

> Every motivation is apperception. The emergence of a lived-experience *A motivates* the lived-experience *B* in the unity of a consciousness; the consciousness of *A* is equipped with an intention that *points beyond*, "indicating" a *coexistence*. But here we must add that every unfulfilled intention, every unfulfilled horizon contains motivations, systems of motivations. It is a *potentiality* of motivation. [...] One can also say that *apperception is itself a motivation*, that it motivates whatever may occur as fulfilling, that it motivates beyond itself into an emptiness.[57]

We must here keep in mind that, at the level of sense perceptual experience of spatiality, motivations are always *embodied*, always pertain to lived bodily corporeity, and are thus *kinaesthetic* motivations. The wind blows as a gust; like the touch sensation of my palm along the surface of the cloth, I experience the tactual sensation of the wind against my skin as a chill and brush my arm, while the vigour of the candles' flames seduces my gaze and my hearing is enticed by the rustling leaves of the large tree in the moonlit night sky, which I see at the edges of my vision through the arched openings. This I experience in the retentional mode: "just a moment ago the room was still, and my gaze was fixed on the illuminated surface of the figurine by the candle's glow against a background of environing things, including what is behind me, the clear night sky, etc."; and also in the protentional mode: "the gust continues—the candles' flames flicker with the vigour of the wind, the figurine recedes, the foliage outside is aurally foregrounded with the vivacity of the candles' glow and the tactual prominence of the cool 'surface' of the wind, etc." The experience is corporeal—I attune my hearing, move my arms, perhaps gesture forward or to the side following the directionality of the candles' flames in tilting my head, and my eyes adjust in modulation to capture the vibrancy of the flames while keeping the environing things in view in varying levels peripherality. More precisely, "I can" accomplish these movements, or others, anticipatorily. I described this motivational structure previously, but here we must keep in mind that the experience of space has an *indexical* character, which points not only to the horizonal extension—the level of the appearance of thing-bodies "having grown together" in their relationality and their internal and environing horizonality—but to the vertical depth of the temporal horizon of the *subject* in its lived bodily corporeity. It is in terms of embodied subjectivity that the *sense* of spatiality not only emerges but is built up as an acquired "history."

To be sure, spatiality implies the givenness beforehand of the sensible, and the discoverability of the given is always in relation to some perceiving lived bodily subject, but this is space in its "ready-made" character rather than its genesis, development, and sedimentation of a sense history. Husserl initially abstracts from this ready-made quality of space to describe its constitution at the level of mere sensual appearance, that is, phantom spatiality. With genetic analyses, the givenness in advance of space in terms of its thingly and environmental quality is shown to be at the same time a givenness beforehand of depths of experiential sense, which at the lowest level of phantom experience has the character of "unfamiliarity," yet I still perceive "something" against a background of "environing things" in its position "there" in relation to my lived bodily "here" in terms of the perspectivity or aspectuality of its "one-sided" appearance—I enter the room at just the moment when the electric lights were out, only the candles' glow and the moon give soft illumination, and the scene appears as "things" on a table, which I do not quite recognise (Figure 2.7). As events unfold, things in their relational givenness and horizonality become recognisable, such that even the intermittent gusts of wind become familiar—after repeated gusts I welcome the cool air on my skin; attuned to the rustling leaves, but as a background of familiar "whistling," I keep my focus on the figurine in spite of the vigorously flickering glow of the candles, which my eyes can easily trace out if enticed (Figure 2.2); I experience the fluttering ceiling in its wave-like movement without having to raise my head and turn my gaze directly towards it, as I can now easily trace its physiognomy in the periphery of my visual and aural fields. My kinaestheses have now a "history," characterised by lived bodily familiarity with the *situation* as a "kinaesthetic situation."[58] Welton thus speaks of Husserl's account of "situations" as "an account of that habitual world over against which individual objects arise and of the temporality of life in terms of which particular acts have their temporal genesis."[59]

"Genetic spatiality" can thus be characterised in terms of the spatiality out of which the natural world—the world of phantom spatiality—accrues sense and historicity at the level of the individual perceiving subject, in the continuous becoming and sedimentation of capacities and habitualities as actual and potential lived bodily kinaesthetic situations. Kinaesthetic situations are temporal—I hear the whistling of the trees in the living now as a rhythm that extends back to the "just now" of a soft breeze and the "coming now" of a rising gust. The temporality is apperceptive; it is not a mere series "after-one-another" (*Nacheinander*) but a becoming "out-of-one-another" (*Auseinander*) such that an actual kinaesthetic situation in the living present *motivates* a possible future kinaesthetic situation in continuity with it in the temporality of protention as the mode of expectation[60]—the "coming now" of the rhythm of the rustling leaves is an aural sensation that I anticipate *out of* the "having been" of the sound, such that if the wind were to abruptly stop my perception would be "disappointed," but then a new motivation arises out of the stillness, perhaps the allure of the figurine draws me back, or having already turned towards the leaves outside I notice their texture emerging more distinctly from the obscurity of the night. By this time, we have developed a particular lived bodily kinaesthetic *style* in the genesis and development of our familiarity with the room in the *typicality* of its appearance as an experiential *norm*.[61] As the gust occurs a second time, and then again, and again, the environmental "constellations" in their *experienced* relationality—rustling leaves, fluttering ceiling, flickering candles' flames, crisp chill of the air, and so forth experienced in perceptual fields—function indexically in their similarity, pointing back to each other as a "history" of situational repetition.[62] This indexicality of the horizon of the similarity and repetition of situations Husserl characterises in terms of the rubric of "association," which has the sense *"this recalls that,"* "one calls attention to the other":

> We can catch sight of this phenomenon only in the concrete, where we have individual prominences, individual data, standing out from a field: the one recalls the other. And this relationship is itself capable of being shown phenomenologically. It presents itself in itself as genesis: one of the elements is characterized relative to consciousness as that which evokes, the other as that which is evoked. [...] There are also cases of mediate association [...]. But *all immediate association is an association in accordance with similarity*. Such association is essentially possible only by virtue of similarities, differing in each case, up to the limit of complete likeness. Thus all original contrast also rests on association: the unlike comes to prominence on the basis of the common. Homogeneity and heterogeneity, therefore, are the result of two different modes of associative unification.[63]

We must keep in mind the *temporality* of association, such that the sense of "similarity"—which can also be understood as a range incorporating "difference," along the lines of the range of spatial affectivity—is understood in terms of the *modificational* continuity characteristic of perception in the living present, that is, its horizons of retention and protention. It is not merely that one thing points to another; rather, the perceptual situation has the character of "constellations," a nexus of spatial relations of varying affective levels of foregrounding from the foggy haze of the retentional horizon of perception, in the protentional mode of *expectation*. Here, recollection is inherent to my lived bodily disposition and capabilities as a becoming, and thus an acquisition of capacities and a history of habitualities—in the animation of the room by the gust of wind in the living present, I am corporeally attuned to the transformation of the space as a "constellation" that is "similar" to when a gust swept through the room previously; whereas the first time, I experienced the animation of the room by the gust as having "instituted" a genesis of the spatial sense, the second and other times I experienced this as part of the "heritage" of my lived bodily familiarity with the space. But this does not merely apply to the event of the gust; rather, winds were moments in the continuity of my becoming familiar with the spatiality of the *caboclo reunião* as a whole—from the early setting of the table with the white cloth, to the figurine illuminated and foreground against a horizon of environing things, the fluttering paper ceiling, crisp intermittent winds, rustling leaves against the clear night sky, and so forth. My habitualities, which have been acquired as lived bodily tendencies, are thus *indices* of my instituted and sedimented spatial experiences—were I to leave the room, my acquired habitualities in their immanence as sedimented kinaestheses facilitate possibilities for me to accommodate myself corporeally to the affective nuances of the space with ease on my return. We can say that I "carry" with me the spatiality of the room in terms of the indexical possibilities of my lived body. We thus can follow Husserl when he says,

> the habitualities that begin with institutive acts of my own and become constituted as abiding convictions in which *I myself* become abidingly convinced of such and such [...] acquire determinations that are specifically Ego-determinations. But *"transcendental objects"* (for example: the objects of *"external" sensuousness*, unities belonging to multiplicities of sensuous modes of appearance) also belong here: if I, as ego, take into account just what is constituted *actually originaliter* as an appearing spatial object by my own sensuousness, my own apperceptions, *as itself concretely inseparable from them*.[64]

This sense of the inseparability of the spatiality within which my habitualities were acquired from the habitualities themselves as immanent becomes clearer when we see this in light of the temporality and indexicality of the lived body. The genesis of tendencies is a function of the affectivity of space as experienced *originaliter*, in the flesh. Welton summarizes this sense in which a

> genetic account of affectivity leads us, then, to a deepening of the notion of protention and, as a consequence, to an integration of the lived-body in its motility into the account. This is part of the background in terms of which all perception is situated. With this the contrast between association and affection becomes integrated into the corporeal movements of appropriation and accommodation.[65]

This genetic characterisation of the role of affective and associative structures in determining the habituality of spatial experience, understood in its relation to the inherent "open intersubjectivity" of the constitution or coming to givenness of the natural world as phantom spatiality, is what I will bring to Husserl's account of the encounter with the other in empathy.

Empathic spatiality

The table has been set—the white cloth is spread, the vase filled with foliage, popcorn scattered on the surface, the jug and glasses filled with water, implements placed at what we will come to understand as the head of the table, the figurine in its place, the candles lit. We are with our hosts, who sit around the table, with the *mãe-de-santo* (mother-of-saint) at the head. Although we have acquired some familiarity with the room, our experience of its spatiality is still embryonic. For us, the space has the character of phantom spatiality—thing-phantoms appear in their mere sensuousness according to their structures of discoverability—aspectuality, positionality, horizontality in the "having grown together" of their coexistence. To help facilitate description I have had cause to qualify these according to familiar terms—"figurine," "candles," "foliage," "wind," and so forth, and where no such familiar types are readily available, more general categories like "implements" and ultimately "things." Even at this low and abstract level—"abstract" in the sense of a "moment" of mere sensibility—we already accrued temporal depth, that is, a familiar sense of the space as characterised by intermittent winds, rustling sounds, flicking lights, cool tactual sensations, and so forth. Within limits the edges of which are not precise—and thus the appropriateness of the descriptive term "phantom"— our *singular* experiences at this level are indices of open intersubjective experienceability, the horizon of the "natural" world as *the* "world" of phantom spatiality previously analysed.[66] But the actual situation is that our spatial experience is *concretely* shared—we are in the room with others, who have different experiences and who experience the space from different perspectives, different spatial orientations, and have different lived bodily capacities and habitualities. The question of difference in concrete experiences of historicity is implicated, but I will take up this problem in the final section of this chapter. The immediate concern is to investigate the character of this experience of shared spatiality, as the possibility of an experience of the spatiality of others.

I have already noted that Husserl's lectures of 1910/1911, "Basic Problems of Phenomenology," begin with the problem of the spatiality of the lived body, and that by this time Husserl had already conducted extensive, detailed research on the constitution of space, exemplified in his "Thing Lectures" of 1907. I emphasised Husserl's thematic concern with a certain qualification of the "natural" world in terms of the perceptual structures of the lived body, and treated these problems, drawing on the analyses of

124 *Space and the other*

Zahavi, as inherently intersubjective—the natural world as *the* "world" of phantom spatiality is structurally intersubjective, whether or not actual others are present to a perceiving subject. Husserl, however, does raise very early on the concrete problem of intersubjectivity as the actual experience of others in *empathy* (*Einfühlung*), in relation to one's own environmental spatiality, understood as the level of the givenness of space in terms of mere sensibility. But even at this level, Husserl notes that others are experienced as *lived bodies*:

> Every I finds in its surrounding, and more often in its surrounding of immediate interest, things which it regards as lived bodies but which it sharply contrasts to its "own" lived body as *other lived bodies*. It does this in such a way that to each such lived body there belongs again an I, but a different, other I. (It regards the lived bodies as "bearers" of I-subjects. But it "sees" the other I's not in the sense that it sees itself or experientially finds itself. Rather it posits ["perception of the other and experience of the other" (*Fremdwahrnehmung und Fremderfahrung*)] them in the manner of "empathy;" hence other lived experiences and other character dispositions are "found" too; but they are not given or had in the sense of one's own.)[67]

Husserl's descriptive insight that I experience others in the *immediacy* of sense perception as other lived bodies, and thus other *subjects*, may appear obvious at first glance, but the issue is one of the most difficult to clarify and lies at the core of this study of spatiality in the *concreteness* of experience. In the ethnographic context and in relation to the historical emergence and development of ethnography as a method, the question is fraught with difficulties. In terms of the historicity of anthropology, as discussed in Chapter 1, Valentin Mudimbe frames *Einfühlung* as being not merely of methodological and hence ethnographic significance, but more fundamentally, as an *ethical* imperative towards the transformation of anthropology into "a more credible *anthropou-logos*, that is a discourse on a human being."[68] As should be clear, Husserl's analyses of spatiality at the level of thing-phantom appearance, and the constitution of space as the givenness beforehand of the sensible world are founding and thus "abstract" levels of phenomenological description, which preserve the ontological sense of the *transcendence* of the "thing." I approach the problems from this level, very slowly, and in this way the phenomenon of empathy presents us first with fundamental problems of a structural nature, before they become concrete problems of genesis, generativity, and thus of history. I believe that this way of approaching the problem of interpreting the spatiality of the Candomblé *caboclo reunião* in its experiential truth is guided by the more concrete, historically situated sense of *Einfühlung* that Mudimbe, rightly, insists on.

Zahavi discusses Husserl's use of the term *Einfühlung* in relation to the theories of Theodor Lipps. According to Zahavi, "Lipps argues that our knowledge of others is a modality of knowledge *sui generis*, something as irreducible and original as our perceptual experience of objects or our memory of our past experiences."[69] This point is not controversial from the phenomenological perspective and, as Michael Andrews notes, Husserl will also characterise empathy as a "found*ing* mode" of experience in terms of the peculiar manner of the givenness of others.[70] What is problematic for Husserl, however, is Lipps's thesis of "imitation" and "projection," that is, the idea that I reproduce the other's expressive gestures, and in so doing evoke their feeling in my own experience, which I then attribute to the other through "projection."[71] What is at stake in the phenomenon of empathy is not a question as to whether or not I experience directly the other's *experiencing*, but rather a more fundamental problem, which is that of how it is that I experience the other as an *other subject*, who has her own lived bodily capacities, habitualities, perceptions, memories, moods, feelings, and so forth—that is, as one who *experiences*. In fact, Husserl points to the impossibility of my experiencing directly the other's experiencing life in the way that I experience my own, as Zahavi notes:

> The fact that my experiential access to the minds of other[s] differs from my experiential access to my own mind is not an imperfection or shortcoming. On the contrary, it is a difference that is constitutional. It is precisely because of this difference, precisely because of this asymmetry, that we can claim that the minds we experience are *other* minds.[72]

This characterisation of empathy has profound implications for our understanding of spatiality, as it is precisely in terms of perception, and thus the structure of spatial constitution, that I experience the givenness of others. Although I address this problem primarily in relation to human community, at the structural level *any* embodied subjectivity is given to me as a *lived body* in terms of its motility—the ant crawling along my skin, the bird in the sky, and so forth. In the ethnographic context we come across further difficulties having to do with the experience of "saints," the *caboclos* and *orixás*, and the status of certain "objects," such as the "figurine." But we will start again from the lowest level, that of the spatiality of the lived body and its structures.

Husserl's most developed presentation of his theory of empathy published in his lifetime is the much debated "Fifth Meditation" of his *Cartesian Meditations*.[73] Certain central concepts for Husserl's elaboration of empathy, for example, those of "apperception" and "association," were worked out in detail in manuscripts published posthumously. These, as I have noted, include lectures published in the *Analyses*, which I drew upon in developing our analyses of "genetic spatiality." Problems of genesis were anticipated in the lectures of 1910/1911, where Husserl drew attention to intersubjectivity and the problem of empathy.[74] Significant also in this regard is Husserl's theory of relation as developed, for example, in the third chapter of part 1

Figure 3.1 *Filho-de-santo* being incensed. Photo by the author

of *Experience and Judgement*, titled "The Apprehension of Relation and Its Foundations in Passivity."[75] Husserl's concept of relationality that he elaborates at the level of "passivity"—of sense perceptual experience—I propose, helps to further clarify aspects of his theory of association that are significant for grasping empathy as a fundamentally embodied, spatial mode of intersubjective communion.

As will be described in intimate detail in Chapter 4, the *caboclo reunião* typically begins with the act of incensation. As we enter the room, it has the sensual quality of a fragrant, smoky haze. Others are present with us, but in the atmospheric cloudiness of the room they appear blurred, like silhouettes in a mist (Figure 3.1). We might describe their hazy, almost immaterial, appearance using the metaphor of the "phantom," a givenness as mere sensuous figuration; however, they are certainly not encountered as "things," as mere material "bodies" (*Körper*). In the immediacy of our perceptual encounter— as others emerge in our visual or tactual fields and we spy their gestures, or in groping through the thick smoke we touch them—we encounter them perceptually, *originaliter*. Even their vague, gestural contours we experience as *lived bodies*. Here, it is useful to quote Husserl at length:

> Experience is original consciousness; and in fact, in the case of experiencing a human being in general [*einem Menschen allgemein*] we say: the other is himself there before us "in the flesh" [*leibhaftig*]. On the other hand, this being there in the flesh does not keep us from admitting forthwith that, properly speaking, neither the Ego himself nor

Figure 3.2 Filha-de-santo incensing. Photo by the author

his lived experiences [*Erlebnisse*] or his appearances themselves [...] becomes given in our experience originally. If it were, if what belongs to the other's own essence were directly accessible, it would be merely a moment of my own essence, and ultimately he himself and I myself would be the same. The situation would be similar as regards his lived body [*Leib*] [...] *A certain mediacy of intentionality* must be present here, going out from the substratum, "primordial world" [...] and making present to consciousness a "there-with" [*Mit da*] which nevertheless is not itself there and can never become an "itself-there." We have here, accordingly, a kind of *making co-present* [*Mitgegenwärtig-machens*], a kind of *"appresentation."*[76]

The gendered sense of Husserl's description should not be misconstrued, and here I follow the careful analyses of the phenomenology of bodily becoming of Sara Heinämaa, to which I refer later.[77] We must not be hasty but continue slowly and with caution. I enter the room and someone approaches. She nears me and as the fragrant smoke recedes, her appearance becomes more distinct, her outstretched arm motions towards me with the censer (Figure 3.2). Through the smoky haze I had already grasped in its gestural figuration her physiognomy, as performing this incensing activity—moving across, away from or towards me she appeared in terms of *her* kinaestheses. This kinaesthetic facility of her corporeal givenness in its appearance to me I do not experience itself, that is, I do not accomplish *her* motility in its modes of actuality or potentiality. Rather, I see her approach which has the sense, "coming towards me to incense my body and my immediate surroundings." In terms of her gestures, I experience not merely the sensuous givenness of her corporeal presence in my visual field, but "there-with" her bodily appearance I experience the "co-presence" of her intentions towards me. The latter is not something "signified" or "represented" by her physical body as a "sign"; on the contrary, her bodily disposition is *one* with her intentions. But it is not merely this that I experience through her bodily "mediation."

She gestures towards my direction from over "there," where she is. She moves across the room with the ease of familiarity; unlike me, as the thickness of the smoke compels me to move slowly and feel my way around, she traverses the room in fluid movements, at once incensing and carving away the smoky haze with her movements. I *see* the familiarity of her spatial experience. In this way, for example, I experience to a certain extent the historicity of her lived body, not in the mode of direct presentation—in the way that I perceive the phantom-like sensuous presence of her bodily physiognomy—but rather, as an "appresentation," inseparable from her lived bodily corporeity. I see to an extent her "having been here for some time," such that her movements are indices of *her* kinaesthetic motivations and spatial constitution. In having been here before, having performed this incensing before, perhaps many times, her movements appear in their having acquired a "history," in the sense of the sedimentation of past experiences as a halo of temporality motivating and orienting experiential possibilities in the present. Here, the past affectivity of space is not absent, but rather it is sedimented as inseparable from the temporality of past experience. Her familiarity could have been acquired in a day, or over years; what is appresented is not a chronology, but a horizon of lived bodily historicity. Let us, however, tarry with the concept of appresentation.

Husserl's discussion of the phenomenon of appresentation in the "Fifth Meditation" is intricate, yet compact. In order to interpret it appropriately, we must refer to his extensive and detailed investigations of space constitution and the self-affection of the lived body, problems explored in the previous chapter. Husserl points to the fundamental significance of the experience of the corporeity and spatiality of one's own lived body for the experience of another. The matter is rudimentary. Recalling the analyses of spatial constitution in the tactual sphere in Chapter 2, in touching the surface of the cloth spread over the table, I experience its "softness" as a tactual sensation localised in my palm in terms of the temporality of the givenness of the sensation.[78] Here, what was shown was that in the touching not only does the object appear—"soft" cloth—but my lived body is also given in the touching; I constitute myself in the kinaesthesis of experiencing the object, although not, in this example, as an "object," but rather, in a certain "hidden" way as *experiencing* subject. I do not objectify my experiencing; rather, I "live through" the act of experiencing. Key to this is the temporal structure of the experience, which, as was noted, is not a juxtaposition of instances but a continuity of phases, continuously modified through which we have the *sense* "soft expanse of fabric." We also noted, however, that I can experience my lived body in a peculiar reflexive mode as an object-like givenness, for example, an area of my skin touches another area (assuming neither touching nor touched surface is numb). And one mode of experience can motivate the other—I experience the tactual sensation of the crisp "surface" of the wind against my skin as a chill and I rub my arms with my palms. Here we must keep in mind the earlier discussion of the problem of receptivity, spontaneity, and affection, that is, problems of the *genesis* of spatiality: in the cloudy, fragrant atmosphere of incense she approaches me with the censer in her outstretched hand. There emerges a distinct hierarchy to the givenness of my surroundings, as the affective allure of her gestures entices me not merely to look, but already to anticipate a horizon of my own movement—a different rhythm of breathing, eyes focusing and refocusing, gesturing towards her yet not quite moving, a kind of liminal kinaesthesis having the sense, "I can move, yet I hesitate," except for a general inclination towards her experienced as a subtle tremor along seemingly the entire surface of my skin. Over "there," from where she approaches, is the centre of my spatial affection. In terms of the latencies of my kinaesthetic situation, which are motivated by the affectivity of the spatiality of the woman who approaches me, I experience directly and immediately *that* I am given to her spatial experience—I am constituted by her—and in a certain mediated way, *how* she experiences me. The structure of this mediation, which is concretely inseparable from the immediacy of my direct sense perceptual apprehension, is what Husserl means by "appresentation." He characterises it as a mode of "apperception," first, as an *"apperceptive transfer from my lived body [Leib]"* such that the other is given to me precisely as *her* lived body, that is, an *other person*.[79]

I first discussed the concept of apperception in relation to the perception of a thing-phantom and spoke of it as a moment of the unity of a perceptual act in which the sides not directly perceived—for instance, the "back" side—are co-perceived with the directly perceived "front" side. It was characterised in relation to the temporal structure of perception, specifically the horizon of expectation or protention; protention is anticipatory precisely because the retentional phases motivate expectations.[80] Insofar as the other is experienced sensuously—in my visual or tactual fields, for example—my perception of her corporeal givenness involves apperception in the abstract sense of phantom spatiality. But Husserl qualifies another sense of apperception in terms of a certain "empathy"—using the term more broadly—with myself in memory or phantasy.

I initially approached the house where the *caboclo reunião* took place from the street. The front gate was slightly ajar and I opened it; in closing the gate, I noticed a peculiar object on the ground in the corner. Stooping and bending forward I looked closer and saw a white substance on a creased leaf (Figure 3.3). Now I am in the room, at the table, and I notice a number

Figure 3.3 Detail at the ground at the front gate. Photo by the author

of things seemingly wrapped in leaves (Figure 2.4). They appear "similar" to what I had seen earlier, and in their apparent similarity awaken a memory in which I re-present to myself in recollection what I had seen earlier. This act of recollection, or reproducing a once-perceived thing in memory, Husserl terms "presentification" or "presentiating" (*Vergegenwärtigung*).[81] Considered closely, it has a peculiar structural and genetic relationship to my spatial experience in the living present. It is not merely that I recall the object; implicated in the recollection is my lived bodily kinaesthesis and orientation *then*, including the affective allure of the white substance against the background horizon of environing things, but as seen from the *current* perception of the things on the table. My previous perception had the sense: "what is this, there?" whereas my presentation in memory has the sense: "that which I saw there then, is like this that I am now seeing here." That is, my current perception is at the same time a modification of my past perception in the mode of recollection. It is not merely that I establish a connection between two "similar" objects; rather, the perceptual and memorial experiences are put into relation in the *entirety of their spatial situations*. The sense of this relationality is not as a juxtaposition; the spatiality of one event is completely enfolded in the spatiality of the other and both conditions determine the sense of each other. But the relation is not merely an interlacing of equivalent experiences; rather, there is a hierarchy and interplay of genesis that has the sense: "this recalls that"—the wrapped leaf I currently see motivates a recollection which, in being foregrounded from the halo of the cloudy past, orients my understanding of my present perception and does this for my embodied spatial experience as a whole. What is important to grasp here is that the idea of "similarity" does not merely pertain to the two objects. We must keep in mind that our entire description remains at the pre-predicative level, that is, the level of sense perceptual experience and its implications for the memorial. To further clarify the sense of Husserl's terms, so that we do not mistake these for acts of predicative judgement or reflection, but understand them as lived bodily spatial accomplishments, we must approach in greater detail Husserl's analyses of relationality in the passivity of perceptual experience.

Our analyses have been concerned with problems of relation from the start, although implicitly; Husserl explicitly addresses the problem of a theory of relation as this pertains to perception in the chapter "The Apprehension of Relation and Its Foundations in Passivity" in *Experience and Judgement*.[82] The analyses of the chapter are not closed onto themselves but reach out in different directions to more detailed analyses found in Husserl's manuscripts, specifically those published in the *Analyses*. I address those concepts that appear explicitly in the "Fifth Meditation," which are significant for Husserl's treatment of the problem of the experience of another in empathy, and thus the constitution of what I have termed empathic spatiality. Husserl begins with the situation in which "another person [*Mensch*] enters our perceptual sphere," such that

> the body over there, which is nevertheless apprehended as a lived body [*Leib*], must have derived this sense by an *apperceptive transfer from my lived body* [*Leib*], and done so in a manner that excludes an actually direct, and hence primordial, showing of the predicates belonging to a lived bodily corporeity [*Leiblichkeit*] specifically, a showing of them in perception proper. It is clear from the very beginning that only a *similarity* connecting, within my primordial sphere, that body over there with my body can serve as the *motivational* basis for the *"analogizing" apprehension* of that body as another lived body [*Leib*].[83]

Husserl goes on to emphasise that we are not here speaking of "inference by analogy. Apperception is not inference, not a thinking act."[84] Husserl's description above functions at the level of the immediacy of experience in perception; it indicates relational structures that can be viewed as having the character of *analogia* in the primary sense of "relationship between relationships."[85] Burt Hopkins draws an explicit parallel between Husserl's phenomenology and Classical Greek thought. His exegeses extend beyond what can be addressed here, but it is useful to draw on his mereological framing of the problem of relationality in Husserl.[86] I have touched on this theme in terms of Husserl's concept of a "moment" as a part that cannot appear independently of the whole, for example, the whiteness of the cloth spread over the table. This relationship is itself enfolded as a moment of other relationships, and there are hierarchies of dependency or foundation, although these are not static and one can speak of a certain interdependency or, following Hopkins's interpretation, "what Husserl characterizes as a 'two sided' or 'reciprocal' foundation relation."[87] Let us recall the phenomenon of the "having grown together" (*zusammengewachsen*) of the coexistence of things in their appearance to perception[88]—we spy the figurine as having a luminous sheen on its "cheek" and already beforehand we are put in relation with its "inner" horizon as the apperceived background of all its other "sides" not directly visible. But the glow on its "cheek" appears with the candle's gently flickering flame just next to it, resting on the table with its shadow folding along the surface of the saucer on which it stands, which we do not focus on but yet still "notice" peripherally, like the relative positions of other environing things in the background, not merely juxtaposed but situated "across" from me, "above," "beneath," and "behind" me in such a way that I apperceive their presence—the floor, the walls surrounding me, the ceiling, the dome of the night sky through the arched openings in its moonlit expanse beyond the frame, and so forth. Already in advance, given with the appearance to perception of the figurine is its *coexistence* with environing things, and this "plurality of what is cogiven in the surroundings is a *plural unity of the affecting*."[89] Thus the relationality of the "inner" horizon of the figurine is itself a "moment" in the relational horizon of the levels of *affectivity* of the surroundings, in which this or that may entice my regard—I notice the vase full of foliage, and in titling my head following its upward directionality I glimpse the fluttering ceiling, or some other possibility. But even this nexus of spatial relations in order to be understood in their affective potentialities is itself given as a "moment" in a relational structure of temporal depth—I first saw the white substance on the seemingly unfolded leaf as I motioned close to the front gate (Figure 3.3); as I currently look at the table, the things wrapped in leaves seduce my vision more than the figurine, which fades into the background (Figure 2.4); the affective force of the things wrapped in leaves is *motivated* by my earlier experience such that they appear "familiar," but it is in turn precisely this appearance to perception in the living present of these things wrapped in leaves that *motivates* or "awakens" this vivid memory. Thus, the relations of temporality—structures of retention-protention in the living present, continuity and continuous modification, the haze of the past, and so forth—that determine horizons of acquired familiarity and expectation function as a mode of relationality structurally inherent to the relationality in which spatiality is given in its levels of affectivity, and the relation between these relations is one of "reciprocal" foundation. In this way, Husserl notes:

> This typical familiarity codetermines the external horizon as that which always contributes, even though it is not copresent, to the

determination of every object of experience. It has its ground in the passive associative relations of likeness and *similarity*, in the "obscure" recollections of the similar. Now, instead of investigating, as in internal explication, the object for itself on the basis of these relations, which remain concealed, *we can also thematize these relations themselves.*[90]

I turn to the *Analyses* to consider Husserl's concept of similarity. In a short section on "syntheses of homogeneity," meaning perceptual appearance in one of the sense fields, for example, the visual, Husserl discusses "similarity" in terms of the temporality of perception.[91] I see the object—its colouration, texture, shape, size—and in the immediacy of perceiving I "see" what I had earlier seen—the white substance in a creased leaf. It is not that two "similar" things lay before me side by side as the basis of a comparison. There is no "comparison," no predicative activity of comparing. Rather, there occurs a fusion, a unity of the perceptual with the memorial, "as the ground of a concealment, and thereby of repression and eruption."[92] Thus, the overlapping of the perceptual and the memorial "is not a pure fusion and formation of unity," but a *conflict* as a "coinciding par distance."[93] In the case of the tactual sphere, I would also feel in the localisation of the touch sensation the overlap and conflict between experiences. I was there *then*, at the gate, my palms pushing its timber surface against the fading luminosity of the evening sky. In the twilight, the colouration of my surroundings blended into monochromaticity, and as I traced the silhouette of the gate I was enticed by a white substance on the ground, at the corner of the gate's frame, resting on a creased leaf. My thoughts and feelings of uncertainty about being here for the event as a guest gave way to curiosity and my body "focused" in a new, directed kinaesthesis as I bent down to see the white substance "clearly." I am presently in the room by the table, feeling "at ease," glancing here and there—at the women dressed in richly embroidered clothing; through the arched window at the barely visible tree in the opacity of dusk; and "now" at the things wrapped in leaves, which awaken the memory of the white substance at the gate at twilight. In this way, there is a coincidence or blending of "now" and "then," not as separate moments, but with the "then" incorporated into the living present *producing* its sense, even as the perceptual apprehension *reproduces* the past experience "then," not "as it was," but rather as it appears again from the perspective of a "familiarity" that it itself instituted. Furthermore, the similarity is not about the things as such—the white substance seemingly wrapped in leaves—rather, the thing *indexes* relations. The full concreteness of this *similarity of relationality* cannot be described in its totality, and this is so not only because of the horizonality of spatial relations—the horizon of environing things cannot be listed because the givenness of their coexistence is a function of the affective structure of space—but because the relations of the spatiality of "now" and the spatiality of "then" are themselves *interrelated*, and this interrelation is related to other relations.

The things wrapped in leaves also have a glowing sheen, from the candles' flickering flames, on their surface and are set just "in front" of the figurine and "before" a candle that softly illuminates a sheet of paper with writing on it. The text exerts an allure, seducing me to read and I barely make out "13 Maio 2010" (Figure 2.4). I glance back at the things wrapped in leaves, which I perceive in terms of this new relation, and so forth. The concept of similarity in Husserl's discussion of "association," therefore, should not be understood in terms of a comparison between reified "bodies"; rather, the complexity of the relational structure of spatiality and the genesis of sense in the blending of spatial, perceptual, and memorial affectivity are implicated. Husserl would thus characterise empathy in the following, concise way:

> In empathy an objective, intersubjectively common time, in which everything individual in lived experiences and temporal objectivities must be capable of being ordered, is constituted. This constitution can be reduced to the fact that for every ego empathy is nothing other than a special group of positional presentifications [*Vergegenwärtigungen*] in relation to memories and expectations.[94]

The woman approaches me, dressed in white, her hand outstretched with the censer swinging as it releases perfumed smoke around me, and the things wrapped in leaves perceived in the conflicting coincidence of an awakened memorial situation recede again into the cloudy haze of memory, just as they dissolve into the smokiness of my current visual field. Just a moment ago she was on the other side of the room, perfuming the body of another (Figure 3.1). As she lifted the censer, swinging it back and forth releasing the fragrant smoke, he raised his arms and turned around until he faced her again, the surface of his whole body now touched by smoke. Now she is before me, in a "similar" way. Through her motion I "see" what was just before me perceptually—the man's gesture towards the source of smoke—but is now a recent past. I do not see it as an awakened memory, as with the white substance on a creased leaf; rather, it is with me more vividly, although neither as a current perception nor as an image in recollection. I "see" the recent past—she incenses as he gestures towards the smoke—through my *kinaestheses*. As she swings the censer towards me releasing the perfumed smoke, I raise my arms and turn around until I face her again, the surface of my whole body now touched by smoke. In the living present I am being perfumed and I actually move my body, but this actual movement is only a "moment" of my kinaestheses, a moment of actual performance. When I had just seen the other person being perfumed, already in the seeing was a kinaesthetic expectation: "I can do just as he is doing." But it is not merely a bodily movement. The potential of similar kinaestheses involves the relationality of the *situation*: "I can respond to her gestures just as he does." This, of course, does not occur to me as a thought; rather, in my perception of the situation in its corporeity in the living present, I *apperceive* the "I can" over "there" —*his* movement—as the kinaesthetic situation of another living bodily "I can," in terms of which the lived bodily kinaestheses of the one performing the incensing is experienced communicatively as the action through which there is similarity—*she* incenses, we are perfumed.

As the smoke around me thins, she passes by me with the censer and motions towards another woman, and with similar gestures directs the fragrant smoke towards her (Figure 3.4). The receiving woman's gestures are more articulate, and she lingers with the perfumed smoke longer, drawing it expressly towards her body by extending her arms and waving her hands, gathering the smoke in its ephemeral substantiality around her as if in an embrace, immersed in its fragrance (Figure 3.5). Her kinaesthetic situation also appears "similar" to what I had just experienced—she is being perfumed, the other incenses—and I similarly apperceive the "I can" of *her* lived body in its expressivity. Husserl describes this, as we saw, as an "apperceptive transfer" of sense, such that I experience her givenness in my perceptual field as "analogous" to my experience of self-affection, and thus I experience her precisely as a *lived body*.[95] I have noted that the concept of "similarity" in Husserl is to be understood in terms of a theory of relation; the "analogizing" apprehension is not between two reified "bodies"—mine and hers—but involves the continuous concretion of the structures of relationality of one's entire temporally unfolding life, which is not to deny the implication of tendencies towards reification and objectification of the other. But the experience of "similarity" does not place our whole lives into relation; the relation is partial and structured by the horizon of the situation, although in such a way that the "part" is inseparable from the whole and is transformative for it. Husserl qualifies this sense as "transferred similarity."[96] In the simple example of the overlapping perceptual and memorial experiences of the white substance seemingly wrapped in leaves, we saw that the entire spatial horizon and my kinaesthetic situation were implicated in the memorially motivated perceptual apprehension and the perceptually motivated memorial presentification, that is, recollective reproduction of the past perception. The phantom appearance of the thing in its mere sensibility to my perceptual field—which means the entire structure of the givenness of spatiality in terms of aspectuality, positionality, horizonality, and lived bodily kinaestheses—is motivated by the affectivity of space, which I experience in terms of my own memorial and expectational life. My life as an experiencing life is always spatially articulated—except perhaps in dreamless sleep, for example.[97] Spatiality, as analysed in the previous chapter, is structurally inherent to my lived bodily constitution, so that the horizon of my past is a halo of spatiality; each spatial experience is a "moment" along a continuum of spatial experience in which sense is continuously accrued and sedimented as embodied habitualities. In seeing the other being perfumed by the smoke, the experience of

136 *Space and the other*

Figure 3.4 *Filha-de-santo* being incensed. Photo by the author

Figure 3.5 *Filha-de-santo* being incensed. Photo by the author

"similarity" extends to the hazy continuity of the overlapping and fusion of past nexuses (*Verkettungen*)[98] of spatial experiences in the memorial conflicts of "concealment," "repression," and "eruption";[99] these exist as the continual sedimentation and becoming of embodied habitualities that function to motivate my anticipatory understandings in the living present, that is, the prejudices inherent in the corporeity of my lived bodily tendencies towards spatial orientation. In this way, in the concreteness of its life, a description of experiencing subjectivity is potentially unending, because the lived body does not merely index the phantom spatiality of the natural world; rather, the natural world as that which appears in pure sensuality is a "moment" of the empathic world, so that a concrete description of subjective experience is necessarily a description of intersubjectivity.

I—speaking concretely as myself, the researcher—come to the *caboclo reunião* with a personal "history" of spatial experience sedimented as lived bodily habitualities extending from my birth and life in the Caribbean. Phantom spatiality and open intersubjectivity appear already saturated with historicity, so that the relationality in terms of which the women in the incense filled room appear in my perceptual field, for example, is one tied to my life horizon of memories and expectations. As the women motion towards each other, the colour of their skins, features and expressions of their faces, their gesturing arms, and their entire physiognomic appearance through the flowing embroidered fabric are given in my visual field as the expressivity of lived bodily kinaestheses in the mode of a typicality that I had experienced, in terms of histories of interrelations that cannot be counted but are rather latent memorial possibilities in the foggy atmospheres of my past, "a thick brume, ethereal like white fungus."[100] At any moment, however, a past experience can be foregrounded in terms of the affectivity of a present perception.

The *mãe-de-santo* herself passes by. When the smoke settles, she walks around the room, her hand outstretched, and at each corner, or perhaps according to the cardinal points, she blows what appears as fine powder from her palm. She appears clearly in my visual field, the fragrant air having wholly dissipated. She is dressed in white, a long flowing dress, her head wrapped in white cloth. We can turn to the exemplarity of literary description to indicate an apperceptive possibility that we can have—and that I myself did have—in the *immediacy* of, and thus as a co-perception *with* the merely sensuous givenness in phantom spatiality of the colouration of the other's skin. Here, as with my opening description in the introductory chapter, I draw on the literature of Simone Schwarz-Bart:

> When she sat in the sun the black lacquer of her skin had glints the color of rosewood, like those you see in old rocking chairs. When she moved, the blood rose near the surface and mingled in the blackness, and glints the color of wine appeared in her cheeks. When she was in the shade she at once colored the air surrounding her, as if her presence created a smoky halo. When she laughed her flesh grew rounded, taut,

and transparent, and a few green veins appeared on the backs of her hands. When she was sad she seemed to be consumed like a wood fire; she went the color of a scorched vine, and as her emotion increased it would turn her almost gray. But it was very rare for her to be seen like this, the color of cold embers, for she was never sad in public, or even in front of her children.[101]

In the corporeity of the appearance of the colouration of the skin—of the *mãe-de-santo*, who is a black woman—lies a style of affectivity, in which my perception is saturated with sedimented experiences of spatiality, inseparable from the affective appearance of feelings and moods in the expressivity of the other's lived bodily "flesh"—*la chair*, as Merleau-Ponty would render *Leib*—and the "occasionality of speech" which implicate a historicity of spatiality *with others*, both for the other and myself.[102] Empathic spatiality, therefore, must extend beyond the I-Thou relation and presupposes a genesis in community. It involves a conception of the world in its continuous concretion and becoming in intersubjective generation as the *life-world*.

Generative space

Our experience of the environment of the *caboclo reunião* is becoming more descriptively concrete. Others are with us. The incensing has ceased, although the fragrance lingers; its givenness to our olfactory sense-field has an analogous quality to its visuality, as a seemingly thick ubiquity that, in its dissipation, also recedes into the fog of memory. We are no longer in the midst of merely sensuous phantoms; rather, our environment has accrued sense. Its character as intersubjective is not merely the open intersubjectivity that qualifies the natural world as the indexical structure of phantom spatiality in its pointing to indeterminate others. Our environment has a qualified sense in concrete relations with others, which is becoming increasingly significant for us, at the very level of our perceptual apprehension. This latter point is important, because even if we were to assume a stance of disinterest, the visual, tactual, aural, and olfactory givenness of the surroundings will continue to be affective and thus our lived bodily relation to the space is sustained. My aim in the following is to describe and explicate the spatiality of concrete intersubjective relations. It will require a clarification of the sense of spatiality on three registers, building on the study of Husserl's static and genetic descriptive analyses of the perceptual and affective givenness of space, and our provisional exploration of "empathic spatiality." I will first consider the significance for a thematisation of *intersubjective spatiality* of "the magic word *Lebenswelt*," Husserl's concept of the life-world.[103] We will explore this in terms of the notion of the *Umwelt*, or "environing world," as a mediating spatial notion through which the natural world—as the perceptual world of open intersubjectivity, accessible to *any* actual or possible perceiving subject—is enfolded into and inseparable from the life-world. The problem of the life-world will lead to the question of its concrete temporality, specifically its intersubjective, intergenerational, and historical constitution. The conception of the spatiality of the life-world will thus expand to address what Husserl terms its *environmentality* (*Umweltlichkeit*), thereby shifting the descriptive register from a genetic to what Anthony Steinbock has characterised as a "generative phenomenology."[104]

The spatiality of the life-world

Husserl's concept of the life-world appears in the third part of his "great last work," *The Crisis of European Sciences and Transcendental Phenomenology*, titled "The Way into Phenomenological Transcendental Philosophy by Inquiring Back from the Pregiven Life-World."[105] The *Crisis* was the last of Husserl's works published during his lifetime, but only the first two parts—where the theme of the life-world was sketched out in a preliminary way in the context of an historical reflection on the emergence of modern mathematical sciences, which is also a reflection on the structure of history—were published in 1936. Husserl's thematisation of history is extremely complex, and as scholars have noted—including Jacques Derrida in his well-known "Introduction" to Husserl's essay "The Origin of Geometry"—his concern in this "inquiring back" is to clarify the more fundamental question concerning the nature of human *historicity* (*Geschichtlichkeit*).[106] The concept of the life-world, however, appears much earlier in Husserl's thought. Welton has proposed that Husserl first introduced the term publicly in his lecture course titled "Nature and Spirit," which was given first in Freiburg in 1919.[107] The course was given again in 1927, and both texts have been published in the Husserliana series in two volumes as *Natur und Geist* (Nature and spirit).[108] Within the context of these lectures Husserl also develops his concept of the "environing world" in terms of "a theory that understood 'nature' and 'spirit' as various 'strata' or 'levels' of the 'environing world' (*Umwelt*) or 'everyday world' (*Alltagswelt*)."[109] Adam Konopka situates Husserl's concept of the environing world in the context of contemporary debates on the question of method in the human and natural sciences (*Geisteswissenschaften* and *Naturwissenschaften*) in relation to one of his main interlocutors, Wilhelm Dilthey.[110] The problem of history is fundamentally implicated.

It is important to have a sense of this background in order to understand the complexity of Husserl's concept of *world*, and its interlaced nuances as the "natural world," "environing world," and "life-world." Husserl's treatment of "the natural concept of the world" and the background of its *critical* relation to Avenarius has already been discussed. The natural world is the perceptual world, what I have termed "phantom spatiality"; it is a structure of appearance pertaining to the regional ontology of the sensible "thing," and as such is an abstract moment of the world. As a structure of appearance, the natural world is not a "thing"; rather, it facilitates the discoverability of things in terms of their structures of aspectuality, positionality, and horizonality as an index of open intersubjectivity, in relation to actual and possible lived bodies.[111] As such, the natural world could be understood as the horizonality of phantom spatiality. If one were tempted to speak in in such a fashion, then what is "unnatural" would be a mode of givenness that is *non-perceptual*. As Husserl treats differentiated modes of non-perceptual givenness and their interlacing with the perceptual using other terms—related to the temporal dimensions of habituality, intersubjectivity, and generativity—I have followed and continue to follow his lead. Clearly, therefore, Husserl's concept of nature is not coincident with "nature" in the naturalistic sense of the positive natural sciences. The *critique* of naturalism, however, is one of the motivations for Husserl's development of the more concrete concept of the world as environing world.

Konopka provides a survey of the problem, which is useful as a point of departure. The core issue concerns "the appropriation of methodological naturalism in what is known today as the human sciences."[112] Konopka identifies two competing approaches to the problem: the Neo-Kantian position of Wilhelm Windelband and Heinrich Rickert, and the hermeneutics of Wilhelm Dilthey. The arguments on both sides are intricate but can be viewed in essence as a tension between epistemological and ontological approaches. Rickert views the problematic as one of "attitude" (*Einstellung*). He considers the attitudinal interest of the natural scientist as "nomological," concerned with general laws, while that of the human scientist is "ideographic," concerned with the particulars of historical knowledge. The empirical realities are the same and, furthermore, in of themselves irrational.[113] Dilthey's position, which would be decisive for the phenomenological hermeneutics of Martin Heidegger, is that the "object" of the human sciences is to be understood in a different way from that of natural science. The former is *historical*, characterised by the nexus of life, what Heidegger would later characterise as the way Dasein "stretches *itself* along."[114] For Dilthey, the life-nexus "is inclusive of a localized milieu or environment (*Umgebung*) that has an intrinsic intelligible structure."[115] It is in terms of this historical sense of life that Dilthey speaks of the environing world (*Umwelt*). Although the concept can be traced to naturalistic and biologistic conceptions of organism-environment relations, Dilthey "rejects this naturalization project" and, in effect, points to the problem of the *historicity* of the environing world.[116] From Husserl's perspective, Dilthey's framing of the problem was insufficiently radical.[117] It is not only that the human sciences derive their sense from the life-nexus and environing world, nor is the problem merely one of "attitude" in an epistemological sense. The *Natur/Geist* divide—as an onto-epistemological dualism that continues to this day in the form of "nature/culture" or "nature/society" binaries, although even here "culture" and "society" are increasingly being incorporated within the naturalistic category of "nature"[118]—calls for clarification in terms of the *priority* of the world as experientially pregiven, always already there.

This is not merely a perceptual world but the *life-world* which can be described, drawing on Welton, as "the nexus of meaning in and through which things have presence."[119] Welton's compact framing points to both the linguality ("nexus of meaning") and the spatiality ("presence") of the life-world. His description as he elaborates, however, suggests a more distinctly spatial conception of the life-world as "horizon," but he also discusses Husserl's theory of meaning in terms of the "genetic analysis of speech" as "an account of the essential temporality and spatiality of meaning."[120] Let us then start with the question of the spatiality of language, or the relationship between the environing world and the occasionality of verbal expression, such as speech or song which, according to Husserl, "in spite of being occasional, have their intersubjective truth or falsity. This truth-value obviously depends on the relatedness of the single subject's and the community's whole daily life to a *typical specific likeness among situations*."[121] Husserl goes on to speak of the genesis, accruing, and sedimentation of sense in terms of which the sense of judgements relates to their occasionality:

> Uncovering the sense-genesis of judgements signifies, more precisely, an unravelling of the sense-moments that are implicit in, and belong essentially to, the sense that has plainly come to light. [...] The essential peculiarity of such products [judgements] is precisely that they are senses that bear within them, as a sense-implicate of their genesis, a sort of historicalness; that in them, level by level, sense points back to original sense [...] that therefore each sense-formation can be asked about its *essentially necessary sense-history [Sinnesgeschichte]*.[122]

Although Husserl speaks of "judgements" in the passage above, we can frame this more generally as "speech" or modes of verbal expression that are implicated in one's experience of the environing world. Husserl qualifies the occasionality of speech in terms of a conception of "normality," which we should be careful not to misconstrue. As Steinbock notes, "Husserl does not mean medicinal or psychological normality, but rather *modalities of sense constitution*."[123] We touched on the concept in a more basic sense in the previous chapter, with reference to the constitution of normative sense perceptual experience related to the optimal appearance of the thing-phantom, visually or tactually. Here, "normativity" must be understood as pertaining to the intersubjective sense of *situations*; perceptual experience is implied, but in terms of orientations that are a function of accrued and sedimented sense. In the Candomblé *reunião*, it is normal that persons "manifest" *caboclos* as lived bodily experiences; this is precisely a constitutive aspect of its environing world as *normative*. Its normativity is tied to its occasionality. Even for us—we who have only been here for a short while

Figure 3.6 *Filhas-de-santo* singing at the table. Photo by the author

and are experiencing the *reunião* for the first time—the surroundings increasingly appear as a familiar environing world. It does not have the "historical" depth for us as it does for our hosts, manifest in the expressivity of their movements and gestures as lived bodily habitualities, and expressly in their speech—songs, prayers, chants, and so forth. Yet, we ourselves have accrued a certain "sense-history." The environing world is not to be understood as an aggregation of spatial phantoms, as if it were an infinite totality of things; rather, the pregiven natural world of phantom spatiality is an abstract moment in the continuous *becoming* of the world as environing world. Borrowing a conceptual distinction from Welton between linguistic meaning and perceptual sense, the environing world can be understood as the interlacing of the linguality of meaning and the corporeity of sense, and in this way can thus be characterised as the spatiality of the life-world.[124] Let us engage our hosts.

The women dressed in white and others are sitting at the table (Figure 3.6). We sit where other guests are, to the side. The affectivity of space has a different character; it is saturated with sound. At the table and beside us, everyone is clapping in continuous rhythm, and we hear the words more or less distinctly:

A bença, a bença meu pai, né?
Bença pai, bença mãe,
A bença meu pai, né?...

[Bless me, bless me father, right?
Bless me father, bless me mother,
Bless me father, right?...][125]

The figurine does not appear to us in the same way, not merely because it is at times obscured from our visual field, but because the entire quality of the space has transformed. The affectivity of the space is expressive and emotive. Things are not encountered in their mere sensible givenness, nor are we involved with things merely "equipmentally," as "ready-to-hand" tools in Heidegger's sense;[126] in fact, insofar as the chants and words may be unfamiliar to us, the mere sensuous quality of the tonality of the sound can enrapture us and we "turn towards" it in "involuntary" kinaestheses—swaying our bodies, tapping our feet, nodding our heads, and so forth. We are instead drawn towards the corporeity and expressivity of others around us. This does not mean, however, that a gust of wind cannot draw us away from the affection of the musicality of the space; still we do not experience the gust in the same way, because as a tactual sensation it is enfolded in the audial. As Filip Mattens notes,

> Sounds do not [...] fill the surfaces of objects like colors and textures do. Sounds do not present corporeal entities but seem to come from a source. Whereas colors are seen *over there*, where the colored object is, the sounds that we hear have reached us and continue behind us [...] *a sound surrounds us*. In this way, sounds do not appear over against us, but approach us, flow around us, and pervade the space in which we find ourselves.[127]

For those at the table, who sing and articulate the words, the audial filling of space is at the same time *lingual*. Not merely sounds, but the chanting *voices* surround us, and although they blend harmoniously, there is still a tonal and thus corporeal hierarchy; what we hear primarily are the *voices of women*, the speech—as music—of women. The communicative sense of space that asks for "the blessing" (*a bença*) of "my father" (*meu pai*) and "mother" (*mãe*) is gendered, and thus the affectivity of space in its sonicity is given as intersubjectively constituted through a certain kind of surrounding feminine style. Insofar as the chanting voices, even as they blend and surround us in a harmony of articulation, appear as coming from a "source," the corporeity of voices are given with the expressivity of bodily gesture and faces. As with the tonality of sound, in which words are articulated in the way that women's voices clothe the surroundings, so too there is a lived bodily style, expressive of sexuality (in the sense of sexual difference) through lived bodily kinaestheses, as Sara Heinämaa describes it, as "a modal or stylistic identity."[128] As we will see when the *caboclos* "arrive," a kinaesthetic process of *becoming* masculine unfolds, and the physiognomic expressions of femininity, including the voice, transform. But we must approach this

144 *Space and the other*

phenomenon slowly, and for the moment we tarry with the affectivity and sensuality of the space.

As the chanting unfolds, not only do things in their structures of relationality as having grown together in simultaneity and succession of coexistence recede, but the very structure of phantom spatiality is given as a *background*. And we ourselves appropriate the clapping gesture imitatively, even the words in their sensuousness as sound. We begin to sing and repeat the basic sonic quality of the chant. Even if we do not clap or sing, the clapping and the articulation of music is something that we come to expect. This happens in the living present, "now" a tone as a word that in the temporal flow of perception is already the running-off "just now" of retention, which stays with us in understanding but gets cloudy even as it motivates our anticipation of the "to come" of the chant as rhythm. In this way, the sense of spatiality develops "genetic density" for each of us together.[129] It is not merely the sound, but words, voices, the source of the voices over "there," in relations with each other and with me "here," appearing in lived bodily kinaestheses "against" an environmental background of "things" in their "thereness for everyone" in terms of structures of relationality and appearance, appearing from different "perspectives" for each experiencing subject. As I hear the songs and recognise this or that rhythm or phrase, my linguistic comprehension or incomprehension is inseparable from my perceptual "immersement" in the situation, to borrow Marilyn Strathern's term, such that the meanings of songs are fused with the occasionality of spatial experience.[130] I too embody this as the genesis, acquisition, and sedimentation of sense.

When the chanting stops, the affectivity of sound recedes, and in the silence, I notice again the rustle and sinuous movement of the ceiling. When the chanting resumes, I engage it with an already acquired sense-history, and I join with greater exuberance, or perhaps, having acquired this familiarity, the allure is now weaker, and I continue my gaze at the ceiling even as I clap and sing. But I am still just learning the songs, the rhythms, the gestures, whereas others in the expressivity of their actions and voices embody the meaning of these *as they articulate the meaning expressively*. Their historicity is embodied in the corporeity of their lived bodily kinaestheses, including the meanings expressed in speech, as Husserl notes:

> In speaking we are continuously performing an internal act of meaning, which fuses with the words and, as it were, animates them. The effect of this animation is that the words and the entire locution, as it were, *embody* in themselves a meaning, and bear it embodied in them as sense.[131]

The corporeity of speech as the sensible bearer of meaning is not indifferent to the spatiality of the environing world that structures the corporeal givenness of the occasion. This is what Husserl means when he raises the question of truth, in relation to the problem of typicality and normativity. Language is implicated insofar as it "precisely belongs (*gehört*) to this *horizon of humanity* (*Menschheitshorizont*). One is conscious of humanity from the start as an immediate and mediate *linguistic community* (*Sprachgemeinschaft*)."[132] With regard to the question of truth—which from the perspective of this study speaks to an ethical situation regarding an understanding of the experience of the "Other," in the critical sense as per Mudimbe's and Fabian's interrogation of anthropology—the fundamental problem concerns the nature of the givenness of the life-world in its concreteness, specifically with regard to problems of genesis and generation. Its spatiality, therefore, must be approached from the perspective of generativity.

The generation of space

Towards the end of the "Fifth Meditation," Husserl points to phenomena—which he notes have not yet been addressed in his analyses of intersubjectivity from the perspective of empathy—that pertain to "generative (*generativen*) problems of birth and death and [the] generational connection (*Generationszusammenhang*) of animality."[133] Anthony Steinbock, in *Home and Beyond: Generative Phenomenology after Husserl*, presents a systematic study of Husserl's treatment of "generative problems" in his late works, demonstrating its relation to and expansion of Husserl's detailed studies of perceptual genesis, for example in the *Analyses* and the manuscripts on space constitution. Husserl's treatment of generative problems, what he terms "generativity" (*Generativität*), is approached by Steinbock through a study of his late writings, specifically those on the phenomenology of intersubjectivity.[134] Steinbock reflects on his own study of the problem of generativity in Husserl, noting that his "task, in part, was to formulate a 'generative phenomenology.' Though Husserl never used an expression like this, this movement in Husserl suggested and called for the positive formulation of a generative phenomenology."[135]

Steinbock, therefore, can be said to have disclosed in a systematic way Husserl's identification and phenomenological treatment of generative problems, and in so doing articulated and thus developed generative phenomenology as a paradigm *after*—in the dual sense of "in the manner of" and "following from"—Husserl.[136] For the purpose of this enquiry into the problem of *spatiality*, Steinbock's study is of particular significance as it situates Husserl's analyses of generativity in relation to his theory and description of normativity at the level of perceptual experience, that is, in terms of the structures of what I have analysed and called phantom spatiality. I note here as well that, although in the following I do not address questions of non-human animal generativity, as indicated in the quote above from the "Fifth Meditation," Husserl's conception of generativity is expansive or "ecological," even enquiring into the generativity of plants and "single-cell organisms."[137]

146 *Space and the other*

To enter into the problem of what we can term "generative space" or the spatiality of generativity, it would be useful to trace the movement of Steinbock's analyses—with the understanding developed through our detailed studies of perceptual space and genetic and empathic spatiality in view—in order to identify the moment in which the theme of generativity emerges in his work in explicit reference to problems of space. In *Home and Beyond*, Steinbock's enquiry shifts from a critical stance directed at problems of the structures and genesis of subjectivity in what he terms Husserl's "Cartesian way"—for example, the approach to the problem of empathy in terms of the method of abstraction to the "sphere of ownness"—to an identification and explication of generative themes in Husserl's characterisation of the concept of the life-world as *"world-horizon"* (*Welthorizont*) and *"earth-ground"* (*Erdboden*). This is the moment when Steinbock's investigations assume a distinctly spatial sense, wherein the life-world is characterised in terms of a phenomenological conception of "territory" (*Territorium*).[138]

Steinbock draws on a remarkable fragment by Husserl from a manuscript of 1934, published posthumously in 1940 as "Grundlegende Untersuchungen zum phänomenologischen Ursprung der Räumlichkeit der Natur," and later translated by Fred Kersten as "Foundational Investigations of the Phenomenological Origin of the Spatiality of Nature."[139] Kersten's introduction to his translation offers valuable insight, not only into this specific fragment but more generally into the development of Husserl's "meditations" on the problem of space constitution in relation to his thought of later years. As we have seen, the latter is marked by problems of phenomenological genesis, empathy, and intersubjectivity. Kersten notes the important contribution of Ulrich Claesges's study—explored in Chapter 2—pointing out, however, "that Claesges does not refer to the manuscript translated here," referring to "Foundational Investigations," or to a continuation of this fragment in a related text, titled "Notizen zur Raumkonstitution" (Notes on the constitution of space).[140] "Foundational Investigations" can thus be seen as lying between the period of Husserl's lectures on problems of the genesis of sense in the *Analyses* and the publication of his *Cartesian Meditations* (1931), and the period that followed a year later when he began work on the *Crisis*, introducing the concept of the life-world and foregrounding the problem of human historicity.[141] As a meditation on *space*, this fragment, even in its very position in the chronology of Husserl's thought, demonstrates the extent to which the problem of space constitution is paradigmatic in the development of Husserl's phenomenology, tying his early work on the phenomenology of perception and lived bodily spatiality to later works on problems of intersubjectivity, historicity, and generativity.[142] Following the path of Steinbock's investigation, therefore, I also approach the problem of the generative constitution of spatiality through this and related fragments.

Husserl begins the "Foundational Investigations" in the following way:

[...] the world in the openness of the *environment* [*Umwelt*] [...] The openness is not given as perfectly conceived, as made objective, but as a horizon already implicitly formed.[143]

Although the word *Umwelt* as used by Husserl is typically translated as "environing world"—which, as emphasised by Cairns, is preferred in order that "the expressed reference to world should be preserved"[144]—I employ the common term "environment" to anticipate and indicate a terminological shift Husserl makes that corresponds to an increasingly intricate and intimate inquiry into the significance of intergenerational relations for the constitution of space. The passage continues:

Openness of the landscape [*Landschaft*]—knowing that I have arrived at the borders of Germany, then arriving at the French, Danish, etc. landscape. I have not paced off and become acquainted with what lies in the horizon, but I know that others have become acquainted with a piece further on, then again others yet another piece—representation [*Vorstellung*] of a synthesis of actual experiential fields which mediately produces the representation of Germany, Germany within the boundaries of Europe, and gives rise to a representation of Europe itself—ultimately of the earth.[145]

Implied in Husserl's description of one's experience of the landscape in the openness of its environmental horizonality is the sense in which this is not merely "my" experience, but the experience that I acquire from and share with many others: "I appropriate to myself the reports of others, their descriptions and ascertainments, and form universal representations."[146] Already in these opening passages, Husserl sets up a relationship between the lived body in its perceptual habitualities and the "earth"; a relationship established in terms of the openness of the landscape as one experiences it immediately in person and mediately through "the reports of others." To a significant extent, the problems that Husserl traces out in this dense fragment anticipate his "inquiry back" (*Rückfrage*) into the formation of modern philosophy and natural science out of the life-world that he develops in the *Crisis*.[147] He does not, however, introduce the concept of the life-world here, but rather teases out a "Copernican" problematic of the constitution of the spatiality of the earth from the point of view of lived bodily spatiality. The fragment gestures towards problems of intersubjective space, intergenerational experience, and historicity, starting with descriptions of the experience of rest and movement peculiar to the lived body—that is, lived bodily kinaestheses as explored in Chapter 2—but here characterised in terms of its grounding in the experience of the earth. The motif of "earth" in this fragment is not easy to elaborate in brief. Although the term suggests questions of spatial scale—as in the expansiveness of a landscape—the matter is equally about the scale of time. This sense is beautifully rendered in an image Husserl provides of one born at sea, which it is useful to quote at length:

> But consider this. Each of us always has his "historicity" [*Historizität*] on the basis of the respective ego which is made at home in it. If I am born a sailor's child, then a part of my development has taken place on the ship. But the ship would not be characterized as a ship for me in relation to the earth [...] the ship would itself be my "earth," my primordial homeland [*Urheimat*]. But my parents are not then primordially at home on the ship, they still have the old home, another primordial homeland. In the changeover [*Wechsel*] of homelands [...] there remains universally stated that each ego has a primordial homeland—and every primordial people with their primordial territory has a primordial homeland. But every people and their historicity and every cosmopolitan people (cosmopolis) [*Uebervolk (Uebernation)*] are themselves ultimately made at home, naturally, on the "earth."[148]

The earth is therefore not originarily experienced (lived experience) in a planetary sense, but rather is given in terms of levels of lived bodily habituality, and thus by extension levels of intersubjective and intergenerational *geo*-historicity. Steinbock develops this geo-historical sense of the earth by focusing on Husserl's characterisation of the earth as *the* "ground" (*Boden*)—the earth is the "earth-ground" (*Erdboden*).[149] Rendered in this way in English, the expression has a feeling of weight and stability, but it can also be rendered, as Kersten does, as "earth-basis," which releases to an extent its reified sense of physicality. In reference to this fragment of Husserl's, Merleau-Ponty introduces the more contingent, temporal notion of "sense-ground" [*Sinnboden*]: "natural *Boden* (the earth) and cultural-historical *Boden* which is built on the earth."[150] Merleau-Ponty's division is somewhat misleading, but the idea of *sense* is key. The matter pertains to the handing down or "changeover" of sense from one generation to the next and so on, which implies problems of tradition and generative phenomena of birth and death. I have followed Kersten in rendering *Uebernation* as "cosmopolis," as I believe that this better captures the *environmental* sense of Husserl's concept of the "earth"—its "cosmic" spatiality. That Husserl conceives these "horizons of earth-space" (*Erdraumhorizont*)[151] as incorporating the spatial experiences of animals is clear in the attention that he pays to the bird's experience of the earth-ground through "its particular kinaesthesis of flying."[152] In this way, we are thus returned to the problem of empathy, which now has a horizon of temporality that stretches beyond the life span of any single individual, and thereby to historical horizons of environmental experience:

> From the starting point of the human being, I am led back to the phylogenetic universal process of living beings and their *environmentalities*

[*Umweltlichkeiten*], as a universal historicity [*Geschichtlichkeit*] [...] It is a historicity of (styles of) lived bodily corporeity [*Leiblichkeiten*], of biological developments—running its course evermore between birth and death—in a generativity that continues on while the individuals die, while animal species are born and die, new ones grow up, etc.[153]

In this dense passage, taken from the posthumously published supplementary volume to the *Crisis*, Husserl relates the problem of embodiment or lived bodily corporeity—its kinaesthetic structures, motivation, affection, and so forth—to intersubjective, intergenerational, and even interspecies relations, through a concept of space that is both historical and environmental.[154] Cairns suggests that the term *Umweltlichkeit* in Husserl be translated as "belonging to the surrounding world."[155] At the risk of obscuring the sense of "world," I have rendered this expression as *environmentality*, in order to characterise not only its intersubjective spatiality but, in relation to this, its *generative* temporality as a geo-spatial inheritance. I want to, therefore, propose Husserl's use of *Umweltlichkeit* as a *phenomenological* concept of environmentality.[156]

Environmentality is space in its most concrete mode of experience, as generative spatiality. It is significant to note that Husserl speaks of *environmentalities* (*Umweltlichkeiten*) in the plural, and thus of multiple styles of lived bodily corporeity (*Leiblichkeiten*) as ways of belonging to surrounding worlds. In this way, the habitualities that I accrue, as my spatial surroundings acquire the sense of familiarity, are not limited to my finitude—to my life that stretches between birth and death; rather, through the environmentality of space my lived body acquires levels of temporal depth that are geo-historical. Environmentality is the geo-historicity of generative spatiality that I experience in terms of lived bodily corporeity and spatiality. Husserl would thus speak of the "living environment" (*Lebensumwelt*) as a horizon of experiential possibilities that are traced out in advance in "preliminary sketches" (*Vorzeichnungen*) as a consequence of finding myself in a world already structured by previous generations and in generative connection (*generativen Zusammenhang*).[157]

In as much as the environing world is pregiven as surroundings, characterised by its traditionality as having been passed on through a generative nexus, this environmentality is still something that each person encounters and must acquire as a familiar world through the accruing of habitualities *individually*, from birth. Husserl even speaks, in this light, of pre-natality and the peculiar kind of intersubjective acquisition that characterises embryonic or foetal lived bodily spatiality—prenatal subjectivity—such that the "pre-ego [...] nevertheless already has in its way—its pre-way—world, in the pointing-ahead [*Vor-Weise*], its world not presently experienceable [*inaktuelle Welt*]" constituting the generative basis of a "first empathy" (*erste Einfühlung*), that between mother and child.[158] Sara Heinämaa draws on Husserl's analyses of lived bodily spatiality and his descriptive gestures

150 *Space and the other*

towards the problem of natality in approaching the work of Simone de Beauvoir, specifically her descriptions of "the body in labor," that is, natality from the point of view of the woman's embodied experience.[159]

Challenging traditional interpretations of Beauvoir's work as empirical studies, Heinämaa situates Beauvoir distinctly within the phenomenological lineage of Husserl and Merleau-Ponty. The body in labour is the concretely embodied moment of generative connection, not as a mere biological process but as a lived bodily experience characterised by its own kinaestheses, affectivities, and pathos:

> the feeling and perception of an uncontrollable process still forms an irreducible part of the experience. And it is exactly this aspect of the experience that makes it difficult for us, if not impossible, to characterize childbirth as an act or deed of the woman.[160]

In approaching Heinämaa's interpretation it is important to keep in mind the analyses of lived bodily spatiality in Chapter 2; the issue concerns *how* a woman's body is given to her in the experience of childbirth, its kinaesthetic modalities of "I can" in relations of affection. These include "the passive body 'I suffer'" in its "two different modes of passivity: the body that suffers from external impact and the body that suffers from internal processes."[161] The latter, Heinämaa explains, "appear as teleological and vital. [...] the processes appear as goal-driven but independently of my goals."[162]

The constitutive phenomenon of birth as a lived bodily experience of sexual difference points to other concretely embodied moments at the limits of the generative nexus: how the newborn is constituted as "child," the woman as "mother" or "parent," others as "father," "grandparent," and so forth. Only through the extended temporality of generational connection, and not merely intersubjective community of persons existing side by side in synchrony, is one given to oneself as "child," "parent," "grandparent," and so forth. As Steinbock notes, "in Generativity, we share with others a 'generatively communicative time.'"[163] Husserl enquires into ways in which the newborn already accrues habitualities in its relations with the parent:

> The child involuntarily utters sounds in involuntary kinaestheses [...] Inherent to the child's sounds are kinaestheses that lie within its ability [*vermögliche Kinästhesen*]. But the mother for her part utters similar sounds, first imitating the child's [...]. The child repeats the sounds—the mother follows suit—what role could this play?[164]

We can follow Husserl's questioning and say that in this fundamental way a generative nexus becomes concretely constituted. When viewed at this level of primacy and intimacy—prior even to language acquisition on the part of the newborn but still corporeally, orally, and aurally communicative—the contingent nature of generativity is glaring. Consider, for example, the problem of generative becoming in the geo-historical situation Toni Morrison presents us with:

> To marry or not. To have children or not. Inevitably these thoughts led me to the different history of black women in this country—a history in which marriage was discouraged, impossible, or illegal; in which birthing children was required, but "having" them, being responsible for them—being, in other words, their parent—was as out of the question as freedom. Assertions of parenthood under conditions peculiar to the logic of institutional enslavement were criminal.[165]

Morrison's description provokes the question: What form can a generative nexus take under such conditions of violence? Following Orlando Patterson, we can say that it takes the negative form of a process of "de-socialization" or "social death" through what he terms "natal alienation": "Not only was the slave denied claims on, and obligations to, his parents and living blood relations but, by extension, all such claims and obligations on his more remote ancestors and on his descendants."[166] Abstractly, this would suggest an absolute severing of the generative nexus, but more concretely the concept of natal alienation points to conditions that limit the "facultative possibility" (*Vermöglichkeit*), to use Husserl's term, or the power of one generation, Patterson continues, "to integrate the experience of their ancestors into their lives, to inform their understanding of social reality with the inherited meanings of their natural forebears, or to anchor the living present in any conscious community of memory."[167] It suggests that the generative nexus would have to be constituted through means that could transgress the limiting conditions of the time, establishing other modalities of filiation and alliance in the formation of intergenerational community. The landscape, and even the seascape, would be implicated. We can think back to Husserl's image of the child born on a ship, and to the bird in flight:

> The horned island sank. This meant they were far out,
> perhaps twenty miles, over the unmarked fathoms
> where the midshipman watched the frigate come about,
>
> where no anchor has enough rope and no plummet plumbs.
> His cold heart was heaving in the ancestral swell
> of the ocean that had widened around the last
>
> point where the Trades bent the almonds like a candle-
> flame. He stood as the swift suddenly shot past
> the hull, so closely that he thought he heard a cry[168]

In the excerpt above from *Omeros*, Derek Walcott points to the soaring swift, as Achille, the protagonist, is guided by the bird's kinaestheses across the Atlantic from his Antillean homeland to Africa. The environmental space itself has a peculiar character as historical:

> our only inheritance that elemental noise
> of the windward, unbroken breakers, Ithaca's
> or Africa's, all joining the ocean's voice,
>
> because this is the Atlantic now, this great design
> of the triangular trade. Achille saw the ghost
> of his father's face shoot up at the end of the line.[169]

The environment is here a geo-historical space that harbours generational experience and trauma as a spectral memory, in and through which one encounters oneself as transcending one's empirical life, and thus one's finitude. Walcott's image is only partially metaphorical; in the intergenerational handing over of experience, the environmental space is also handed over as an inheritance, as a mode of relating to the environment. Through the image of Achille being guided back across the Atlantic to Africa, by "the sea-swift as a pilot," Walcott foregrounds the environmental reverberations of historical experience.[170] "The sea is History."[171] Édouard Glissant speaks of this relation through the image of a "fibril," a connective tissue that can be understood as a figure of generative intertwining characteristic of the specificity of the Antilles, a specificity "of its own landscape and lived existential history."[172]

The reverberation of this history in the changeover from one "earth" to another and the ship as a "flying ark" points to a certain pregivenness of the environment in *levels of environmentality*.[173] I do not experience the "living environment" (*Lebensumwelt*) of previous generations as lived by them in its immediacy. Not even my own spatial past do I experience immediately as it was lived; rather, it is clouded in the haze of memory.[174] It is the affectivity of the environment experienced in the living present that motivates my kinaestheses—I habitually turn my head and my eyes follow the waves of paper streamers as the wind blows and the ceiling rustles[175]—and in so doing foregrounds distant images, feelings, moods, and so forth out of the fog of memory. Consider again natality, the experience of pregnant (inter)subjectivity as described by Iris Young:

> For the pregnant subject [...] pregnancy has a temporality of movement, growth, and change. The pregnant subject is not simply a splitting in which the two halves lie open and still, but a dialectic. The pregnant woman experiences herself as a source and participant in a creative process. Though she does not plan and direct it, neither does it merely wash over her; rather, she *is* this process, this change.[176]

Lived bodily habitualities accrue and natality acquires the sense of familiarity and even facility, for example, through "altering between movement and rest and by varying her breathing and changing her position, she can influence the way that her labor proceeds."[177] Already, the temporality of natality that characterises the accruing of lived bodily habituality and familiarity with an "inner" environmental affectivity points to the constitution of a generative nexus in potentiality. Husserl begins, however, from the point of view of the lived bodily corporeity of the yet to be born "pre-ego" and the newborn, the manner in which it already experiences itself as part of a generative nexus at the level of lived bodily kinaestheses and affection, that is, at a level analogous to phantom spatiality in which the accruing of sense is "embryonic." Of course, we are not speaking here of self-awareness in an explicit sense, but again imply the question Husserl rhetorically asks: "what role can that play" in the generative constitution of space?[178] Natality, therefore, is a level of environmentality that involves a mode of intersubjective and intergenerational experience of space as a potential link in the generative nexus. This potentiality becomes increasingly realised through processes of acquisition and accruing of sense through iterative structures of "institution" (*stiften, Stiftung*), that is, of establishing and renewing the inherited sense of the surrounding world within which the coming generation will find itself immersed already, in advance.[179]

Here, I am concerned with the manner in which this generative horizon is constituted in lived experience, how the corporeity and spatiality of the lived body is given to itself environmentally as *historical* in its kinaestheses, affections, habitualities, and so forth. It is a question that pertains to the historicity of the lived body in the living present. The living present is the ongoing, flowing perceptual present in which my surroundings, including other people, are given to me in their corporeal appearance. I described its basic structures—temporal, kinaesthetic, affective, and habitual—in depth in Chapter 2. Of the environment given to one in the flow of the living present, Husserl states:

> The world familiar to us through experience, our life world, is in every present; and in every overview the unity of spatiotemporality that inheres in our experience is found in the unitary world, which is ours not only through a flowing present, but also as our spatiotemporal world of experience. Thanks further to past events which memory can find anew and to experience that prefigures a living future for us, this is a world thoroughly *typified*.[180]

We approached the idea of the typicality of spatial experience earlier, in terms of lived bodily motility having acquired a particular "style" of experiencing situations, that is, the lived body in its habitual tendencies in relation to spatial affections.[181] We saw further that my empathic experiences of others and of being with others are inextricably interlaced with my habitualities in their genesis, acquisition, and development or transformation.[182] In this way and reciprocally, others acquire and accrue lived bodily habitualities in an affective relation to their spatial surroundings as I do. The surrounding world is thus constituted and *actively* appropriated in intersubjective community in levels of relative environmentality, that is, relative modes of belonging to the environment. This thus implies a historically situated, intersubjective, and intergenerationally mediated relationship between individual subjectivity as necessarily embodied and the environment. At the level of sense perceptual experience—which means lived bodily kinaestheses, habitualities, and affections—the environment is given to an experiencing human subject as historical. But, as we saw, Husserl does not neglect the birds; they also have environmental experiences in their lived bodily kinaestheses being "borne by the wind" in flight.[183] We experience the bird empathically as well, its lived bodily "I can" and its peculiar environmentality, in terms of empathic spatiality. The bird in flight against the blue sky is part of the *typification* of our environment, in which we are in intersubjective, interspecific communion with it. Husserl draws our attention to the bird as a means of directing our regard towards the earth:

> All developments, all relative histories have [...] a single originary history [*Urhistorie*] of which they are episodes. In that connection it is indeed possible that this originary history would be a togetherness of people living and developing completely separated, except that they all exist for one another in the open, indeterminate horizons of earth-space.[184]

The spatiality of the earth, however, is not extrinsic to its historicity; rather, we might say that it is analogous to the phantom spatiality of the natural world, which is space as a horizon-structure of affectivity, in terms of which the sense perceptible surrounding world appears in modes of discoverability to the lived body.[185] But phantom spatiality is an abstract moment of concrete spatial experience, the latter being spatiality saturated with significance—emotive, social, historical, and so forth—afforded possibility and experienceablity by the earth. The spatiality of the earth is thus not merely analogous to the spatiality of nature (phantom spatiality), but includes it as inherent to its structure as horizon. The spatiality of the earth can be characterized as vertical or as having a depth-structure, that is, a temporal horizon-structure as that which makes possible affective spatio-corporeal appearances of environing worlds in their *historicity*. Intrinsic to such appearance is embodied subjectivity as the lived body. This sense of subjectivity is *empathic* (intersubjective) and generative: it is always already with others, whether they are present in the flesh; as having been present during or before one's lifetime; or those yet to be encountered. This being-with-others is inherent to lived bodily experience, in the spatiality, historicity, and futurity of the living present.[186] Space is therefore fundamentally *earth-space*:

> Bodies are given as having the sense of being earthly bodies and space is given as having the sense of being *earth-space*. The totality of the

We, of human beings or "animate beings," is in this sense *earthly*—and immediately has no contrary in the nonearthly.[187]

Levels of environmentality accrue: the surroundings become a familiar landscape, reified in its familiarity as "objective" in its "thereness-for-everyone"; language is acquired, customs learned as habit, familial and social bonds formed, deepened, but also transformed, ruptured, repaired, and so forth. There is thus implied the generative phenomena of growth, ageing, and death. The generative problems here are substantial and are addressed by Steinbock in great detail.[188] I have traced them out in order to identify and formulate a distinct conception of spatiality in Husserl that concerns the geo-historicity of intergenerational experience of space, which I have rendered as environmentality. Spatial experience is constituted through sedimented layers of generative sense—social and cultural meaning, for example—that resonate in the living present. These meanings recede into the background like a fog, and yet are experienced as a prepossession in a generative sense, that is, as a mode of traditionality and thus having the character of a heritage. Working with the poetic image from Walcott quoted above we can say that, in the context of the Americas, within the interlacing of relations the pregivenness that inheres and makes possible the givenness in the living present of the surrounding world in levels of environmentality is paradoxical: it manifests as a geo-spatial inheritance *through* a historical process intended to annihilate the geo-historicity of generations of persons. The problem of the constitution of the spatiality of the living present in this intersubjective and generative sense is what I aim to describe concretely, through the example of the ritual event of the *caboclo reunião*. Let us see, therefore, the extent to which we can grasp the spatiality of the event as generative, that is, its pregiven levels of environmentality and geo-historicity constituted in the lived bodily experience of its space.

Notes

1 This is what Dan Zahavi points to when he notes, in his study of Husserl's phenomenology of the body, that

> the following considerations do not express empirical-mundane (not to speak of anthropological) statements. Quite to the contrary, the analysis of the body's functions as a condition of possibility for the experience of objects is as well an analysis of the body's function as a condition of possibility for objects of experience.

See Zahavi, "Husserl's Phenomenology of the Body," *Études Phénoménologiques* 19 (1994): 64.

2 Edmund Husserl, *Cartesian Meditations: An Introduction to Phenomenology*, trans. Dorion Cairns (Dordrecht: Kluwer, 1999), 92–99 [124–30]. Hereafter cited as *Cartesian Meditations*, followed by the page number of the English translation and, where intended, pagination of the corresponding Husserliana volume in brackets; idem., *Cartesianische Meditationen und Pariser Vorträge*, Husserliana, vol. 1, ed. Stephan Strasser (Dordrecht: Kluwer, 1950, rpt. 1991).

3 See the detailed presentation by Don Welton, "Cartesian Enclosures," in *The Other Husserl: The Horizons of Transcendental Phenomenology* (Bloomington: Indiana University Press, 2000), 96–130.
4 See, for example, Edmund Husserl, "The Transcendental Problems of Intersubjectivity and of the Intersubjective World," in *Formal and Transcendental Logic*, trans. Dorion Cairns (The Hague: Martinus Nijhoff, 1969), 237–44; idem., "Fifth Meditation. Uncovering the Sphere of Transcendental Being as Monadological Intersubjectivity," in *Cartesian Meditations*, 89–151; idem., "The Way into Phenomenological Transcendental Philosophy by Inquiring Back from the Pregiven Life-World," in *The Crisis of European Sciences and Transcendental Phenomenology: An Introduction to Phenomenological Philosophy*, trans. David Carr (Evanston, IL: Northwestern University Press, 1970), 103–89 (hereafter cited as *Crisis*).
5 Dan Zahavi, *Husserl and Transcendental Intersubjectivity: A Response to the Linguistic-Pragmatic Critique*, trans. Elizabeth A. Behnke (Athens: Ohio University Press, 2001).
6 Zahavi, *Husserl and Transcendental Intersubjectivity*, xx. Zahavi also notes Husserl's *Ideas II*, *Erste Philosophie II*, *Phenomenological Psychology*, and unpublished research manuscripts. See the following three volumes of Husserliana: *Zur Phänomenologie der Intersubjektivität. Texte aus dem Nachlass. Erster Teil: 1905–1920*, Husserliana, vol. 13, ed. Iso Kern (The Hague: Martinus Nijhoff, 1973); *Zur Phänomenologie der Intersubjektivität. Texte aus dem Nachlass. Zweiter Teil: 1921–1928*, Husserliana, vol. 14, edited by Iso Kern (The Hague: Martinus Nijhoff, 1973); *Zur Phänomenologie der Intersubjektivität. Texte aus dem Nachlass. Dritter Teil: 1929–1935*, Husserliana, vol. 15, ed. Iso Kern (The Hague: Martinus Nijhoff, 1973). Hereafter cited as *Intersubjektivität I*, *Intersubjektivität II*, and *Intersubjektivität III*, respectively.
7 See Kern's discussion in Husserl, *Intersubjektivität I*, xv–lxx. These lectures appear in Husserl, *Intersubjektivität I*, 111–94. They have been translated into English as a separate volume as Edmund Husserl, *The Basic Problems of Phenomenology: From the Lectures, Winter Semester, 1910–1911*, trans. Ingo Farin and James G. Hart (Dordrecht: Springer, 2006).
8 See Welton, *The Other Husserl*, 111–30.
9 See the discussion in Kern's introduction to *Intersubjektivität II*, xxiv–xxvi. See also the short explanation given by Drummond under "Primordial" in *Historical Dictionary of Husserl's Philosophy* (Lanham, MD: Scarecrow Press, 2008), 170.
10 Husserl, *Basic Problems of Phenomenology*, 3–5; *Intersubjektivität I*, 113–15.
11 *Basic Problems of Phenomenology*, 4, emphasis added; *Intersubjektivität I*, 114.
12 David Carr, "The 'Fifth Meditation' and Husserl's Cartesianism," *Philosophy and Phenomenological Research* 34, no. 1 (September 1973): 23. See also the summary definition in Dermot Moran and Joseph Cohen, *The Husserl Dictionary* (London: Continuum, 2012), 260–61.
13 Husserl, *Cartesian Meditations*, 96.
14 *Basic Problems of Phenomenology*, 1; *Intersubjektivität I*, 111.
15 See Iso Kern's introduction to *Intersubjektivität I*, xxxvi.
16 David Carr, *Phenomenology and the Problem of History: A Study of Husserl's Transcendental Philosophy* (Evanston, IL: Northwestern University Press, 1974), 151. For Husserl's discussions of Avenarius see, for example, Husserl, *Basic Problems of Phenomenology*, 22–28 and idem., "Appendix III(XXII)," *Basic Problems of Phenomenology*, 107–11; idem. *Intersubjektivität I*, 131–138 and idem., "Beilage XXII," *Intersubjektivität I*, 196–99. See also Patricio Agustín Perkins, "La relación filosófica entre Husserl y Avenarius

en Problemas fundamentales de la fenomenología," *Diánoia* 59, no. 72 (May 2014): 25–48.
17 *Basic Problems of Phenomenology*, 108; *Intersubjektivität I*, 197.
18 John Scanlon, "Husserl's *Ideas* and the Natural Concept of the World," in *Edmund Husserl and the Phenomenological Tradition*, ed. Robert Sokolowski (Washington, DC: Catholic University of America Press, 1988), 217.
19 Scanlon, "Husserl's *Ideas*," 220.
20 Scanlon, 220.
21 Scanlon notes that this is the insight that serves as the starting point for Avenarius: "We already have the natural concept of the world available to us. It has been formed automatically, as the very sense of our experience […] it is understood as natural in opposition to all philosophical theory." Avenarius's response, however, is unacceptable to Husserl. Scanlon notes of Avenarius's approach:

> In proposing a cure for the delusions of subjective idealism and skeptical materialism, the therapeutic process never questions the unexpressed motivations for mechanistic naturalism. The cure, if accepted, would repress subjectivity so completely as to leave us with a world from which we are effectively alienated in favor of a mechanical process involving a principle coordination of a central nervous system with its environment as all that can be experienced, strictly speaking.
> (Scanlon, 223 and 225, respectively)

22 Maurice Merleau-Ponty, "La foi perceptive et son obscurité," in *Le visible et l'invisible* (Paris: Gallimard, 1964), 17–30.
23 *Basic Problems of Phenomenology*, 109; *Intersubjektivität I*, 197, emphasis added.
24 As I noted in the Introduction, this is the source for the concept of "the 'natural' world" in the philosophy of Jan Patočka, and thus of Dalibor Vesely; although related in this way, Husserl's use of the term is not coincident with Patočka's or Vesely's use. See Dalibor Vesely, *Architecture in the Age of Divided Representation: The Question of Creativity in the Shadow of Production* (Cambridge, MA: MIT Press, 2004), 398 note 54. For Patočka see Jan Patočka, *The Natural World as a Philosophical Problem*, ed. Ivan Chvatík and Ľubica Učník, trans. Erika Abrams (Evanston, IL: Northwestern University Press, 2016). See my discussion in Tao DuFour, "Toward a Somatology of Landscape: Anthropological Multinaturalism and The 'Natural' World," in *Routledge Research Companion to Landscape Architecture*, ed. Ellen Braae and Henriette Steiner (London: Routledge, 2019), 156–70.
25 Maurice Merleau-Ponty, "Husserl's Concept of Nature (Merleau-Ponty's 1957–58 Lectures)," in Merleau-Ponty, *Texts and Dialogues: On Philosophy, Politics, and Culture*, ed. Hugh J. Silverman and James Barry Jr. (Amherst, NY: Humanity Books, 2005), 164.
26 See Husserl's discussion in "The A Priori of Nature, the Natural-World Concept, and the Natural Sciences. Avenarius' 'Critique of Pure Experience'," in *Basic Problems of Phenomenology*, 22–28.
27 Zahavi, *Husserl and Transcendental Intersubjectivity*, 25–61.
28 Iso Kern notes that Husserl uses multiple terms equivalent to "sphere of ownness" (*Eigenheitssphäre*) and "primordial sphere," including "original sphere" (*Originalsphäre*) and "solipsistic sphere" (*solipsistische Sphäre*). See Kern's introduction to *Intersubjektivität I*, xlv. Kern uses the contrived term "primordinal" in reference to the sphere of ownness, saving "primordial" for the sense of Husserl's "*ursprünglich*" or "originary." In Zahavi's *Husserl and Transcendental Intersubjectivity* "primordial" is used to refer to the sphere of ownness and I follow this usage. See Rudolf Bernet, Iso Kern, and Eduard Marbach,

158 *Space and the other*

    An Introduction to Husserlian Phenomenology (Evanston, IL: Northwestern University Press, 1999), 261 note 13.
29 Zahavi, *Husserl and Transcendental Intersubjectivity*, 28.
30 Eduardo Viveiros de Castro, *Cannibal Metaphysics*, trans. Peter Skafish (Minneapolis, MN: Univocal, 2009), 87. In the context of his research on Amazonia and thesis of "Amerindian perspectivism," Viveiros de Castro describes "controlled equivocation" as a mode of translation, in recognition of the limits of anthropological knowledge. For a phenomenological sense of linguistic equivocation comparable to Viveiros de Castro's ethnographic characterisation, compare André de Muralt, "Equivocations of Language and Shifting of Intentionality," in *The Idea of Phenomenology: Husserlian Exemplarism*, trans. Garry L. Breckon (Evanston, IL: Northwestern University Press, 1974), 205–10. See also DuFour, "Toward a Somatology of Landscape," 161–63, 168 note 54.
31 Zahavi, *Husserl and Transcendental Intersubjectivity*, 40.
32 *Husserl and Transcendental Intersubjectivity*, 40–41.
33 According to Zahavi, Husserl's position on the possibility of a disembodied subject would be that "we are then dealing with an impoverished subject which has a very limited field of experience." See Zahavi, "Husserl's Phenomenology of the Body," 77.
34 See Chapter 2, "The spatial phantom and time."
35 See, for example, Edmund Husserl, "Horizon-Consciousness and Relational Contemplation," in *Experience and Judgement*, ed. Ludwig Landgrebe, trans. James S. Churchill and Karl Ameriks (Evanston, IL: Northwestern University Press, 1973), 149ff.
36 Husserl, *Experience and Judgement*, 155.
37 Zahavi, *Husserl and Transcendental Intersubjectivity*, 48.
38 See the discussion in Chapter 2 of the present work, under the heading "The spatial phantom and time."
39 Zahavi, *Husserl and Transcendental Intersubjectivity*, 50.
40 In characterising the retentional-protentional structure of the living present, Husserl refers to the retentional phases as a "heritage," anticipating later genetic analyses: "each [retentional] memory is in itself continuous modification that carries within, so to speak, the heritage [*Erbe*] of the whole preceding development in the form of a series of adumbrations." Husserl, *On the Phenomenology of the Consciousness of Internal Time (1893–1917)*, trans. John Barnett Brough (Dordrecht: Kluwer), 339 [327]. Hereafter cited as *Consciousness of Internal Time*, followed by the page number of the English translation and, where intended, pagination of the corresponding Husserliana volume in brackets; idem., *Zur Phänomenologie des inneren Zeitbewusstseins (1893–1917)*, ed. Rudolf Boehm (The Hague: Martinus Nijhoff, 1966). In preparing the "abstraction" to the sphere of ownness, Husserl speaks of a "sense history" ("*Sinngeschichte*") that emanates from others; see Husserl, *Cartesian Meditations*, 92 note 1.
41 Welton, "Part I. Contours: The Emergence of Husserl's Systematic Phenomenology," in *The Other Husserl*, 13–256.
42 Bernet, Kern, and Marbach, *An Introduction to Husserlian Phenomenology*, 196. Welton describes static phenomenology succinctly as follows:

> The task of a static phenomenology is to *secure* that structure (intentionality) that provides the irreducible ground to the various regions, which then allows us to frame each as a sphere of constitution. The method that secures the ground of all regions in intentionality also provides each with its basic form of analysis. Since the as-structure of appearances is

understood in terms of the one to whom or for whom objects and complexes are manifest, all intentional analysis is 'correlational'.

My focus on space, from the point of view of static phenomenology, would be framed as concerned with the regional ontology of the "thing," apprehended through "acts" of sense perception. Welton's characterisation of genetic phenomenology is what we are exploring in this section. See *The Other Husserl*, 249.

43 See specifically the section in Chapter 2, "Tactual Space, Motility, and the Lived Body." The scope of this study does not allow for a discussion of Husserl's conception of phenomenology as transcendental philosophy, but see my brief presentation in the Introduction. For a detailed discussion of Husserl's place within the tradition of transcendental philosophy, see David Carr, "Transcendental and Empirical Subjectivity: The Self in the Transcendental Tradition," in *The New Husserl: A Critical Reader*, ed. Donn Welton (Bloomington: Indiana University Press, 2003), 181–98, and David Carr, *The Paradox of Subjectivity: The Self in the Transcendental Tradition* (Oxford: Oxford University Press, 1999).
44 Welton, *The Other Husserl*, 249–56.
45 Robert Sokolowski, *The Formation of Husserl's Concept of Constitution* (The Hague: Martinus Nijhoff, 1970), 173–77.
46 Welton, *The Other Husserl*, 249–51.
47 Sokolowski, *Formation*, 174.
48 Welton, *The Other Husserl*, 237–46; Dalibor Vesely, "The Place of Architecture in the Life of Culture," in *Architecture in the Age of Divided Representation*, 96–107.
49 In reference to Heidegger's approach to questions of affectivity and understanding, Welton notes that "while the notion of moods or attunement is alien to Husserl we might even argue that Husserl expands the domain of affectivity, placing here one thing that Heidegger wants to locate in understanding (the theory of perception) and one thing he avoids altogether (the body). One can almost hear him complain of Heidegger, as he did of Kant, that he does not 'suspect the magnitude' of the 'lower levels of experience'" (*The Other Husserl*, 234).
50 Sokolowski, *Formation*, 175.
51 *The Other Husserl*, 251–54.
52 *The Other Husserl*, 254–55. Welton does not mention problems of plant and animal generativity, but see Mario Vergani, "Husserl's Hesitant Attempts to Extend Personhood to Animals," *Husserl Studies* 1–17, 28 April 2020, https://doi.org/10.1007/s10743-020-09263-w.
53 Anthony Steinbock, *Home and Beyond: Generative Phenomenology after Husserl* (Evanston, IL: Northwestern University Press, 1995).
54 Edmund Husserl, *Analyses Concerning Passive and Active Synthesis: Lectures on Transcendental Logic*, trans. Anthony J. Steinbock (Dordrecht: Kluwer, 2001), 624–34 [336–45]. Hereafter cited as *Analyses*, followed by the page number of the English translation and, where intended, pagination of the corresponding Husserliana volume in brackets; idem., *Analysen zur passiven Synthesis. Aus Vorlesungs- und Forschungsmanuskripten 1918–1926*, Husserliana, vol. 11, ed. Margot Fleischer (The Hague: Martinus Nijhoff, 1966).
55 Donn Welton, "The Systematicity of Husserl's Transcendental Philosophy: From Static to Genetic Method," in *The New Husserl*, 255–88.
56 See my presentation in Chapter 2, "The spatial phantom and time" and "Corporeity and time."
57 Husserl, *Analyses*, 625 note 98, my emphasis.
58 See Chapter 2 of the present work, "Visual space."

59 Welton, *The Other Husserl*, 246.
60 See Welton, *The Other Husserl*, 247 and Husserl, *Analyses*, 628 [339].
61 On the sense of the expectational horizon of apperception, Husserl says,

> The expectation is generally not plain and clear; it has its apperceptive horizon of indeterminate determinability within an intentional framework that circumscribes it, and it concerns precisely one of the modes of behavior which corresponds to the style [of the person].

See *Ideas Pertaining to a Pure Phenomenology and to a Phenomenological Philosophy: Second Book*, trans. R. Rojcewicz and A. Schuwer (Dordrecht: Kluwer, 1989), 283. Hereafter cited as *Ideas II*, followed by the page number of the English translation and, where intended, pagination of the corresponding Husserliana volume in brackets; idem., *Ideen zu einer reinen Phänomenologie und phänomenologischen Philosophie: Zweites Buch: Phänomenologische Untersuchungen zur Konstitution*, Husserliana, vol. 4, ed. Marly Biemel (The Hague: Martinus Nijhoff, 1976). Merleau-Ponty draws on Husserl in his discussion of the "style" of the world as analogous to an individual's "style" as "a certain manner of dealing with situations." See Maurice Merleau-Ponty, *Phenomenology of Perception*, trans. Colin Smith (London: Routledge, 1989), 327.

62 "At each place in the stream [of consciousness] it is possible for constellations that are similar [...] to be produced again with earlier ones, to recall the earlier similar ones, to point back to them, perhaps to bring them to intuitive presence, and then as fulfillments, to show them synthetically unified with present ones, etc." Husserl, *Analyses*, 626.
63 Husserl, *Experience and Judgement*, 75. On Husserl's appropriation and complete transformation of the sense of the term "association" as used in the tradition of empirical psychology, see Steinbock's introduction to *Analyses*, liv–lv.
64 Husserl, *Cartesian Meditations*, 104. On "immanence" see Zahavi, *Husserl and Transcendental Intersubjectivity*, 29–32.
65 Welton, *The Other Husserl*, 245.
66 See above, the section "The Natural World," in this chapter.
67 Husserl, *Basic Problems of Phenomenology*, 5. The note in square brackets was later added by Husserl to the manuscript, this according to the editor of the Husserliana volume, Iso Kern. See Husserl, *Intersubjektivität I*, 115.
68 V. Y. Mudimbe, *The Invention of Africa* (Bloomington: Indiana University Press, 1988), 186. See Chapter 1 of the present work for my discussion of Mudimbe's notion of *Einfühlung*.
69 Dan Zahavi, "Empathy, Embodiment and Interpersonal Understanding: From Lipps to Schutz," *Inquiry* 53, no. 3 (June 2010): 288.
70 Michael F. Andrews, "Edmund Husserl: Empathy and the Transcendental Constitution of the World," in *Does the World Exist? Plurisignificant Ciphering of Reality*, ed. Anna-Teresa Tymieniecka (Dordrecht: Springer, 2004), 218.
71 Zahavi, "Empathy, Embodiment and Interpersonal Understanding," 288.
72 Zahavi, "Empathy, Embodiment and Interpersonal Understanding," 295.
73 Husserl, *Cartesian Meditations*, 89–157. See, for example, Carr, "The 'Fifth Meditation' and Husserl's Cartesianism," 14–35.
74 Welton, *The Other Husserl*, 115.
75 Husserl, *Experience and Judgement*, 149–94.
76 Husserl, *Cartesian Meditations*, 108–9 [139]. I have modified aspects of the translation as indicated. Cairns's translation is gendered in a way that the

German text is not, specifically his rendering of the term *Mensch*, which I have rendered as "human," "human being," or "person."

77 Heinämaa notes, for example, that the

> Husserlian account of embodiment offers the possibility of conceptualizing the question of sexual identity and sexual difference in a new way. We do not need to restrict ourselves to explaining such identities and differences by empirical realities [...]. More fundamentally, we can understand sexual difference by intentional and temporal concepts as a difference between two different modes or styles of intentionally relating.

See Sara Heinämaa, "Embodiment and Bodily Becoming," in *The Oxford Handbook of the History of Phenomenology*, ed. Dan Zahavi (Oxford: Oxford University Press, 2018), 545.

78 See Chapter 2, "Tactual space, motility, and the lived body."
79 Husserl, *Cartesian Meditations*, 110 [140], translation modified as indicated.
80 See Chapter 2. See, for example, Husserl's discussion in the section, "Laws of the Propagation of Affection," in *Analyses*, 198–206.
81 Dorian Cairns renders this term as "presentation" or "presentiating," while David Carr translates it as "presentification." See Cairns, *Guide for Translating Husserl* (The Hague: Martinus Nijhoff, 1973), 123, and Carr, "The 'Fifth Meditation' and Husserl's Cartesianism," 23. See also note 12 above.
82 Husserl, *Experience and Judgement*, 149–94.
83 Husserl, *Cartesian Meditations*, 110–11 [140], translation altered as indicated by the German terms in brackets, and emphases modified.
84 *Cartesian Meditations*, 111.
85 Alain de Libera, "Analogy," in *Dictionary of Untranslatables: A Philosophical Lexicon*, ed. Barbara Cassin, trans. Emily Apter, Jacques Lezra, and Michael Wood (Princeton, NJ: Princeton University Press, 2014), 31.
86 Burt C. Hopkins, "Parts and Wholes: Foundational Relations," in *The Philosophy of Husserl* (Durham, UK: Acumen, 2011), 105–6.
87 Hopkins, *The Philosophy of Husserl*, 105.
88 See Chapter 2 of the present work, "The spatial phantom and time."
89 Husserl, *Experience and Judgement*, 149.
90 Husserl, *Experience and Judgement*, 150; emphases modified.
91 Husserl, "Syntheses of Homogeneity in the Unity of a Streaming Present," in *Analyses*, 174–79.
92 Husserl, *Analyses*, 177.
93 *Analyses*, 177.
94 Husserl, *Experience and Judgement*, 165 [192], emphasis added.
95 Husserl, *Cartesian Meditations*, 110.
96 Husserl, *Experience and Judgement*, 192–93.
97 See Saulius Geniusas, "On Birth, Death, and Sleep in Husserl's Late Manuscripts on Time," in *On Time: New Contributions to the Husserlian Phenomenology of Time*, ed. Dieter Lohmar and Ichiro Yamaguchi (Dordrecht: Springer, 2010), 71–89.
98 *Experience and Judgement*, 166.
99 *Analyses*, 176–77.
100 Edgar Mittelholzer, *Corentyne Thunder* (Leeds: Peepal Tree, 2009), 201.
101 Simone Schwarz-Bart, *The Bridge of Beyond*, trans. Barbara Bray (New York: New York Review Book, 2013), 25. See the opening paragraph of the Introduction of the present work.
102 Welton, *The Other Husserl*, 237–42.

103 Hans-Georg Gadamer, quoted in Dermot Moran, *Husserl's Crisis of the European Sciences and Transcendental Phenomenology: An Introduction* (Cambridge, UK: Cambridge University Press, 2012), 178.
104 Steinbock, *Home and Beyond*.
105 Husserl, *Crisis*, 103–89; idem, xv, for the expression "great last work" used by Carr.
106 Derrida notes the problem, for instance, that in order "to be able 'to establish' facts as facts *of* history, we must always already know what history is and under what conditions—concrete conditions—it is possible. We must already be engaged in a precomprehension of historicity, i.e., of the invariants of history that language, tradition, community, and so forth are." Jacques Derrida, *Edmund Husserl's Origin of Geometry: An Introduction*, trans. John P. Leavey Jr. (Lincoln: University of Nebraska Press, 1989), 110.
107 Welton, *The Other Husserl*, 339. Steinbock dates the appearance of the term in Husserl's manuscripts to an appendix to *Ideas II* dating from 1916/17 (*Home and Beyond*), 87.
108 Edmund Husserl, *Natur und Geist: Vorlesungen Sommersemester 1919*, Husserliana Materialien 4, ed. Michael Weiler (Dordrecht: Springer, 2002); idem., *Natur und Geist: Vorlesungen Sommersemester 1927*, Husserliana, vol. 32, ed. Michael Weiler (Dordrecht: Springer, 2001).
109 Welton, *The Other Husserl*, 339.
110 Adam Konopka, "The Role of *Umwelt* in Husserl's *Aufbau* and *Abbau* of the *Natur/Geist* Distinction," *Human Studies* 32, no. 3 (September 2009): 313–33. See also the discussion in Hans-Georg Gadamer, "The Extension of the Question of Truth to Understanding in the Human Sciences," in *Truth and Method*, trans. Joel Weinsheimer and Donald G. Marshall (New York: Continuum, 2000), 173–264.
111 In a remarkable passage, Husserl frames the question of "nature" in this way:

> What sense does the in-itself of nature have in relation to the actual and possible intervention of subjects, apart from which nature cannot at all be conceived? What kind of an in-itself is this that is included (and, as idea, is construable) in the idea of the concordance of possible experience—experiencing subjects?
>
> (*Analyses*, 545 [435])

112 Konopka, "Role of *Umwelt*," 315.
113 Konopka, 318.
114 Martin Heidegger, *Being and Time*, trans. John Macquarrie and Edward Robinson (Oxford: Blackwell, 1962), 426.
115 Konopka, 318.
116 Konopka, 321. Here I am working between Gadamer's interpretation of Dilthey's investigation of historical consciousness, and Konopka's study of Dilthey's critical appropriation of the concept of the environing world. See Gadamer, "Extension of the Question of Truth."
117 Konopka, "Role of *Umwelt*," 322. See also Rudolf A. Makkreel, "Husserl, Dilthey, and the Relation of the Life-World to History," in *Husserl and Contemporary Thought*, ed. John Sallis (Atlantic Highlands, NJ: Humanities Press, 1983), 39–58.
118 James G. Hart speaks of "an ever more hegemonic materialistic natural-scientific world view." James G. Hart, "Review of *Grenzprobleme der Phänomenologie*, by Edmund Husserl," *Husserl Studies* 31 (2015): 249.
119 Welton, *The Other Husserl*, 326.
120 *The Other Husserl*, 242.
121 Husserl, *Formal and Transcendental Logic*, 199.

122 *Formal and Transcendental Logic*, 207–8. Edmund Husserl, *Formale und transzendentale Logik: Versuch einer Kritik der logischen Vernunft*, Husserliana, vol. 17, ed. Paul Janssen (The Hague: Martinus Nijhoff, 1974), 215.
123 Steinbock, *Home and Beyond*, 179, my emphasis.
124 Donn Welton, "Intentionality and Language in Husserl's Phenomenology," *Review of Metaphysics* 27, no. 2 (December 1973): 295ff. For a detailed discussion of Husserl philosophy of language focused on his Logical Investigations, see Peer F. Bundgaard, "Husserl and Language," in *Handbook of Phenomenology and Cognitive Science*, eds. S. Gallagher and D. Schmicking (Dordrecht: Springer, 2010), 369–99.
125 The song is noted in Jim Wafer, *The Taste of Blood: Spirit Possession in Brazilian Candomblé* (Philadelphia: University of Pennsylvania Press, 1991), 73. I thank anthropologist Moises Lino e Silva for clarifying the sense of this song in explaining the everyday sense of the expressions *"a bença"* and *"né?"*; my transcription and translation of the song thus differs from that given by Wafer.
126 Heidegger, *Being and Time*, 95–102.
127 Filip Mattens, "From the Origin of Spatiality to a Variety of Spaces," in Zahavi, *Oxford Handbook*, 568.
128 Sara Heniämaa, "Embodiment and Bodily Becoming," 546.
129 Anthony J. Steinbock, *Limit-Phenomena and Phenomenology in Husserl* (London: Rowman & Littlefield, 2017), 27.
130 On Strathern, see my presentation in the Introduction of the present work.
131 Husserl, *Formal and Transcendental Logic*, 22.
132 Edmund Husserl, "The Origin of Geometry," in Maurice Merleau-Ponty, *Husserl at the Limits of Phenomenology*, ed. Leonard Lawlor and Bettina Bergo (Evanston, IL: Northwestern University Press, 2002), 98.
133 Husserl, *Cartesianische Meditationen*, 169: "Nur daß damit freilich noch die oben bezeichneten generativen Probleme von Geburt und Tod und Generationszusammenhang der Animalität nicht berührt sind." Here, I do not follow Cairns's translation. See *Cartesian Meditations*, 142, for comparison.
134 Husserl, *Intersubjektivität I*, *Intersubjektivität II*, and *Intersubjektivität III*.
135 Steinbock, *Limit-Phenomena and Phenomenology in Husserl*, xiii.
136 Steinbock, *Limit-Phenomena*, xiii. Steinbock continues: "So in some sense, generative phenomenology was already present in Husserl [...] in another sense, "generative phenomenology" as such emerged *after* Husserl."
137 See Steinbock, *Home and Beyond*, 280 note 13. The passage in Husserl quoted by Steinbock reads:

> [...] parallel zur menschlichen Generativität die tierische Generativität. Universum der Tiere, die noch psychophysische Analoga von Menschen sind. [Demgegenüber die Pflanzen?] ... Parallele bei allen Tieren, die Analoga der Menschen sind: Leiber haben mit sinnlichen Organen wie der Mensch. Aber wo endet die Analogie? Sind Einzeller nicht auch psychophysisch, haben sie nicht auch ihre Leiber als Organe ihres 'Ich-pols'?

An alternative translation to Steinbock's suggested to me by Maximilian Sternberg reads:

> In parallel with the human generativity the animal generativity. Universe of the animals that are still psychophysical analogies to the human. [Footnote 1: next to this plants?] [...] Parallel with all the animals, that are analogies to humans: that have lived bodies with sensuous organs like the human. But where does the analogy end? Are single-cell organisms

not also psychophysical, do they not also have bodies as organs of their I-poles?

See *III*, 173. For specific treatment of the problem, see Mario Vergani, "Husserl's Hesitant Attempts to Extend Personhood to Animals," *Husserl Studies*, 28 April 2020, https://doi.org/10.1007/s10743-020-09263-w.

138 In rough terms, we can say that "Part 1: From Consciousness to World" functions as a *critical* preparatory introduction, tracing Husserl's thematic and methodological concerns with intersubjectivity in terms of the concretion of "monadic" subjectivity, whereas "Part 2: Normality, Abnormality, and Normative Territories: Toward a Generative Phenomenology" shifts the register to a positive development of his treatment of generative problems. This transition occurs in the last chapter of part 1, in the section titled "The Lifeworld as Territory"; Steinbock, *Home and Beyond*, 102–22. The scope of the present work does not allow me to engage with the spatial implications of Steinbock's rich phenomenological concepts of "terrain" and "territory."

139 Steinbock, *Home and Beyond*, 287 note 16. The manuscript was published as Edmund Husserl, "Grundlegende Untersuchungen zum phänomenologischen Ursprung der Räumlichkeit der Natur," in *Philosophical Essays in Memory of Edmund Husserl*, ed. Marvin Farber (Cambridge, MA: Harvard University Press, 1940), 307–25 (hereafter cited as "Grundlegende Untersuchungen"). The English translation by Fred Kersten was published in Peter McCormick and Frederick Elliston, eds., *Husserl: Shorter Works* (Notre Dame: Indiana University Press, 1981), 222–23. Hereafter cited as *Shorter Works*, followed by the page number of the English translation and, where indicated, corresponding pagination of the German text in brackets. The translation was revised by Leonard Lawlor as Edmund Husserl, "Foundational Investigations of the Phenomenological Origin of the Spatiality of Nature: The Originary Ark, the Earth, Does Not Move," in Merleau-Ponty, *Husserl at the Limits of Phenomenology*, 117–31. Hereafter cited as "Foundational Investigations" followed by the page number of the English translation and, where indicated, corresponding pagination of the German text in brackets.

140 Fred Kersten, "Introduction," in McCormick and Elliston, *Shorter Works*, 214. Husserl's fragment "Notizen zur Raumkonstitution" was edited posthumously by Alfred Schutz and published as Edmund Husserl, "Notizen zur Raumkonstitution," *Philosophy and Phenomenological Research* 1, no. 1 (September 1940): 21–7, 217–26.

141 Kersten, "Introduction," 215.

142 As Kersten notes, "Space was not only an important philosophical problem in its own right [...] but its phenomenological investigation was paradigmatic" ("Introduction," 214).

143 Husserl, *Shorter Works*, 222 [307], translation modified.

144 Cairns, *Guide for Translating Husserl*, 115.

145 *Shorter Works*, 222 [307]. I am drawing here on both Kersten's translation and Lawlor's revision, with reference to the original German text. For the Lawlor revisions see, Husserl, "Foundational Investigations," 117–18 [307].

146 Husserl, "Foundational Investigations," 118 [308].

147 See David Carr, "Husserl's *Crisis* and the Problem of History," *Southwestern Journal of Philosophy* 5, no. 3 (Fall 1974): 139.

148 *Shorter Works*, 228 [319], translation modified. See also Husserl, "Foundational Investigations," 126 [319].

149 Steinbock, *Home and Beyond*, 109–22.

150 Merleau-Ponty, *Husserl at the Limits of Phenomenology*, 67–68. See also the discussion in Henriette Steiner, "The Earth Does Not Move and the Ground of the City," *Journal of Comparative Cultural Studies in Architecture* (June 2012): 46–55.

151 *Shorter Works*, 228 [319].
152 *Shorter Works*, 226.
153 Edmund Husserl, *Die Krisis der Europäischen Wissenschaften und die Transzendentale Phänomenologie: Ergänzungsband Texte aus dem Nachlass 1934–1937*, Husserliana, vol. 29 (Dordrecht: Kluwer, 1993), 333–34 (hereafter cited as *Krisis*):

> Ich werde von den Menschen aus zurückgeführt auf den phylogenetischen universalen Prozeß der Lebewesen und ihrer Umweltlichkeiten, als eine universale Geschichtlichkeit [...] Es ist eine Geschichtlichkeit der Leiblichkeiten, der biologischen Entwicklungen, immerfort zwischen Geburt und Tod verlaufend, in einer Generativität, die fortläuft, während die Individuen sterben, während auch Tierarten geboren werden und sterben, neue erwachsen usw.

154 On the supplementary volume to the *Crisis*, published as Husserliana, vol. 29, see Anthony J. Steinbock, "The New 'Crisis' Contribution: A Supplementary Edition of Edmund Husserl's 'Crisis' Texts," *Review of Metaphysics* 47, no. 3 (March 1994): 557–84.
155 Cairns, *Guide for Translating Husserl*, 115.
156 My rendering of *Umweltlichkeit* as "environmentality" is a literal translation in English of Husserl's formation of the adjective *umweltlich* (environmental) into an abstract noun by adding the suffix "-keit." As in English, the German noun *Umwelt* (environment) and adjective *umweltlich* are common terms, but in forming the noun *Umweltlichkeit* Husserl is indicating a meaning that is philosophically technical and conceptual in intent. My use of the term "environmentality" is thus distinct from its established usage by Arun Agrawal, for whom the term is conceptually derived from Foucault's notion of "governmentality." See Arun Agrawal, *Environmentality: Technologies of Government and the Making of Subjects* (Durham, NC: Duke University Press, 2005). Heidegger also uses the term *Umweltlichkeit*, which Macquarrie and Robinson translate as "environmentality," but he uses the term in a purely spatio-practical sense in elaborating his doctrine of "readiness-to-hand" (*Zuhandenheit*). See Heidegger, *Being and Time*, 200; idem., *Sein und Zeit* (Tübingen: Max Niemeyer Verlag, 2006), 158.
157 See Husserl, *Krisis*, 70: "Die Lebensumwelt, die Welt der Erfahrung, der intersubjektiv verbundenen [...] in ihrer Raum-Zeitlichkeit." (The living environment, the world of experience, of the intersubjectively connected [...] in their spatio-temporality.); and idem., 88: "Auch mein eingeborener Charakter, stammt er nicht aus dem generativen Zusammenhang [...] die Horizonte sind keine offenen Möglichkeiten, welche die Phantasie füllen könnte, sondern Horizonte als Formen für apodiktische Vorzeichnungen." (Also my innate character, does it not stem from a generative connection [...] the horizons are not open possibilities which phantasy could fill, but horizons as forms traced out in advance for apodictic preliminary sketches.) Shaun Gallagher's presentation of the "lived body-environment" relation he develops from his reading of Merleau-Ponty is relevant to my discussion, however, the concept of *environmentality* in Husserl that I am foregrounding addresses problems of temporality beyond the environmental situation of the individual subject as lived body; it extends to problems of intersubjective, intergenerational, and historical situation. See Shaun Gallagher, "Lived Body and Environment," in *Research in Phenomenology*, Vol. 16 (1986), 139–70.
158 *Intersubjektivität III*, 604: "das Vor-Ich [...] hat doch in seiner Weise schon Welt, in der Vor-Weise, seine inaktuelle Welt [...]." Husserl's use of the German *"inaktuelle"* suggests that the foetal subject's world as a spatial horizon is not experienceable by others, except perhaps through the haptic, etc.

experience of the mother. Cairns offers various options for rendering *"aktuell"* including "in present experience." See Cairns, *Guide for Translating Husserl*, 5. Merleau-Ponty also comments on the embryonic stage:

> In between the microscopic facts, global reality is delineated like a watermark, never graspable for objectivizing-particular thinking [...] we had only a bit of a protoplasmic jelly, and then we have an embryo, by a transformation which [...] we were never witness to in our investment in a biological field.

See Maurice Merleau-Ponty, *Nature: Course Notes from the Collège de France*, ed. Dominique Séglard, trans. Robert Vallier (Evanston, IL: Northwestern University Press, 2003), 207.
159 Sara Heinämaa, *Toward a Phenomenology of Sexual Difference: Husserl, Merleau-Ponty, Beauvoir* (Lanham, MD: Rowman & Littlefield, 2003), 109–14.
160 Heinämaa, *Toward a Phenomenology of Sexual Difference*, 110–11.
161 Heinämaa, *Phenomenology of Sexual Difference*, 131.
162 *Phenomenology of Sexual Difference*, 131.
163 Steinbock, *Limit-Phenomena*, 30.
164 *Intersubjektivität III*, 606:

> Das Kind äussert unwillkürlich Laute in unwillkürlicher Kinästhese [...] Zu seinen Lauten gehören vermögliche Kinästhesen. Aber die Mutter äussert ihrerseits ähnliche Laute, zunächst Nachahmungen der kindlichen [...] Das Kind wiederholt selbst—die Mutter ebenso—, welche Rolle könnte das spielen?

Cairns renders *"vermöglich"* as "lying within one's ability (*or* power)." See Cairns, *Guide for Translating Husserl*, 125.
165 Toni Morrison, *Beloved* (New York: Vintage, 2004), xvi–xvii. This includes the practice of *partus sequitur ventrem* in which the child "inherits" the mother's legal status as "slave." I thank Gerard Aching, who investigates the profound, dehumanizing implications of this legal practice, for sharing his recent work on the Underground Railroad in conversations with me.
166 Orlando Patterson, *Slavery and Social Death: A Comparative Study* (Cambridge, MA: Harvard University Press, 2018), 5. To this, Luis Nicoulau Parés adds a process of "depersonalization." See Luis Nicolau Parés, *The Formation of Candomblé: Vodun History and Ritual in Brazil*, trans. Richard Vernon (Chapel Hill: University of North Carolina Press, 2013), 47. For an overview of the concept and sources see Perry Zurn, "Social Death," in *50 Concepts for a Critical Phenomenology*, ed. Gail Weiss, et al. (Evanston, IL: Northwestern University Press, 2020), 309–14.
167 Patterson, *Slavery and Social Death*, 5.
168 Derek Walcott, *Omeros* (London: Faber and Faber, 1990), 127. Excerpts from *Omeros* by Derek Walcott. Copyright © 1990 by Derek Walcott. Reprinted by permission of Farrar, Straus, and Giroux. All Rights Reserved. This and the following excerpt from *Omeros* by Derek Walcott reproduced with the permission of Faber and Faber Ltd., and Farrar, Straus, and Giroux.
169 Walcott, *Omeros*, 130.
170 *Omeros*, 134.
171 Derek Walcott, *Selected Poems*, ed. Edward Baugh (London: Faber and Faber, 2007), 123.
172 Sylvia Wynter, "Beyond the Word of Man: Glissant and the New Discourse of the Antilles," *World Literature Today* 63, no. 4 (Autumn 1989): 643. On the figure of the "fibril" see Édward Glissant, *Poetics of Relation*, trans. Betsy

Wing (Ann Arbor: University of Michigan Press, 2010), 5. I thank Natalie Melas for enriching conversations on Walcott and Glissant, as well as Schwarz-Bart, Aimé Césaire, and other Caribbean writers. On Glissant and Walcott see Natalie Melas, *All the Difference in the World: Postcoloniality and the Ends of Comparison* (Stanford, CA: Stanford University Press, 2007), 103–69.

173 Husserl speaks of "die Vorgegebenheit und Gegebenheit der Welt in *Stufen der Umweltlichkeit*" (the givenness beforehand and the givenness [in the present] of the world in *levels of environmentality*.) *Intersubjektivität III*, 218.

174 *Intersubjektivität III*, 176 note 1.

175 My reference here is to the *caboclo* ritual; see earlier sections of this chapter.

176 Iris M. Young, "Pregnant Subjectivity and the Limits of Existential Phenomenology," in *Descriptions*, ed. Don Ihde and Hugh J. Silverman (Albany: SUNY Press, 1985), 32–33.

177 Heinämaa, *Phenomenology of Sexual Difference*, 112. See also Jonna Bornemark and Nicholas Smith, eds., *Phenomenology of Pregnancy* (Huddinge: Södertörn University Press, 2016).

178 See above, note 164.

179 I am drawing on Merleau-Ponty's interpretation of Husserl's fragment, "The Origin of Geometry," in which he elaborates on the structure of "institution" [*Stiftung*] in Husserl's work as *Urstiftung—Nachstiftung—Endstiftung* ("primal institution"—"reinstitution"—"final institution"). See Merleau-Ponty, *Husserl at the Limits of Phenomenology*, 17–19. See my discussion of Merleau-Ponty's readings of Husserl's fragments in Tao Sule-DuFour, "The Sense of Architecture in Husserlian Phenomenology: The Example of a Candomblé-Caboclo Ritual of Tupinikim," (PhD diss., University of Cambridge, 2012), 53–89.

180 Edmund Husserl, "The World of the Living Present and the Constitution of the Surrounding World That Is Outside the Flesh," in *Husserl at the Limits of Phenomenology*, 142.

181 See this chapter, the section "The genesis of space," above.

182 See "Empathic spatiality," above.

183 *Shorter Works*, 226.

184 *Shorter Works*, 228 [319].

185 See my presentation in Chapter 2 of the present work, "The spatial phantom and time."

186 Implied here is also the sense of the *spectrality* of the living present. See Jacques Derrida, *Specters of Marx: The State of the Debt, the Work of Mourning, and the New International*, trans. Peggy Kamuf (New York: Routledge, 1994), xvii–xx, and the discussion in Janet Donohoe, "The Nonpresence of the Living Present," *Southern Journal of Philosophy* 38 (2000): 221–30.

187 *Shorter Works*, 227, emphasis added.

188 Steinbock, *Home and Beyond*, see specifically "Part 2: Normality, Abnormality, and Normative Territories: Toward a Generative Phenomenology," 123–270. See also Steinbock, "From Immortality to Natality in Phenomenology: The Liminal Character of Birth and Death," in *Limit-Phenomena*, 21–35. Although I have foregrounded the question of birth, this is not separate, as Steinbock shows, from that of ageing and death. For phenomenological perspectives on ageing see, for example, the contributions of Michael Bavidge and David Carr in Geoffrey Scarre, ed., *The Palgrave Handbook of the Philosophy of Aging* (London: Palgrave Macmillan, 2016). An extraordinary work on generative themes is Matthias Fritsch, *Taking Turns with the Earth: Phenomenology, Deconstruction, and Intergenerational Justice* (Stanford, CA: Stanford University Press, 2018).

4 A phenomenological ethnography of space

In this chapter, we encounter our hosts—the *mãe-de-santo* and her household—in the concreteness of the spatiality of the event of the ritual. This calls for a shift in the approach to spatial description, from one that weaves between analyses of Husserl's phenomenology of space and examples of spatial experience drawn from moments of the Candomblé ritual—which I have referred to in its Portuguese expression as a *reunião* (a "gathering")[1]—to a style that aims at the experienced event itself. In my references thus far to moments of the ritual or *reunião*, I have described certain situations—the candles' flickering flames or the rustling of the ceiling—as if I am presently in the room, and the reader is there with me, pointing at times to photographic images in order to bring us closer to things. In writing, I turn towards past sense perceptual experiences in recollection.[2] Memory is also implicated in the perceptual encounter in the living now—for example, the white substance I "now" see on the table, I had just seen on the floor at the gate[3]—and I describe this as if the reader is there with me, both in the remembering and the sense perceptual experiencing in what was then the living, perceptually unfolding present. Guided by the written description, we tarry with the photographic image, stretching it out as if it were the living moment itself. The written description as taken up in the process of reading is a mode of experiencing through acts of imagination, related to my memorial aiming at a once perceptual present. To properly flesh out this tangled skein of relations, problems of experience pertaining to imagination, phantasy, and what Husserl terms "picture-" or "image-consciousness" (*Bildbewusstsein*) would have to be considered. An in-depth investigation of these phenomenological themes is beyond the scope of this book; an outline of the issues, however, would assist in clarifying the stylistic transition I make in this chapter to a spatial ethnography that is related to phenomenological description in the manner of an example.

Husserl's analyses of imagination, phantasy, and what he identifies as the peculiar manner in which images are experienced were published posthumously as volume 23 of the Husserliana series, translated as *Phantasy, Image Consciousness, and Memory (1898–1925)*.[4] The volume brings

DOI: 10.4324/9781351116145-5

together Husserl's lecture notes and unpublished research manuscripts on these themes so that, rather than a polished work intended for publication, it presents Husserl at work engaged in phenomenological analyses. Julia Jansen takes up the question of imagination in Husserl's thought, foregrounding his attention to the experiential act of imagining, and thus to the imagined object as being given in its own peculiar way. Jansen notes that it is important to attend to:

> the distinct awareness of objects that is characteristic of imagining, to the various modes in which imagined objects manifest themselves to us, and to what kinds of operations and achievements this awareness and these distinct objects enable us to perform.[5]

In phenomenological description, what is aimed at is not that which is imagined as such, an imagined object, but through the latter as an *example* the way in which the imagined as a class of phenomena is constituted or given in the experience of imagining. This is also the case for the perceived, the remembered, and so forth, that is, phenomenological descriptions are aimed at structures *through* the examples. For instance, the example of a moment of the *reunião*—such as the givenness in the visual field of the figurine resting on the white spread of cloth amidst environing things—is used to ask the reader to imagine a sense perceptual experience through the image I offer descriptively in writing and in reference to photographs. I use the image—literary and photographic—to direct the reader's imagining towards perception; not the things perceived, but the structure of perceptual experience in its role in the constitution of space: lived bodily kinaestheses, perspectivity, positionality, the horizonality of the givenness of things, and so forth.[6] I have not explored problems of imagination or phantasy in the strict sense, in terms of the "*protean*" and "*optional*" character of imagining, which is marked by a certain freedom from the constitutional constraints of perceptual or memorial givenness determined by the affectivity of space and things.[7] Through the examples drawn from moments of the *reunião*, I have attempted to ground the reader's imagining in the perceptual and memorial situation of the lived experience of the spatiality of the event.

The sense in which the reader has been with me imaginatively, "as if" we are together in the space of the *reunião* in the living present, is not, therefore, one purely of the free play of phantasy. As I am constrained by memory, which is grounded by its reference to the actuality of my past perceptual experience of the event, so too the reader's imagination is weighted by my descriptions. But this is only the case for the descriptions of the examples drawn from the *reunião*, which may be put out of play once they have successfully helped in clarifying the phenomenologically structural or "static" description. But the example was also used as a kind of guiding thread, leading to problems of increasing "genetic" and "generative" complexity: from mere phantom spatiality, to problems of spatial affectivity and the genesis, accrual, and sedimentation of sense; to being in communion with others and thus the empathic, intersubjective quality of space; to problems of intergenerationality and thus the generativity and geo-historicity of space experienced in levels of environmentality.[8] In relation to this—the increasing thematic concreteness of the phenomenological enquiry into space—the *reunião* still serves as an "example." But because the problem of the description of spatiality extends to incorporate these themes as outlined, the example takes root due to its *specific* generative and historical situation; a situation in relation to which I myself as the researcher am implicated, including *my* historical situation inherent to my lived bodily corporeity and spatiality. In this way, we are not merely dealing with a methodological use of the example of the *reunião* as if it could be any example; rather, the *reunião* is implicated in the possibility of deepening phenomenological description as itself a *situated* practice.[9]

Phenomenological description is concerned with the modes of givenness of the things themselves, which imply the experiencing subject to and for whom things appear. In the previous two chapters I have teased out the intricacies and complexity of this relationship, including reference to the manner in which the historicity I myself habitually bear is implicated in the experiential givenness of the spatiality of the *reunião* in intersubjective community. In the following, the phenomenological description of the example takes on the quality of ethnography. As I have noted, it aims to ground the reader's imagination in the actuality of the event, as if she were herself there, with me in person. My description is primarily textual, but also includes photographs. The writing and the photographs work together, figuring the *reunião* in "images."

In discussing Husserl's analyses of what he terms "image-consciousness," Javier Carreño points out the problem of grasping "the unique way in which an image refers me to an object."[10] Husserl speaks of "images" in the strict sense that implies sense perceptual apprehension, for example, the reproduced photographs of moments of the *reunião*. My textual description is not an image in this sense, but it can be understood in an analogous way, in that it points the reader's imagination to a perceptual situation that is *absent*. The photograph, unlike the text, has the peculiar feature of doing this through its actual perceptual givenness. The photographic image does not lie alongside the experienced situation, nor does it indicate it in the manner of a sign; rather, it gives the lived moment itself *in image*. As John Brough notes,

> it is this element of seeing the subject *in* the image that distinguishes image consciousness from signifying or symbolizing consciousness, the sort of consciousness at work when I understand a highway sign or a symbol in an airport.[11]

In an analogous way, the written description gives the lived experience of the event in the living present in the "literary image." Insofar as we have

(I describe) the event textually and with photographs, we precisely are not given the *reunião* itself originarily, in person in perception. Rather, the perceptual encounter in the full concreteness of spatiality must be, in a certain qualified sense, "imagined." Imagination is here implicated in an intricate and dependent way, involving the modes of self-disclosure of the *reunião* itself in relation to my perceptual experience in person and then in recollection, the givenness of moments of the event photographically *in image*, and the event's givenness through literary "images." The reader is carried along towards the living present of perceptual encounter imaginatively, not in free phantasy but grounded by the manners in which the *reunião* presences itself in levels of mediated givenness. The reader's experience in imagination is thus guided towards "reproduction" or "re-presentation"—what Husserl terms "presentification" (*Vergegenwärtigung*)[12]—of the living present *as if* a perceptual encounter; thus, as Jansen notes, in imagination constrained in this way,

> we imagine not an image, neither merely the imagined object, but we also, often tacitly, quasi-experience *seeing*, *smelling*, *tasting*, and/or *touching* it. An imagined object or scene is, in other words, imagined "*as if*" *being seen, heard, smelled, tasted*, and/or *touched*. It is thus not the viewing of mental images that characterizes imagining, but the *simulation* of possible experiences of thus imagined objects.[13]

In the following, I develop a phenomenological description of the spatiality of the *reunião* in its intersubjective concreteness. Through the written description and photographs the reader is invited to re-present the event imaginatively, *as if* there in person in the perceptual concreteness and environmentality (*Umweltlichkeit* as discussed in Chapter 3) of its spatiality. In this way, phenomenological description acquires generative density ("generativity" as presented in Chapter 3), taking on an ethnographic style and texture that I term a phenomenological ethnography of space.

Before we enter directly into the space, I introduce the contours of the Afro-Brazilian religion of Candomblé again, to remind and re-familiarise the reader with the topic of the *reunião*.

*

Brazilian anthropologist Marcio Goldman offers a concise description of Candomblé as follows:

> Candomblé is one of the many Brazilian religions that display elements of African origins. Probably formed from the nineteenth century onwards, Candomblé—at least as we know it today—also embodies, to different degrees, elements of Native American practices and cosmologies, as well as that of popular Catholicism and European Spiritism. In addition, it is possible to observe more or less marked differences

among various cult groups, depending on the African regions from which came the larger part of its repertoire, and on the modalities and intensities of its "syncretic" connections with other religious traditions.

Roughly speaking, followers of Candomblé tend to classify their *terreiros* (temples or cult houses) into three great *nations* [...] derived in theory from the different African origins of their founders. Thus, the Ketu nation originated from the Yoruba of Nigeria and Benin; the Jeje from the Fon of Benin; and the Angola nation from the Bantu of Angola and Congo.[14]

In the unfolding of my descriptions of the spatiality of the ritual thus far, I have referred to a class of entities called *caboclos*; they would correspond to what Goldman characterizes above as "elements of Native American practices and cosmologies" within Candomblé praxis. Jim Wafer describes the presence of *caboclos* in the structure of Candomblé using the motifs of the "carnivalesque" or "heteroglot," after literary theorist Mikhail Bakhtin.[15] Following Wafer, this understanding of the presence of *caboclos* in Candomblé suggests a certain dialogical openness and permeability, which would seem to run counter to the idea of "nation," in the sense indicated by Goldman above. This notion—of "nation"—in the particular manner used in Candomblé can be traced, according to Luis Nicolau Parés, to the conditions that characterized the transatlantic slave trade in the seventeenth and eighteenth centuries in which "*nation* was used at that time by slave traders, missionaries, and administrative officials from the European factories along the Mina Coast to designate diverse autochthonous populations."[16] As discussed in Chapter 1, the historical sense of the term reflects a tension between "internal" (*ethnonym*) and "external" (*meta-ethnic*) denominations.[17] Wafer's Bakhtinian notion of *caboclo* "heteroglossia" thus suggests a certain multivalence characteristic of *caboclos* that would make them "transnational." Jocélio Teles dos Santos, drawing on the work of Antonio Geraldo da Cunha, traces the expression *caboclo* to the late eighteenth century, signifying rural persons of indigenous and white racial mixture from the *sertão*—a hinterland region in the Brazilian Northeast—"of sunburned skin."[18] The mid-nineteenth-century term acquired the everyday sense, still resonant today, of a rustic person of the hinterland.[19] The word takes on a more specific sense in the context of Candomblé, which Wafer describes as an "entity belonging to a class that includes primarily spirits of Indians and cowboys, but also spirits of royal personages, Brazilian folk heroes, sailors, mermaids, etc."[20] In light of the associations with ideas of indigeneity, the *caboclo* is described as the "*dono da terra*," the "ruler or owner of the earth": "Caboclos are owners of the earth, of the forests. They are the first inhabitants of the land."[21] The *candomblé* Centro do Caboclo Tupiniquim—where my field work was conducted and whose ritual practice is the focus of my description—is thus the religious house or *terreiro* dedicated to the "Indian spirit" called Tupiniquim. This specific *candomblé* of Tupiniquim is also a Candomblé Angola, that is, a *terreiro* classified according to its Congo-Angola significance, as per Goldman's description above. The name "Tupiniquim" is itself one among a number of typical *caboclo* names, which Wafer describes as "the name of an Indian tribe, also colloquially used to mean 'Brazilian.'"[22] Regarding Candomblé in general, Goldman speaks of the "existence of deities (*orishas*, *voduns*, or *inkices*) that possess previously prepared followers during specific ceremonies."[23] The *inkices* is the name given to the deities of the Angola "nation" in particular, although throughout all Candomblés one finds major *orixás* (or *orishas*). The Yorùbá *orixás* are encountered as having a certain priority in Candomblé.[24] In light of this, more detailed comments are appropriate. I should note, however, that the *caboclo reunião* is an event in which the *orixás* do not participate "in person," that is, they do not "manifest." Their "presence," however, is still an issue that appears as a theme in my description, insofar as certain objects and articulations of the room indicate their significance.

The term *orixá* is derived from the Yorùbá word, *òrìṣà*.[25] The noun *orí* is Yorùbá for "head," through which one finds verb-compounds, such as *borí*, a word used in Candomblé meaning, literally, "to feed the head" (in Portuguese, *dar de comer à cabeça*).[26] The *borí* is one of the rites of initiation in Candomblé, the goal of which is to "fix" (*fixar*) the *orixá* in the head of the initiate, and thus to "make the saint" (*fazer o santo*). The term "saint," used to refer to the *orixás*, and reflected in noun-compounds such as mother-of-saint or *mãe-de-santo*, points to the complex historical phenomenon of syncretism and problems of its interpretation.[27] Certain *orixás* are identified/associated with certain Catholic saints, and the word saint in Candomblé generally indicates *orixás*. As Goldman has suggested, what an *orixá is* is perhaps best thought of in terms of action, that is, a process of becoming.[28] In this regard, by describing the process of its being "made" through rites of initiation, ethnographic description qualifies the name *orixá* in concrete terms.

The initiate is called in Portuguese a *filha-de-santo* (daughter-of-saint) or *filho-de-santo* (son-of-saint). The head of a *terreiro* is called the *mãe-de-santo* (mother-of-saint) or, if a male head, *pai-de-santo* (father-of-saint). As discussed in Chapter 1, heads of *candomblés* are in the majority women, although the evidence suggests that this was not historically the case. This shift in the gender composition of Candomblé leadership, according to Parés, corresponded to the post-abolition period (after 1888) in which "the era of terreiros [...] led largely by African men, had ended, and the epoch of candomblés led largely by Creole women had begun."[29] On the process of initiation, Bastide provides the following description:

> Fixing the *orixá* in the head of the *filha* happens slowly, step by step, from entering the sanctuary until the dark plunge which she makes in the end. The progressive character of these steps shows itself by a set of symbols: her hairs are first cut with scissors, after shaven; her head is moistened with the blood of two-legged animals, after four-legged; her body is first tattooed, after opening incisions, etc. During all of

these steps, the candidate lives in a small room [...] under the care of a priestess, "the *mãe-pequena*." She [the candidate] cannot speak to visitors from the candomblé, she can only communicate with them by beating one of her hands against the other, or a gesture called *paó*.[30]

On the state of hebetude experienced by the initiate, and the phenomenon of "possession" that ensues, Pierre Verger states:

> In the eyes of the believer, the crisis of possession represents the action of the spirit on the body which serves at that moment there as the temporary receptacle. He ceases to be himself [...] he is the god in flesh and bone...[31]

The above descriptions by Bastide and Verger point to the sense in which the *orixá* is corporeally *made*, present in "flesh and bone" in the living bodies of the *filhas-* and *filhos-de-santo*. The initiation process of making the saint involves responsibility on the part of the initiate towards a number of "objects": beads, stones, clothing, food, and so forth. Fundamental to all of this is *axé*, which is perhaps best qualified in the negative: "There cannot be candomblé without *axé*."[32] Quoting a proverb, Bastide simply states that "the blood is the *axé* of all that breathes."[33] Rather than offer definitions, I refer to these ethnographic fragments in order to highlight the sense in which the ontological question of the being of the *orixás* is fundamentally tied to their corporeal appearance: in "things," flesh, and blood.[34] As mentioned, the *orixás* do not manifest "in person" in the *caboclo reunião*; the *reunião* is precisely for the *caboclos*. This does not, however, rule out the possibility of the appearance "in the flesh" of an *orixá* "in" her *filha*, which I witnessed and include in my description, but this is anomalous. What we do find in the room where the *reunião* takes place, called the *barracão*, are "things" that "indicate" various *orixás*. A clarification of the mode of givenness of these things in the intersubjective constitution of the spatiality of the *reunião* will have to come from the unfolding of the event itself. The reader, however, would be helped along by having a preliminary sketch of the room in advance, which I draft in the following section. Here, in describing the room, I allude to the association of objects with the following names of *orixás*: Exu, Oxalá, Oxóssi, Xangô, Oxum, Ogum, Ossâim, and Omolu. This description, however, is preparatory, anticipating a style of phenomenological description aimed at the concreteness of the event of the *reunião* in its performance that follows.

As noted in Chapter 1, Santos offers a description of a *caboclo* "sessão," or "session."[35] The *sessão*, like the *reunião*, is different in scale and structure from the grand public *festas* or festivals for the *orixás*, which have been the topic of many ethnographies.[36] Similar public festivals are also held for *caboclos*.[37] Santos notes that aspects of the more intimate *sessão* suggest the influence of European Spiritism. However, the manifest presence of *caboclos* and *orixá* implements is abhorred in the context of Spiritism, so that its influence is ambiguous.[38]

*

The Centro do Caboclo Tupiniquim is headed by a *mãe-de-santo* called Mãe Juta. Mãe Juta's daughter, Gilmara, who is also a *filha-de-santo*, would at times sit with me and explain things during the event, and I will intermittently refer to her. With regard to documentation, I was permitted to photograph the *reunião* until the "manifestation" of Tupiniquim. When Mãe Juta "manifests" Tupiniquim, he is said to have "*chegou*" ("arrived"). With these reintroductory comments in mind, let us enter the *reunião*.

*

The *reunião* takes place for the most part every Thursday.[39] Each event is of course unique in its actual enactment, but there appears to be a definite structure that gives the ritual its typical character. It is this typicality that I will attempt to describe, by drawing on various happenings at specific meetings that I was present at as examples.

Certain preparatory activities take place, on the same day, before the ritual begins. I was able to witness one Thursday some of these activities, and to help with one of them. Close to the house is an area of growth called the *mato*. Mato is a Portuguese word meaning bush or shrubbery, as in a thicket. In Candomblé the term takes on particular significance.[40] For the moment, we will stick to its naïve everyday meaning, and consider it as merely referring to an area of bushes from where leaves of a specific kind were taken. In terms of our particular spatial concern, we see that the *mato* has a certain immediate topographical value precisely because it has a *practical* significance: it serves as the source of certain leaves.[41] The leaves themselves would in turn articulate a spatial topography of the ritual in a very direct way. To describe this vividly, we need to first have a general picture of the house and to locate the site of the main room in which the *reunião* takes place.

The house is located in a *bairro*, or district, of Salvador some distance away from the coastal areas of the city, several kilometres inland to the east of the historic centre. The general sense of scale of the area is roughly that of two- to three-storey dwellings, relatively compact as an urban fabric, but reflecting neither the density nor the absence of infrastructure of a favela. The house sits off a short street that connects to a major road. Not far from the house and along the main road is an open area of growth sloping downwards towards a river; this is, for the purposes of the *reunião*, the *mato*. The house itself does not stand out from the fabric of which it is a part. Viewed from the street, it has three visible storeys, with a fourth level not visible to the rear. Immediately in front and rooted at the pavement is a grand and lush tree, extending almost twice the height of the house and branching out beyond its width at the top. The front wall (west facing) is punctured by four large rectilinear openings above the ground floor, each shallowly arched at the top. On the first floor, the rectilinear "punctures" are clearly two windows; on the floor above they are more like mere "openings," two vast holes in the wall that invite the wind. From the street, it is possible to see quite clearly the ceiling of the room in which the *reunião* takes place through these openings: it appears as a sky of white, fluttering paper leaves. Extended from the north wall and set back significantly from the line of the front wall is a covered porch. From the street, a staircase ascending towards it at the first floor is visible. It is defined by a white wall, broken by a middle band consisting of a white iron grille that wraps around the volume of the protruding porch. At the level above is a high railing of similar ironwork extending from the wall, suggesting an upper floor that is open to the sky. At the edge of this railing where it turns the corner is attached a wooden flagpole carrying a white flag. This is a general background picture of the house. I will focus on a detail significant for entering the *reunião*, literally, the front gate of the house.

The *reunião* takes place at night, starting more or less between seven and eight o'clock in the evening, when it is already dark. The entrance to the house from the street is offset from the north wall of the house. It is a white rectangular portal and has the appearance of a free-standing figure. Atop the lintel and visible from the street is a small clay vase. The dark timber gate is set against the backdrop of white structure; the floor is tiled with yellowish, patterned clay tiles. During the *reunião* at the foot of the door is placed a hand-full size of soft, solid, white substance on an unwrapped section of a palm leaf. At the other end, just beyond the arc of the door-swing, is a lit white candle on the ground, illuminating to the left of it another white substance in an unwrapped palm leaf (Figure 3.3). Just beyond is a tap protruding from the wall close to the ground, and to its left, a small clay vase similar to the one on the lintel of the archway. Just further beyond, on the ground, is a shallow earthen bowl filled with popcorn and bits of grated coconut. This is a picture of the entrance from the street. I observed the activities that anticipate this image in their unfolding from the main room of the *reunião* towards this entrance, in terms of "preparation." The following description will focus on this anticipatory preparation.

The preparatory activities that would ultimately terminate at the entrance to the house from the street refer us to their beginning in the room of the *reunião* proper (Figure 4.1). Here, I take up where we left off with the leaves from the *mato*. I said that the leaves articulate a topography: they are scattered, spread out on the floor of the ritual room or *barracão*. The room proper in which the *reunião* happens is on the second floor, the ceiling of which we saw earlier from the street through the arched, rectilinear openings in the wall. The leaves from the *mato* are initially encountered—within the horizon of the event—as scattered about the floor; they will be encountered again in more intimate ways. The room is not always articulated in

A phenomenological ethnography of space 177

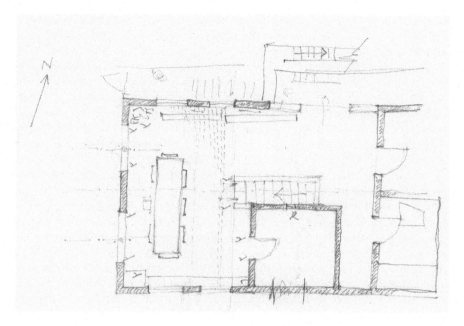

Figure 4.1 Plan of the room where the *reunião* takes place. Sketch by the author.

the way I am describing. Rather, my description is circumscribed by the horizon of the *reunião* in its performance. We are trying to enter into this horizon precisely through its beginning, but this start lies within vague edges of preparatory activities. These activities involve the following "things": (1) the leaves of the *mato*; (2) the white substance we saw at the entrance from the street, white candles, white spirits or *cachaça* (a distilled spirit) and water; (3) white clothing; (4) the setting of the table; and (5) incense. As we will see, the table is the "object-pole," the central *topos* towards which all the preparation is oriented and around which the *reunião* is performed. Furthermore, the division reflected in the numbering above is merely for the sake of convenience for my description; everything is interrelated. This total interweaving is exemplified at the site of the set table.

(1) We arrive into the ritual room via a staircase planted in the centre of the house, from the first floor. The first floor itself displays the house in the fullness of domesticity, and the staircase sits in a type of foyer, unfurnished at the stair and becoming a living room at its west (street) end. The axis of the stair is east–west. Ascending the stair, one's first view of the ritual room is towards the ceiling, into a sea of fluttering paper whiteness, or, more aptly, a "sky": the *orixá* "Oxalá" (Figures 2.8 and 2.10). The inverted commas here indicate an ambiguity regarding the relation between the object—white paper ceiling—the name Oxalá, and the entity so named; they point to a need for *clarification*, either in terms of the actual presence

or "descent" of the *orixá*—the *orixás* are said to "descend" (*descer*) in the heads of their *filhas-de-santo*—or the actual utterance of the name in some defining situation.[42] The ceiling delimits the room in part, and in terms of arrival is the first articulation of the pre-eminence of this room in relation to the house as a whole. It is made of innumerous strips of white paper, suspended from thin wires running the width of the room (north–south) and extending from the inner face of the west (street) wall to just before the final step onto the floor of the room proper. Beyond this edge, we simply find the underside of the clay shingled roof, which, in its contrast with the paper's whiteness, has its own earthy, haptic quality, in terms of colour and visual texture. The ceiling has a translucent, ephemeral quality.

Atop the staircase and arriving in the room of the *reunião*, we meet a forest of leaves, scattered about a white ground: the *mato* in its presence as the *orixá* "Oxóssi."[43] The floor is first encountered as a field of leaves against a background of whiteness; even the lines that express the individual glazed tiles are present more as a grid than expressing the joints of a material surface; in other words, it is precisely the presence of the leaves, that is, the "indication" of the *orixá*, that matters. This ground, in its continuous articulation by scattered leaves, extends beyond the limit implied by the white paper ceiling to the rear (east) wall of the room, behind the central penetration in the floor that accommodates the staircase. A low white barrier defines the edge of the floor slab through which the stair is punctured. At the top of the stairs is a small, white picket gate; on the ground and to either side of this gate rests a handful of *milho* (white maize); but before we find this, we meet on either side of the low barrier where the gate hinges and locks, the white substance, as at the entrance to the house from the street.

The walls are white. The west wall (towards the street) stands out in a way that calls for attention. The large arched openings that we saw from the street present even more so from within the sense of opening onto an emptiness, that is, the opacity of night. The immense tree outside, however, qualifies this background as "foliated."[44] This lushness is even more present with the wind. Centred between the openings is a line-drawn image on the wall of a face, generically that of a *caboclo*, in profile with a crown of feathers. Immediately above it and partially obscured by a bundle of foliage—the same as the leaves on the floor—are images of mythical figures, one on either side. They are depictions of the *orixás* Xangô and Oxum, the latter of which will "interrupt" the *reunião*, which will have the sense of an apparent anomaly that is opportune for us. Typically, the *orixás* do not explicitly participate, that is, "descend" into the bodies of their "daughters" and "sons," in the *caboclo reunião*.[45] For the moment, these images are merely there, as "pictures." Placed centrally on the bottom ledge of each opening is a clear glass of water; on either side and at the corners is placed a handful of *milho*: this is the "food" of Oxalá called *êbô*, which we encountered earlier.[46] The arch of each opening is marked by a length of dried, stripped palm leaf: the *orixá* "Exu."[47]

This wall, with its openings onto the foliated night, emerges as a background for the table, the primary *topos*, which we will explore further along. The south wall in contrast has a certain merely "functional" presence. There are two large rectangular sash windows marked along the top of the frame by a similar length of dried palm leaf. Centred on the part of the wall that divides the windows is hung a fragment of coloured cloth, though obscured by a bunch of leaves, again, the same as on the ground. Running the full length of the wall and against it are sewing machines and other bits—including a fabric doll of a *bruxa* (witch)—all covered with white cloth. On the ground at the western end rests a handful of *milho*, similar to what we saw earlier. The adjoining wall (east) ends at the stair, delimiting a private room. A door centred in it is marked on the ground on either side by *milho*; from this room the *mãe-de-santo* emerges. But it is in the direction of the north wall that the room is animated, competing with the table, which is like a theatrical set over against the audience.

In the northwest corner of the room stands the *caboclo*; flanking him are the *orixás* "Xangô" and "Oxum," the images painted on the west wall that we saw repeat themselves in sculptural dimension, although in this respect Xangô "*is*" corporeally a stone: a meteor. This corner could claim a pre-eminence equal to the table; it is too a *topos* that seems to have its own peculiar autonomy. The *caboclo* stands in the form of a life-sized sculpted figure of the indigenous "spirit," romanticised or stylised—with feathered diadem, bare torso, armed with a bow and gesturing as if towards the sky.[48] Much like the images on the wall, though with a different perceptual force, the *caboclo* here appears to us as a kind of sculpted "picture." As we enter the *reunião* in its dynamic, temporal performance, such a static picture might be proven false. This life-sized *caboclo* repeats itself at a smaller scale. Immediately in front and on the ground is another sculptural "representation" of a *caboclo*, a few centimetres tall and holding the head of a snake, whose body is depicted coiled around something like a tree stump.[49] Resting west of the large *caboclo* on a columnar stand that is itself in the form of a classical column is a shallow bowl containing a meteor, and facing it is a photograph of a man, with the attributes of Xangô.[50] Mirroring this column to the side of the *caboclo* against the north wall is another, with a small ceramic figure of a woman resting atop it: Oxum.[51] Placed in the outstretched arm of the *caboclo* is a bundle of foliage—the leaves from the *mato*—and immediately before his miniature repetition on the ground are a handful of *milho* and a lit white candle.

The north wall is the place for those who for the most part "witness" the event. Against it are two long benches where I typically sat with others, looking on and at times clapping, singing, and reciting prayers. This wall mirrors the south wall, though it extends further towards the rear of the room and is broken by a wide opening onto a deck outside, which is the roof of the porch on the first floor. Centred on the section of the wall between the windows is a timber relief carving of an "old black man": *preto-velho*.[52]

180   *A phenomenological ethnography of space*

Beneath him and pinned to the wall is bush from the *mato*. We will see that these bundles of leaves—fixed to the primary walls of the ritual space as demarked implicitly by the area of the white paper canopy—play a significant and direct role during the *reunião*. On the table rests a vase, also filled with bush from the *mato*. In this way, the *mato*, at least in terms of its actual foliage, appears to have a total presence in a room whose spatial horizon it delimits. A description of the rear (east) wall, with its door to the sanctuary or shrine, I must postpone until the end.

(2) Our description will see us return to where we started, at the entrance to the house from the street. We have just seen that the north wall of the ritual room stops far short of the rear (east) wall, and that there is a wide opening onto an outside deck, which also serves as the roof of the porch on the first floor. This area was alluded to by the white flag, which we saw from the street. The deck is dark—the *reunião* takes place at night we recall—and the only direct source of light is from candles. The white candles qualify the deck's illumination in relation to certain objects, but also in a manner that anticipates a peculiar division of the floor into two places designated for a kind of ritual "dusting," "fumigation," and "beating." For the moment, I merely note where the candles are placed. The deck is defined by a wall and a high railing above it to the west (street facing) and north; against the north wall is a staircase that leads to what appears to be a small room on the floor above, which I was not privy to. Against the west wall are three large plant pots. In the pot at the north end of the wall are iron implements that stand erect: "Ogum." Before this *orixá* is placed a lit white candle on the ground.[53] The other two pots sit at floor level against the wall; in the one farthest left (south) is the thin, dried trunk of a plant, and the other holds a pole wrapped by a vine with leaves with a bird figure atop, all made of iron: the *orixá* "Ossâim."[54] A single lit candle marks these two pots. Lastly, two lit candles stand isolated on the ground, more or less implying centre points of the floor area, as if it were divided into two—indeed this will amount to an actual division in praxis. The leaves from the *mato* do not extend onto this deck.

The room of the *reunião* proper, delimited by the leaves from the *mato*, and the outside deck and the sanctuary, can be said to together constitute a tripartite structuring of the second floor as a literal and ontological horizon of the ritual: a *topos* within which there are further divisions and preeminent sites. In terms of preparation, this horizon—practically, the second floor—was in fact and for the most part made ready for the event of the ritual first. But there is also and necessarily a vertical movement, which too is ontological in a way that is still for us obscure. The *mãe-de-santo*, with one of her *filhas-de-santo*, would articulate this vertical descent—that is, literally and in terms of preparation down towards the street entrance—with white candles, the white substance wrapped in leaves, *cachaça*, and water.

The white substance wrapped in a section of palm leaf that we have noted in various places is called *acaçá*. It is made from *milho* and is certainly edible, although at the *caboclo reunião* it is not eaten in an "actual" sense;

A phenomenological ethnography of space 181

we will see in a very explicit, bodily manner one of its functions when we come to the ritual in full performance.[55] It is placed unwrapped and with a lit white candle near to it, at the entrance to the foyer from the porch on the first floor; we first saw this combination at the timber gate at the street entrance. In the porch is also placed a shallow white basin of whitish water— that is, *acaçá* dissolved in cold water—on a low stool: to calm Exú and the *eguns* (the dead ancestors).[56] Against the wall shared with the foyer are objects: a red timber figure of a devil-like head, a small earthen vase, a small figurine of a red devil with an empty glass and coins on a book, a partially filled bottle of red wine, three clay bricks near a red and a black candle— both unlit, and at the corner to the east a large plant-pot holding an erect iron stand with iron implements similar in texture—though not form—to the one we saw on the north corner of the deck. Immediately before the red-devil figurine the *filha-de-santo* places and lights a white candle and then fills Exú's glass with *cachaça*. At the bottom of the staircase from the porch, we arrive again at the portal and timber gate, and thus to our description of the entrance to the house at street level with which we had begun: the *mãe-de-santo* fills the small earthen vase with water from the tap against the wall and pours the water on the pavement immediately before the gate.

(3) In the room of the *reunião*, everyone, for the most part, is dressed in white, myself included. It appears that the very act of *changing* clothes— into whiteness—is significant. At the very least and in quite a general sense, it is anticipatory of the ritual. The act of dressing ends in a mist of perfume, as we shall see when we come to describe the total incensing that qualifies the space of the *reunião*. The clothing of the men is relatively simple: white trousers and a white shirt. But it is with the women that the clothing appears architectonically. There is a hierarchy expressed in the layering of the women's clothing: the full-length white dress or blouse and skirt—typically frilled and patterned—closest to the body, and the white wrap of cloth that covers this primary layer at the torso, up to the chest and extending just above the knees, where the fabric is at times ornate with embroidery. This description implies variation, and applies rigidly in the case of the *mãe-de-santo*, who in addition always has her head wrapped with white cloth, at least until the arrival of Tupiniquim. Both women and men—although not the *mãe-de-santo* herself—tend to wear also long beaded necklaces (Figure 4.2). I was given one by Tupiniquim during a *reunião*, made of small, deep-blue beads, joined at its ends by a large deep-blue glass bead, spherical in overall appearance but carved in such a way as to form a cross-shape in section; this large bead sits at the nape of the neck, I was shown. The necklace was a gift from the *orixá* Ogum.

In addition to the actual clothing, there is the marking of the body with a gritty, scented powder, typically as follows: the wrists, marked with a cross; the palms with a small circle; the top of the bare feet with a cross; the chest, close to the neck, with a cross; the nape, and the forehead (Figure 4.3).[57] The descriptions above should be taken as "more or less" the case; at times the marking of the body occurred during the *reunião* in full play, at times

182 *A phenomenological ethnography of space*

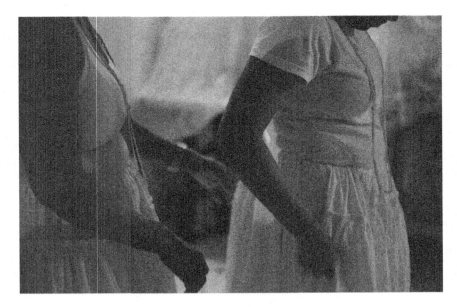

Figure 4.2 *Filhas-de-santo* attending to dress. Photo by the author

Figure 4.3 *Filha-de-santo* marking her body with scented powder. Photo by the author

prior as I am describing. In the former case, Tupiniquim himself often marked the bodies with figures more or less as I have described, though not the feet. Otherwise, only those who would "fully" participate marked themselves in this way.[58]

(4) The solid wooden table, like the floor, walls, and ceiling, is white. It is rectangular, oriented in its length along the north–south axis of the room, and is relatively centred underneath the white paper canopy. The head of the table is at the south end and is where the *mãe-de-santo* and, later, Tupiniquim sit. Seven white timber chairs surround it: one at the head, one at the opposite end, three along the east edge, and two on the other side, separated by a stool that is not visible from the north wall, where the benches for "spectators" are. The chairs are uniform.

The setting of the table happens gradually, in layers like the making of a painting. It is done neither mechanically nor with haste, as though each layer needs to "dry." First, a white tablecloth is laid; following this and not necessarily in the order that I shall describe, various objects are placed or "spread." As I noted earlier, a white vase filled with foliage from the *mato* is centred on the table; scattered about it and spread across the whole surface of the table are leaves and popcorn: "Omolu." This *orixá* articulates the table in a manner analogous to the leaves on the ground.[59] On either side of the vase is placed a wide plate, filled with wrapped *acaçá* (Figure 2.9). Six white candles will illuminate the top surface of the table, and ultimately the entire room; they are arranged, one at the head and foot, and two on either side of the table's length. A seventh candle stands on the ground, directly below the vase: it too will be lit, illuminating the underside of the table, and next to it a wrapped *acaçá* on a white plate. From this point, the symmetry of our layering is interrupted, and above this "primer" the hierarchy of the image is constructed with elaborate detail. The setting of the table has the feel of a creative work, as I suggested, like producing an oil painting, building it up in layers: the white timber surface, the white tablecloth, and the spread of popcorn all articulate and anticipate a horizon of communion. This articulation thickens as the vertical elements project towards the ceiling: the white plate just implying a relief, the white candles, and the white vase penetrating towards the sky as an implied vertical axis that bursts into foliage.

At the far end of the table protruding like a plateau rests a deep wicker bowl of popcorn, wrapped in white cloth, and next to it a rattle made of a calabash gourd (Figure 2.6). Ascending towards the table's head is a small white plate, filled with uncooked white rice. Beyond the vase is a clear glass pitcher of water.[60] With his back to the water and ahead of it stands, or more precisely stoops with eyes directed forward, a miniature reflection of the *caboclo*. In relation to this figurine, Tupiniquim will be face to face with his "image" (Figure 2.2). During the *reunião*, the *mãe-de-santo* will sit at the head of the table and will have immediately before her some sheets of paper with prayers and notes written. Encircling these sheets we find a small, organic-shaped wooden container that will serve as an ashtray; a box or stack of large cigars; and a glass of water and implements of the *mãe-de-santo*. The latter include a calabash rattle, a smaller wicker case with a handle, and, covered with a white cloth, the *adjá*—a small silver bell in the form of two adjacent cones that merge to form a handle (Figures 2.1 and 2.4).[61] This is the articulation of the table's surface as the primary *topos*, as we shall see (Figure 4.4).

(5) Lastly, we have the presence of incense. Already, with the burning of incense, the whole space is enlivened in an extraordinary way; it seems we are at the common horizon of preparation and participation.[62] Everything and everyone is fragranced. What I have termed the tripartite spatial horizon of the *reunião* is totally perfumed; the smoke is ubiquitous. The same *filha-de-santo* whom we met earlier performs the incensing. She holds with her arm outstretched a simple metal censer, through which she bathes the room in smoke and its diffuse light (Figure 3.2). As this happens, the *mãe-de-santo* blows powder from the palm of her hands into the air in the direction of the corners of the room. But it is in terms of the censer that the ritual as a community in dialogue first shows itself amidst the haze. Everyone orients themselves towards the censer, and through various gestures of drawing the smoke towards their bodies, everyone is in communion with each other and with the *filha-de-santo*, her motion itself determined by the task of perfuming. This implicit reference to Catholic rite will be made transparent through prayer when all are around the table, at which point we will certainly have crossed the limit of preparation.

*

In the unfolding of my description, I have alluded to certain significances—particularly the identification of *orixás*—as they appeared as "objects." I have not elaborated on these because our concern is not to explicate an assemblage of things, but to understand their significance for the event of the *reunião* as a dynamic, temporal horizon. What I have attempted to do is to anticipate the possibility of their relevance in terms of the more or less static description I have offered, meant not in a phenomenological sense, but as if the space were a still "image." In the following the descriptive register changes, and we find ourselves within the space imaginatively re-enlivened.

The *reunião*

The previous section was preparative in two overlapping senses: (1) it described preparatory activities of the ritual, taking apart the spatiality of the room and presenting it for the most part as a static scene, which (2) served a methodologically descriptive purpose, giving us a preliminary "picture" of the room and its "contents" in order to return, through a necessarily

A *phenomenological ethnography of space* 185

Figure 4.4 View towards the table. Photo by the author

reflective description, to a more original sense of the experience as temporally animated in communicative relations with others.

*

The room is thick with the perfumed smoke of incense.

As I noted in Chapter 1, Tupiniquim shows himself through the mediation or "medium" (*médium*) of Mãe Juta to be an "indoctrinated" (*doutrinado*) indigenous "spirit" (*espírito*).[63] Tupiniquim, therefore, shows up as, in some indeterminate manner, Catholic. We must keep this in mind as the cloud of incense thins, and we arrive firmly into the horizon of the performance of the *reunião*.

The use of incense to mark the introit of a Catholic mass is well known; its symbolic significance is archaic and pre-Christian.[64] My interest, however, is in its significance for the event in its performativity and presence, happening "here and now." It appears that the act of incensing functions as a kind of threshold, instituting the beginning of the *reunião*. I will use one primary example to enquire more deeply into its significance in this regard, that is, as initiatory and oriented by the practical *telos* of the *reunião*'s enactment. The incensation does not take place, for the most part, until after the room is "decorated" and clothing is changed. There is a general sense, therefore, of the priority of dressing—of "ornamenting" the room and the body in readiness for the occasion of the *reunião*. The example I will use is that of the *filha-de-santo* who carries the censer and performs the incensation, hence its primacy. She dresses herself and is dressed—in white and with necklaces—prior to taking up the censer. Her clothing becomes a "theme" in the very basic sense that it is something explicit towards which her actions, and therefore her body, is oriented (Figure 4.2). *How* this whiteness of her clothing shows itself in the ritual performance is our concern.[65] We know that in general the entire scene is qualified by whiteness, and we will have to allow the ritual itself to tell us "why." The moment the *filha-de-santo* takes up the censer, her clothes are no longer "thematic" for her. The censer itself is a simple, shallow cylindrical tin with a long metal wire handle. The *filha* holds it in her outstretched right hand and swings the censer as she circles the room, anticlockwise starting from the north wall (Figure 3.2). The room fills with the perfumed smoke such that the air "thickens." Over against the "objective" quality of things in the room—the table, the *caboclo* in the north-west corner, and so forth—we have the ephemeral objectivity of smoke, such that we no longer have a "picture" of anything, like the experience of walking through a dense fog. But unlike a fog, here it is precisely the smoke that becomes what is sought after; this is clear from the gestures of people: they wave their hands, lift their arms, and turn their bodies in such a way as to draw the smoke towards them. They precisely do not walk through the smoke but are oriented towards it through these gestures that bring it close (Figures 3.4 and 3.5). But the smoke *is* its very ephemerality: as quickly as it is "had," it is gone. Once it has been "had," when the body has been completely perfumed, it is truly "gone" in terms of its purpose and can itself become a visual spectacle, a "picture." At the end, the *filha-de-santo* incenses her own body—making present again to herself her clothes—and we know that the *reunião* has begun.

> *Pai nosso, que estais no céu*
> *Santificado seja o Vosso nome...*
> [Our Farther, who art in heaven,
> hallowed be thy name...]
>
> *Ave Maria, cheia de graça,*
> *O Senhor é convosco...*
> [Hail Mary, full of grace,
> Our Lord is with thee...]

With *Mãe-Juta* and others seated around the table, the *reunião* typically begins as all those present recite the Lord's Prayer and the Ave Maria, repeated several times. This fact seems to implicate the Catholic doctrine of prayer. Both prayers point to the issue of God's grace; St. Augustine would even suggest the status of a sacrament for the Lord's Prayer.[66] In Catholic doctrinal terms, therefore, the *telos* of this situation is the communication of God's grace through prayer. I can say in advance that this is apparently not the case, or at least not absolutely. The Catholic dimension of the *reunião* pertains to the "fact" of the *caboclo*—Tupiniquim—as having been "indoctrinated," and it is to *his* Catholicism that the prayer is addressed, in order that he might "arrive" (*chegar*). It is not the case that he is being called to participate in a Catholic ritual that would have as its goal God's grace as such. Rather, Tupiniquim's presence *is* the *telos* in terms of such Catholic practice. But if Tupiquinim's Catholicism were on some level "true," then the concern with communicating God's grace must be present in the *reunião* more than merely instrumentally. The setting of the table, not in terms of the actual objects, but its general sense as a setting for a meal, a "supper," would suggest the presence of prayer as a liturgical institution, whose fulfilment, rather than being the Eucharist, is ultimately Tupiniquim's incarnation.

After the prayers have been recited a few times, everyone present claps in an evidently prescribed way. The palms are arched and crossed so that a low, deep tone resounds when they clasp; the rhythm is somewhat fragmented: two slow claps, followed by three or four more rapid ones, a pause, then a final clap, after which the pattern is repeated. The entire gesture is oriented downwards through the subtle movement and positioning of the body as a whole. We will come to this clapping gesture (called *paó*) again shortly; here, it seems to mark an interstice between the prayers and the singing that will follow.[67] After the prayers, everyone in the room begins

188 A *phenomenological ethnography of space*

to sing and mark the rhythm of the songs with clapping in the more typical sense, that is, as rhythmic accompaniment (Figure 3.6):

A bença, a bença meu pai, né?
Bença pai, bença mãe,
A bença meu pai, né?...

[Bless me, bless me father, right?
Bless me father, bless me mother,
Bless me father, right?...][68]

As these words are chanted, those around the table and some other participants—those of us sitting against the north wall—individually and in turns begin to greet the *mãe-de-santo* in an elaborate and structured manner. I should note here that the order in which these actions take place is not rigid. It happened at least once that Tupiniquim "arrived" towards the beginning of a *reunião* during the recital of Catholic prayers; in that event, it was Tupiniquim who was greeted in the manner that I am about to describe. I will use again the *filha-de-santo* who performed the incensing as an example; we will see why for other reasons she is exemplary. Her place at the table is to the right of the *mãe-de-santo*. During the singing, she leaves her seat and first addresses the "entrances," or more precisely, "thresholds"—the door to the *mãe-de-santo*'s room, the gate at the stair, the opening to the deck outside, the door to the sanctuary—by bending and touching the ground before the entrances with her right hand, then with this hand touching her forehead and the back of her head. She then greets those around the table and some of us who "spectate" by gently touching the palms of their hands with hers as they both say "*a bença*" (blessing). Finally, she greets the *mãe-de-santo* in the following way: kneeling at the head of the table, with the *mãe* sitting, they embrace. The *filha* then lies on the ground, her body outstretched, first on one side, with her head resting on clasped hands, then repeating the gesture on the other; she lies then on her front, bringing her palms to her forehead and repeats the gesture of the clap or *paó* that we encountered, before lying prostrate before the *mãe-de-santo*. In the latter position, the *mãe* gently touches her back with her right hand, making a cross (Figure 4.5). After the "blessing," the *filha* returns to her seat at the table. The prostration of the *filhos-de-santo* (sons-of-saint) differs; I will use the example of the *filho* who typically sits directly across from the *mãe-de-santo*, at the "foot" of the table. After addressing the entrance thresholds and greeting others—exactly as the *filha-de-santo* did—he approaches the *mãe-de-santo* from a distance, crouched on his knees and elbows, and extends his body towards her by dragging his lower arm forward until he is prostrate.[69]

The gesture of lying prostrate before the *mãe-de-santo* or other senior dignitaries in Candomblé is typical and is also performed by the *orixás*

A phenomenological ethnography of space 189

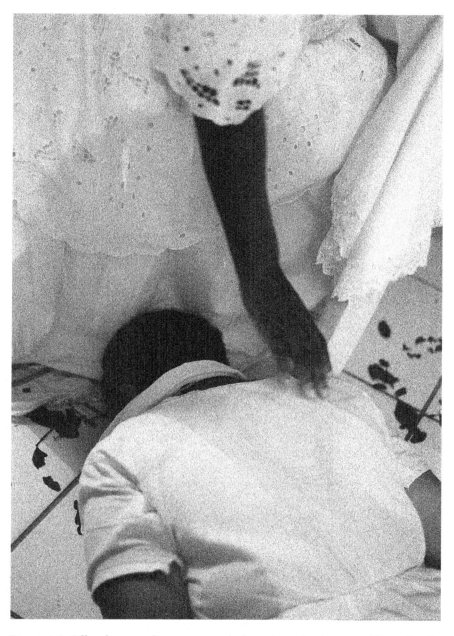

Figure 4.5 Filha-de-santo lies prostrate before the *mãe-de-santo*. Photo by the author

"themselves," that is, persons in trance during public festivals.[70] It suggests a rupture in the ritual between the Pater Noster and the gestures of "blessing"—what we might call the "*bênção* greeting"—perhaps effected through the peculiar clapping. But we saw that the clapping gesture is repeated in the act of prostration, so it seems to not signify a complete break in general. Furthermore, the Lord's Prayer and the Ave Maria are repeated once the *bênção* is completed. Whatever fragmentation might be implied, the ritual performance is clearly continuous in general, with the clapping integrated into this continuity. The *orixás* do not manifest, so we can only validly assume their *explicit* absence, which means that the articulation of the ritual situation in terms of mythology is effectively "open." We can contrast this with the relatively "closed" articulation of the Pater Noster and the Ave Maria, and their implicit doctrinal determination. As regards the implicit presence of the *orixás*—Exú at the thresholds, and Oxalá in terms of the *êbô* and *acaçá*—the presence of myth could perhaps be delimited, but without linguistic articulation of the myth, this would take the corresponding form of an implied but indefinite horizon of meaning.[71] The articulation of the situation of the *bênção* happens fundamentally in terms of ritual action, which we have in an originary way through perception. The most articulate dimension is the language of the song itself—we know that it involves the "blessing" of the *mãe-de-santo*. As our interest is in the experience of space, we must begin from the bottom, which coincides with the very first gesture: touching the ground at the thresholds. I will attempt to draw out from the *bênção* situation a fundamental mode of spatial givenness, which we can call the *ground*.

The ritual itself has beforehand established for us the ground as a *thesis*; we are merely following this phenomenal thread reflectively. It is clear that the entrances, and specifically the floor at the entrances—for the *filhas-* and *filhos-de-santo* could have addressed the lintel, for example—become pre-eminent sites during the *bênção* greeting; they are in this manner "posited" through the gesture described; the gesture is *thetic*. These words I use in a basic sense, implying merely *orientation*. Behind what may be the express symbolic value of the thresholds—the *orixás* Exú, Oxalá, Oxóssi, and so forth—the gestures reveal the orientation of the ritual performance within the horizon of the *bênção* greeting. The entrance thresholds were always there, but now they are made present explicitly in the form of a prescribed gesture that links them, through the right hand, to the head. Within the context of the ritual action, they form the necessary antecedent to the communal act of exchanging *bênçãos* (blessings).

In addressing the thresholds, the floor is expressly touched—with the hands—in a similar way as the palms of those around the table, for example, would be; it is the floor itself *as* some significance—Exú, Oxalá, Oxóssi, and so forth—that is brought to attention. With the gesture of prostration, however, this is not the case. At all times, the attention is directed towards the *mãe-de-santo*, *by means of* the floor, this even when the *filho-de-santo* is face down. But as a secondary *telos*, that is, quite literally a horizontal level that affords the gesture of prostration, the floor is not "addressed"; rather, it is laboured, *worked*. The "working" of the floor is precisely the gesture of prostration as it unfolds as a *technique*, oriented towards the accomplishment of *bênçãos*. I witnessed the *mãe-de-santo* explicitly showing one of the "novice" *filhas* how to perform the clapping gesture while prostrate. The labour that accomplishes the blessings is most clearly shown by the *filho-de-santo* crouched on his knees and elbows; he drew out his body until his posture was literally horizontal. The *telos* of the horizontality of the body was the same for the *filha-de-santo*, whose preparatory work seemed less laborious, that is, resting her weight on one side, then the next before actual prostration. In this position, the *mãe-de-santo* would complete the *bênção* by crossing the backs of the *filhas*, that is, bending to touch them with her hands, like the manner in which the *filha* before had bent to touch the floor at the thresholds. Whatever may be the symbolic meaning—reverence or submission—we have witnessed in the unfolding of the *bênção* greeting a *historicity* rooted in the phenomenon of the greeting itself. In quite a literal way, the lowest horizon of the room—the horizontal level of the floor—becomes a pre-eminent presence, to the extent that in the end, the body of the *filha-de-santo* is horizontal, "like" the floor. This dynamic, temporal unfolding of the *bênção* greeting is historical in a fundamental sense: the first instituting or *thetic* act was addressing the floor at the thresholds—an act that in fact was already anticipated by the song—in terms of the unfolding of a prescribed and thus already anticipated technique or manner of enactment; this aspect of the *reunião* ended with the accomplishment of the *thesis*, in the basic sense of an orientation: the crossing of the back on the prostrate body in blessing. Without asserting the symbolic meaning explicitly, we have been shown by the unfolding of the phenomenon itself that there is a prescribed context of sense—an "institution"—determined by the *telos* of *bênçãos* that is to be technically accomplished through the *ground* as a spatial horizon—experientially and literally—of labour.

Pai nosso, que estais no céu...
[Our Farther, who art in heaven...]

Ave Maria, cheia de graça...
[Hail Mary, full of grace...]

After the blessings, and everyone is again seated, the *mãe-de-santo* leads the recital of the Lord's Prayer and the Ave Maria. During the prayer—though, as I noted, not always—Tupiniquim "arrives." His arrival initiates a remarkable transformation, not only of the *mãe-de-santo* but of the entire *topos*; we will observe first the former.

Figure 4.6 Filhas-de-santo in prayer at the table. Photo by the author

The prayers are recited just as we saw them before: solemnly, in the Catholic posture of clasped hands and bowed heads (Figure 4.6). In the instance where Tupiniquim does not arrive during prayer, playful songs are sung about the *caboclo*, explicitly calling him by name as everyone claps in rhythmic accompaniment; but we will continue with the example of Tupiniquim's arrival during prayer, as it ultimately anticipates our description of the end of the *reunião*, as we will see. In either case, the gesture of the *mãe-de-santo* is consistent. At a certain point in the recital of the prayers, the *mãe-de-santo* stops praying and begins to rub her forehead, typically removing her spectacles. At the table on her left sits the *equede*, her assistant in the praxis of the ritual who, though praying, has her eye on the *mãe*—in a sense, everyone does in general anticipation.[72] Tupiniquim's arrival is marked by a certain gestural force, in the sense of a transgression: the *mãe-de-santo*'s entire body shakes *once*, it seems, yet it is as though only her head moves—in an instant, a sudden jolt; the ambiguity of my description reflects the visceral ephemerality of the event, experienced in a blink. In the instant—which is understood by all—the lights are switched off and only the flicker of the candles' light remains.[73]

The instant that marks the arrival of Tupiniquim introduces for us a methodological difficulty, because it appears to be totally *concrete*, like a kind of "death," yet in the same instant a "genesis."[74] By concreteness I am referring to the phenomenon as an instantaneous event that is, by itself in a certain way complete, expressed by the "jolt" of the *mãe-de-santo* and

A phenomenological ethnography of space 193

complemented by the switching off of the lights. We appear to be here at an edge, a seam.[75] Thus far, we have approached this edge from one direction, that is, in a linear, descriptive manner moving forward in time. This means that our understanding is already prejudiced in favour of this instant as a *telos*. But clearly it is transgressed, as the *reunião* continues, or we could say begins qualitatively anew. In the latter sense, this instant marks a genesis. The methodological difficulty lies in the status of the instant as an apparently autonomous whole that does not seem to have a temporal and thus perceptual unfolding like the "*bênçãos*," for example. Its *instantaneity* makes phenomenological clarification difficult. The visual texture of the whole scene: the "adorned" table surrounded by the whiteness of clothing and lit by flickering candles against the lush blackness of night is evocative of a Caravaggio—*Supper at Emmaus*.[76] My reference to the painting is not merely visual. Rather, I am drawing a parallel with the instantaneous, revelatory significance of the event that it depicts: "And their eyes were opened, and they knew him; and he vanished out of their sight."[77] It is the obscure temporality, or even atemporality, of the *jolt* of the body of Mãe Juta, which at the same time inaugurated her "absence," that speaks to the narrative of Christ's vanishing. But here we are faced with the persistence of the body of "Mãe Juta" cum "Tupiniquim," and the transformation of the whole scene into the unequivocal appearance of the *head of the table* as pre-eminent. Within the horizon of the event of Tupiniquim having *chegou* (arrived), it is also unequivocal that "he" is bodily present, in the flesh.

With Tupiniquim now at the head of the table, the *equede* attends: she takes off the white headwrap of the *mãe-de-santo* and removes the white blouse—s/he is wearing a white dress underneath—and wraps his/her torso from the chest with white cloth, tied at the back. The *equede* then removes the feathered crown from the "image" of the *caboclo* at the northwest corner of the room and fixes it on Tupiniquim's head.[78] Finally, she takes one of the cigars that we saw on the table, lights it, and offers it to Tupiniquim with a respectful gesture. With the first puff, we seem to be taken back to the image of the incensing—an appearance that will prove ever more true, as we will see—only the lighting is much changed, like mist before our Caravaggio. Tupiniquim leads the recital of a prayer.

Tupiniquim's face is uplit from the candles' light on the table, which ascends with the smoke from the cigar joining the white ceiling-sky as a cloud. His eyes are open but almost squinting, and his face seems slightly drawn downward, though complemented by the upright posture of his frame.[79] He speaks a Portuguese that anthropologist Jim Wafer describes as "*caboclo* talk," slowly, softly, and with a low, husky, monotone voice, typically in a gregarious and jovial manner.[80] Although this did not occur at the *reuniões* I attended, there are apparently instances in which Tupiniquim speaks "Tupi."[81] His overall demeanour is much like his speech, and he makes few gestures with his hands; while he is seated, we notice perhaps only the measure that accompanies holding and smoking a cigar.

The table is set as I have described, except that the vase of foliage is removed—we will witness again the removal of the *mato*'s leaves. In the darkness, more than before, the lit candle under the table stands out, although still in a secondary way. After the prayer, Tupiniquim chats casually, enquiring first after the well-being of those around the table, greeting everyone in the room from his seat, and making jokes. Let us consider this conversation as general talk and draw from the scene aspects of its spatial significance.[82]

Our first clue is the removal of the vase of leaves, which happens as the lights go off. Let us assume, naïvely, that the leaves were a visual obstruction; Tupiniquim can be more or less clearly seen by all, and he in turn can glance at whom he wishes. While the general talk happens, those around the table "fiddle" with things in quite a casual way. There are usually two small dogs in the room, one white and the other black. Loosened from the prayer, some at the table, particularly the *filho-de-santo* across from the head of the table, would typically throw some of the popcorn spread on the tabletop onto the floor for the dogs. Others simply fiddle with the popcorn or sometimes with the beads of their necklaces. Apart from this, the table is for the most part "still"; attention is not even paid to the jug of water, for example. The scene of the objects on the table has the atmosphere of a painting, a still life. Nothing on the table is eaten at the table; the bowl of popcorn at some point is passed around, not at the table, but to the "audience" (those of us against the north wall). Unlike at a dinner—where, for example, utensils are at hand for the purpose of eating—for the most part, nothing appears to be "to hand," in the sense in which they would be moved. It is as though the whole table were an *ornament*. But we are certainly not in the presence of a mere painterly *natura morta*, if only because the table is not present as a spectacle, for were this the case there could be no dialogue; those at the table would merely be looking. The table is lit; the candles' flames flicker with the wind. In contrast to this, the background—the walls, the windows, the "punctures"—is as dark as the shadows; its presence is more deeply felt as the sound of the rustling leaves of the tree outside. But this sound is secondary to the speech of the general talk. All of this talking happens above the level of the table, obviously. As lips move, there are smiles or laughter, Tupiniquim blows smoke, there is movement. But it appears as though this movement does not involve doing anything with the "objects" on the table; we may say that they are "symbolic" —the popcorn Omolu, the *acaçá* Oxalá, the "figurine" of the *caboclo*, and so forth—but this clarifies little for us in terms of the *event* itself. The table with its "ornament" is itself like a background, though not as obscure as the walls. The dogs, as they are fed, tend to go towards the lit candle underneath the table; their movement is like a secondary "dialogue," one that increases the visibility of the floor such that it is not a "shadow" like the walls. The perceptual apprehension of the spatiality of the room is here constructed from the general talk instituted by Tupiniquim, the one towards which all attention was directed immediately as the lights were turned off and the vase of leaves was removed; the perception of the room *was* the instantaneous perception of Tupiniquim, and all else was experientially obscure. The prayer drew this attention away from Tupiniquim—this even as he led it—making language—the *speech* of the praying act—into a presence that established communion; as such, even Tupiniquim became part of the obscure background, but in this regard not like a shadow over against light, but as and with the *monotonic* quality of the recital. This is perhaps as close as we might get to something like a homogeneous "space," as a complement to the monotonic speech; yet, there was still a spatial hierarchy, and the head of the table maintained its pre-eminence even in this "neutralness." To grasp this more fully, it will be instructive to compare this situation to the event of the arrival of another *caboclo*, which we will come to.

When the prayer ended, conversation began. As the general talk unfolded, the clarity of Tupiniquim's presence extended towards the table; its surface was like a clearing that made others around it present to each other, presenting as well what lay on it as things to "fiddle" with. This meant that with the passing of time, there emerged from obscurity persons other than Tupiniquim, "things" and other subjects that could be attended to, if only in a secondary manner, such as the popcorn and the dogs. What is exemplary about this situation is how it accommodates the language of description: the background—the walls, windows, and the black foliated night—is unattended to and in this sense obscure during the talk, but it is also quite literally obscure, built of shadows. We saw, however, that the table was not only a clearing for dialogue, but that it too emerged as a kind of background, presenting itself as *ornament*. The meaning of this we cannot yet clarify, because the activity is still unfolding—the general talk is not an end in itself but leads to other things—and it is possible that the "objects" on the table anticipate an end that we are at present blind to. The talking does not go on in this manner perpetually; it is broken by singing and clapping—as rhythmic accompaniment—that lead to other events which call for description.

- *Você gostou de mim?*
- *Gostei, sim senhor.*
- *Então me dê um abraço.*
- *Eu dou, sim senhor.*

[- Did you like me?
- Yes sir, I did.
- Then give me an embrace.
- Yes sir, I will.][83]

At some point during the singing, Tupiniquim leaves his seat and embraces everyone, starting with those at the table, then moving to those of us against the north wall. He even at times playfully repeats the words of the song above, which is an example of many, imitating a dialogue with the person meeting his embrace. The gesture of the embrace is quite particular:

both parties stoop slightly as Tupiniquim extends his right hand to meet the right hand of the one he faces; he enquires briefly about the other's well-being; then in one fluid movement they lift their hands, releasing their grip as they embrace twice, first right cheek to right cheek, then left. During these individual greetings and in this atmosphere of singing, two other *caboclos* would "arrive." Their arrival is not marked by the attention which defined that of Tupiniquim; rather, it happens in the background of Tupiniquim's activity. But it is worth describing in some detail.

We return once again to the example of the *filha-de-santo* who performed the incensing. "Her" *caboclo* typically arrives first, followed by that of another *filha-de-santo* who sits to the right of the *filho-de-santo*. The case of the latter is more vigorous in comparison, but the manner is in principle similar. As the music is sung with its rhythmic clapping and the embraces of Tupiniquim continue, the *filha-de-santo* bends forward at the table, rubbing her forehead as the *mãe-de-santo* had done; then there is a sudden shriek from her place, and her body is thrust back, the legs of the chair making a sharp sound against the floor as it is pushed aside in the movement. The *caboclo* rises, first unbalanced and almost hopping on one foot as "he" rubs the flat surfaces of "his" palms together. In the force of the event the *filha-de-santo's* headwrap is flung onto the floor. By this time, the *equede* is close at hand with a coloured length of cloth, which she wraps around the *caboclo*'s chest; she hands him a shorter length of coloured cloth, which he ties in a band around his forehead. The *caboclo* who has just arrived then motions towards Tupiniquim's empty seat at the head of the table and kneels on one leg with clasped hands against his forehead in a gesture of prayer. The singing and the embracing stop, and all clap in the peculiar prescribed way that we met earlier. The *caboclo* recites a prayer in a low tone, as if dragging the oration. After the prayer, the *caboclo* rises and begins to sing and to dance:[84]

Ô boa noite senhor,
Boa noite, senhora...

[Oh good evening sir,
Good evening ma'am...][85]

The *caboclo* greets us in song, and although everyone sings and claps, only the *caboclos* dance—the second which we spoke of will "arrive" shortly thereafter, marked by the shriek: "*Isa!*", which will again interrupt the event through prayer at Tupiniquim's seat, before we are back to singing and dancing.[86] Tupiniquim, however, does not dance; he will take his place outside, and so too will the first *caboclo*. We have arrived by this point at what may be called the main body of the *reunião*, if only because the actions that unfold—singing, dancing, and a kind of individual "beating" outside that I will describe—last for the most extended period. Two kinds of activity qualify this part: one public, communal and inside; the other private, intimate and outside. The former we have already begun to explicate as generally dancing—the *caboclos* only—and singing; it calls for more attention before we turn to the latter.

Tupiniquim's action of embracing introduces an anticipation, which is precisely the anticipation of this individual acknowledgement of one's bodily presence in the form of an embrace. The song itself has beforehand communalised this anticipation. This situation is different from the prayer recital that Tupiniquim initiated in a way that I will describe in relation to the *caboclos*' praying. Tupiniquim is away from his seat, walking around the room, as everyone claps and sings. The activity of clapping and singing tempers the anticipation insofar as it calls attention to itself as an activity, and to others apart from Tupiniquim who are similarly clapping and singing. This means that the background, as a background sound of music and clapping, becomes more present and the room "opens up"; the clarity and literal visibility that characterises one's experience of the table extends to the floor, walls, and benches where the "audience" sit, the site of those who "spectate." Those "looking on" as they clap and sing are mostly against the north wall, but some are also on the other side—against the south wall at the eastern end, away from the table—as the benches are filled. But it is precisely *what* they are "looking on" at that is put into question for us. There emerges a certain fluidity of attention: one's glance can be called by another's gesture—a smile or an overly enthusiastic clapping, for example—the dogs' animation by the music, Tupiniquim's embracing of another, the flickering candles' light, the rustle of the trees outside, and so forth. In other words, the hierarchy of the event is loosened, which means that the spatiality of the room is more homogeneous, even allowing extension to the "picture" of the night outside seen through the arched openings in the wall. In meeting Tupiniquim's embrace, the openness of the room is not lost, but let us save this interpretation for the intimacy that we will experience with Tupiniquim outside.

This scene, qualified by clapping and singing, changes once the other *caboclo* arrives and is kneeling at the seat at the head of the table. Most obviously, the prescribed clapping initiates a break, and apart from its measured slowness and fragmented rhythm, there is silence; in fact, it draws attention to the silence as a prelude to the prayer recital. The *caboclo* is oriented towards an absence: Tupiniquim is not at his seat. It is precisely Tupiniquim's bodily absence that draws attention to the pre-eminence of the head of the table as a site. Earlier I spoke of a "neutralness"; it is "as if" Tupiniquim were at his seat and being addressed. Even though he is in the room, his bodily presence is paid no mind during the recital, and yet he is attended to in terms of his place at the head of the table. At this point, where Tupiniquim happens to be bodily is accidental in relation to the pre-eminence of the head of the table, whereas before it was coincident. After the prayer, the *caboclo*'s actions—dancing—draw out the floor over against the table in a remarkable way.

As we will also see when we are called outside, the presence of the other *caboclos* initiates a kind of spatial "competition" or "conflict." Outside, even in its obscurity, or precisely because of the darkness, this sense of space as *agōn* was anticipatorily articulated by the two isolated candles we spoke of earlier. Inside and upon reflection, it was alluded to by the very location of the table. The table rests closer to the west wall, on axis with one of the two pairs of windows that mirror each other in the north and south walls. This placement allows for an expanse of floor before it, an area that the *caboclos* would "clarify," that is, establish as a clearing for the sake of dancing.

The *caboclos* appear to dance in a spontaneous manner; their movements do not seem "prescribed." We will witness later an extraordinary contrast with the gesture of an *orixá* that pierces, as the pitch of a sound, through the *reunião*.[87] The *caboclos* dance and sing, but they tend not to clap; rather, they smoke cigars.[88] They typically dance on one spot, at times turning or spinning, or gesturing forward and backward with a kind of jerky hop. Their manner while dancing is always jovial, festive, and "unconcerned." Their feet are bare and land heavily on the ground as they dance, in loud thumps, while up above the rising smoke imitates their gestures in its own way. In terms of this dancing, the floor competes with the table for our attention in a spatial conflict. But it is not only this competing activity that compels our regard. Typically, only one *caboclo* holds the floor, dancing; the other is towards the outside, where Tupiniquim is. When the dancing had begun, and after the embracing, Tupiniquim had taken from the walls—the west wall where we saw the line drawing of the *caboclo*, and the north wall, below the "image" of Preto-velho—the bundles of leaves from the *mato* that we saw earlier. As one *caboclo* dances in the clearing before the table, each individual is called, one at a time, to Tupiniquim and to the other *caboclo*, who have taken their places by the two isolated candles on the deck outside. Here, I will use my experience as an example, not only because this event was not communally witnessed but primarily for the sake of descriptive convenience.

I am called by one of the *filhos-de-santo*—the one who had before laid prostrate on the ground—to the *caboclo*. Leaving the place on the bench where I sit, the *filho-de-santo* gently gestures to me to remove my sandals, my necklace of blue glass beads, spectacles, keys, and so forth. I then step outside—over a threshold expressed on the ground by the thickness of the wall—towards the *caboclo* who was at one point our exemplary *filha-de-santo*. The *caboclo* stands by the candle further east, and I before him with my back to Tupiniquim, who is attending to another. I am told to close my eyes as he begins to "brush" my body with leaves. From my shoulders, he firmly rubs downward my arms, then my legs at the sides; he then takes my hands and pulls sharply at each finger, before holding my hands firmly and "flapping" my arms; the *caboclo* then holds my clasped hands as I feel the heat of his cigar and its smoke blown onto my hands; he speaks a few words and I recognise the name "Oxalá"; I am gestured to turn around as he brushes again my body with the bush, before rubbing my arms and legs as before; at this point, I am delivered over to Tupiniquim. I face Tupiniquim at the other candle, who holds an *acaçá*. My eyes are again closed as Tupiniquim rubs the length of my body with the unwrapped white *acaçá*; he then, with his hands to either side, rubs my head from the top down at the sides, and snaps his fingers two or three times as his hands part around my ears—this action is performed a few times and very quickly. I am gestured to turn around, and Tupiniquim rubs my body again with *acaçá*. Facing him after this, and sensing the heat from his cigar, he blows smoke towards my torso, and a cloud smothers my face; he then embraces me twice—first right cheek to right cheek, then left—and he says a brief word. I recover my things and return to my seat on the bench, amidst the singing and clapping as before.[89]

We were led to a description of the intimacy of outside not merely by a goal of showing the *reunião's* "components," but rather out of a methodological necessity. To grasp correctly the spatial significance of the event of dancing and singing, which I qualified as spatial competition or conflict, it was necessary to widen the horizon of description to include the events outside, such that we grasp the situational unity of the *reunião* in this aspect. But we are still in the presence of dancing and singing even as I return to my seat on the bench; the dancing and singing was simply going on all the while, and our horizon is not yet adequately determined until this activity is at an end. This end coincides with a sense of the general completion of the *reunião* that we will ultimately come to. But before we get to this point, I will describe an anomaly, which will prove methodologically useful for clarifying the *reunião* in its normalcy, in one of its more articulate aspects.

> She [Oxum] comforted him [Orixalá] singing a song.
> Whenever Orixalá was in need of her
> he could sing this song to call her ...
>
> Then Orixalá began to cry of the great pain that he felt.
> He sung the song of Oxum.
> And Oxum came with her jar of water,
> washed the wound with water from the river
> and covered it with dressings of herbs
> that grew close to the source of the river.
>
> She bound the wound with the white cloth of Orixalá.
> Oxalá later healed.
> Orixalá adores Oxum because she is kind to him.[90]

The above myth fragment serves as an example of one possible articulation—in the sense of speech—that offers us a clue as to the meaning of the anomalous event; in a circular manner, the event itself as having occurred is precisely the clue to the presence of myth; in other words, the perceived bodily action that qualified the event (and with this what was actually uttered) points to some more elaborate articulation in language. I chose this myth because it expressly concerns the relationship between Oxum and Oxalá/Orixalá.[91] The details of the narrative content that links these names are not the primary concern for us; the myth is rather like a broad speech gesture that gives us a vague orientation. We are not concerned with textual exegesis per se; the priority of our glance is towards the explication of this anomalous occurrence in its experience as an *event*, open to perception.

During one of the *reuniões* I attended, there was an extraordinary happening. The *reunião* was going on as I have described, up to the recital of the Lord's Prayer and the Ave Maria by the *mãe-de-santo* after the *bênçãos* ("blessings"). Tupiniquim was taking an inordinately long time to "arrive." The evening was windy, the trees rustled, and the white paper ceiling rippled like waves. Immediately to my right sat the daughter and *filha-de-santo* of the *mãe-de-santo*; she would typically sit next to me, on the benches against the wall, to see that I was comfortable. I noticed, as the wind was blowing, that her eyes were closed and that her body swayed gently as she sat. Quite discretely at first, but with an increasingly sharp and loud pitch, she began to moan; the sound was piercing, like the sound recordings of dolphins. The *mãe-de-santo* approached her daughter; she very gently lay her head against her chest and stroked her hair as the *filha-de-santo*'s body began to slither—her arms as though sewn to her sides—against the *mãe-de-santo* in sinuous gestures. With time, the movements became more vigorous as the *filha* slid off her seat, though the sinuosity of her motion was not compromised, but further exaggerated as the pitch of the sound emanating from her became more piercing. Mãe Juta disclosed that "Oxum" was present. She gestured and a large sheet of plain white cloth was brought to her; she draped the fabric completely over the slithering body of her *filha-de-santo*/Oxum and—while gently stroking her head—called the name "Oxalá" a few times. Within a few moments, the sinuous movement ceased; the *mãe-de-santo* removed the cloth and her daughter eased back onto the bench, seeming a bit dazed but with eyes opened.[92]

Both the myth fragment and the anomalous event described above should be seen in relation to our principal task of explicating the intersubjective constitution of spatiality in the progress of the *reunião* in its *normalcy*; I stated that this was the reason for interrupting our description of the dancing and singing of the *caboclos* in the *reunião*. I also stated that we must see the description through to its end. We will see that the reason for interrupting the description of the *reunião* in its normal progression with the narrative of the anomalous intrusion is tied to the need to make an approximate qualification of the presence of myth in terms of the name "Oxalá," which

A phenomenological ethnography of space 201

we recall was uttered by the *caboclo* outside. My description of this event is complete, in the sense that I went from the beginning to the end. But we still have not arrived at the end of the event of the singing and dancing of the *caboclos*, which I said was methodologically necessary in order to have a horizon that recalls its situational unity. We must therefore continue with the description of the *reunião* in its normalcy, and with this in hand take up again the apparent anomaly, in order to qualify the former.

Pai nosso, que estais no céu
Santificado seja o Vosso nome...
[Our Farther, who art in heaven,
hallowed be thy name...]

Ave Maria, cheia de graça,
O Senhor é convosco...
[Hail Mary, full of grace,
Our Lord is with thee...]

When all have been attended to by Tupiniquim in the intimacy of outside, the singing and dancing stops. The *caboclos* return to their seats around the table, and Tupiniquim to the head. Before this he gives each of us one wrapped *acaçá*.[93] From the head of the table, Tupiniquim leads the recital of the Pater Noster and the Ave Maria, repeated several times. During the prayer recital the two *caboclos* typically "depart"—the *filhas-de-santo* fall out of trance—but not so Tupiniquim. After the prayer, all perform the peculiar clapping gesture. With everyone standing, Tupiniquim takes the bowl of popcorn from the table and smears its contents on the heads and shoulders of each one, in a clockwise motion. Tupiniquim then retires into the sanctuary; the candles and cigars and other items from the table are taken into the sanctuary by the *filhas-de-santo*, but not the things that are "spread"—the leaves and the popcorn. The lights are switched on.

—

I said that the end of the event of the dancing and singing of the *caboclo* coincides with the end of the *reunião* in its public ritual aspect in general; this we now see is determined by Tupiniquim retiring into the sanctuary. The *caboclo* actually stopped dancing just before returning to his seat at the table to recite the Pater Noster and the Ave Maria. The actual beginning of the dancing occurred just after the *caboclo* recited a prayer while kneeling at the head of the table. Both actual instances of the beginning and the end of the event of dancing were marked by a "just after" and a "just before," which are to be understood in relation to some activity—prayer—performed in explicit reference to the table. The horizon of ritual action with which we are concerned—in terms of our task of explicating its spatiality—is therefore to be understood as existing within the limits of this "just after" and "just before." Within this horizon of activity, we are concerned with the meaning of the situation as it shows itself to perception, which is necessarily a *spatial* showing and it is the *meaning as spatiality* that we are after. Therefore, in terms of phenomenological method, what has priority for us is the perceptual unfolding of the situation, because this is the phenomenon that we are reflectively seeking to clarify. The symbolic dimension is part of the perceptually experienced continuum that qualifies the temporal unfolding of the event, and thus the significance of the spatial environment. Here, spoken utterances stand out from the mute background of the architectural environment, insofar as they are expressly articulate actions; this is the reason why certain uttered names—"Pai Nosso," "Ave Maria," "Tupiniquim," "Oxalá"—are privileged and direct my description at certain points. It is in terms of this original perceptual movement that all present share in the meaning common to the event, in terms of its spatiality, even though the depth of understanding may vary from one person to the next.

Just after the *caboclo* recited the prayer while kneeling at the head of the table, he began singing and dancing, clarifying through these gestures that a certain part of the floor was for the purpose of dancing. During this time, Tupiniquim was outside, on the deck at the site of an isolated candle; the other *caboclo* would join him at the location of the other candle. While in the room and sitting on the bench, our attention—that is, that of those present—is drawn to the visual spectacle of the *caboclo* dancing and the aural homogeneity of the singing and clapping, which extends all around the room. In this environment, the hold of ritual action on our glance is loosened; we can attend to other aspects of the room while singing and clapping, without disturbing the overall rhythmic flow of the music and dancing. Tupiniquim's absence from the visual and aural scene, however, is for us an anticipatory presence, as one by one we are called outside. Each of us walks past the "dance floor," interrupting the view of the other for an instant. We arrive quickly to the area of the room just before the outside deck, where we remove our shoes, small items, and accessories in a shuffling manner; in fact, during the singing and dancing there is a constant shuffling in the background that, in its very indeterminacy as action, competes for our attention. We experience a certain "conflict of interest," as a "passion"—suffering the anticipatory distractions made manifest by the shuffling of others as they prepare to step outside—and as an "action" directing our attention to the primary spectacle of the *caboclo* dancing. One of us is now called: I rise from the bench and like those before me, walk past others. The scene of the "dance floor"—its pre-eminence qualified by the *caboclo*'s gestures in relation to a homogeneous background of clapping and singing—is now for me a background as a whole. For me, the environment of dancing has been radically interrupted, insofar as its "root" was in fact the moment "just after" the action of the *caboclo* praying at Tupiniquim's empty seat; in other words, I am now before Tupiniquim's bodily presence.

A phenomenological ethnography of space 203

For simplicity, let us conflate the experience I described with Tupiniquim and the *caboclo* outside as if it were *one* event; I will therefore refer to the actions of Tupiniquim and the *caboclo*, as if they were performed by one *caboclo*, using the names interchangeably.[94]

In this place—outside in the dark by the candle—my individual body becomes expressly the "object" of attention, like being measured by a tailor. My eyes are closed, I do not "spectate" nor is anything "to hand"; *as my body*, it seems I am acted upon. But even in this intimate relation with Tupiniquim, I continue to hear the singing and dancing taking place inside; my current inaction or "passivity" continues to refer to the ongoing activity inside, which is now for me more indefinite. In other words, the continuity of my experience of the spatiality of the *reunião* in its aspect of dancing and singing is not absolutely broken; rather, the current experience modifies my understanding of this continuity. The modification is actually a clarification: when I was in the room sitting on the bench, the shuffling activity to the side instituted a passive interest in what was happening outside which conflicted with my active engagement with the *caboclo*'s dancing gestures. Once called outside, I begin the concrete process of fulfilling this institution and progressively realise in the clarity of actual presence what was only anticipatory and imaginary. But this clarification does not have the sense of simply adding something to something else that remains as it was. The *whole* experience of the spatiality of the *reunião* has been modified and continues to be modified as a whole until it is complete. Even if the explicit meaning of the symbolic actions of Tupiniquim towards my body is not known by me, I still have an original understanding of the experience as an *event*, and furthermore, this original understanding becomes *habitual*.

I have stated that the limit of my enquiry is the *reunião* in its performance, and furthermore that I am drawing out from within this limit the significance of its spatiality. The historical dimension, too, is qualified from within this limit, and this qualification is in terms of *perceptual genesis*. It is in fact the perceptual genesis of the experience of the event that points us towards the relativism of historical significance in the wider hermeneutic sense. Therefore, to justify an historical enquiry that goes beyond the limit of the perceptual experience of the *reunião* in its performance, activities within this horizon have themselves to point us in this direction. The clearest indicator in this regard is speech, and more precisely the speaking of proper names. It is for this reason that I have introduced the "historical" problem of myth in relation to the name "Oxalá," which was uttered outside. I use Oxalá as an *example* of the utterance of names in general and do not mean to imply that his is the only *orixá* name called, or that *caboclo* or even Catholic saint names are not mentioned; we have already seen that "Tupiniquim" and "Maria" are called, for example. As a clue to the meaning of the name "Oxalá" for the *reunião* in its *normalcy*, and thus the presence of myth as a norm, I have turned to the seemingly anomalous event in which he was most explicitly presenced, in the form of the white sheet.

It was in fact Oxum who first "descended" ("*desceu*"). The "saint" or *orixá* who is "fixed" in the "head" of the daughter of the *mãe-de-santo* is Oxum.[95] The question of the being of the *orixás* is fraught with difficulties;[96] rather than make ontological claims, I am concerned with the manner in which the *orixás* are experientially and intersubjectively given. As far as the *reunião* in its performance is concerned, we witness the gestures of the *filha-de-santo*, and the proper name "Oxum" as a qualification. When the white sheet was draped over the body of the *filha-de-santo*/Oxum, this gesture was tied to the proper name "Oxalá." It is in terms of these names that we were directed to myth, and more specifically, a myth fragment about them. The myth discloses for us a closeness or affinity between the names, but in the general sense of "affection" or *pathos*, as simply suffering the effect of some other presence in a prescribed way. Beyond this sense of *pathos*, I project no further into the possible meaning of the myth; what appears before us perceptually is the *belonging* of the name to the *filha-de-santo*, and that the names and the gestures are interlaced. What motivated this concern with the name was the distinct utterance by the *caboclo* outside of "Oxalá." We are turning away from this normal aspect of the praxis of the *reunião*—that is, the intimate relation with Tupiniquim outside—to the apparently intrusive event of the "descent" of "Oxum," in order to clarify the significance of the name "Oxalá" for the modification of our understanding of the situational unity of the event of dancing, and by extension the *reunião* as a whole in its *typical* praxis.

Just before the *mãe-de-santo*'s daughter and *filha-de-santo* began swaying her body beside me on the bench, all present were anticipating Tupiniquim's "arrival," as is typical during the recital of the Pater Noster and Ave Maria after the *bênçãos*. As we saw, the *bênçãos* made the floor thematic as the laboured site of the technical accomplishment of blessings. As the *mãe-de-santo* leads the prayer recital, her disposition normally changes, as we saw—she begins by rubbing her forehead, for example. Typically, except for the *mãe-de-santo*, everyone is engaged in the same activity of prayer, or, as I noted, of calling Tupiniquim through song. During all of this action, the head of the table retains its pre-eminence as anticipatory, even with the electric lights still on. But as her daughter's gestures gradually became more visible and audible, she drew the *mãe-de-santo* herself away from the task of "calling" Tupiniquim, towards a new task of attending to the "descending" "Oxum." As the *filha-de-santo* slithered against the body of the *mãe* and pierced the room with the sound of her wailing, she broke through the *reunião* and ruptured its spatial continuity. But even this rift was a modification, though of a more severe manner. Its severity can be measured in relation to one place: the head of the table. The *telos* of the *bênçãos* was ultimately the blessing received from the *mãe-de-santo* at the head of the table, even though this was achieved by the technical working of the ground. The "arrival" of Tupiniquim *was* the articulation of space, and everything else was a background until Tupiniquim extended the clearing

A phenomenological ethnography of space 205

of his presence towards the table. The "arrival" of the other *caboclos* was marked by their kneeling and praying gesture at Tupiniquim's empty seat, that is, his *absence* qualified the pre-eminence of the head of the table "itself"; the "itself" here is of course not the head of the table as a "thing," but as a *telos* whose fulfilment is the bodily presence of Tupiniquim sitting there within the horizon of the *reunião* in full play. The intimacy of outside was already anticipated in terms of Tupiniquim's absence from the scene of the *caboclo* dancing, an absence which means an absence at the table. Only the moment after the final recital of the Lord's Prayer and the Ave Maria, where Tupiniquim retired into the sanctuary, devalued the pre-eminence of head of the table. But this also marked the completion of the *reunião* as having accomplished its task of performance; this was not an interruption, not a breaking through the situational unity but constitutive of this unity as the *end*. The modification instituted by the "descent" of "Oxum" was not an end but a rupture that had to be overcome to secure the continuity of the *reunião*. Over against the head of the table, the spot on the bench where the *filha-de-santo* sat asserted its presence as a *telos*; let us attempt to describe it on its own terms, with a view to drawing out the spatial significance.

As we sit in prayer or call Tupiniquim expressly in song, our collective utterance is gradually taken out of its harmony by the high-pitched wailing of the *filha-de-santo*. Our attention is divided; though we can perhaps choose not to look, the sound surrounds us as it calls from the bench on the side of the room across from the *mãe-de-santo*. The room expands laterally as at some point we attend to both cries, just before the wail of the *filha* asserts itself over above all else. Mãe Juta walks towards her daughter and embraces her as the *filha*'s sinuous movement takes her body off the bench. By this time, the table with its "ornament" is fully in the background, and the utterance of the name "Oxum" by the *mãe-de-santo* throws us into the historicity of myth, *vaguely* for those of us for whom the name is a vague reference to some meaning "*orixá*," or *deeply* for those who—like the *mãe-de-santo* herself, or more so her *filha-de-santo* "in" whose "head" Oxum is "fixed"—embody and *live* the myth. When the *mãe* is brought the white sheet and she covers the body of her *filha* with it and the name "Oxalá," we see this mythic-historical reference *as* this very action of *covering with white cloth*. In other words, we experience the *verticality* of the *reunião* expressly, in two senses: (1) the historical depth of speech that opens up the mythic horizon of the proper name, even if only vaguely, and (2) the spatial height of the action of covering: it is the white cloth over the *filha-de-santo*'s body that is worked or that *works*, and not the laboured floor as with the *bênçãos*, for example. Covering the *filha-de-santo*'s body in the whiteness of the name "Oxalá" ends this interruption; here, the white cloth appears as a ritual implement, as a kind of "technology." Although the event of Oxum's "descent" appears as an anomaly, it is not necessarily the case that Oxum was unwelcome; after all, the *mãe-de-santo*'s actions towards her *filha* were loving and gentle. The simultaneous gestures of speech—calling

"Oxalá"—and movement—spreading the white cloth—appeared together as a mode of hospitality, welcoming Oxum's "surprise visit" through the reassurance of Oxalá's care, protection, and literal "covering." We can now leave this example and take up again the task of clarifying the sense of the modification introduced in the intimacy of the outside in its typicality.

Typically, as I stand face to face with Tupiniquim outside, he *covers* my body: either "brushing" my body with leaves from the *mato*, rubbing my sides with his hands, tracing my head until the "snap" at my ear, covering me with *acaçá*, with smoke, or through the utterance of the name "Oxalá." I experience Tupiniquim's concern for my bodily presence in a certain way; earlier I used the image of being measured by a tailor. In fact, the Portuguese expression "*fazer um 'trabalho*,'" literally, "to make a 'work,'" is used in describing Tupiniquim's "vocation."[97] Tupiniquim does not measure my body with the concern of a tailor; his "equipment" consists of leaves from the *mato*, smoke, *acaçá*, and even the very name "Oxalá," and the *topos* of this working is marked by a lit candle on the ground. The "dress" that he covers me with as he practises his calling on my body is apparently not useful in an instrumental sense. This "covering" of my body rather seems "ornamental," comparable to the objects on the "dinner" table, which are not there to be eaten. This comparison is also a coincidence: the leaves, the smoke—that is, the cigars—the *acaçá*, and the candles are also to be found at the table—in the context of the occasionality of the event of the *reunião*—as "decorative." The depth of my understanding of the significance of this "ornamental" situation is dependent on the depth of my involvement in the ritual praxis. By the terms "decorative" and "ornamental," I do not mean to suggest something superfluous; on the contrary, I am pointing towards the expression and articulation of the situation through bodily gesture, the mediation of implements, and speech, as precisely what make possible my participation in and access to its significance and occasionality. In this way its ritual and practical functions, as aspects of Tupiniquim's vocation, are inherent to its communicative and expressive givenness as *embodied*, including the palpable qualities of smoke and the sound of speech.[98]

When Tupiniquim has ended his vocational practice concerning my bodily presence, I return to my seat on the bench inside, after having recovered my things. Typically, I rejoin the others inside, and like everyone else on the bench, I clap and watch the *caboclo* dancing and singing. If I am not the last, other people leave the bench and shuffle about before being attended to by Tupiniquim outside. I do not experience their shuffling in the same way as before, insofar as I no longer anticipate being called outside. I have already accomplished the task of handing my bodily self over to Tupiniquim to be "adorned" and can now be more or less wholly claimed by the spectacle before me. The "conflict of interest" that I experienced earlier has now been resolved by the absorption of the experience outside into the continuity of the ritual, as a fulfilled task; yet, I can still free myself from this claim of the inside spectacle and direct my attention to others outside as, for example, a researcher might.

When Tupiniquim has completed his work outside and has attended to everyone, he returns to his seat, as do the other *caboclos*. We are taken back to a similar scene as at the beginning: the monotonic quality of the recital of the Lord's Prayer and the Ave Maria. But this situation is not the same as before; we do not anticipate Tupiniquim's "departure" as a *telos*. In fact, after the recital, Tupiniquim performs a few brief actions—rubbing the popcorn and giving out the *acaçá*—before retiring into the sanctuary or shrine.[99] There seems to be, therefore, a certain "open endedness" to this ending of the *reunião*, and the prayers are not oriented to a *telos* in the same way as at the beginning. Let us pay closer attention. During prayer, typically—though not always—the two other *caboclos* "depart" with a less vigorous bodily gesture as per their "arrival," although they still shriek. Similar to the beginning, there is a certain "neutralness" to the room, qualified by the monotonic speech, yet the table is still more of a foreground. When the prayer is ended and Tupiniquim attends to everyone with the popcorn, the situation resembles the earlier event when he embraced everyone to the chanting of "*Você gostou de mim?...*"; in walking around, he "foregrounds" the background and by this time—just before the lights go on—the head of the table is already losing its pre-eminence. When Tupiniquim finally retires to the sanctuary and the lights go on, the room becomes "ordinary": the table is "merely" a table, as also the chairs, and so forth. The *filhas-de-santo* begin sweeping the leaves off the floor and gathering the spread popcorn and leaves off the table.[100] Tupiniquim remains in the sanctuary, with the doors closed or slightly ajar, until at some point he "departs," and a loud shriek is heard from within the room.

*

On some occasions, family friends or other persons come to the *reunião* specifically to consult with Tupiniquim on seemingly mundane matters, such as financial, relationship, or work problems. They often come towards the end, but sometimes are there earlier. If they are there early enough, they speak with Tupiniquim when he is at the table. One of the *filhas-de-santo* places a small stool to the right of Tupiniquim, where the guest would sit. If the guest is female, she must wrap a length of cloth around her body from her chest, similar to the dress of the *filhas-de-santo*, prior to sitting with Tupiniquim. If the "visitors" arrive late, they would see Tupiniquim after he retires to the sanctuary, and therefore in the sanctuary. In my experience, only one or two persons would come to see Tupiniquim in this capacity at any one event. There appears, therefore, to be an important social function that Tupiniquim fulfils, an analysis of which would thicken our description of intersubjective spatial constitution but is beyond the scope of the current enquiry. Jocélio Teles dos Santos notes the *caboclo*'s role as a "guide" or "godfather," for which one of the functions of the "*sessão*" is to offer counsel.[101]

Earlier in the text, I described Tupiniquim's "arrival" as a "seam," the instant of which I said was difficult to phenomenologically clarify because of its seemingly complete nature. We know now what lies on the other side of this "edge," and we can confirm the situational unity of the *reunião* as a whole. Therefore, we can clarify this seam as a *modification* of the orientation of the *reunião*. This modification has a value different to the "rift" of "Oxum's" "descent," and also different to the fulfilment of the vocational attention paid to one's bodily presence by Tupiniquim outside. It is more radical in that it points to an *absence*. We now see that the *telos* of Tupiniquim's arrival is his retiring into the sanctuary. This means that the *reunião* as a whole was always oriented to its completion in terms of this room at every step, even from the preparatory start, the description of which we began with in an anticipatory way. The "ornament" at the table—apart from the popcorn and the leaves, which in the end did have a "use"—"retires" into the sanctuary with Tupiniquim, including the candles. The sanctuary is lit by these candles. Typically, its interior is not in view, although one gets a glimpse as things are taken into it. In principle, the pre-eminence of the sanctuary is as an absence to perceptual clarification. Like the instant of the "arrival" of Tupiniquim, it stands out, apart from our experience of the spatiality of the *reunião* in its unfolding. It is a pre-eminent "background," which only comes to light as having been a "proscribed" *telos*; the end is "not in sight," quite literally.

Finally, the *filhas-de-santo* share out *munguzá*, a sweet porridge made with *milho*, to all in the room.[102] Everyone chats in a relaxed manner, and the situation has the ease of everydayness, except for the fact that there is a sense that something transmundane is still happening in the sanctuary, which is now an *ecstatic* background.

Notes

1 See Chapter 1, "Fieldwork as Methodological Clue."
2 The issue is not purely one of memory without material "supports," as I also made notes and sketches in the field. It was not possible within the scope of this book to elaborate on the role of making field notes and drawing for my fieldwork, and their relation to photography. I was given the opportunity to discuss these more practical aspects of documentation—including my choice to use black and white film photography and even technical aspects of this—in a lecture for a joint seminar at the Graduate School of Architecture at the University of Johannesburg (GSA) and the School of Architecture at the University of Illinois Urbana-Champaign in the spring of 2021. I thank the Director of the GSA, Mark Raymond, for the invitation, and the students for their lively engagement with the material.
3 See Chapter 3, "Empathic Spatiality."
4 Edmund Husserl, *Phantasy, Image Consciousness, and Memory (1898–1925)*, trans. John B. Brough (Dordrecht: Springer, 2005). In German as Husserl, *Phantasie, Bildbewusstsein, Erinnerung: Zur Phänomenologie der anschaulichen Vergegenwärtigungen. Texte aus dem Nachlass (1898–1925)*, Husserliana, vol. 23, ed. Eduard Marbach (The Hague: Martinus Nijhoff, 1980).

A phenomenological ethnography of space 209

5 Julia Jansen, "Imagination De-Naturalized: Phantasy, the Imaginary, and Imaginative Ontology," in *The Oxford Handbook of the History of Phenomenology*, ed. Dan Zahavi (Oxford: Oxford University Press, 2018), 683.
6 See Chapter 2.
7 John B. Brough's introduction to Husserl, *Phantasy, Image Consciousness, and Memory*, xxxvii–xl.
8 See Chapter 3, specifically the sections on "Empathic Spatiality" and "Generative Space."
9 Regarding the question of the status of the example for phenomenological description, an analysis of the relationship between the phenomenology of phantasy and that of history, which is beyond the scope of this study, is implicated. On the former, see Richard M. Zaner, "Examples and Possibles: A Criticism of Husserl's Theory of Free-Phantasy Variation," *Research in Phenomenology* 3 (1973): 29–43. On the question of history see David Carr, *Phenomenology and the Problem of History: A Study of Husserl's Transcendental Philosophy* (Evanston, IL: Northwestern University Press, 1974).
10 Javier Carreño, "On the Temporality of Images According to Husserl," *New Yearbook for Phenomenology and Phenomenological Philosophy*, 8 (2008): 74.
11 Brough's introduction to *Phantasy, Image Consciousness, and Memory*, xlvi. Husserl develops detailed analyses of this, differentiating between: "1) the physical image, the physical thing made from canvas, marble, and so on; 2) the representing or depicting object; and 3) the represented or depicted object. For the latter, we prefer to say simply '*image subject*'; for the first object [...] 'physical image'; for the second [...] 'image object'." Husserl, *Phantasy, Image Consciousness, and Memory*, 21. See Carreño's analyses, cited above, for a detailed introduction to the theory of image consciousness in Husserl.
12 See the discussion in Chapter 3 of the present work, "The Genesis of Space."
13 Jansen, "Imagination De-Naturalized," 685–86.
14 Marcio Goldman, "How to Learn in an Afro-Brazilian Spirit Possession Religion: Ontology and Multiplicity in Candomblé," in *Learning Religion: Anthropological Approaches*, ed. Ramón Sarró and David Berliner (Oxford: Berghahn, 2007), 103–4. The etymology of the word *"candomblé"* itself is disputed. Roger Bastide and William Megenney claim that it was the name of a dance, Rachel Harding suggests it is of Bantu origin, while Pedro McGregor notes that the "problem [...] is that the two consonants 'b' and 'l,' together, simply do not exist either in Sudanese or in Bantu languages." See Bastide, *African Religions of Brazil*, 191; William Megenney, *A Bahian Heritage* (Chapel Hill: University of North Carolina Press, 1978), 97; Rachel Harding, *A Refuge in Thunder: Candomblé and Alternative Spaces of Blackness* (Bloomington: Indiana University Press, 2003), 45; Pedro McGregor, *A Moon and Two Mountains: The Myths, Ritual and Magic of Brazilian Spiritism* (London: Souvenir Press, 1996), 70.
15 Jim Wafer, *The Taste of Blood: Spirit Possession in Brazilian Candomblé* (Philadelphia: University of Pennsylvania Press, 1991), 55–62.
16 Luis Nicolau Parés, *The Formation of Candomblé: Vodun History and Ritual in Brazil*, trans. Richard Vernon (Chapel Hill, NC: University of North Carolina Press, 2013), 1.
17 Parés, *The Formation of Candomblé*, 3; see the first part of Chapter 1 of the present work.
18 See Jocélio Teles dos Santos, "O termo e as definições de Caboclo," in *O Dono da Terra: O Caboclo nos Candomblés da Bahia* (Salvador: SarahLetras, 1995), 53. Similarly, regarding the etymology of the word, Jim Wafer notes that "the term *caboclo* (which in Candomblé is usually pronounced without the *l*, as *caboco*) is said to come from the Tupi word *kari'boka*, meaning 'deriving from

210   *A phenomenological ethnography of space*

the white.' Thus its primary meaning is 'mestizo,' 'a person of part Indian and part European descent.'" Wafer, *The Taste of Blood*, 55.
19   Santos, *O Dono da Terra*, 53.
20   Wafer, *The Taste of Blood*, 197.
21   Santos, 56.
22   Wafer, 89. Santos lists typical *caboclo* names, Tupiniquim among them, in Santos, 149–52. The *mãe-de-santo* herself once told me that Tupiniquim dwells in the forests of Angola. Wafer notes that "the *caboclos*, who are the spirits of dead Indians and backwoodsmen [...] dwell in a forest land of beauty and abundance called Aruanda (The name probably comes from the city of Luanda, in Angola)" (Wafer, 63).
  On the historical association of *caboclos* with Congo-Angola *candomblés*, Parés notes the "general expansion of candomblés in the postabolition period that included [...] an increase in Nagô terreiros, as well as others exhibiting a Congo-Angola influence, that for their part aided the expansion of the so-called *Cabaclo* Candomblé." Parés, *The Formation of Candomblé*, 155–56.
23   Goldman, 104.
24   Bastide offers a sociological explanation for this, which has been challenged by recent scholarship. See Bastide, "Geography and the Afro-Brazilian Religions," in *African Religions of Brazil*, 173–219; Harding, *A Refuge in Thunder*, 64–67; and Parés, *The Formation of Candomblé*, 87–123 on the significance of *vodun*. Compare the focus on Yorùbá traditions in Mikelle Smith Omari-Tunkara, *Manipulating the Sacred: Yorùbá Art, Ritual, and Resistance in Brazilian Candomblé* (Detroit, MI: Wayne State University Press, 2005).
25   Roy Clive Abraham, *Dictionary of Modern Yoruba* (London: University of London Press, 1958), 483.
26   See Roger Bastide, "O borí," in Bastide, *O Candomblé da Bahia: Rito Nagô*, trans. Maria Isaura Pereira de Queiroz (São Paulo: Compahnia das Letras, 2005), 42–45. See also Abraham, *Dictionary of Modern Yoruba*, 479, 480 for "*orí*" and "*borí*" respectively.
27   See Bastide, "Problems of Religious Syncretism," in *African Religions of Brazil*, 260–84.
28   Goldman, 115–18. See my discussion in Chapter 1 of the present work, "The Systematic Study of Candomblé: Some Theoretical Issues."
29   Parés, *The Formation of Candomblé*, 155. For a detailed presentation see Parés, "The Candomblés Social Composition and Its Increasing Racial Mixing," in *The Formation of Candomblé*, 94–100, and Harding, "The Nineteenth-Century Development of Candomble," in *A Refuge in Thunder*, 68–76.
30   Bastide, *O Candomblé da Bahia*, 49–50.
31   Pierre Verger, "Rôle joué par l'état d'hébétude au cours de l'initiation des novices aux Cultes des Orisha et Vodun," *Bulletin de l'Institut Français d'Afrique Noire* 16, nos. 3–4 (July–October 1954): 335.
32   Bastide, *O Candomblé da Bahia*, 77.
33   *O Candomblé da Bahia*, 77. See also Pierre Verger, "The Yoruba High God—A Review of the Sources," *Odu* 2, no. 2 (January 1966): 19–40.
34   Wole Soyinka notes that "for the Yorùbá, the gods are the final measure of eternity, as humans are of earthly transcendence. To think, because of this, that the Yorùbá mind reaches intuitively towards absorption in godlike essence is to misunderstand the principle of religious rites, and to misread [...] the significance of religious possession." Quoted in Olufemi Taiwo, "Òrìsà: A Prolegomenon to a Philosophy of Yorùbá Religion," in *Òrìsà Devotion as*

A phenomenological ethnography of space 211

World Religion: The Globalization of Yorùbá Religious Culture, ed. Jacob K. Olupona and Terry Rey (Madison: University of Wisconsin Press, 2008), 101.
35 Santos, *O Dono da Terra*, 119–22.
36 For example, the detailed descriptions in Bastide, *O Candomblé da Bahia*, and more recent ethnographies of Rosamaria Barbara, "A danças das Aiabás, Dança, corpo e cotidiano das mulheres de candomblé" (PhD diss., University of São Paulo, 2002) and Gisèle Binon Cossard, "Contribution a l'étude des Candomblés au Brésil: Le Candomblé Angola" (PhD diss., University of Paris, 1970).
37 See the descriptions in Wafer, *The Taste of Blood*, 68–83, and Santos, 91–115.
38 See Santos, 116–17, Bastide, *African Religions of Brazil*, 60–61, and McGregor, *A Moon and Two Mountains*, 86ff.
39 In Candomblé, each day of the week is consecrated to one or more *orixás*. Thursday is consecrated to the *orixás* Oxóssi and Ogum. Oxóssi in particular is understood as having an affinity with the *caboclo*, as the *orixá* associated with hunting and the forest, armed with a bow and arrow. As I noted in Chapter 1, Candomblé is for the most part a secretive religion, and I even at times had a sense that *reuniões* took place on other days, which I was not told about. On the affinity of the *caboclo* with Oxóssi, see Santos, "Oxossi/Caboclo," in *O Dono da Terra*, 142–46. See also Paul Christopher Johnson, "Secrecy and Ritual Practice," in *Secrets, Gossip, and Gods: The Transformation of Brazilian Candomblé* (Oxford: Oxford University Press 2002), 103–47.
40 In a conversation I had with anthropologist Juana Elbein dos Santos in March 2008, she spoke of the relation between the *mato* of a Candomblé *terreiro* and the tropical forest of Africa. Santos explained that the *mato* is meant to symbolise the forest, and it need not be an actual area of growth. Bastide notes that "the *orixás* live neither in the *mato* nor in the forest; they live always in Africa [...] Thus, the first opposition between sacred and profane is the opposition between Africa and Brazil." For both Bastide and Santos, therefore, the sense of the *mato* in some way is a reference to Africa. In relation to Candomblé *caboclo*, however, the issue appears more complex insofar as the apparently autochthonous *caboclos* are also closely associated with the *mato*, in its specifically Brazilian actuality. See Bastide, *O Candomblé da Bahia*, 73; on the *caboclos* see Santos, *O Dono da Terra*, 49.
41 The vernacular name of the leaf is *murici* (Byrsonima sericea DC.) of the Malpighiaceae family. See Robert A. Voeks, *Sacred Leaves of Candomblé: African Magic, Medicine and Religion in Brazil* (Austin: University of Texas Press, 1997), 182 and Santos, 120.
42 The expression of the ceiling in this way is typical for the public ritual room or *barracão* of Candomblé *terreiros*. In a conversation I had with anthropologist Fábio Lima in 2010, he pointed out to me that the ceiling as articulated in this way refers to Oxalá. The *orixá* Oxalá in Brazil is associated with the colour white and with the sky; syncretised with Christ and, through his iconographic representation as a bird, with the Holy Spirit (as a dove); attributed the quality of wisdom; and symbolically related to water. For a rich description and allegorical interpretation of two significant rituals of Oxalá—the Waters of Oxalá and the *Lavagem do Bonfim*—see Roberto Strongman, "Transatlantic Waters of Oxalá: Pierre Verger, Mário de Andrade, and Candomblé in Europe," in *Queering Black Atlantic Religions: Transcorporeality in Candomblé, Santería, and Vodou* (Durham, NC: Duke University Press, 2019), 212–30. On Oxalá as "the sky-father of the orixás" see Johnson, *Secrets, Gossip, and Gods*, 137. Regarding terms used to describe states of trance, see Wafer, 101.

43 The *murici* leaves are also associated with the *orixás* Ogun and Xangô. The mythic-historical understanding of these three *orixás* and their interrelation is complex. According to Renato da Silveira, Oxóssi was the first Nagô (Yorùbá) *orixá* to be cultivated in the Candomblé of the Barroquinha. In Africa, Oxóssi was originally a quality of Odé, the *orixá* of the hunt in the Nagô region of Africa, the word *ode* meaning "hunter" in Yorùbá. In Brazil, however, the name "Oxóssi" became more important. The cult of Oxóssi also refers to a quality of the *orixá* Exu, called Adetá. Both the *orixás* Oxóssi and Exu, according to Santos, are seen as having affinities with the *caboclo*. On the *murici* leaves see Voeks, *Sacred leaves of Candomblé*, 182–83. On the cult of Oxóssi, see Renato da Silveira, *O Candomblé da Barroquinha: Processo de constituição do primeiro terreiro baiano da keto* (Salvador: Edições Maianga, 2006), 396–97. On Oxóssi, Exu, and the *caboclo*, see Santos, 139–46.

44 According to Voeks, the tree species *gameleira branca* (*Ficus sp.*) was adopted in Brazil as the *orixá* Iroko (Yorùbá name) or Tempo, who "became the god of time and eternity." Although the word "tempo" is Portuguese for time, the etymology of the name points to that of a Bantu deity named Zaratempo. While not the species *gameleira branca*, during the *reunião* this majestic and lush tree is a constant and at times alluring presence in the background, visually and aurally. I thank anthropologist Moises Lino e Silva for identifying the tree, via images I sent, as Indian almond (*Terminalia catappa*) or *amendoeira* in Brazil. See Voeks, 163–65; Wafer, 166.

45 Conversation with Gilmara; but also from my own observation. On the public *caboclo* festivals, Wafer notes that "the *orixás* are not expected to descend, and if they do, they are 'suspended,' without being given the opportunity to dance." Wafer, *The Taste of Blood*, 69.

46 Edison Carneiro, *Candomblés da Bahia* (Bahia: Brasileira de Ouro, 1948), 82.

47 Exu is a particularly difficult *orixá* to qualify. He is known as the "trickster" and generally associated with thresholds, literally and metaphorically. Insofar as no aspect of life escapes passage in some form or other, Exu's presence seems always implied. This is revealed most markedly in his role in divination, called Ifa, thus his close association with the phenomenon of language. In addition, there are multiple *exus* or *exuas*, the feminine version. See Bastide, "Exu," in *O Candomblé da Bahia*, 161–186; Wafer, "Part 1: Exu," in *The Taste of Blood*, 1–49. See also Henry Louis Gates Jr., "A Myth of Origin: Esu-Elegbara and the Signifying Monkey," in *The Signifying Monkey: A Theory of African-American Literary Criticism* (Oxford: Oxford University Press, 1988), 3–43, and Robert D. Pelton, "Legba and Eshu: Writers of Destiny," in *The Trickster in West Africa: A Study of Mythic Irony and Sacred Delight* (Berkeley: University of California Press, 1980), 113–63. On Ifa divination, see Martin Holbraad, *Truth in Motion: The Recursive Anthropology of Cuban Divination* (Chicago, IL: University of Chicago Press, 2012).

48 See the similar description in Santos, 22, 32. The representation of the *caboclo* in this way is typical and refers to the wider historical issue of the image of the "Indian" in the formation of Brazilian national identity. One of the main points of reference is the work of the influential Brazilian historian, Gilberto Freyre. The discourse regarding the status of the indigenous person is of course layered and complex; see, for example, Wafer, 53–87 and Santos, 31–52. On the historical context of Brazilian nationalism see F. W. O Morton, "The Conservative Revolution of Independence" (PhD diss., Oxford University, 1971). On Amazonian anthropology see Edwardo Viveiros de Castro, *From the Enemy's Point of View: Humanity and Divinity in an Amazonian Society*, trans. Catherine V. Howard (Chicago, IL: University of Chicago Press, 1992).

49 The image of the *caboclo* with the snake is considered to be a nationalist reference to Bahian Independence, in which the snake represents the defeated governor of the city, being "crushed under the feet." But the snake is also an important symbol in Candomblé that refers to the *orixá/vodun* Oxumaré, the rainbow-snake. On the *caboclo* and Bahian Independence, see Santos "O dois de Julho," in *O Dono da Terra*, 35. On Oxumaré, see E. Bolasi Idowu, *Olódùmarè* (London: Longmans, 1962), 34; J. Melville Herskovits, *An Outline of Dahomean Religious Belief* (Menasha, WI: American Anthropological Association, 1933), 56–57; and Pierre Verger, "Yoruba Influences in Brazil," *Odu*, no. 1 (January 1995): 10.

50 For the attributes and place of Xangô in terms of the cardinal points, see Bastide, *O Candomblé da Bahia*, 106–8, 115–24. On myths involving Xangô, see Reginaldo Prandi, "Xangô," in *Mitologia dos Orixás* (São Paulo: Companhia das Letras, 2011), 242–91. Xangô is considered the Yorùbá equivalent to the Dahomean *vodun* Sogbo, who is female while Xangô is male. There are also multiple modes or "qualities" of Xangô. In other words, the understanding of the *orixás* and their interrelation is fluid. On Sogbo see Herskovits, *An Outline of Dahomean Religious Belief*, 19–22.

51 We will meet this *orixá* of sweet (fresh) water—"identified" with Our Lady of Candlemass—in person as the *reunião* unfolds. See Verger, "Yoruba Influences in Brazil," 10.

52 The presence of *preto-velho*, literally "old black" man, points to the dimension of this *terreiro* that includes Umbanda, an Afro-Brazilian religion with elements of Spiritism. Paul C. Johnson notes that *"pretos velhos* (old blacks) are the spirits of former slaves." See Johnson, *Secrets, Gossip, and Gods*, 52. On the sense of *"preto"* in relation to African and Creole identity in nineteenth-century Brazil see Parés, *The Formation of Candomblé*, 47–52.

53 The significance of the presence of Ogum, like that of the other *orixás* we have encountered—Exu, Oxalá, Oxóssi, Xangô, and Oxum—for the *reunião* as it is accomplished, is a question that the *reunião* itself must suggest and disclose. On the *orixás* in Brazil and their link with Africa, see Silveira, "As tradições jeje-nagô, iorubá-tapá, aon Efan, ijexá," in *O Candomblé da Barroquinha*, 457–76. On Ògŭn (Ogum) as "the divinity to whom belong iron and steel," see Idowu, *Olódùmarè*, 85–89.

54 On Ossâim, "guardian of the sacred leaves and medicine" and his "symbol" of "a piece of iron with seven points, with the central point mounted by a magical bird," see Voeks, 115–19.

55 *Acaçá* was noted as early as the original ethnography in 1900 of Nina Rodrigues (2005, 100). On *acaçá* and "mythological bodies," see Fabio Lima, *As Quartas-feiras de Xangô: Ritual e Cotidiano* (João Pessoa: Editora Grafset, 2010), 89–94.

56 Lima, *As Quartas-feiras de Xangô*, 94. On the *eguns*, see Bastide, "A Sociedade dos Eguns," in *O Candomblé da Bahia*, 133–43.

57 In speaking of the "coming-out" rituals of new Candomblé initiates, in which they incorporate their respective *orixás* in a public festival, Wafer observes that each "had a white cross on the top of each foot" (137).

58 The question of initiation for the *caboclo reunião* ritual seems less involved than initiation pertaining to the *orixás* in Candomblé; in fact, the word "initiation" in this case may be misleading. Gilmara explained to me that the *caboclos* are "free," and persons who are appropriate "mediums" will simply find their "heads" entered by the "saint." The *mãe-de-santo* can "fix" the *caboclo* in the head, but this requires only a few visits and is far less involved than "fixing" an *orixá* in the head of the *filha-de-santo*, as I discussed earlier. On initiation pertaining to *caboclos* see Santos, 67–69. Parés notes that "it is also said that

the *caboclos* have no initiation, that is, *vodunsis* do not go through any special preparation in order to be consecrated to their *caboclos*. It is accepted, however, that these entities may manifest themselves in specific situations in order to warn of some danger, give counsel, or admonish." See Parés, *The Formation of Candomblé*, 242–43. On the elaborate rites of initiation in Candomblé, see Binon Cossard, "Contribution a l'étude des Candomblés au Brésil," 157–217.

59 Edison Carneiro notes that in the festival of Ômòlu-Óbaluyê—the *ôlubajé*—the principal element is popcorn. Carneiro, 82. The domain of Omolu (the *vodun* Sakpata, a name that is taboo), is "earth," and he is the "god of smallpox and infectious disease"; the St. Lazarus of the *orixás*. See Voeks, 79–80; Idowu, "Sòpòná," in *Olódùmarè*, 95–101; Bastide, *African Religions of Brazil*, 195, 264.

60 This apparently suggests the Spiritist "element"; see Santos, 116–17; also in McGregor, plate 4 above, shows a Spiritist gathering with glasses of water on a table.

61 The *adjá* is the implement of the *mãe-de-santo* of a Candomblé *terreiro* and is used in the grand public festivals to direct the orchestra, and therefore the *orixás* who manifest, and the ritual as a whole. Carneiro, 51.

62 Santos also notes the use of incense in the *caboclo* "sessions" (116).

63 This, according to Gilmara. For a broader discussion see Wafer, "Order and Progress," in *The Taste of Blood*, 53–87. Wafer, for instance, states that "there are two basic categories of *caboclo* spirits: those called *boiadeiros* or 'cowboys,' 'backwoodsmen' [...] and those called 'Indians,' [...] However, I have heard of others. There are, for example, various foreign *caboclos*, such as the King of Hungary [...], and Italian and Japanese *caboclos*." Wafer, 55.

64 M. McCance, "Incense," in *New Catholic Encyclopedia*, vol. 7, Catholic University of America (Detroit, MI: Thomson/Gale, 2003), 376–77; E. G. Cuthbert F. Atchley, *A History of the Use of Incense in Divine Worship* (London: Longmans, 1909).

65 Gilmara explained that the origin of the white dress is Islamic, implying that it dates to the presence of African Muslims brought to Brazil in the nineteenth century. We have descriptions of the nineteenth-century clothing from contemporary European travellers: "The gala dress of the black woman is very peculiar and very elegant. The upper part of the dress [...] is made of fine muslin [...] The skirt of the dress [...] has a white arabesque pattern sewed upon it [...] A large handkerchief of white net [...] is most gracefully made into a turban." James Wetherell, *Stray Notes from Bahia: Being Extracts from Letters, etc., during a Residence of Fifteen Years* (Liverpool: Birkenhead printed, 1860), 72–73. See also Harding, *A Refuge in Thunder*, 49–50; Bastide, *African Religions of Brazil*, 146–48. This thesis, however, is to an extent speculative, particularly in light of the historical disintegration of the "veneer of Mohammedanism" in Brazil; see Bastide, *The African Religions of Brazil*, 154. In addition, Adepegba makes no reference to the influence of Islam, when he notes that "the association of Obàtálá [Oxalá] with white cloth situates him within the Yorùbá epoch of a more advanced technological age than the epoch of Ògún or Ifá, who are associated with the earlier technology of intricately woven palm frond designs." Cornelius Adepegba, "Associated Place-Names and Sacred Icons of Seven Yorùbá Deities," in Olupona and Rey, *Òrìsà Devotion as World Religion*, 114.

66 On Augustine's doctrine of grace see Jaroslav Pelikan, *The Christian Tradition*, vol. 1 (Chicago, IL: University of Chicago Press, 1971), 305–6. On the Ave Maria and the status of the Virgin Mary as "full of grace" see Pelikan, *The Christian Tradition*, vol. 4 (Chicago, IL: University of Chicago Press, 1984), 39.

A phenomenological ethnography of space 215

67 Wafer describes *paó* as a "ritual gesture that involves clapping the hands in a rhythm that begins slowly and gradually increases in tempo" (201); also Santos, 119.
68 I noted this song in Chapter 3, and again thank Moises Lino e Silva for clarifying its sense. See Wafer, 73.
69 Wafer describes the "*Rezas e salvas de agradecimento* ('Prayers and greetings of thanks')" of a typical *caboclo* festival. These greetings are performed by the *caboclos* who manifest, and the structure of the festival is very different from the *reunião* (72–74).
70 This gesture, called *padê* and directed towards the *orixá* Exu, I witnessed myself several times at the public festivals of the grand *terreiros*. Of its character and significance, Binon Cossard notes, "Elles vont s'incliner devant les tambours en portant la main à terre, puis à leur tête. Ensuite, elles s'inclinent devant le père de saint qui, de sa main levée, leur donne sa bénédiction. Pendant le *pade* tous les assistants restent debout, à la fois par respect et par crainte d'un *oriSa* redouté, ombrageux, dont il est plus prudent de se méfier." (They [the initiates], bringing their hands and heads to the ground, prostrate themselves before the drums. Then they prostrate before the father-of-saint who, with his hands raised, confers blessings. During the *pade* all the assistants remain erect, both out of respect and fear of the dreaded, tenebrous *oriSa*, of whom it is prudent to beware.) See Binon Cossard, "Contribution a l'étude des Candomblés au Brésil," 102. See also Bastide, "O *padê* de Exu," in *O Candomblé da Bahia*, 34.
71 The phrase "presence of myth" is inspired by Leszek Kolakowski's short treatise. See Leszek Kolakowski, *The Presence of Myth*, trans. Adam Czerniawski (Chicago, IL: University of Chicago Press, 1989). For a selection of myths on Exu and Oxalá, see Prandi, *Mitologia dos Orixás*, 38–83, 500–523.
72 On the *equede* see Wafer, 16, and Bastide, *O Candomblé da Bahia*, 36.
73 Santos gives a description of the "manifestation" of *caboclos* (73–75). I asked Gilmara why the electric lights are turned off, and her reply was simply that Tupiniquim does not like them.
74 According to Wafer, "the state of vertigo that precedes trance" in a *caboclo* festival is called *barravento*; the person experiencing trance "partially loses consciousness and muscular control, and begins to lurch. With the onset of the trance state proper, the body control returns." See Wafer, 80–81.
75 As I noted, typically from this point until the end of the *reunião*—that is, in the presence of Tupiniquim—I was not permitted to take photographs.
76 Peter Carl, in his seminars for the History and Philosophy of Architecture MPhil at Cambridge University, often referred to this painting when speaking of the temporal, embodying structure of "situation," the latter in the sense used by Heidegger. Christ's head is framed by a halo, not of light, but of the shadow of the standing servant—a shadow as mute as the wall—his face in contrast is luminous, his eyes appear closed or looking downward, and his lips are shut; his gesturing hands are most articulate.
77 Luke 24: 31. Robert Carroll and Stephen Prickett, eds., *The Bible: Authorized King James Version with Apocrypha* (Oxford: Oxford University Press, 2008), 113.
78 Santos describes the clothes of the "Indians" worn by Candomblé "people of the saint" during the Bahian Independence Day parade, and Wafer notes the dress of "those [*caboclos*] called 'Indians,' who often wear feather headdresses, and may be costumed in feathers, fur, or hide." See Santos, 43 and Wafer, 55.

216   *A phenomenological ethnography of space*

79 This is quite different from the "descent" of an *orixá* into the body of a *filha-de-santo*. Typically, when *orixás* "descend into 'matter,' they keep their mouths and eyes closed" (Wafer, 62).
80 Wafer describes "*Caboclo talk*" as "distorted in a way that is meant to imitate the speech of bumpkins" (64–68).
81 When I was first introduced to Tupiniquim, I found it difficult to understand his Portuguese, which seemed even more confusing for him. Gilmara "translated" (she told me what he said in "*caboclo* talk" that was unintelligible to me) and explained to him that the situation was similar to when he spoke "Tupi" to them; I assume that by this she meant a Tupi-Guarani language.
82 Although it was difficult for me to understand Tupiniquim's speech, I typically sat next to Gilmara, who would tell me intermittently what was being discussed.
83 See Wafer, 80. The song I heard is slightly varied from the one noted by Wafer.
84 It was difficult for me to grasp the words of this prayer. Santos (43), in speaking of the Bahian Independence parade, notes that the "Indians," that is, the followers of Candomblé who "cultivate *caboclos*" "before the beginning of the parade [...] remain in front of the Church of Lapinha, kneeling in a semicircular position, praying in a language called *cabocla*, with some words in Portuguese, others offered as of Tupi origin. The prayers have a low melody and tone of lamentation." Santos goes on to note that "when the procession of the parade starts, they dance as if they were warring." These descriptions of particular details are evocative of what I witnessed and am describing of the *reunião*.
85 See Wafer, 70.
86 On the exclamation "*Isa!*", Wafer notes that it "is one of the interjections used by the *caboclos* as an expression of their 'Indian-ness'" (73).
87 In general, the dances of the *orixás* as manifest through their *filhas-de-santo* in the grand public festivals of "traditional" Candomblés are very specific and recognisable to those familiar in their distinct "styles." See Barbara, "A danças das Aiabás." The dances or sambas of *caboclos*, although not as formalized as those of the *orixás*, still have a typical character. Wafer identifies three types: "*the samba de sotaque* ('banter samba'); *the samba de roda* ('circle samba'); and *the samba de barravento* ('*barravento* samba,' for calling other *caboclos*)." The dances I witnessed seem closest to the *samba de roda*. See Wafer, 73–82.
88 In one of the *reuniãos* I attended there was a third *caboclo* who characteristically drank beer; in offering him the drink, the bottle was always placed before him on the ground with a respectful gesture, never handed to him directly.
89 This is referred to as *sacudimento*, or "leaf whipping." Voeks notes that it is "employed to neutralize negative energies and to restore spiritual equilibrium" (93). See also Santos, 120.
90 For the full text of the myth, see Prandi, "*Oxum recupera o báculo de Orixalá que Iansã joga no mar* [Oxum recovers the staff of Orixalá that Iansã throws in the sea]," in *Mitologia dos Orixás*, 333–34.
91 On the *orixás* Oxum and Oxalá/Orixalá see above note 51 and note 42.
92 It appears that this particular manifestation of Oxum has a quite different gestural character to that which one would typically find in the highly structured public Candomblé festivals. The latter I have witnessed on several occasions. See, for example, Barbara, 167–68.
93 This did not always happen.
94 It was sometimes the case that only Tupiniquim would attend to persons outside, so the "as if" here is not purely a case of descriptive simplification.

95 These are typical expressions in Candomblé. See, for example, the description of initiation in Bastide, *O Candomblé da Bahia*, 45–70; and Pierre Verger, "Première Cérémonie d'initiation au culte des orishas nago à Bahia au Brésil," *Revista do Museu Paulista* 9, Nova Série (1955): 269–91.
96 See Pierre Verger, *Notes sur le culte des Orisa et Vodun: À Bahia, la Baie de tous les saints, au Brésil et à l'ancienne Côte des esclaves en Afrique* (Dakar: IFAN 1957), 27–32, and Ulli Beier, *The Return of the Gods: The Sacred Art of Susanne Wenger* (Cambridge, UK: Cambridge University Press, 1975), 33. Goldman discusses the "ontological" question in terms of *process*, thus shifting the issue away from the implication of "substantiality" to a thesis of *action*. See Goldman, 110–18.
97 Santos, 120.
98 See my discussion in Chapter 3 of the present work on the notions of "occasionality" and "sense-history" (*Sinnesgeschichte*) in Husserl, specifically the section "The spatiality of the life-world." See also Hans-Georg Gadamer, "The Ontological Foundation of the Occasional and the Decorative," in *Truth and Method*, trans. Joel Weinsheimer and Donald G. Marshall (New York: Continuum, 2000), 138–52.
99 I use "sanctuary" and "shrine" interchangeably. The place where the implements of the *caboclo* live is called the "*assentamento*" or "seat" of the *caboclo*. On the "*assentamento*," Santos states that it "signifies the representation of his force and of the implements which to him are sacred [...] In many *terreiros*, the *assentamento* is located in a room called a *cabana*" (65).
100 I was told that the symbolic value of this is the casting away of negative energies.
101 Santos, 120–21.
102 Santos, 121.

Epilogue
Umweltlichkeit

Twilight deepened and the space appeared as if seen through a blue-grey brume. The twilight would eventually defer to the moon's light.[1] Amidst the sonority of chanting voices and the percussive vibrations of the air could be heard the shrill cries of an infant. I was already in the room, to which I must have been drawn by the peculiar curiosity and "lust of the eyes" that mark a child's first experience of something.[2] Typically, children "were sent to play behind the house."[3] I must have gone unnoticed in the interstice of moods; anticipating her incorporation of the saints, "everybody was tense. It seemed that the saints were already in the room. Necks were becoming stiff and eyes were shining, but nobody went into a trance" as yet.[4] Nenny, my paternal grandmother, held the newborn by its arms.[5] Just before, "they would strip the child naked, oil it down, pray, chant, sprinkle water over its head, and smoke it with incense; drums are always a part of such feasts."[6] Here I rely on my aunt's recollection and understanding, for the memory that holds me has the character of an impression, seen through the overcast atmospheres of remembrance. It is not a static portrait, but rather an impression of *movements*, of gestures. Holding the baby by its arms, its deep brown skin glistening and luminous with the oil like a saint's halo, my grandmother entranced swung her arms into the air lifting the infant above the horizon of everyone's gaze. My aunt explained this event to me as what "could have been a thanksgiving and blessing/offering up in one, what you may call a christening."[7]

In this book, I have ventured to interpret Husserl's meditations on space through an example that is typical of a style of experience one finds in Latin America and the Caribbean that indicates, more broadly, lived experiential dilations of the geo-historical horizons of transatlantic space.[8] My grandmother would have recognised the *mãe-de-santo*'s manner immediately—the whiteness of her dress, the "black lacquer of her skin," her gestures of welcome, her voice as she uttered the names "Oxalá" and "Oxum," the figuration and corporeity of her physiognomic transformation as Tupiniquim *chegou*.[9] In a similar fashion, the *mãe-de-santo* would have recognised the world of the "shacks buried in the ravines" in the village of Carenage in Trinidad and its enchanted population as "homecomrades"

DOI: 10.4324/9781351116145-6

Epilogue: Umweltlichkeit 219

(*Heimgenosse*).[10] Inherent to this mutual recognition would be latent communicative possibilities in speech—even if initially limited to the lingual and rhythmic articulations of music, due to linguistic difference—that would be present in advance, in terms of the historicity, lived bodily corporeity, and spatiality of the occasion of encounter.

The first time I met Mãe Juta it was early afternoon. A Trinidadian friend who had travelled with me to Brazil introduced me to someone whom she had met there, whom I also befriended, and who introduced me to the *mãe-de-santo*.[11] I met her at her home. Mãe Juta and her daughter, Gilmara, sat with me at the same table around which the *reunião* would, unbeknown to me, later unfold. At this time the table was covered by a fine green tablecloth. Despite the linguistic gaps—they didn't speak English and I struggled with Portuguese—the encounter had for me a general feeling of familiarity, of being at home.

In recounting this moment of fieldwork and the memorial image from my childhood, it is not merely the particular relation to me as an individual that I am pointing to; rather, I am indicating a historical quality that can only be experienced environmentally, even in imagination. The literary image is aimed at the evocation of lived experience, and thus of space. I have attempted in this study to describe the layers, textures, and sedimentations of spatial experience that constitute an intersubjective, generative, and historical density of spatiality that I have termed *environmentality*. This is my rendering of Husserl's term in German, *Umweltlichkeit*. I have proposed that there is a continuity of the conception of space in Husserl's work, which extends from his early descriptions of "phantoms" to his late articulations of "earth." I have explored Husserl's phenomenology of space, from its givenness as an abstract moment in phantom experience (visually and tactually in the corporeity of lived bodily kinaestheses); to its givenness as having accrued sense in the genesis and acquisition of habitualities; to its empathic and intersubjective constitution; and ultimately spatiality as experienced in its generativity and geo-historicity. The concept of enviornmentality that I propose expresses this full, concrete movement of the sense of spatiality. I have chosen to render *Umweltlichkeit* as environmentality, at the risk of losing its German articulation of "world" (*Welt*), in order to foreground through this terminological shift Husserl's attention to the contingency, intimacy, and even precarity of space in its embodied experience and intergenerational transfer. Environmentality as a spatial concept in a Husserlian sense foregrounds lived bodily spatiality. To conceptualise subjectivity in terms of embodiment is to recognise the particularities of the affectivity and allure of space, the manner in which space enchants and motivates one's kinaestheses. As I have demonstrated in this work, lived bodily kinaesthesis is not mere movement, but the potentiality for, and the genesis, acquisition, and accruing of, a sense-history as habitualities. Through the phenomenological register of *empathy* (*Einfühlung*), I described the relationality of space, its constitution in intersubjective community. In this way, space is also and fundamentally an inheritance, thus the generativity of space.

I don't recall having seen the *mãe-de-santo* leave the sanctuary after the *reunião* appears to have ended, as I would typically leave after helping to sweep the leaves off the floor. Perhaps on one or two occasions I felt it appropriate to linger long enough to see her afterwards, but in any event, I never entered or saw clearly the inside of the sanctuary during the *reunião*. I did, however, see it once during the day. It was perhaps an early afternoon, when the *reunião* was not in play, and Mãe Juta permitted me to see and to document the interior of the sanctuary. I found it extraordinary. It was a simple room, large enough to fit comfortably a small desk and chair, with a window to the east, which was at the time blacked out. All the surfaces, apart from the ceiling, were tiled with white tiles. The desk was covered with white cloth, with the little silver bell—the *adjá*—that was on the table to the left of the *mãe-de-santo* during the *reunião*, resting atop, covered by a patterned cloth and encircled by coloured, beaded necklaces. Across from the desk and resting on a built-out and stepped surface, low to the ground, were the objects and ritual implements that I had seen on the table during the *reunião*, and many others that I had not seen. I recognised the figurine of the *caboclo*, no longer illuminated by the candle's flickering light and centrally situated; rather, here it was part of a constellation of figures and statuary in miniature. Among these were doll-like figurines elaborately articulated according to attributes, which I came to recognise as those of *orixás*—growing up in Trinidad and Tobago, I do not recall seeing anthropomorphic articulations of orishas at feasts or ceremonies—and variations of the *caboclo* with an archer's (warrior or hunter) gesture. It struck me that I was not merely in the presence of a collection of things simply juxtaposed. The *caboclo* figurine pointed to an entire environmental transformation: the homogenisation of the space of the room by means of incense, in tension with the bodily desire to draw the perfumed smoke towards oneself; the articulation of the *worked* floor as the site of blessings (*bênçãos*); the pre-eminence of the head of the table during prayer, at the instant of Tupiniquim's "arrival," and in his bodily absence; the gradual rise to pre-eminence of the site on the bench through the sinuous gestures of the *filha-de-santo*/Oxum; the clearing that instituted the conflict between the floor as the site where the *caboclo* danced, over against the head of the table as the site of Tupiniquim's bodily absence; the latent desire for the intimate encounter with Tupiniquim such that "outside" is manifest as the site of his "covering" one's body with smoke, *acaçá*, and the name "Oxalá"; and the "ecstatic" presence of the inside of the sanctuary in the mode of a not-visible *telos* of the event. As with the *caboclo* figurine, each item in the sanctuary was potentially an index to a lived experiential transformation and articulation of spatiality, analogous to the *reunião*. Within the sanctuary was thus a constellation of spatial and cosmic possibilities.[12] Each object can be understood as involved in an anticipatory structuring of spatial relationships, constitutive of an ecology of intersubjective lived-experiential situations in reserve historically and in potentiality. The matter is not merely one of symbolism or of religiosity, but of the corporeity of the inherence of lived experience in such a way that one bears the environment in its historicity habitually and bodily.

We began with a description of the appearance to perception of mere visual phantoms, of "things" laid out on the table. These things are no longer as unfamiliar to us as when we first entered the room in Chapter 2 and laid our gaze to rest on the figurine, which did not initially appear with the familiarity, for example, of the candles. This means that we ourselves brought our own habitual modes of seeing to the table, not as something private or merely "subjective," but as a habitually inherited way of seeing tied to our historically situated "earth-space." From the start, therefore, phantom spatiality was geo-spatiality experienced in levels of familiarity and unfamiliarity, of recognisability and strangeness. Revisiting our first welcome at the table, following our "immersement" in the *reunião* in Chapter 4, we can no longer experience the environing world of the room in the same way. Perhaps it may have been for us typical that some persons would, in the corporeal expressivity of their bodies and speech, be given to us as other entities, for example *orixás*, *voduns*, or saints. The *caboclo reunião* would have thus appeared with a level of familiarity from the start, requiring special effort to see certain objects—the *acaçá* for example—as mere phantoms ("things" wrapped in leaves) in the way the candles would have to be imagined as-if unfamiliar. Perhaps we ourselves have the capacity to "manifest" a *caboclo* "in" our lived bodily being in its sexuality, in which case the entire unfolding of my description would be familiar in its typicality and normativity. As we witness the liminal moment just prior to Tupiniquim's "arrival," perhaps Simone Schwarz-Bart's description registers with us intimately so that it appeared to us that as the *mãe-de-santo* moved "the blood rose near the surface and mingled in the blackness" of her skin and "glints the color of wine appeared in her cheeks."[13] Here, following Caroline Humphrey, the literary imagination points not merely to "fiction" but to the typicality and historical density of intersubjective experience.[14] On the other hand, it may be that we are only familiar with the typicality of candles, tables, chairs, and so forth in this situation, and that the appearance of the figurine, the *acaçá,* the rustling sound of the ceiling, the draught blowing through the room, and perhaps even the night sky of Salvador have an unfamiliar quality.

The surrounding world appears in levels of familiarity and unfamiliarity; the levels are not fixed, but rather interlace and affect each other in their givenness as and through "sedimentations [*Niederschläge*] of experiential sense."[15] The geological (and also atmospheric) image that Husserl uses in speaking of the genesis, accrual, and transformation of sense as habitual also indicates generative phenomena of birth, ageing, and death in the intergenerational handing over of sense. The latter implies continuity, but in its precarity also rupture, transformation, suture, and repair—even

222 *Epilogue*: Umweltlichkeit

in relation to that which appears inexpiable—as inheritances and potentialities inherent to lived experience, which is itself an ongoing process of becoming. The concept and phenomenon of environmentality directs us to processes of generation that are necessarily relative and contingent. It points to a phenomenological conception of spatiality as the corporeity and historicity of space as environmental:

> Human existence, human life is played out as horizonal (to/for itself) in the constant and constantly moving tension of familiarity and unfamiliarity, nearness and distance—that is, always "environmentally"—in a relativity of this *environmentality*, in other words, in the relativity of the worldly situation, and in this movement lies its constant *historicity*, its own and that of its environment.[16]

*

I have not been back to Salvador since my travels for fieldwork, and thus have not seen Mãe Juta and her family in quite some time. There are moments when I think I encounter Tupiniquim in dreams. I write to Gilmara every so often to see how the family is doing, most recently to enquire after their health as we all try to make our way through the pandemic. I was happy to hear that the family is well, and from her that *"lembramos sempre de você."*[17]

Notes

1 I draw here on Edgar Mittelholzer's vivid evocations of the mood of weather in the tropics. See, for example, Edgar Mittelholzer, *Corentyne Thunder* (Leeds: Peepal Tree, 2009), 201–12.
2 Saint Augustine, *Confessions*, trans. R. S. Pine-Coffin (London: Penguin Books, 1961), 242.
3 Jacques Stephen Alexis, *General Sun, My Brother*, trans. Carrol F. Coates (Charlottesville: University Press of Virginia, 1999), 96.
4 Alexis, *General Sun, My Brother*, 100.
5 See the opening paragraph of the Introduction of the present work.
6 Maria Dürsteler, email message to author, January 24, 2021. I thank my aunt, Maria, for her thoughtful responses to my questions.
7 Dürsteler, email message to author, January 24, 2021.
8 See Paul Gilroy, *The Black Atlantic: Modernity and Double-Consciousness* (Cambridge, MA: Harvard University Press, 1993) and Édouard Glissant, *Caribbean Discourse: Selected Essays*, trans. J. Michael Dash (Charlottesville: University of Virginia Press, 1999). Husserl speaks of the "expansion" or "dilation of the world" (*"die Erweiterung der Welt"*) through the experience of others. See Edmund Husserl, *Zur Phänomenologie der Intersubjektivität. Texte aus dem Nachlass. Dritter Teil: 1929–1928*, Husserliana, vol. 15, ed. Iso Kern (The Hague: Martinus Nijhoff, 1973), 492. I am alluding here to the manner in which the lived body is inherent to the socio-historical sense of "world"; Merleau-Ponty, for example, speaks of acquired "habit" as expressing "our power of

dilating [*dilater*] our being-in-the-world." See Maurice Merleau-Ponty, *Phenomenology of Perception*, trans. Colin Smith (London: Routledge, 1989), 143; idem, *Phénoménologie de la perception* (Paris: Éditions Gallimard, 1945), 179.
9 Simone Schwarz-Bart, *The Bridge of Beyond*, trans. Barbara Bray (New York: New York Review Books, 2013), 25.
10 See Anthony J. Steinbock, "Homecomrades," in Steinbock, *Home and Beyond: Generative Phenomenology after Husserl* (Evanston, IL: Northwestern University Press, 1995), 222–32. For the first quote see Stuart Hall, *Familiar Stranger: A Life between Two Islands*, ed. Bill Schwarz (Durham, NC: Duke University Press, 2017), 35.
11 I thank Nnandi and Viviane for their help during fieldwork.
12 Husserl speaks of "constellations" of experiences; see Edmund Husserl, *Analyses Concerning Passive and Active Synthesis: Lectures on Transcendental Logic*, trans. Anthony J. Steinbock (Dordrecht: Kluwer, 2001), 626.
13 Schwarz-Bart, *The Bridge of Beyond*, 25.
14 See my discussion in the Introduction of the present work.
15 Husserl, "The World of the Living Present and the Constitution of the Surrounding World That is Outside the Flesh," in Maurice Merleau-Ponty, *Husserl at the Limits of Phenomenology*, ed. Leonard Lawlor and Bettina Bergo (Evanston, IL: Northwestern University Press, 2002), 140; Edmund Husserl, "Die Welt der lebendigen Gegenwart und die Konstitution der ausserleiblichen Umwelt," ed. Alfred Schuetz, *Philosophy and Phenomenological Research* 6, no. 3 (March 1946): 331. Bergo and Lawlor render "*Niederschläge*" as "sedimentations," but the term can also be translated as "precipitations," that is, with an atmospheric sense in the way that Husserl uses the image of "fog" when describing the temporality of perception (see Figure 2.11) and memory.
16 Husserl, *Zur Phänomenologie der Intersubjektivität. Texte aus dem Nachlass. Dritter Teil: 1929–1928*, 395:

> Menschliches Dasein, menschliches Leben spielt sich als ihm selbst horizonthaft in der beständigen und beständig beweglichen Spannung der Bekanntheit und Unbekanntheit, der Nähe und Ferne ab, also immer „umweltlich", in einer Relativität dieser Umweltlichkeit, oder was nur ein anderes Wort ist, in der Relativität der weltlichen Situation, und in dieser Beweglichkeit besteht seine beständige *Historizität*, seine und seiner Umwelt.

17 Email correspondence to the author, January 25, 2021.

Glossary

The following lists terms specific to the ritual that appear frequently in the ethnography (Chapter 4). It is not an exhaustive glossary of Candomblé terms.

bênção. Indicates gestures requesting or conferring "blessing."
acaçá. Ritual food made of fine white maize meal (*milho*) as a gelatinous cake wrapped in a palm leaf.
adjá. Ritual implement of the *mãe-de-santo* in the shape of a small bell with two chambers.
caboclo. An entity experienced by participants in the *reunião* as an indigenous "spirit."
candomblé. When italicised refers to a specific Candomblé community.
Candomblé. When capitalised refers to the Afro-Brazilian religion.
Candomblé *caboclo*. Refers to the aspect of Candomblé praxis devoted to the ritual manifestation of *caboclos*.
êbô. Ritual food of the *orixá* Oxalá made of white maize meal (*milho*).
equede. Assistant to the *mãe-de-santo* in the performance of the ritual.
filha-de-santo (daughter-of-saint) or *filho-de-santo* (son-of-saint). An initiate of Candomblé; in my descriptions, I at times simply use *filha* or *filho*.
mãe-de-santo (mother-of-saint) or *pai-de-santo* (father-of-saint). A religious leader of a *candomblé*; in my descriptions, I at times simply use *mãe* for the specific *candomblé* of Tupiniquim.
mato. A ritual area of vegetation, actual or symbolic.
milho. White maze meal.
orixá. A class of divine being, from the Yorùbá, *òrìṣà*.
Oxalá/Orixalá. An *orixá* whose attributes include the colour white and the sky.
Oxum. An *orixá* whose attribute is "sweet water."
paó. A ritual gesture involving a particular style of clapping.

reunião. Used in the ethnography to refer to the specific ritual being described, meaning a "gathering."
terreiro. The physical environment of the *candomblé*, which can also refer to it as a community.
Tupiniquim. The name of the *caboclo* whom the *mãe-de-santo* "manifests."

Bibliography

Abraham, Roy Clive. *Dictionary of Modern Yoruba*. London: University of London Press, 1958.
Adepegba, Cornelius. "Associated Place-Names and Sacred Icons of Seven Yorùbá Deities." In Olupona and Rey, *Òrìsà Devotion as World Religion*, 106–27.
Agier, Michel. "Between Affliction and Politics: A Case Study of Bahian Candomblé." In *Afro-Brazilian Culture and Politics: Bahia, 1970s to 1990s*, edited by Hendrik Kraayb, 134–57. Armonk, NY: M. E. Sharpe, 1990.
Agrawal, Arun. *Environmentality: Technologies of Government and the Making of Subjects*. Durham, NC: Duke University Press, 2005.
Ahmed, Sara. *Queer Phenomenology: Orientations, Objects, Others*. Durham: Duke University Press, 2006.
Alexis, Jacques Stephen. *General Sun, My Brother*. Translated by Carrol F. Coates. Charlottesville: University Press of Virginia, 1999.
Andrews, Michael F. "Edmund Husserl: Empathy and the Transcendental Constitution of the World." In *Does the World Exist? Plurisignificant Ciphering of Reality*, edited by Amma-Teresa Tymieniecka, 217–37. Dordrecht: Springer, 2004.
Atchley, E. G. Cuthbert F. *A History of the Use of Incense in Divine Worship*. London: Longmans, 1909.
Augustine, Saint. *Confessions*. Translated by R. S. Pine-Coffin. London: Penguin, 1961.
Barbara, Rosamaria. "A danças das Aiabás, Dança, corpo e cotidiano das mulheres de candomblé." PhD diss., University of São Paulo, 2002.
Bastide, Roger. *The African Religions of Brazil: Toward a Sociology of the Interpenetration of Civilizations*. Translated by Helen Sebba. Baltimore, MD: John Hopkins University Press, 1978.
———. *O Candomblé da Bahia: Rito Nagô*. Translated by Maria Isaura Pereira de Queiroz. São Paulo: Compahnia das Letras, 2005.
Bedford, Joseph. "Creativity's Shadow: Dalibor Vesely, Phenomenology and Architectural Education (1968–1998)." PhD diss., Princeton University, 2018.
Beier, Ulli. *The Return of the Gods: The Sacred Art of Susanne Wenger*. Cambridge, UK: Cambridge University Press, 1975.
Benjamin, Andrew. *Architectural Philosophy: Form, Function and Alterity*. London: Athlone Press, 2001.
Benjamin, Walter. *Illuminations: Essays and Reflections*. Edited by Hannah Arendt. New York: Schocken, 2007.
Bernet, Rudolf, Iso Kern, and Edward Marbach. *An Introduction to Husserlian Phenomenology*. Evanston, IL: Northwestern University Press, 1993.

Bornemark, Jonna, and Nicholas Smith, eds. *Phenomenology of Pregnancy*. Huddenge: Södertörn University Press, 2016.
Bundgaard, Peer F. "Husserl and Language." In *Handbook of Phenomenology and Cognitive Science*, edited by S. Gallagher and D. Schmicking, 369–99. Dordrecht: Springer, 2010.
Burke, Patrick. "Merleau-Ponty's Appropriation of Husserl's Notion of 'Präsenzfeld'." In *Husserl in Contemporary Context*, edited by Burt C. Hopkins, 37–58. Dordrecht: Springer, 1997.
Cairns, Dorion. *Guide for Translating Husserl*. The Hague: Martinus Nijhoff, 1973.
Carneiro, Edison. *Candomblés da Bahia*. Bahia: Brasileira de Ouro, 1948.
Carr, David. "The 'Fifth Meditation' and Husserl's Cartesianism." *Philosophy and Phenomenological Research* 34, no. 1 (September 1973): 14–35.
———. "Husserl's *Crisis* and the Problem of History." *Southwestern Journal of Philosophy* 5, no. 3 (Fall 1974): 127–48.
———. *The Paradox of Subjectivity: The Self in the Transcendental Tradition*. Oxford: Oxford University Press, 1999.
———. *Phenomenology and the Problem of History: A Study of Husserl's Transcendental Philosophy*. Evanston, IL: Northwestern University Press, 1974.
Carreño, Javier. "On the Temporality of Images According to Husserl." *New Yearbook for Phenomenology and Phenomenological Philosophy* 8 (2008): 73–92.
Carroll, Robert, and Stephen Prickett, eds. *The Bible: Authorized King James Version with Apocrypha*. Oxford: Oxford University Press, 2008.
Casey, Edward. *The Fate of Place: A Philosophical History*. Berkeley: University of California Press, 1998.
———. *Getting Back into Place*. Bloomington: Indiana University Press, 1993.
Castillo, Lisa Earl. "The 'Ketu Nation' of Brazilian Candomblé in Historical Context." *History in Africa* 0, (2021): 1–41.
Castro, Eduardo Viveiros de. *Cannibal Metaphysics*. Translated by Peter Skafish. Minneapolis: Univocal, 2009.
———. *From the Enemy's Point of View: Humanity and Divinity in an Amazonian Society*. Translated by Catherine V. Howard. Chicago, IL: University of Chicago Press, 1992.
Castro, Eduardo Viveiros de, and Marcio Goldman. "Slow Motions: Comments on a Few Texts by Marilyn Strathern." *Cambridge Anthropology* 28, no. 3 (January 2008): 23–42.
Claesges, Ulrich. *Edmund Husserls Theorie der Raumkonstitution*. The Hague: Martinus Nijhoff, 1964.
Clifford, James, and George E. Marcus, eds. *Writing Culture: The Poetics and Politics of Ethnography*. Berkeley: University of California Press, 1986.
Cossard, Gisèle Binon. "Contribution a l'étude des Candomblés au Brésil: Le Candomblé Angola." PhD diss., University of Paris, 1970.
Crowell, Steven. 2002. "Does the Husserl/Heidegger Feud Rest on a Mistake? An Essay on Psychological and Transcendental Phenomenology." *Husserl Studies* 18, no. 2 (2002): 123–140.
———. "'Idealities of Nature': Jan Patočka on Reflection and the Three Movements of Human Life." In *Jan Patočka and the Heritage of Phenomenology: Centenary Papers*. Edited by Ivan Chvatik and Erika Abrams, 7–22. Dordrecht: Springer, 2011.
Davidson, Cynthia, and Bryan E. Norwood, eds. *Disorienting Phenomenology, Log 42*. New York: Anyone Corporation, 2018.

Derrida, Jacques. *Edmund Husserl's Origin of Geometry: An Introduction*. Translated by John P. Leavey. Lincoln: University of Nebraska, 1989.

———. *Limited Inc*. Evanston, IL: Northwestern University Press, 1988.

———. "Limited Inc abc ...". Baltimore, MD: Johns Hopkins University Press, 1977.

———. *Speech and Phenomena: And Other Essays on Husserl's Theory of Signs*. Translated by David B. Allison. Evanston, IL: Northwestern University Press, 1973.

———. *Specters of Marx: The State of the Debt, the Work of Mourning, and the New International*, Translated by Peggy Kamuf. New York: Routledge, 1994.

Desjarlais, Robert and C. Jason Throop. "Phenomenological Approaches in Anthropology." *Annual Review of Anthropology* 40 (October, 2011): 87–102.

Dodd, James. *Phenomenology, Architecture and the Built World: Exercises in Philosophical Anthropology*. Leiden: Brill, 2017.

Donohoe, Janet. *Husserl on Ethics and Intersubjectivity: From Static to Genetic Phenomenology*. Toronto: University of Toronto Press, 2016.

———. "The Nonpresence of the Living Present." *Southern Journal of Philosophy* 38, no. 2 (Summer 2000): 221–30.

Drummond, John J. *Historical Dictionary of Husserl's Philosophy*. Lanham, MD: Scarecrow, 2008.

DuFour, Tao. "Toward a Somatology of Landscape: Anthropological Multinaturalism and the 'Natural' World." In *Routledge Research Companion to Landscape Architecture*, edited by Ellen Braae and Henriette Steiner, 156–70. London: Routledge, 2019.

Duranti, Alessandro. *The Anthropology of Intentions: Language in a World of Others*. Cambridge, UK: Cambridge University Press, 2015.

Evans-Pritchard, E. E. "Lévy-Bruhl's Theory of Primitive Mentality." *Bulletin of the Faculty of Arts of the Egyptian University* 2 (1934): 1–36.

Fabian, Johannes. "An African Gnosis: For a Reconstruction of an Authoritative Definition." *History of Religions* 9, no.1 (August 1969): 42–58.

———. *Time and the Other: How Anthropology Makes Its Object*. New York: Columbia University Press, 2002.

Fausto, Boris. *A Concise History of Brazil*. Cambridge, UK: Cambridge University Press, 1999.

Fernandes, Ana, and Marco A. A. de Filgueiras Gomes. "Revisiting the Pelourinho: Preservation, Cultural Heritage, and Place Marketing in Salvador, Bahia." In del Rio and Siembieda, *Contemporary Urbanism in Brazil: Beyond Brasília*, 144–63. Gainesville: University Press of Florida, 2009.

Fink, Eugen. "Operative Concepts in Husserl's Phenomenology." In *Apriori and World: European Contributions to Husserlian Phenomenology*, edited by William McKenna, Robert M. Harlan, and Laurence E. Winters, 56–70. The Hague: Martinus Nijhoff, 1981.

Fritsch, Matthias. *Taking Turns with the Earth: Phenomenology, Deconstruction, and Intergenerational Justice*. Stanford, CA: Stanford University Press, 2018.

Gadamer, Hans-Georg. *Philosophical Hermeneutics*. Translated by David E. Linge. Berkeley: University of California Press, 1976.

———. *Reason in the Age of Science*. Translated by Frederick G. Lawrence (Cambridge, MA.: The MIT Press, 2001.

———. *The Relevance of the Beautiful and Other Essays*. Edited by Robert Bernasconi. Cambridge, UK: Cambridge University Press, 2002.

———. *Truth and Method*. Translated by Joel Weinsheimer and Donald G. Marshall. New York: Continuum, 2000.

Gallagher, Shaun. "Lived Body and Environment." *Research in Phenomenology* 16 (1986): 139–70.
Gates, Henry Louis, Jr. *The Signifying Monkey: A Theory of African-American Literary Criticism.* Oxford: Oxford University Press, 1988.
Geniusas, Saulius. "On Birth, Death, and Sleep in Husserl's Late Manuscripts on Time." In *On Time: New Contributions to the Husserlian Phenomenology of Time*, edited by Dieter Lohmar and Ichiro Yamaguchi, 71–89. Dordrecht: Springer, 2010.
Gilroy, Paul. *The Black Atlantic: Modernity and Double-Consciousness.* Cambridge, MA: Harvard University Press, 1993.
Glissant, Édouard. *Caribbean Discourse: Selected Essays.* Translated by J. Michael Dash. Charlottesville: University of Virginia Press, 1999.
———. *Poetics of Relation.* Translated by Betsy Wing. Ann Arbor: University of Michigan Press, 2010.
Goldman, Marcio. "An Ethnographic Theory of Democracy: Politics from the Viewpoint of Ilhéus's Black Movement (Bahia, Brazil)." *Ethnos* 66, no. 2 (2001): 157–80.
———. "How to Learn in an Afro-Brazilian Spirit Possession Religion: Ontology and Multiplicity in Candomblé." In *Learning Religion: Anthropological Approaches*, edited by Ramón Sarró and David Berliner, 103–19. Oxford: Berghahn, 2007.
Goonewardena, Kanishka, Stefan Kipfer, Richard Milgrom, and Christian Schmid, eds. *Space, Difference, Everyday Life: Reading Henri Lefebvre.* New York: Routledge, 2008.
Hall, Stuart. *Familiar Stranger: A Life between Two Islands.* Edited by Bill Schwarz. Durham, NC: Duke University Press, 2017.
Harding, Rachel E. *A Refuge in Thunder: Candomblé and Alternative Spaces of Blackness.* Bloomington: Indiana University Press, 2003.
Harries, Karsten. *The Ethical Function of Architecture.* Cambridge, MA: MIT Press, 1997.
Hart, James G. "Review of *Grenzprobleme der Phänomenologie*, by Edmund Husserl." *Husserl Studies* 31 (2015): 245–60.
Heidegger, Martin. *Being and Time.* Translated by John Macquarrie and Edward Robinson. Oxford: Blackwell, 2002.
———. *Sein und Zeit.* Tübingen: Max Niemeyer Verlag, 2006.
Heinämaa, Sara. "Embodiment and Bodily Becoming." In Zahavi, *Oxford Handbook*, 533–57.
———. *Toward a Phenomenology of Sexual Difference: Husserl, Merleau-Ponty, Beauvoir.* Lanham, MD: Rowman & Littlefield, 2003.
Held, Klaus. "Husserl's Phenomenological Method." In *The New Husserl: A Critical Reader*, edited by Donn Welton, 3–31. Bloomington: Indiana University Press, 2003.
Henare, Amiria, Martin Holbraad, and Sari Wastel, eds. *Thinking through Things: Theorising Artefacts Ethnographically.* London: Routledge, 2007.
Herskovits, J. Melville. *An Outline of Dahomean Religious Belief.* Menasha, WI: American Anthropological Association, 1933.
Holbraad, Martin. *Truth in Motion: The Recursive Anthropology of Cuban Divination.* Chicago, IL: University of Chicago Press, 2012.
Holbraad, Martin, and Morten Axel Pedersen. *The Ontological Turn: An Anthropological Exposition.* Cambridge, UK: Cambridge University Press, 2017.

Bibliography 231

Holenstein, Elmar. *Roman Jakobson's Approach to Language: Phenomenological Structuralism.* Translated by Catherine Schelbert and Tarcisius Schelbert. Bloomington: Indiana University Press, 1976.

Holl, Steven, Juhani Pallasmaa, and Alberto Pérez-Gómez. *Questions of Perception: Phenomenology of Architecture.* San Francisco, CA: William Stout, 2006.

Holston, James. *Insurgent Citizenship: Disjunctions of Democracy and Modernity in Brazil.* Princeton, NJ: Princeton University Press, 2008.

Hopkins, Burt C. *Intentionality in Husserl and Heidegger: The Problem of the Original Method and Phenomenon of Phenomenology.* Dordrecht: Kluwer, 1993.

———. *The Philosophy of Husserl.* Durham, UK: Acumen, 2011.

Humphrey, Caroline. "Ideology in Infrastructure: Architecture and Soviet Imagination." *Journal of the Royal Anthropological Institute* 11, no. 1 (March 2005): 39–58.

Husserl, Edmund. "Allgemeines zur Theorie der Erfahrung von *Realem.* [...] Auslegung der logischen Ideen *Reales der Welt* und *Welt selbst.* [...]." Unpublished manuscript D 1, 1932. 18 pages. Transcribed by L. Landgrebe (Prague).

———. *Analysen zur passiven Synthesis. Aus Vorlesungs- und Forschungsmanuskripten 1918–1926.* Husserliana, vol. 11. Edited by Margot Fleischer. The Hague: Martinus Nijhoff, 1966.

———. *Analyses Concerning Passive and Active Synthesis: Lectures on Transcendental Logic.* Translated by Anthony Steinbock. Dordrecht: Kluwer, 2001.

———. *Aufsätze und Vorträge (1922-1937).* Husserliana, vol. 27. Edited by Thomas Nenon and Hans Rainer Sepp. Dordrecht: Kluwer, 1989.

———. *The Basic Problems of Phenomenology: From the Lectures, Winter Semester, 1910–1911.* Translated by Ingo Farin and James G. Hart. Dordrecht: Springer, 2006.

———. *Cartesianische Meditationen und Pariser Vorträge.* Husserliana, vol. 1. Edited by Stephan Strasser. 1950. Reprint, Dordrecht: Kluwer, 1991.

———. *Cartesian Meditations: An Introduction to Phenomenology.* Translated by Dorion Cairns. Dordrecht: Kluwer, 1999.

———. *The Crisis of European Sciences and Transcendental Phenomenology: An Introduction to Phenomenological Philosophy.* Translated by David Carr. Evanston, IL: Northwestern University Press, 1970.

———. *Die Krisis der europäischen Wissenschaften und die transzendentale Phänomenologie. Eine Einleitung in die phänomenologische Philosophie.* Husserliana, vol. 6. Edited by Walter Biemel. The Hague: Martinus Nijhoff, 1976.

———. *Die Krisis der europäischen Wissenschaften und die transzendentale Phänomenologie: Ergänzungsband Texte aus dem Nachlass 1934–1937.* Husserliana, vol. 29. Edited by Reinhold N. Smid. Dordrecht: Kluwer, 1993.

———. "Die Welt der lebendigen Gegenwart und die Konstitution der ausserleiblichen Umwelt." Edited by Alfred Schuetz. *Philosophy and Phenomenological Research* 6, no. 3 (March 1946): 323–43.

———. *Ding und Raum: Vorlesungen 1907.* Husserliana, vol. 16. Edited by Iso Kern. The Hague: Martinus Nijhoff, 1973.

———. "Edmund Husserl's Letter to Lucien Lévy-Bruhl." Translated by Lukas Steinacher and Dermot Moran. *New Yearbook for Phenomenology and Phenomenological Philosophy* 8 (2008): 349–54.

———. *Experience and Judgement.* Edited by Ludwig Landgrebe. Translated by James S. Churchill and Karl Ameriks. Evanston, IL: Northwestern University Press, 1973.

———. *Formal and Transcendental Logic*. Translated by Dorion Cairns. The Hague: Martinus Nijhoff, 1969.

———. *Formale und transzendentale Logik. Versuch einer Kritik der logischen Vernunft*. Husserliana, vol. 17. Edited by Paul Janssen. The Hague: Martinus Nijhoff, 1974.

———. "Foundational Investigations of the Phenomenological Origin of the Spatiality of Nature." In McCormick and Elliston, 222–33.

———. "Foundational Investigations of the Phenomenological Origin of the Spatiality of Nature: The Originary Ark, the Earth, Does Not Move." In Merleau-Ponty, *Husserl at the Limits of Phenomenology*, 117–31.

———. "Grundlegende Untersuchungen zum phänomenologischen Ursprung der Räumlichkeit der Natur." In *Philosophical Essays in Memory of Edmund Husserl*, edited by Marvin Farber, 307–25. Cambridge, MA: Harvard University Press, 1940.

———. *Ideas: General Introduction to Pure Phenomenology*. Translated by W. R. Boyce Gibson. London: Routledge, 2012.

———. *Ideas Pertaining to a Pure Phenomenology and to Phenomenological Philosophy. First Book: General Introduction to a Pure Phenomenology*. Translated by F. Kersten. The Hague: Martinus Nijhoff, 1983.

———. *Ideas Pertaining to a Pure Phenomenology and to a Phenomenological Philosophy: Second Book*. Translated by R. Rojcewicz and A. Schuwer. Dordrecht: Kluwer, 1989.

———. *Ideen zu einer reinen Phänomenologie und phänomenologischen Philosophie. Drittes Buch: Die Phänomenologie und die Fundamente der Wissenschaften*. Husserliana, vol. 5. Edited by Marly Biemel. 1952. Reprint, The Hague: Martinus Nijhoff, 1971.

———. *Ideen zu einer reinen Phänomenologie und phänomenologischen Philosophie. Erstes Buch. Allgemeine Einführung in die reine Phänomenologie*. Husserliana, vol. 3. Edited by Karl Schuhmann. The Hague: Martinus Nijhoff, 1976.

———. *Ideen zu einer reinen Phänomenologie und phänomenologischen Philosophie: Zweites Buch: Phänomenologische Untersuchungen zur Konstitution*. Husserliana, vol. 4. Edited by Marly Biemel. The Hague: Martinus Nijhoff, 1976.

———. "Individuation, das *Tode-ti*." Unpublished manuscript D8, 1918. 66 pages. Transcribed by E. Fink.

———. *Logical Investigations*. Vol. 1. Edited by Dermot Moran. Translated by J. N. Findlay. New York: Routledge, 2001.

———. *Logical Investigations*. Vol. 2. Edited by Dermot Moran. Translated by J. N. Findlay. London: Routledge, 2001.

———. *Natur und Geist: Vorlesungen Sommersemester 1927*. Husserliana, vol. 32. Edited by Michael Weiler. Dordrecht: Springer, 2001.

———. *Natur und Geist: Vorlesungen Sommersemester 1919*. Husserliana Materialien, vol. 4. Edited by Michael Weiler. Dordrecht: Springer, 2002.

———. "Notizen zur Raumkonstitution." *Philosophy and Phenomenological Research* 1, no. 1 (September 1940): 21–37, 217–26.

———. "Objektivität, *objektive* oder Wahrheit an sich. Objekt, Gegenstand an sich." Unpublished manuscript D3, 1920. 20 pages. Transcribed by E. Fink.

———. *On the Phenomenology of the Consciousness of Internal Time (1893–1917)*. Translated by John Barnett Brough. Dordrecht: Kluwer, 1991.

———. "The Origin of Geometry." In Merleau-Ponty, *Husserl at the Limits of Phenomenology*, 93–116.

———. *Phantasie, Bildbewusstsein, Erinnerung: Zur Phänomenologie der anschaulichen Vergegenwärtigungen. Texte aus dem Nachlass (1898–1925)*. Husserliana, vol. 23. Edited by Eduard Marbach. The Hague: Martinus Nijhoff, 1980.

———. *Phantasy, Image Consciousness, and Memory (1898–1925)*. Translated by John B. Brough. Dordrecht: Springer, 2005.

———. "Phenomenology and Anthropology." In *Psychological and Transcendental Phenomenology and the Confrontation with Heidegger (1927–1931)*. Translated and edited by Thomas Sheehan and Richard E. Palmer, 458–500. Dordrecht: Kluwer 1997.

———. *Phenomenology and the Foundations of the Sciences: Ideas Pertaining to a Pure Phenomenology and to a Phenomenological Philosophy: Third Book*. Translated by Ted E. Klein and Williame E. Pohl. The Hague: Martinus Nijhoff, 1980.

———. *Thing and Space: Lectures of 1907*. Translated by Richard Rojcewicz. Dordrecht: Kluwer, 2010.

———. "The World of the Living Present and the Constitution of the Surrounding World That Is Outside the Flesh." In Merleau-Ponty, *Husserl at the Limits of Phenomenology*, 132–54.

———. "The World of the Living Present and the Constitution of the Surrounding World External to the Organism." In McCormick and Elliston, *Husserl: Shorter Works*, 238–50.

———. "Zur Konstitution der physischen Natur. Zuerst Leib Aussending. dann rückführend auf Hyle und Kinästhese." Unpublished manuscript D10 I, 1932. 68 pages. Transcribed by E. Fink.

———. *Zur Phänomenologie der Intersubjektivität. Texte aus dem Nachlass. Dritter Teil: 1929–1928*. Husserliana, vol. 15. Edited by Iso Kern. The Hague: Martinus Nijhoff, 1973.

———. *Zur Phänomenologie der Intersubjektivität. Texte aus dem Nachlass. Erster Teil: 1905–1920*. Husserliana, vol. 13. Edited by Iso Kern. The Hague: Martinus Nijhoff, 1973.

———. *Zur Phänomenologie der Intersubjektivität. Texte aus dem Nachlass. Zweiter Teil: 1921–1928*. Husserliana, vol. 14. Edited by Iso Kern. The Hague: Martinus Nijhoff, 1973.

———. *Zur Phänomenologie des inneren Zeitbewusstseins (1893–1917)*. Husserliana, vol. 10. Edited by Rudolf Boehm. The Hague: Martinus Nijhoff, 1966.

Huizinga, Johann. *Homo Ludens*. London: Routledge, 1980.

Idowu, E. Bolasi. *Olódùmarè*. London: Longmans, 1962.

Ingold, Tim. *Making: Anthropology, Archaeology, Art and Architecture*. London: Routledge, 2013.

———. *The Perception of the Environment: Essays on Livelihood, Dwelling and Skill*. London: Routledge, 2000.

Jackson, Michael, ed. *Things as They Are: New Directions in Phenomenological Anthropology*. Bloomington: Indiana University Press, 1996.

James, C. L. R. *Beyond a Boundary*. London: Serpent's Tail, 1994.

Jansen, Julia. "Imagination De-Naturalized: Phantasy, the Imaginary, and Imaginative Ontology." In Zahavi, *Oxford Handbook*, 676–95.

Jarzombek, Mark. "Husserl and The Problem of Worldliness." In Davidson and Norwood, *Disorienting Phenomenology*, 67–79.

Johnson, Paul Christopher. *Secrets, Gossip, and Gods: The Transformation of Brazilian Candomblé.* Oxford: Oxford University Press 2002.
Jonas, Hans. *The Gnostic Religion: The Message of the Alien God and the Beginnings of Christianity.* London: Routledge, 1992.
Ihde, Don, and Hugh J. Silverman, eds. *Descriptions.* Albany: SUNY Press, 1985.
Katz, Jack and Thomas J. Csordas. "Phenomenological Ethnography in Sociology and Anthropology." *Ethnography* 4, no. 3 (September, 2003): 275–288.
Kersten, Frederick Irving. "Husserl's Investigations Toward a Phenomenology of Space." PhD diss., New School for Social Research, 1964.
Khalfa, Jean. "Fanon and Psychiatry." *Nottingham French Studies* 54, no. 1 (2015): 52–71.
Kolakowski, Leszek. *The Presence of Myth.* Translated by Adam Czerniawski. Chicago, IL: University of Chicago Press, 1989.
Konopka, Adam. "The Role of *Umwelt* in Husserl's *Aufbau* and *Abbau* of the *Natur/Geist* Distinction." *Human Studies* 32, no. 3 (September 2009): 313–33.
Kortooms, Toine. *Phenomenology of Time: Edmund Husserl's Analysis of Time-Consciousness.* Dordrecht: Springer, 2002.
Lammi, Walter. "Gadamer's Debt to Husserl." In *Passions of the Earth in Human Existence, Creativity, and Literature*, edited by A. T. Tymieniecka, 167–79. Dordrecht: Kluwer Academic Publishers, 2001.
Landes, Donald A. "Merleau-Ponty from 1945 to 1952: The Ontological Weight of Perception and the Transcendental Force of Description," in Zahavi, *Oxford Handbook*, 360–79.
Landes, Ruth. *The City of Women.* Albuquerque: University of New Mexico Press, 1994.
Larrabee, Mary Jeanne. "Husserl's Static and Genetic Phenomenology." *Man and World* 9 (June 1976): 163–74.
Lau, Kwok-Ying, and Chung-Chi Yu, eds. *Border-Crossings: Phenomenology, Interculturality and Interdisciplinarity.* Würzburg: Königshausen & Neumann, 2014.
Lau, Kwok-Ying, Chan-Fai Cheung, and Tze-Wan Kwan, eds. *Identity and Alterity: Phenomenology and Cultural Traditions.* Würzburg: Königshausen & Neumann, 2010.
Lefebvre, Henri. *The Production of Space.* Translated by Donald Nicholson-Smith. Oxford: Blackwell, 1991.
Lévy-Bruhl, Lucien. "A Letter to E. E. Evans-Pritchard." *British Journal of Sociology* 3, no. 2 (June 1952): 117–23.
Libera, Alain de. "Analogy." In *Dictionary of Untranslatables: A Philosophical Lexicon*, edited by Barbara Cassin and translated by Emily Apter, Jacques Lezra, and Michael Wood, 31–33. Princeton, NJ: Princeton University Press, 2014.
Lima, Fabio. *As Quartas-feiras de Xangô: Ritual e Cotidiano.* João Pessoa: Editora Grafset, 2010.
Lobkowicz, Nicholas. *Theory and Practice: History of a Concept from Aristotle to Marx.* Notre Dame, IN: University of Notre Dame Press, 1967.
MacDonald, Sharon. "British Social Anthropology." In *Handbook of Ethnography*, edited by Paul Atkinson et al., 60–79. London: Sage, 2002.
Makkreel, Rudolf A. "Husserl, Dilthey, and the Relation of the Life-World to History." In *Husserl and Contemporary Thought*, edited by John Sallis, 39–58. Atlantic Highlands, NJ: Humanities Press, 1983.

Mattens, Filip. "From the Origin of Spatiality to a Variety of Spaces." In Zahavi, *Oxford Handbook*, 558–78.

———. "Spatial Phenomena in Material Places: Reflections on Sensory Substitution, Shape Perception, and the External Nature of the Senses." *Phenomenology and the Cognitive Sciences* 18 (2019): 833–854.

Malpas, Jeff. *Place and Experience: A Philosophical Topography*. Cambridge, UK: Cambridge University Press, 1999.

Matory, J. Lorand. "Gendered Agendas: The Secrets Scholars Keep about Yorùbá-Atlantic Religion." *Gender & History* 15, no. 3 (November 2003): 409–439.

Mbembe, Achille. *Necropolitics*. Translated by Steven Corcoran. Durham, NC: Duke University Press, 2019.

McCance, M. "Incense." In Catholic University of America, *New Catholic Encyclopedia*, vol. 7, edited by Thomas Carson and Joann Cerrito, 376–77. Detroit: Thomson/Gale, 2003.

McCormick, Peter, and Frederick Elliston, eds. *Husserl: Shorter Works*. Notre Dame, IN: University of Notre Dame Press, 1981.

McGregor, Pedro. *A Moon and Two Mountains: The Myths, Ritual and Magic of Brazilian Spiritism*. London: Souvenir Press, 1996.

Megenney, William. *A Bahian Heritage*. Chapel Hill: University of North Carolina Press, 1978.

Melas, Natalie. *All the Difference in the World: Postcoloniality and the Ends of Comparison*. Stanford, CA: Stanford University Press, 2007.

Merleau-Ponty, Maurice. *Husserl at the Limits of Phenomenology: Including Texts by Edmund Husserl*. Edited by Leonard Lawlor with Bettina Bergo. Evanston, IL: Northwestern University Press, 2002.

———. *Le visible et l'invisible*. Paris: Éditions Gallimard, 1964.

———. *Nature: Course Notes from the Collège de France*. Edited by Dominique Séglard. Translated by Robert Vallier. Evanston, IL: Northwestern University Press, 2003.

———. *Phénoménologie de la perception*. Paris: Gallimard, 1945.

———. *Phenomenology of Perception*. Translated by Donald A. Landes. London: Routledge, 2014.

———. *Phenomenology of Perception*. Translated by Colin Smith. London: Routledge, 1989.

———. *Texts and Dialogues: On Philosophy, Politics, and Culture*. Edited by Hugh J. Silverman and James Barry Jr. Amherst, NY: Humanity Books, 2005.

———. *The Visible and the Invisible*. Translated by Alphonso Lingis. Evanston, IL: Northwestern University Press, 1968.

Miettinen, Timo. *Husserl and the Idea of Europe*. Evanston, IL: Northwestern University Press, 2020.

Mittelholzer, Edgar. *Corentyne Thunder*. Leeds: Peepal Tree, 2009.

Moran, Dermot. "Edith Stein's Encounter with Edmund Husserl and Her Phenomenology of the Person." In *Empathy, Sociality, and Personhood: Essays on Edith Stein's Phenomenological Investigations*, edited by Elisa Magrì and Dermot Moran, 31–47. Cham, Switzerland: Springer, 2017.

———. *Edmund Husserl: Founder of Phenomenology*. Cambridge, UK: Polity Press, 2005.

———. "Edmund Husserl's Phenomenology of Habituality and Habitus." *Journal of the British Society for Phenomenology* 42, no. 1 (January 2011): 53–76.

———. "'Even the Papuan is a Man and not a Beast': Husserl on Universalism and the Relativity of Cultures." *Journal of the History of Philosophy* 49, no. 4 (October 2011): 463–494.

———. "Heidegger's Critique of Husserl's and Brentano's Accounts of Intentionality." *Inquiry* 43, no. 1 (March 2000): 39–66.

———. *Husserl's Crisis of the European Sciences and Transcendental Phenomenology: An Introduction.* Cambridge, UK: Cambridge University Press, 2012.

———. *Introduction to Phenomenology.* London: Routledge, 2000.

———. "The Phenomenology of Embodiment: Intertwining and Reflexivity." In *The Phenomenology of Embodied Subjectivity*, edited by Rasmus Thybo Jensen and Dermot Moran, 285–303. Dordrecht: Springer, 2013.

Moran, Dermot, and Joseph Cohen. *The Husserl Dictionary.* London: Continuum, 2012.

Moran, Dermot, and Lukas Steinacher. "Husserl's Letter to Lévy-Bruhl: Introduction." *New Yearbook for Phenomenology and Phenomenological Philosophy* 8 (2008): 325–47.

Morrison, Toni. *Beloved.* New York: Vintage, 2004.

Morton, F. W. O. "The Conservative Revolution of Independence." PhD diss., Oxford University, 1971.

Mouloud, Noel. "Le principe spatial d'individuation: Fondement phénoménologique et signification géométrique." *Revue de Métaphysique et de Morale* 1 (January– March 1956): 259–82.

Mudimbe, V. Y. *The Invention of Africa: Gnosis, Philosophy, and the Order of Knowledge.* Bloomington: Indiana University Press, 1988.

Muralt, André de. *The Idea of Phenomenology: Husserlian Exemplarism.* Translated by Garry L. Breckon. Evanston, IL: Northwestern University Press, 1974.

Najman, Charles, and Frankétienne, dir. *Une étrange cathédrale dans la graisse des ténèbres.* 2011. La Huit Productions. YouTube video. https://www.youtube.com/watch?v=U8RbFX3G2t0.

Oliveira, Rafael Soares de. "Feitiço de Oxum: Um estudo sobre o Ilê Axé Iyá Nassô Oká e suas relações em rede com outros terreiros." PhD diss., Federal University of Bahia, 2005.

Olupona, Jacob K. and Terry Rey, eds. *Òrìsà Devotion as World Religion: The Globalization of Yorùbá Religious Culture.* Madison: University of Wisconsin Press, 2008.

Omari-Tunkara, Mikelle Smith. *Manipulating the Sacred: Yorùbá Art, Ritual, and Resistance in Brazilian Candomblé.* Detroit, MI: Wayne State University Press, 2005.

Otero-Pailos, Jorge. *Architecture's Historical Turn: Phenomenology and the Rise of the Postmodern.* Minneapolis: University of Minnesota Press, 2010.

Paiva, José de, ed. *The Living Tradition of Architecture.* London: Routledge, 2017.

Parés, Luis Nicolau. *The Formation of Candomblé: Vodun History and Ritual in Brazil.* Translated by Richard Vernon. Chapel Hill, NC: University of North Carolina Press, 2013.

Parviainen, Jaana. "Choreographing Resistances: Spatial-Kinaesthetic Intelligence and Bodily Knowledge as Political Tools in Activist Work." *Mobilities* 5, no. 3 (September 2010): 311–29.

Patočka, Jan. *Body, Community, Language, World.* Edited by James Dodd. Chicago: Open Court, 1998.

———. *The Natural World as a Philosophical Problem*. Edited by Ivan Chvatík and Ľubica Učník. Translated by Erika Abrams. Evanston, IL: Northwestern University Press, 2016.
Patterson, Orlando. *Slavery and Social Death: A Comparative Study*. Cambridge, MA: Harvard University Press, 2018.
Pelikan, Jaroslav. *The Christian Tradition*. Vol. 1. Chicago, IL: University of Chicago Press, 1971.
———. *The Christian Tradition*. Vol. 4. Chicago, IL: University of Chicago Press, 1984.
Pelton, Robert D. *The Trickster in West Africa: A Study of Mythic Irony and Sacred Delight*. Berkeley: University of California Press, 1980.
Pérez-Gómez, Alberto. *Architecture and the Crisis of Modern Science*. Cambridge, MA: MIT Press, 1985.
Perkins, Patricio Agustín. "La relación filosófica entre Husserl y Avenarius en Problemas fundamentales de la fenomenología." *Diánoia* 59, no. 72 (May 2014): 25–48.
Prandi, Reginaldo. *Mitologia dos Orixás*. São Paulo: Companhia das Letras, 2011.
Prefeitura da Cidade do Salvador. *Lei do Ordenamento do Uso e da Ocupação do Solo de Salvador, Versão 1.2*. Salvador: Fundação Mário Leal Ferreira, 2001–2004.
Price, Richard, ed. *Maroon Societies: Rebel Slave Communities in the Americas*. Baltimore, MD: John Hopkins University Press, 1996.
Ram, Kalpana, and Christopher Houston, eds. *Phenomenology in Anthropology: A Sense of Perspective*. Bloomington: Indiana University Press, 2015.
Reis, João José. *Slave Rebellion in Brazil*. Translated by Arthur Brakel. Baltimore, MD: John Hopkins University Press, 1993.
Ricoeur, Paul. *From Text to Action: Essays in Hermeneutics, II*. Translated by Kathleen Blamey and John B. Thompson. Evanston, IL: Northwestern University Press, 1991.
———. *Memory, History, Forgetting*. Translated by Kathleen Blamey and David Pellauer. Chicago, IL: University of Chicago Press, 2006.
Rio, Vicente del, and William Siembieda. *Contemporary Urbanism in Brazil*. Gainesville: University Press of Florida, 2009.
Risério, Antonio. *Uma História da Cidade da Bahia*. Rio de Janeiro: Versal Editores, 2004.
Rodrigues, Raymundo Nina. *L'Animisme fétichiste des Nègres de Bahia*. Bahia: Reis, 1900.
———. *O Animismo fetichista dos Negros baianos*. Salvador: P555 Edições, 2005.
Rush, Fred. *On Architecture*. London: Routledge, 2008.
San Martin, Javier. "Husserl and Cultural Anthropology, Commentary on Husserl's Letter to Lévy-Bruhl." *Recherches husserliennes* 7 (1997): 87–115.
Santos, Maria Stella de Azevedo. "Iansã Is Not Saint Barbara." In *The Brazil Reader*, edited by Robert M. Levine and John J. Crocitti, 408–10. London: Latin American Bureau 1999.
———. *Meu tempo é agora*. Curitiba: Projeto Centrhu 1995.
Santos, Jocélio Teles dos. "Os Candomblés da Bahia no século XXI." *Mapeamento dos terreiros de Salvador*. Salvador: Centro de Estudos Afro-Orientais, 2007. http://www.terreiros.ceao.ufba.br/pdf/Os_candombles_no_seculo_XXI.pdf
———. *O Dono da Terra: O Caboclo nos Candomblés da Bahia*. Salvador: SarahLetras, 1995.

Santos, Juana Elbein dos, and Deoscóredes M. dos Santos. "O culto dos ancestrais na Bahia: O culto dos égun." In *Olóòrişa: Escritos sobre a religião dos orixás*, edited by Carlos E. M. de Moura, 153–88. São Paulo: Agora, 1981.

Scanlon, John. "Husserl's *Ideas* and the Natural Concept of the World." In *Edmund Husserl and the Phenomenological Tradition*, edited by Robert Sokolowski, 217–33. Washington, DC: Catholic University of America Press, 1988.

———. "A Transcendentalist's Manifesto: Introduction to 'Phenomenology and Anthropology'." In McCormick and Elliston, *Husserl: Shorter Works*, 311–14.

Scarre, Geoffrey, ed. *The Palgrave Handbook of the Philosophy of Aging*. London: Palgrave Macmillan, 2016.

Schwartz, Stuart B. *Sugar Plantations in the Formation of Brazilian Society*. Cambridge, UK: Cambridge University Press, 1985.

Schwarz-Bart, Simone. *The Bridge of Beyond*. Translated by Barbara Bray. New York: New York Review Books, 2013.

Scott, David. *Conscripts of Modernity: The Tragedy of Colonial Enlightenment*. Durham, NC: Duke University Press, 2004.

Shirazi, M. Reza. *Towards an Articulated Phenomenological Interpretation of Architecture: Phenomenal Phenomenology*. London: Routledge, 2014.

Siebers, Tobin. *Disability Theory*. Ann Arbor, MI: University of Michigan Press, 2008.

Silveira, Renato da. *O Candomblé da Barroquinha: Processo de constituição do primeiro terreiro baiano da keto*. Salvador: Edições Maianga, 2006.

Sokolowski, Robert. *The Formation of Husserl's Concept of Constitution*. The Hague: Martinus Nijhoff, 1970.

———. "Review of *Edmund Husserls Theorie der Raumkonstitution*, by Ulrich Claesges." *Journal of the History of Philosophy* 6, no. 3 (July 1968): 305–7.

———. "The Theory of Phenomenological Description." In Ihde and Silverman, *Descriptions*, 14–24.

Stawarska, Beata. *Saussure's Philosophy of Language as Phenomenology: Undoing the Doctrine of the Course in General Linguistics*. Oxford: Oxford University Press, 2015.

Stein, Edith. *On the Problem of Empathy*. Translated by Waltraut Stein. Washington, DC: ICS, 1989.

———. *Zum Problem der Einfühlung*. e-artnow, 2018.

Steinbock, Anthony J. *Home and Beyond: Generative Phenomenology after Husserl*. Evanston, IL: Northwestern University Press, 1995.

———. *Limit-Phenomena and Phenomenology in Husserl*. London: Rowman & Littlefield, 2017.

———. "The New 'Crisis' Contribution: A Supplementary Edition of Edmund Husserl's 'Crisis' Texts." *Review of Metaphysics* 47, no. 3 (March 1994): 557–84.

Steiner, Henriette. "The Earth Does Not Move and the Ground of the City." *Journal of Comparative Cultural Studies in Architecture* (June 2012): 46–55.

Steiner, Henriette, and Maximilian Sternberg, eds. *Phenomenologies of the City: Studies in the History and Philosophy of Architecture*. Farnham: Ashgate, 2015.

Strathern, Marilyn. *Property, Substance and Effect: Anthropological Essays on Persons and Things*. London: Athlone, 1999.

Strongman, Roberto. *Queering Black Atlantic Religions: Transcorporeality in Candomblé, Santería, and Vodou*. Durham, NC: Duke University Press, 2019.

Sule-DuFour, Tao N. "The Sense of Architecture in Husserlian Phenomenology: The Example of a Candomblé-Caboclo Ritual of Tupinikim." PhD diss., University of Cambridge, 2012.
Taiwo, Olufemi. "Òrìsà: A Prolegomenon to a Philosophy of Yorùbá Religion." In Olupona and Rey, *Òrìsà Devotion as World Religion*, 84–105.
Tarkovsky, Andrei, dir. *Nostalghia*. 1983. Grange Communications.
Tempels, Placide. *La philosophie bantoue*. Paris: Présence Africaine, 1949.
Van Breda, H. L. "Merleau-Ponty and the Husserl Archives at Louvain." In Merleau-Ponty, *Texts and Dialogues*, 150–61.
———. "Le Sauvetage de l'héritage husserlien et la fondation des Archives-Husserl." In *Husserl et la pensée moderne/Husserl und das Denken der Neuzeit*, edited by H. L. Van Breda and Jacques Taminiaux. The Hague: Martinus Nijhoff, 1959, 1–42.
Vasconcelos, Pedro de Almeida. *Salvador: Transformações e permanências 1549–1999*. Ilhéus: Editus, 2002.
Vergani, Mario. "Husserl's Hesitant Attempts to Extend Personhood to Animals." *Husserl Studies*, 28 April 2020. https://doi.org/10.1007/s10743-020-09263-w.
Verger, Pierre. *Notes sur le culte des Orisa et Vodun: À Bahia, la Baie de tous les saints, au Brésil et à l'ancienne Côte des esclaves en Afrique*. Dakar: IFAN 1957.
———. "Première Cérémonie d'initiation au culte des orishas nago à Bahia au Brésil." *Revista do Museu Paulista* 9, Nova Série (1955): 269–91.
———. "Rôle joué par l'état d'hébétude au cours de l'initiation des novices aux Cultes des Orisha et Vodun." *Bulletin de l'Institut Français d'Afrique Noire* 16, nos. 3-4 (July–October 1954): 322–40.
———. *Trade Relations between the Bight of Benin and Bahia from the 17th to the 19th Centuries*. Ibadan: Ibadan University Press, 1976.
———. "The Yoruba High God—A Review of the Sources." *Odu* 2, no. 2 (January 1966): 19–40.
———. "Yoruba Influences in Brazil." *Odu*, no.1 (January 1995): 3–11.
Vesely, Dalibor. *Architecture in the Age of Divided Representation: The Question of Creativity in the Shadow of Production*. Cambridge, MA: MIT Pres, 2004.
Vessey, David. "Who Was Gadamer's Husserl?" *New Yearbook for Phenomenology and Phenomenological Philosophy* 7 (2007): 1–23.
Vidler, Anthony. *The Architectural Uncanny: Essays in the Modern Unhomely*. Cambridge, MA: MIT Press, 1992.
Voeks, Robert A. *Sacred Leaves of Candomblé: African Magic, Medicine and Religion in Brazil*. Austin: University of Texas Press, 1997.
Wafer, Jim. *The Taste of Blood: Spirit Possession in Brazilian Candomblé*. Philadelphia: University of Pennsylvania Press, 1991.
Walcott, Derek. *Omeros*. London: Faber and Faber, 1990.
———. *Selected Poems*. Edited by Edward Baugh. London: Faber and Faber, 2007.
Weiss, Gail, Ann V. Murphy, and Gayle Salamon, eds. *50 Concepts for a Critical Phenomenology*. Evanston, Illinois: Northwestern University Press, 2020.
Welton, Donn. "Intentionality and Language in Husserl's Phenomenology." *Review of Metaphysics* 27, no. 2 (December 1973): 260–97.
———. *The Other Husserl: The Horizons of Transcendental Phenomenology*. Bloomington: Indiana University Press, 2000.
Welton, Donn, ed. *The New Husserl: A Critical Reader*. Bloomington: Indiana University Press, 2003.

Wetherell, James. *Stray Notes from Bahia: Being Extracts from Letters, etc., during a Residence of Fifteen Years.* Liverpool: Birkenhead, 1860.

Wigley, Mark. *The Architecture of Deconstruction: Derrida's Haunt.* Cambridge, MA: MIT Press, 1993.

Wynter, Sylvia. "Beyond the Word of Man: Glissant and the New Discourse of the Antilles." *World Literature Today* 63, no. 4 (Autumn 1989): 637–648.

Young, Iris M. "Pregnant Subjectivity and the Limits of Existential Phenomenology." In Ihde and Silverman, *Descriptions*, 25–34.

Zahavi, Dan. "Empathy, Embodiment and Interpersonal Understanding: From Lipps to Schutz." *Inquiry* 53, no. 3 (June 2010): 285–306.

———. *Husserl and Transcendental Intersubjectivity: A Response to the Linguistic-Pragmatic Critique.* Translated by Elizabeth A. Behnke. Athens: Ohio University Press, 2001.

———. "Husserl's Phenomenology of the Body." *Études Phênoménologiques*, no. 19 (1994): 63–84.

———. "The End of What? Phenomenology vs. Speculative Realism." *International Journal of Philosophical Studies* 24, no. 3 (2016): 289–309.

Zahavi, Dan, ed. *The Oxford Handbook of the History of Phenomenology.* Oxford: Oxford University Press, 2018.

Zahavi, D. and S. Loidolt. "Critical Phenomenology and Psychiatry." *Continental Philosophy Review* (in press, 2022).

Zaner, Richard M. "Examples and Possibles: A Criticism of Husserl's Theory of Free-Phantasy Variation." *Research in Phenomenology* 3 (1973): 29–43.

Zumthor, Peter. *Atmospheres: Architectural Environments, Surrounding Objects.* Basel: Birkhäuser, 2006.

Index

Note: Page number followed by "n" refer to end notes.

abstract moment 54, 62, 139, 142, 154, 219
accomplishment (*Leistung*) 53, 80, 81, 131, 191, 204
activity: constitution 51; of description 10; prayer, clapping and singing 197, 201, 204; touch sensation 52, 76, 78; of writing 3
adumbration (*Abschattung*) 64, 70, 84, 113
affect 56, 81, 221
affection (*Affektion*) 49, 80, 114
Africa, Gbe-speaking areas 27
African gnosis 32, 36, 37
African gods 35, 36, 46n96
African philosophy 32
African religious traditions 25
Afro-Brazilian religion 5, 8, 14, 23, 29, 171
after-one-another (*Nacheinander*) 121
Agrawal, Arun 165n156
Ahmed, Sara 20n40
allure (*Reiz*) 4, 83–9, 107, 109, 114, 114, 134
"Amerindian perspectivism" thesis 158n30
analogizing apprehension 131, 135
analogy 131, 161n85
Analysen zur passiven Synthesis see Analyses Concerning Passive and Active Synthesis
Analyses Concerning Passive and Active Synthesis (Husserl) 9, 81, 102n122, 104n138
Andrews, Michael 125
Annales school 30
The Anthropology of Intentions (Duranti) 13

anthropou-logos 34, 124
anticipation: of movement 87; horizon of 113; kinaesthetic 116; ritual context 197
appearance 11, 16, 51–71, 73–5, 87, 174, 193
appearing-of-the-tone 54
apperception (*Apperzeption*) 59, 63, 118, 125, 128
archaeology 31
architectonics of space 2
architectural phenomenology 7–9, 19n34, 20n41
architectural theory 7
Architecture in the Age of Divided Representation (Vesely) 8
Architecture's Historical Turn (Otero-Pailos) 7
"art" notion 33, 34, 91n16
aspectuality 62, 65, 70, 106, 111, 120, 123
association 118, 121, 122, 125, 134
attitude (*Einstellung*) 56, 140
auditory field 62
Ave Maria 190, 191, 205, 207
Avenarius, Richard 110, 139, 157n21
axiological/practical relations 82; significance 106

Baía de Todos os Santos (Bay of All Saints) 23
Bantu linguistic group 24
barracão 28, 174, 176, 211n42
Barroquinha *candomblé* 27, 212n43
"Basic Problems of Phenomenology" (Husserl) 108, 109, 110, 123
Bastide, Roger 14, 26, 39, 174
Beauvoir, Simone de 150

Bedford, Joseph 19n34
Being and Time (Heidegger) 82
belief *see* originary "belief"; primal belief
bênção (blessing) 143, 188–91, 204, 220
Blyden, E.W. 31
body/bodily: corporeity 49; as inanimate (*Körper*) 74; as lived bodily corporeity (*Leiblichkeit*) 131, 149; as lived body, animate organism (*Leib*) (*see* lived body); mediation 128; motility 9, 50, 72; movement 62; as self-movement 74; as spatial phantom 75; tactile sensations 75; *see also* lived body
Brentano, Franz 10
Bunzl, Matti 37, 38

caboclo festival 36, 215n69
caboclo reunião 5, 6, 10, 15, 23, 28, 29, 34, 38, 51, 122, 124, 126, 128, 137, 178; *see also* Candomblé ritual; Tupiniquim
"*Caboclo* talk" 193, 216n80
Cairns, Dorion 14, 52, 147; *Guide for Translating Husserl* 14
Candomblé 5, 8, 23, 50, 73, 107, 172, 188; Barroquinha 27; epistemological framework 30; evolution of 27; formation and development 27; interpretation of ritual 32–4; ritual and liturgical structure 27; systematic study 26, 29–32; theoretical issues 29–32; Yorùbá divinities 27
Caravaggio 193
Carl, Peter 8, 215n76
Carr, David 9, 11, 53, 110, 156n16
Carreño, Javier 93n33, 170
Cartesian Meditations (Husserl) 10, 107, 118
"Cartesian way" (Husserl) 146
Casa Branca 27
Casey, Edward 2, 8; *The Fate of Place* 8, 17n7; *Getting Back into Place* 8
Castro, Eduardo Viveiros de 24, 42n4, 113, 158n30
Catholicism 172, 187
Catholic mass 186
Centro do Caboclo Tupiniquim xiv, 172
Cheung, Chan-Fai 13
The City of Women (Landes) 28

Claesges, Ulrich 9, 49, 50, 59, 74, 76, 77, 80, 86, 90n1, 90n4, 112
coevalness 14, 37, 38, 68
coexistence 70, 71, 81, 109, 114, 116, 133
Cohen, Joseph 51
colour sensation 55, 56
common present 37–9
common space 39
community 25, 27, 35, 118, 138, 150, 170, 219
comparison 112, 133, 134, 196, 206
concrete/concreteness: body in labour 150; environing world 140; environmentality 149; experience of others 116; intersubjectivity 124, 137; life-world and generativity 145; object 54, 93n32; person 102n113
conflict as "coinciding *par distance*" 133–4, 137; ritual context 198, 202–3, 206, 220
conflict/tension 5, 133, 206
constellations 68, 121, 122, 220
constitution 15, 50, 51–3, 74; analyses of 113; intersubjective 107
"corporeal schema" 8
corporeity 49, 106, 109, 114; concept of 51; constitution and experience 51–3; corporeity and time 78–90; lived body 72–8; "manifests itself" (*sichbekunden*) 51; motility 72–68; spatiality constitution 50; spatial phantom and time 68–71; of speech 144; tactual space 72–8; visual space 53–68
"cosmic" spatiality 148
Cossard, Gisèle Binon 26
The Crisis of European Sciences and Transcendental Phenomenology (Husserl) 7, 10, 18n29, 39, 108, 139
Crowell, Steven 99n81
Csordas, Thomas J. 13

Davidson, Cynthia 19n29
depth sociology 30, 45n53
Derrida, Jacques 7, 22n65, 40, 41, 80, 139, 161n106, 167n186
description: ethnographic 15; experience description 110; phenomenological description 11, 15; spatial experience 10; "static" description 106

Desjarlais, Robert 13
de-socialization process 151; *see also* social death
Dilthey, Wilhelm 31, 140
Ding und Raum: Vorlesungen 1907 (Husserl) 50
discoverability (*Vorfindlichkeit*) 69, 74, 80, 83, 123
Disorienting Phenomenology (Norwood) 8
distance principle (*Entfernung*) 60, 72, 73, 106
distanciation, critique of ideology 33
D manuscripts 50, 81, 108, 117
Dodd, James 9; *Phenomenology, Architecture and the Built World* 9
Donohoe, Janet 18n28
double continuity 84, 98n77, 101n104
double sensation (*Doppelempfindung*) 52, 73
Drummond, John 54, 81, 92n25, 93n32
DuFour, Tao 19n35
Duranti, Alessandro 13; *The Anthropology of Intentions* 13

earth 7, 16, 147, 148, 154, 172
earth-ground (*Erdboden*) 16, 146, 148, 154
earth-space 16, 148, 154, 221
êbô 178, 221
Edmund Husserls Theorie der Raumkonstitution (Edmund Husserl's Theory of the Constitution of Space) 9
ego (*Ich*) 74, 102n113, 126
Elliston, Frederick 9
embodiment 2, 4, 6–8, 10, 12, 60, 72, 82, 114, 117, 149, 219
empathic spatiality 107, 118, 123–38
empathy (*Einfühlung*) 7, 14, 16, 29, 32, 36, 68, 90, 104n141, 107, 118, 124, 125, 128, 219
enigma 40, 98n76
enquiry, "zigzag" (*Zickzack*) manner 51
"environing things" 60, 62
environing world (*Umwelt*) 16, 138–42, 139, 144, 147, 149, 221
environmentality (*Umweltlichkeit*) 16, 107, 139, 147, 148, 149, 165n156, 219
episteme concept 31, 34
"epistemological" framework 30
"epochē" 12

equivocation 113, 157–8n30
The Ethical Function of Architecture (Harries) 8
ethical imperative 124
ethnographic method 3
ethnographic "Other" 112, 145
ethnography: description 15; development 124; fieldwork and writing 4, 13; historicity of 114; reality 113; spatial description 4; texture 60
Ethnography journal 13
ethnonym 25
"Ethnophilosophical School" 32
ethnopragmatics 13
European colonialism 36
European Spiritism 174
Europe *Annales* school 30; Husserl's idea of 48n127, 48n128
expectation 84, 121, 122, 134, 159–60n61
experience (*Erfahrung*) 15, 51–3, 56, 74, 110
experience (*Erlebnis*) *see* lived experience
experienceability principle of 16, 115–16, 122–3
Experience and Judgement (Husserl) 81, 105n150, 126, 131
experiencing body *see* lived body

Fabian, Johannes 14, 37, 68, 114; *Time and the Other* 37
facticity (*Faktizität*) 81, 102n120
facultative possibility (*Vermöglichkeit*) 151
"familiar stranger" (Hall) 34
Fang, Xianghong 13
Fanon, Frantz 8
farness thing 62
The Fate of Place (Casey) 8
feelings sensations 79
femininity 143–4
Fernandes, Ana 43n25
"field of thermal sensation" 62
fieldwork 14, 219; Candomblé systematic study 29–32; experiences 3; interpretation of ritual 32–3; as methodological clue 29; methodological problem 34–6; priority of perception 38–9
"Fifth Meditation" (Husserl) 108, 125, 131, 145

"figure seen twice" (Strathern, Riles) 3 de Filgueiras Gomes, Marco A. A. 43n25
filha-de-santo (daughter-of-saint) 29, 173, 186, 187, 188, 196
filho-de-santo (son-of-saint) 173, 194
F manuscripts 54
fog/haze of memory 88, 105n149, 137, 152, 223n15; of retention 110, 121
Formal and Transcendental Logic (Husserl) 10, 81, 108
Foucault/Foucauldian 31, 45n67, 165n156
Frampton, Kenneth 7
Frankétienne 89

Gadamer, Hans-Georg 8, 32–4
Gantois 29
generational connection 145
generative phenomenology 107, 118, 145, 149
generative space 138–55; life-world, spatiality of 139–45; space generation 145–55
generativity 7, 9, 50, 118, 145, 146, 151
genesis 81; of community 118; genetic spatiality 116–23; natural world 110–16; of space 109–10; of spatiality 128; of spatial sense 122; of subjectivity 146; theme of 116
"genetic analysis of speech" 141
genetic density 144
genetic method 80
genetic phenomenology 16, 102n113, 116–18
genetic spatiality 80, 116–23, 120, 125
geo-historical sense 148
geo-historical space 152
geo-historicity 107, 170
Getting Back into Place (Casey) 8
Gibson, W. R. Boyce 18n29
Gilroy, Paul 222n8
givenness 59, 62, 74, 74, 75, 78, 81, 120, 170, 219, 221
givenness beforehand (*Vorgegebenheit*) 69
Glissant, Édouard 47n100, 152, 222n8
gnosis concept 31, 32, 34, 36
Goldman, Marcio 14, 26, 30, 31, 35, 173
Good Lord Jesus of the Martyrdoms 27
Goonewardena, Kanishka 17n6
ground 7, 62, 129, 133, 176–80, 183
Guide for Translating Husserl (Cairns) 14

habitualities 15, 49, 87, 109, 118, 122, 123, 136, 219
habitus 15, 41, 49, 89
Hall, Stuart 1, 2, 17n1, 34, 47n100
Harding, Rachel 25
Harries, Karsten 8; *The Ethical Function of Architecture* 8
"having grown together" (*zusammengewachsen*) 70, 97n72, 114
hazy (*diesig*) 105n149
Heidegger, Martin 7–9, 10, 13, 140, 143, 159n49; *Being and Time* 82
Heinämaa, Sara 2, 9, 17n9, 127, 143, 160n77
Held, Klaus 6, 10, 18n20
Henare, Amiria 18n20
heritage (*Erbe*) 106, 116, 122
"Hermeneutics and the Critique of Ideology" (Ricoeur) 32
historicity 7, 34, 37, 39, 50, 80, 83, 90, 114, 118, 120, 138, 222
Holbraad, Martin 18n20
Holl, Steven 7, 19n33
Holston, James 25, 43n26
"holy play" notion 33
Home and Beyond (Steinbock) 146
Hopkins, Burt 131
horizon 16, 33, 36, 41, 62, 70, 110, 119, 147, 198, 201–3, 205, 218
horizonality 15, 49, 59, 62–3, 66, 111, 115, 120, 123, 140, 147, 169
horizon intentionality 112, 116
horizon perception 16, 114
"horizons of earth-space" 148
"Horizons of Knowledge" (Mudimbe) 32
horizon-structure (*Horizontstruktur*) 59, 112, 116, 154
Houston, Christopher 13
Howard, Catherine V. 42n4
Huizinga, Johan 33
human historicity 139, 146
humanity 145
Humphrey, Caroline 3–4, 221; imaginative literature 4
Husserl and Transcendental Intersubjectivity (Zahavi) 108
Husserl Archives in Louvain 6, 10, 50
Husserl, Edmund: *Analyses Concerning Passive and Active Synthesis* 9, 81; "Basic Problems of Phenomenology" 108, 109, 110, 123; biography 10; *Cartesian Meditations* 10,

107, 108, 118; "Cartesian way" 146; constitution of space 49; *The Crisis of European Sciences and Transcendental Phenomenology* 7, 10, 28n29, 39, 108, 139; *Ding und Raum: Vorlesungen 1907* 50; earth motif 147–8, 154; embodiment and perception 6; "Europe," idea of 48n127, 48n128; *Experience and Judgement* 81, 126, 131; "Fifth Meditation" 108, 125, 131, 145; *Formal and Transcendental Logic* 10, 81, 108; "Foundational Investigations" 146; *Husserl: Shorter Works* 9, 164n139; *Ideas Pertaining to a Pure Phenomenology and to Phenomenological Philosophy* 7, 10, 18n29, 73; *Lectures on Internal Time Consciousness* 10; letter to Lucien Lévy-Bruhl 39–42; *Logical Investigations* 10, 103n127, 162n124; "The Natural Attitude and the 'Natural Concept of the World" 110; "Nature and Spirit" 139; "The Origin of Geometry" 139; *Phantasy, Image Consciousness, and Memory* 168; *On the Phenomenology of the Consciousness of Internal Time* 69; space and embodiment 7, 49; space constitution/constitution of space 9, 15, 50–1, 74, 80–3, 108, 146–7, 153; "Static and Genetic Phenomenological Method" 118; "systematic" phenomenology 9, 117; *Thing and Space* 9, 41; transcendental subjectivity, intentionality 11–12; *Zur Phänomenologie der Intersubjektivität* 108
Husserl: Shorter Works (Husserl) 9, 164n139
"Husserl's Investigations toward a Phenomenology of Space" (Kersten) 9

"I can" of spontaneity 86–87
Ideas Pertaining to a Pure Phenomenology and to Phenomenological Philosophy (Husserl) 7, 10, 18n29, 73
Identity and Alterity: Phenomenology and Cultural Traditions (Lau, Cheung and Kwan) 13
Ilé Axé Iyá Nassô Oká 27, 28

image (*Bild*) 70, 71, 98n73; photographic image 170
image-consciousness 170
image-phases 70
imagination 168, 169, 221; experience of 169; imaginative literature 3; literary and photographic 169
imitation and projection thesis 125
immanence/immanent 15, 82, 110, 117, 122, 160n64
immediacy 31, 34, 38, 74, 79, 83, 111, 124, 126, 129, 137, 152
immersement 3, 4, 144, 221
"improper" appearances 59
indeterminate others 116
indexicality 121, 122
Indian spirit 29, 34, 35, 114, 172
indigenous "spirit" 179, 186
Ingold, Tim 13; *Phenomenology in Anthropology* 13
inner horizon 59, 60, 66, 86
inquiry back (*Rückfrage*) 147
institution (*Stiftung*) 87, 104n147, 153, 167n179
intentionality 11–13, 117
intergenerationality 7, 118
internal time-consciousness (*inneres Zeitbewusstsein*) 69
interpretative mode 82, 103n127
interspecies relations 7
intersubjectivity 7, 9, 50, 80, 83, 107, 108, 112, 118, 137, 138, 145, 154
intra-African 28
The Invention of Africa: Gnosis, Philosophy, and the Order of Knowledge (Mudimbe) 31, 32

Jackson, Michael 13; *Things as They Are: New Directions in Phenomenological Anthropology* 13
James, C. L. R. 2, 17n5
Jansen, Julia 169
Jarzombek, Mark 19n29
judgements, occasionality of 141

Katz, Jack 13
Kern, Iso 108, 116, 117, 157n28
Kersten, Fred 9, 22n81, 90n2, 146, 148
Khalfa, Jean 8
kinaestheses 109
kinaesthetic consciousness 86
kinaesthetic motivation 109, 112, 115, 119
kinaesthetic sensations 75, 74, 78

kinaesthetic situation 120, 128, 135
knowledge as *gnosis* and *episteme* 31
Konopka, Adam 140
Kwan, Tze-Wan 13

Labatut, Jean 7
Lammi, Walter 105n149
Landes, Ruth 28; *The City of Women* 28
landscape experience 147
language 145, 154
Lau, Kwok-Ying 13
"leading clue" (*Leitfaden*) 83
Lefebvre, Henri 2, 17n6
"Le principe spatial d'individuation" ("The spatial principle of individuation") (Mouloud) 9
Levinas, Emanuel 10
Lévy-Bruhl, Lucien 30, 32, 40, 41
life-world (*Lebenswelt*) 108; concept 139–45; as earth-ground 146; linguality (nexus of meaning) 141; spatiality (presence) 141; as world-horizon 146
linguistic anthropology 13
linguistic community 145
literary image 170
lived bodily corporeity (*Leiblichkeiten*) 115, 128, 149
lived bodily sensations (*Empfindnissen*) 76, 77, 79
lived body (*Leib*) 12, 15, 49, 66, 72–6, 73, 79, 122, 135, 138; concept of 72; corporeity 137, 219; habituality 153; heritage 116; horizon intentionality 112; indexicality 122; kinaesthetic motivation 109, 136; motility 86; self-affection 109; sexuality expressive 143; tactual body 106
lived experience (*Erlebnis*) 4, 5, 52, 53, 56, 91n16; of the earth 148; for *Erlebnis* 53; generative horizon of 153; *habitus* 89; "literary image" 170, 219; sensing history 14
living environment 4, 149, 152
living present 119; corporeity in 135; retentional-protentional structure 119; running off phases 119
living through process 12; processual sense 53
localised lived bodily sensations (*Empfindnissen*) 77
Logical Investigations (Husserl) 10
Log journal 8

Loidolt, S. 8, 20n41
Lord's Prayer 187, 190, 191, 205, 207

mãe-de-santo (mother-of-saint) 5, 23, 28, 34, 35, 89, 107, 118, 123, 137, 168, 183, 187, 188, 189, 220
Mãe Juta 174, 186, 193, 219, 220
Malinowski, Bronisław 17n14
Malpas, Jeff 9; *Place and Experience* 8
material object (Körper) 109
Mattens, Filip 7, 9, 54, 56, 93n30, 143
Mauss, Marcel 36
Mbembe, Achille 20n42
McCormick, Peter 9
meaning as linguality of the life-world 141
"melting wax" 70
memory 1, 53, 81, 87, 110, 129, 130, 132, 133, 168, 218
mentality 29, 30, 32, 40
mental process 52
Merleau-Ponty, Maurice 6–9, 13, 40, 50, 84, 111, 138, 148
meta-ethnic denomination 25
methodological "reduction" 107
methodological shift, "genetic" phenomenology 107
Miettinen, Timo 48n127
mimēsis 33
Mittelholzer, Edgar 222n1
modificational continuity 121
moment concept 3, 93n32, 131, 132, 134
monotonic quality 195
"moods" 82
Moran, Dermot 9, 40, 41, 48n128, 51, 78
Morrison, Toni 151
motility 72–8
motivation 86, 109
Mouloud, Noel 9
movement anticipation 86
Mudimbe, Valentin 14, 31, 34, 37, 40, 68, 114, 124; *Einfühlung* notion 36; *gnosis* concept 34; *The Invention of Africa: Gnosis, Philosophy, and the Order of Knowledge* 31, 32
mutual externality (*Außereinander*) 69
mutual presence 37
mythos theme 33

Najman, Charles 89
natal alienation 151
natality 150, 152–3

"The Natural Attitude and the 'Natural Concept of the World" (Husserl) 110
natural world 8, 110–16
nature/culture-nature/society 111, 140
nature, Husserl's concept of 110–12, 140; "*mere Nature*" 110
nearness thing 62
near-sense (Nahsinn) 73
Nenny (Orisha devotee) 1, 17n2, 218
neo-Kantian tradition 51
Nicholson-Smith, Donald 17n6
Nina Rodrigues, Raimundo 29
Norberg-Schulz, Christian 7
normality 66, 141, 163n138, 167n187
normativity 141, 145, 221
Norwood, Bryan 8, 19n29; *Disorienting Phenomenology* 8
Nostalghia film 89

objects 74, 118, 128, 140, 174, 184, 195
occasionality of speech 117, 138
O Dono da Terra: O Caboclo nos Candomblés da Bahia (dos Santos) 35
Ogum 180, 181
olfactory field 62
"one-sidedness of outer perception" 59
open intersubjectivity 116, 118, 123, 140
operative concept 51, 54
organism-environment relations 140
originaliter (*ursprünglich*) 78
originary "belief" (*Urdoxa*) 67, 68
"The Origin of Geometry" (Husserl) 80, 139
orixá Dadá (god of new-born children) 29
orixá 173, 174, 178, 220; identification of 184
ornamental/decorative 206
"Ossâim" 180
Otero-Pailos, Jorge 7, 19n32; *Architecture's Historical Turn* 7
Other *see* ethnographic "Other"
other/others experience of 108, 145; being-with-others 154; colouration of skin 137; empathic spatiality 118; generativity 150; indeterminate 116; reports of 147; spatiality of 123; as subjects and lived bodies 124–5, 126, 129
The Other Husserl (Welton) 116
out-of-one-another (*Auseinander*) 121

Oxalá 218, 221
Oxum 178, 179, 206, 208, 218, 221
Oxumare 27

Paci, Enzo 40, 41
pai-de-santo (father-of-saint) 173
Pallasmaa, Juhani 7, 19n33
paó 187, 188, 221
Parés, Luis Nicolau 25, 28, 173
Parviainen, Jaana 9
passive genesis 80, 81
passive synthesis 80, 81, 118
passivity 52
Patočka, Jan 7, 99n81, 157n24
Patterson, Orlando 151
PEACE ("Phenomenology for East-Asian CirclE") 13
Peiffer, Gabrielle 10
perception 38–41, 54; direct perception 62–3; and discourse 117; experience of others 124; as habitual 84; horizon perception 114; intersubjectivity of 112; living present 110; one-sidedness of 59; presence 69; retention-protention structure of 88; visual *vs.* tactile 75
"perceptual faith" 111
perceptual situations 117
Pérez-Gómez, Alberto 7, 19n33
perspectivity 60, 62
phantasy 53, 56, 110, 129, 168, 169, 171
Phantasy, Image Consciousness, and Memory (Husserl) 168
phantom body 50, 59, 114
phantom spatiality 15, 49, 60, 62, 112, 118, 120, 123, 138, 139
"Phenomenological Approaches in Anthropology" (Throop) 13
phenomenological ethnography 5, 11, 13, 15, 171
phenomenological method 116
Phenomenologies of the City (Steiner and Sternberg) 8
Phenomenology, Architecture and the Built World (Dodd) 9
Phenomenology in Anthropology (Ingold) 13
Phenomenology of Perception (Merleau-Ponty) 6, 18n23, 93n28, 96n58, 98n77, 99n78, 99n85, 104n136, 104n139, 104n143, 104n145, 105n148, 160n61, 223n8
philosophical anthropology 73

photographic image 170
physicality 52, 148
picture/image-consciousness 168, 197
Place and Experience (Malpas) 8
play concept 33
plurality 25; of the cogiven 132; of subjects 116
positionality 59, 60, 62, 123
possession 174
post-structuralism 7
potentiality 82, 83; generativity 153; lived body 95n56; motivation 119; ritual context 127
"practicing phenomenology" 5
praxis 27, 44n36
prayers 187, 191, 196
preferred appearances 66
"preliminary sketches" (*Vorzeichnungen*) 149
prenatal subjectivity 149
pre-predicative experience 81, 82, 117
presence *see* living present
presentification (*Vergegenwärtigung*) 110, 128, 171
primal belief (*Urglaube*) notion of sense perception 67
"primitive mankind" theme 42
primitive mentality 40
primitivism 112
primordiality 108, 112
"primordial modes of constitution" (*Urkonstitutionen*) 50, 80
primordial sphere 112, 116
primordinal 157n28
processual sense of *Erlebnis* 53
"proper" appearances 59
protention 121, 122, 129; *see also* retention-protention structure
protodoxa (*Urdoxa*) 67
Pullan, Wendy 8

qualitative problem, spatial description 2, 66
quasi-perceiving 53

race 8, 25, 48n128, 73
Ram, Kalpana 13
receptivity 15, 49, 54, 80, 81
"reciprocal" foundation 132
"reduction" 12
Reis, João José 25
relationality 120, 126, 131, 134

relationship 11, 170
relation Husserl's theory 131–3, 134, 135
representation 29, 34, 51, 179
reproduction/re-presentation 171
retention 84, 88, 103n136, 144; *see also* retention-protention structure
retention-protention structure 84, 88, 92n28, 97n68, 105n148, 110, 119, 121–2, 158n40
reuniaõ, gathering 5, 23, 35, 184, 220
Rickert, Heinrich 140
Ricoeur, Paul 32, 33
Riles, Annelise 3
Risério, Antonio 24, 42n1
ritual implement 106
running-off phenomena (*Ablaufsphänomene*) 69, 110, 119

Salvador 23–4; Candomblé *terreiros* in 29; *cidade alta*/high city 24; *cidade baixa*/low city 24; population of 25; port and regional administrative centre 24
San Martín, Javier 40
Santos, Jocélio Teles dos 35, 172; *O Dono da Terra: O Caboclo nos Candomblés da Bahia* 35
Santos, Juana Elbein dos 172, 174, 207
Scanlon, John 111, 155n18, 157n21
Schwarz-Bart, Simone 2, 221
scope/optic leeway (*Spielraum*) 73, 86
Scott, David 17n13
Searle, John 22n65
sedimentation 81
self-givenness 15, 80
self-identification 25
self-presentation 33
sense: apperceptive transfer of 135; changeover of 148; immediacy of 124; of nature/world 107; of normality 66; sedimentation of 118; of self-movement 74; similarity 121; of spatial experience 81; of spatiality 120; "temporal generation and coming-to-be" 116; of things 106; "transferred similarity" 136
sense-bestowing subjects 41
sense-fields 62
sense giving 53
sense history (*Sinngeschichte*) 116
sense perception 6, 39, 41, 69, 80, 108

sensibility 4, 49, 52, 54, 60, 113, 123
sensory experience 54
sensual appearance 120
"sensual feelings" 82
sensuality 86
sensuous schema 50
sessão 36
sexual difference phenomenology 2, 143
sexuality expressive 143
Shirazi, M. Reza 7, 19n32; *Towards an Articulated Phenomenological Interpretation of Architecture* 7
Siebers, Tobin 104n143
similarity 121; concept 133–5; experience of 136; idea 131; relationality 133
simultaneity (*Gleichzeitigkeit*) 37, 70
singular experiences 123
slave trade 24
smoothness 53, 56, 119
social death 151, 166n166
socio-economic structure, nineteenth-century Salvador 25, 26
softness, tactile sensation 74, 76, 128
Sokolowski, Robert 9, 11, 50–2, 73, 82, 91n12, 91n15, 117–18
space 66; affectivity of 15, 49, 112, 136, 143; architectonics of 2; concept of 9, 113; constellations 121, 122; corporeal experience of 51; distance (Entfernung) 106; earth (*see* earth-space); empathic spatiality 123–38; environmentality of 149, 155, 170; ethnography of 5; experienceability of 16; experience of 120; generative space 138–55; genesis of 16, 109–10; genetic spatiality 116–23; geo-historicity of 107, 170; horizonality of 112; as intersubjective 147; intersubjectivity inherent to 112; modern mathematico-epistemic sense 2; natural world 110–16; phenomenology 13, 219; problem of 3; "ready-made" character 120; systematic descriptions 15
space-of-potential/leeway (*Spielraum*) 67
spatial construction 3, 6, 51; problem of 14; style of 13
spatial ethnography 9
spatial experiences 3, 7, 53; activity of 10; bodily tactility and motility 50; constitution of space 9, 50–1; description of 10; habituality of 123; Husserl's theory of experience 107; investigation of 107; lived bodily motility 153; living present 128; memorial conflicts 137; phenomenology 50; sense perception and embodiment 6; temporality of 50; visual and tactual modes 54
spatial figure (*Raumgestalt*) 70
spatiality 2, 54, 59, 73; of Candomblé ritual 23; constitution of 54; description of 170; of the earth 154; "environmental experience" 148; environmentality 149; experience of 123; generativity 146; givenness of 10, 136; historicity 120; Husserl's phenomenology of 50; intersubjective problem 80; intersubjectivity 50; phenomenology of 81; problem of 145; relational structure of 134; sense and structure 3, 5; structure of 4, 111
spatial nexus 60, 62
spatial phantoms 54, 68–71, 142
spatial sphere 108
spatialty, "static" description 106
spatio-perceptual theme 14
spectral/spectrality 152, 154
speech 141–3, 205
sphere of ownness (*Eigenheitssphäre*) 108, 112; abstraction method 146; primordial sphere 116
spontaneity 15, 49, 50, 80, 86, 109, 112 "Static and Genetic Phenomenological Method" (Husserl) 118
static phenomenology 16, 117, 158n42
"static" structure 87
Steinacher, Lukas 40, 41
Steinbock, Anthony 2, 5, 9, 18n28, 66, 81, 91n13, 102n122, 107, 118, 141, 145, 146, 163n137; generativity 150; geo-historical sense 148; *Home and Beyond* 146
Stein, Edith 9, 10, 79, 81, 82
Steiner, Henriette 8
Sternberg, Maximilian 8, 163n137; *Phenomenologies of the City* 8
Strathern, Marilyn 3, 4, 17n10, 18n20, 144; fieldwork and writing 5; "moment of immersement" 3
Strauss, Erwin 7

250 Index

structure 2; affective 133, 154; of appearance 52, 59; of "depth," vertical 117; as horizon 154; lived body 72; of phantom spatiality 60; of relation 131; of retention-protention 88; temporality 78, 80; of thing perception 63
"structure" notion 33
Stumpf, Carl 7
style: expressive of sexuality 143; environmentalities (*Umweltlichkeiten*) 149; as habit, habituality, and *habitus* 84, 87, 89
subject 106, 118, 120, 124
subjective mental process 52
subjective sensations 79
subjectivity 11, 72, 117, 146, 221
subject-object dichotomy 78
Sule-DuFour, Tao 167n179
Supper at Emmaus (Caravaggio) 193
surrounding world (*Umwelt*) 2, 4, 12, 51, 149, 153–5, 221
symbol 106
sympathy 32
synesthetic perceptions 54
"syntheses of homogeneity" 133
systematic phenomenology 9, 117
systematization 80

"tactile field" 62
tactility 50, 75
tactual experience 80
tactual field 73, 75, 76, 80
tactual phantom 73
tactual space 72–8
Tarkovsky, Andrei 89, 105n151
The Taste of Blood: Spirit Possession in Brazilian Candomblé (Wafer) 35
telos of play 33
temporality 3, 16, 54, 56, 83, 106, 107, 109, 110, 114, 119, 121, 153
tendency towards 86
tension 31, 52
terreiro, religious household 5, 28, 35
territory conception 146
thickening of "now" 84
Thing and Space (Husserl) 9
things 54, 56, 59, 120, 174, 195, 205, 221; appearance of 62, 70; aspectual appearance of 59; discoverability of 140; experience of 106; farness thing 62; givenness of 60, 62, 112; horizonality of 59–66; "inner horizon" 60; nearness thing 62; "objective" quality of 186; perspectivity of 65; sense of 106; spatiality of 67; spatial structure 63; transcendence of 124; visual space, appearance of 63
Things as They Are: New Directions in Phenomenological Anthropology (Jackson) 13
Throop, C. Jason 13
time: corporeity 78–90; and corporeity 78–90; problem of 68; spatial phantom 68–71
Time and the Other (Fabian) 37
topographic integrity 25
touch: auto-affection of 87; "double sensation" (*Doppelempfindung*) of 52; experienced identity of 78; imagination 171; kinaesthesis of 75; localisation of sensation 133; as a *near-sense* (*Nahsinn*) 73; ritual context 188, 190–1
touching sensation 53, 78, 81
Towards an Articulated Phenomenological Interpretation of Architecture (Shirazi) 7
transcendence concept 12
"transcendental logic" 81
transcendental structures 11
transcendental subjectivity 12
"transferred similarity" 136
"transformation into structure" 33
truth 38, 68, 112, 145
Tupiniquim 5, 23, 24, 35, 172, 183, 186, 191, 193–6, 220
turning towards 82
Tymieniecka, Anna-Teresa 105n149

"Uma sessão de caboclo" (A secession of caboclo) (Santos) 35
Umweltlichkeit (environmentality) 16, 149, 164n156, 219
unfamiliarity 120
urban conflict 8

Van Breda, Hermann Leo Fr. 6, 10, 50, 90n6
verbal expression 141
verbal sense 52
Verger, Pierre 24, 26, 174
Vesely, Dalibor 7, 8, 157n24; *Architecture in the Age of Divided*

Representation 8, 19n36; "natural world" concept 19n35
visibility 52
visual appearances 59
visual field 62, 70, 73, 74
visual givenness 62
visual space 50, 53–68; appearance of 63; consideration of 72; constitution of 63; distance principle 60, 72, 73; givenness of 62; temporality of 63
visual phantom 56
vodun 27

Wafer, Jim 35, 172, 193; *The Taste of Blood: Spirit Possession in Brazilian Candomblé* 35
Walcott, Derek 151, 152, 155
Wastel, Sari 18n20
Weltanschauung notion 31
Welton, Donn 9, 80, 107, 108, 116–18, 120; genetic phenomenology 116–18; life-world 141; linguistic meaning and perceptual sense 142; *The Other Husserl* 116; static phenomenology 158n42; systematic phenomenology 117
Windelband, Wilhelm 140
world, Husserl's concept of 139; as environing world 138–42; as life-world 138–42, 145, 146; as natural world 110–12, 114–16
Wynter, Sylvia 47n100

"Xangô" 178, 179

Yorùbá 24, 28; *orixás* 27, 35, 173, 212, 213
Young, Iris 152

Zahavi, Dan 2, 6, 8, 9, 11, 16, 20n41, 60, 72, 80, 90, 100n97, 108, 112, 114, 115, 116, 124, 125, 155n1; *Husserl and Transcendental Intersubjectivity* 108
"zig-zag" process 10
Zoogodô Bogum Malê Rundô 27